Unity and Polemic in the International Communist Movement

Yogendra Dhakal

Unity and Polemic in the International Communist Movement
Yogendra Dhakal

First English Edition 2016

ISBN : 978-93-5002-458-4 (Hb)

Layout Design
Saman Shrestha

Published by

AAKAR BOOKS
28 E Pkt. IV, Mayur Vihar Phase I, Delhi 110 091
Phone: 011 2279 5505 Telefax: 011 2279 5641
aakarbooks@gmail.com; www.aakarbooks.com

Printed at
Sapra Brothers, Delhi 110 092

Dedicated to my sister
Bidya Dhakal,
also known as Jaljala,
who sacrificed her life to the
cause of revolution.

Contents

Preface

This book is a collection of articles written over the period of three decades at different times against the non-Marxist-Leninist thoughts and trends, especially within the Revolutionary Internationalist Movement (RIM). Before and in the immediate aftermath of the foundation of RIM, the focus of the two-line struggle within the RIM was mainly between the Communist Party of Nepal (Mashal) and the Revolutionary Communist Party of the USA. However, its non-Marxist views were contested and opposed by out of the RIM Marxist-Leninist parties and organizations, including the Communist Party of India (Maoist). After the expulsion of CPN (Mashal) from the RIM, the RCP, USA almost exercised monopoly in the RIM and other parties could not take a stand against it. With Bob Avakian's attempt to pass the New Synthesis of Communism (NSC) from the CoRIM, the two-line struggle once again sharpened. The struggle to a great extent saved the CoRIM from the Marxist-Leninist deviation propounded by Bob Avakian. However, from the Marxist-Leninist perspective, it was not appropriate to merely oppose the NSC, without analysing his earlier works since the 1980s and taking it as a climax of the chain of his earlier views.

This book does not include the entire struggle against all the non-Marxist-Leninist thoughts and trends seen in the international communist movement during the period. So, I urge the readers not to expect a comprehensive presentation of the subject as suggested by the title. I would be happy and satisfied if this book could give even elementary information about some aspects of controversy raised in the international communist movement. Except for Bob Avakian's NSC, all the other articles in this book had already been published in Nepali. 'On Bob Avakian's NSC' is an unpublished one, written by me in English. I could not publish it earlier because our party had taken no decision on it. I am making it public in the book form now after the party's decision in this regard.

I was directly involved for almost two and a half decades with the two-line struggle of the international communist movement, especially RIM, mainly because of my association as a member with CPN (Mashal). So, the thoughts and perceptions presented in this book are not personal or independent. Controversies raised in the period were the stand and views of the party. I have given a theoretical shape to the stance and views of the party and also a theoretical basis to silence the opponents.

The party is not an abstract thing; it is a concrete one. An abstract party cannot represent its class and achieve its goal. Party leadership is also a concrete concept. So, my involvement in the international communist movement, especially in the two-line struggle within the RIM, was under the initiative and guidance of the party. During that period, Comrade Mohan Bikram Singh led the party and I was associated with that glorious struggle under his leadership. In that struggle, I contributed ideologically to sharpen the debate within the RIM. Bob Avakian's NSC, written after my breaking away with CPN (Mashal), is also not out of the periphery of the same thought. I am grateful to Mohan Bikram Singh for writing an introduction to this book. Comrade Mohan Bikram Singh uncompromisingly led the almost two decades long struggle based on principle against the Revolutionary Communist Party, USA, and its Chairman Bob Avakin to counter their non-Marxist-Leninist thoughts and trends. I hope the introduction written by the veteran Comrade will make the book an authentic source to readers. In fact, Bob Avakian's 'New Synthesis' is the climax of his non-Marxist-Leninist thought series advocated in the last three decades. So, the struggle against it should be viewed as the highest form of struggle. I consider that my book is an attempt to fulfil this responsibility with full sincerity and seriousness.

In the context of misleading propaganda spearheaded unprecedentedly about Marxism, it is our moral responsibility to revive the correct teachings of Marxism-Leninism regarding the fundamental questions, and for this even long statements from the works of Marx, Engels, Lenin, Stalin and Mao need to be extracted. I realize the pitfalls of such an exercise as they may make the reading more complex, even inviting a negative impact on the popularity of the book itself. However, it cannot be avoided in order to make the work (book) authentic and reliable. Similarly, I have referred to long statements made by RCP, USA and its Chairman Bob Avakin, Enver Hoxha, K.Venu, CoRIM documents, PCP and its Chairman Comrade Gonzalo, and RIM's other parties and organizations so that readers themselves can grasp the holistic perspective of the proponents of scientific socialism on the one hand, and on the other to counter the false notions advanced by the above with sufficient proof and evidence.

The first and third write-ups in this book are translated respectively by my colleague Krishna Pahadi and my cousin Murari Mani Aryal, Marxist intellectuals. I am indebted to the late Comrade Viswanath Pathak who translated the greater part of this book from Nepali into English; to Comrade Roshan Kissoon and Peter Tobin for editing the book. I thank them all from the core of my heart for their cooperation. Words are not sufficient to express my thanks to Saman Shrestha who handled the entire typing work of my project (books) efficiently, tirelessly, timely spending days and nights. This book is no exception to other books regarding the problems faced in the course of publishing from one language into another language. Moreover, my own long sentence structure as well as definitive words of Nepali language complicated the process of translation. I appreciate my colleague Prof. Dr. Shreedhar Gautam's contribution in minimizing the lapses between the original Nepali text and its English translation to ensure that the intended meaning of the first text is not distorted. I thank all critics for sparing their valuable time to read and critique the book.

May 20, 2016 Yogendra Dhakal

Introduction

1

The book, *Unity and Polemic in the International Communist Movement* by Comrade Yogendra Dhakal, known by his pen name Ajay Sharma, is a collection of articles written in the last three decades. The importance of the book lies in its ideological appraisal of the revisionist, anti-communist and metaphysical thinking of Bob Avakian, the chairman of the Revolutionary Communist Party of the USA (RCP, USA). In the present International Communist Movement (ICM), his ideas are almost defunct and they have little impact. The Revolutionary Internationalist Movement (RIM) founded in 1984 by the initiative of RCP, USA is almost extinct. However, a critical study of his ideas will be helpful to understand the various types of revisionist trends appearing in the history of ICM including the present time.

With the emergence of communist ideology, various types of revisionist or opportunist trends also appeared in the international communist movement. The revolutionary communist movement cannot go ahead without a tough ideological struggle against them. When Marxist-Leninists lose sight of it, compromise with them, or become weak ideologically or organizationally to struggle against them, those (revisionists or opportunists) succeed in making a revolutionary party deviate from the revolutionary line, and turn it into an opportunist one to serve the interests of reactionary forces. At times they succeed even to achieve revolution. The collapse of the world socialist system before us is an example. It suffered a setback not only because of the attacks by the external enemies, but because of the weaknesses of Marxist-Leninists to fight successfully against the revisionism within their parties and the socialist system.

Because of the deviations from the Marxist-Leninist ideals, anti-people or petty bourgeoisie trends were dominant in the communist parties or former socialist parties. All these flaws propelled the former revolutionary communist parties or socialist countries towards the breakdown of the system. Communists should learn their lessons from all these experiences of the history of the ICM and should be careful enough not to weaken or slacken their struggle against the revisionists in whatever forms they appear. But such a struggle cannot go ahead successfully without having a clear-cut ideological knowledge of the opportunist trends. If this aspect is overlooked, or we lag behind in enriching ourselves with Marxist-Leninist ideology, we would not be able to fight effectively against revisionism. To enrich ourselves, it is necessary to have an adequate knowledge of classical Marxism-Leninism-Mao-Tse tung Thought. But that is not enough. Revisionism always tries to creep into the communist movement in new or disguised forms. To make ourselves able to meet new challenges posed by revisionists in new forms, we should familiarize ourselves with every new trend of revisionism.

The book written by Comrade Dhakal helps us understand the revisionist theory developed by Bob, although it has lost the importance at present in the international communist movement. In the 1980s and 90s it created an illusion in the international communist movement, especially among the Marxist-Leninists who were in the frontline to fight the Chinese revisionism. Now it has become a matter of history. However, a correct understanding of that will help us to understand the various forms of revisionism in the present world communist movement and fight against that too.

Bob, in his own words, after 35 years of summing up historical experience, positive and negative of Marxism-Leninism has come to the conclusion that firstly, the "whole stage of the communist revolution has ended, and it ended with defeat". Secondly, "a new stage of the communist revolution" has begun. Thirdly, this "new stage of the communist revolution" "cannot embark" under the guidance of Marxism-Leninism", and fourthly, that deficiency can be fulfilled by the New Synthesis of Communism (NSC), an alternative theory propounded by him.

The analysis and conclusions he has drawn from that indicates that Marxism-Leninism had neither played a successful role in the past, nor has the ability to play such a role at present or in future. He has thrown the whole of Marxism-Leninism into a dustbin. According to his study of thirty-five years, Marxism-Leninism or the communist movement as a whole is nothing, but a failure.

It is claimed that the NSC is the outcome of the criticism and analysis of the mistakes of the international communist movement, former socialist countries, and the method that led to those mistakes or failures. Bob Avakian pleads that his theory, NSC, is more than that. It is reviving the experience of the past on a new and advanced basis, placing "on an even firmer foundation of materialism and dialectics". After analysing Bob's whole "coherent, comprehensive and overarching theoretical framework", it is not difficult to understand that the crux of his theoretical framework is to negate the Marxism-Leninism-Mao Tse-tung Thought (MLM), and the communist movement in totality.

Bob Avakian in his different articles published in the *Revolution*, organ of the RCP, USA in 1980 and 1981 has made an all-round attack on Stalin, in "an antagonistic way". The views Bob Avakian has expressed against Stalin are nothing new, but they are stale ones brought against Stalin by Trotsky and he (Bob) simply copied them. Thus, it is not difficult to understand that his entire theoretical framework, NSC, is borrowed from Trotsky.

Comrade Dhakal is correct when he summarizes Bob Avakian's view as such: "On the question of the relation between maintaining of power in the Soviet Union and the advance of the world revolution, Bob Avakian has opposed Stalin in an antagonistic way. Doing this, he stands with Trotskyites. Actually, Bob Avakin's views on the historical experience of ICM are basically on Stalin. As he (Bob Avakian) has said, 'the basic overview can be expressed by using Stalin as the focus.' Comrade Dhakal explains correctly, 'this is the heart of his analysis.' " Yes, on the question of Stalin, he (Bob) completely stands with Trotsky.

Bob Avakian has gone a step ahead of Trotsky. He has criticized Marx, Engels, and Lenin in various ways. His ultimate aim is to negate them totally.

Bob Avakian supported Mao mainly and raised the banner of Maoism high. But owing to his metaphysical way of thinking, he could not spare Mao either. As his thinking is metaphysical, he is unable to grasp the dialectical concepts of Marx, Engels, Lenin, Stalin and Mao too. In fact, his thinking basically was non-Marxist-Leninist from the very beginning, which is clear from the articles published in *Revolution* in 1980 and 1981. Bob's thinking made him reach the NSC and openly stand against Marxism-Leninism and against the banner of Maoism, which 'once upon a time' he raised high. Comrade Dhakal has elaborated extensively the metaphysical, anti-Marxist-Leninist and anti-communist ideology of the NSC propounded by Bob.

The role of Stalin is of outstanding importance in the world communist movement. Firstly, his extraordinary role to defeat fascism and, secondly, building socialism first of all in the history of mankind. It was a great blow to the world capitalism. It was because of such a great contribution that he was hated the most by the imperialists and all reactionaries in the world. Khrushchev condemned Stalin and did his best to downgrade him. Soon it was revealed that his denunciation of Stalin was only a part of his long-term strategy to denounce the entire socialist system and communist movement. In such a background what was needed was to defend Stalin and that was done by the communist party of China under the leadership of Mao.

After the counter-revolution in China in 1976, Bob Avakian appeared on the scene of ICM raising high the banner of Mao Tse-tung thought. At that time, his contributions were praiseworthy. But soon it became obvious that Mao's high handed advocacy was only a rehearsal to prepare the ground to attack the whole communist movement, Marxism-Leninism-Mao Tse-tung Thought was also not spared.

I am happy to see that Comrade Dhakal has undertaken the two fold tasks of defending Marxism-Leninism-Mao Tse-tung Thought and repudiating the metaphysical, anti-Marxist-Leninist trends expressed by Bob. He with vast ideological materials quoted both from authentic Marxist-Leninist literature and the articles or publications of Bob Avakian and RCP, USA and sound logic has shown that on the one side, the charges levelled against Marx, Engels, Lenin, Stalin and Mao are baseless and, on the other, the thinking of Bob Avakian or that of NSC are nothing, but a by-product of Trotskyism proven wrong by the history of the international communist movement.

2

CPN (Mashal) (hereafter only Mashal) has a long history of about three decades of struggle against the Neo-Trotskyite line of RCP, led by Bob. It started with the publication of articles of Bob Avakian and other leaders of RCP, USA in *Revolution*, the central organ of the RCP, USA in 1981. The June issue of *Revolution* in 1981 contained a long article entitled "Outline of Views on the Historical Experience of the ICM and the Lessons for Today", by Bob Avakian which was an excerpt from "Decades to Come on the World Scale", report-adopted by the Central Committee of the RCP, USA at the end of 1980. The same issue contained articles of a similar nature by many other members of the RCP. The No. 50 of *Revolution* contained an article entitled "Conquer the World-the International Proletariat Must and Will" by Bob.

All these articles mentioned above attacked Stalin in an antagonistic way or, to be frank enough, by following the line of Trotsky. Likewise, the RCP, USA tried to negate Marx, Engels, Lenin and Mao too in one or another way. They created great confusion in the international communist movement. However, they had played a very positive role to overhaul the damage done to ICM by the counter-revolution in China. But the loss caused by their Neo-Trotskyite line to the ICM was many times more than what they contributed by the struggle against Chinese revisionism. Soon after it was found that their main strategy was to shake the very foundation of the Marxism-Leninism-Mao-Tse-tung thought and international communist movement. To achieve this objective, they put forth the theory of the NSC. Comrade Dhakal has critically analysed his theory in detail in his book. In the first part of this Introduction, I have tried to throw some light on his praiseworthy work. So, I shall try to confine myself to give a short description of the role played by our Party, Mashal, in the struggle against the Neo-Trotskyite line of Bob Avakian and RCP.

In 1984, the Founding Conference of the RIM (Revolutionary Internationalist Movement) took place in a remote rural area of France, and our party presented a document, "Resolution on International Communist

Movement". (Only Resolution hereafter) The document first of all was prepared as a draft document in 1981 to be presented at the fifth Congress of the Mashal. The document explicitly criticized the danger posed by the Neo-Trotskyitism to the international communist movement. Thus, the struggle of our party against the Neo-Trotskyite line of RCP, USA dates back to 1981. The document criticized many of the Neo-Trotskyite concepts of RCP, which were published in the magazine *Revolution* in 1980 and at the beginning of June 1981, although without mentioning the name of the RCP. The document with a few amendments was endorsed by the fifth Congress of the Mashal held at January 1985. The document was published in 1990 in a book form entitled *Revolutionary Perspectives in the ICM after Counter Revolution in China.*

The Convening Committee (CC) of the Conference consisted of RCP, CRC (India) and TKP (ML), led by RCP. As the Resolution fundamentally took a line different than that of RCP, the CC put aside our Resolution and did not present it for discussion. It was not included even in the agenda of the Conference. At the last Conference I had presented a Note of Dissent (ND) to the International Conference. The ND was circulated among all parties and organizations of the RIM by CoRIM. The ND contains a passage the first sentence of which is such as "I would like to cite the following paragraph from the "Resolution on the International Communist Movement" of Mashal presented to this International Conference." (*Two-Line Struggle within RIM*, edited by M. B. Singh, June 2009 p. 137). This indicates that the document (Resolution) was presented at the Conference.

In the articles written by Bob Avakian and other leaders of the RCP, USA published in the *Revolution* expressed the view that "after Stalin's influence became dominant" in the Comintern "economists, reformist and bourgeois democratic deviations" were "developing in the international communist movement". After the rise of the fascist form of bourgeois dictatorship (1933) in Germany, "heavy defensive and defeatist tendencies grew in the leadership of the Soviet Union and the Comintern" and everything was subordinated to "the defence of the Soviet Union". The RCP, USA disagreed with the view that after the invasion of the USSR by Germany the principal aspect of the war changed from "inter imperialist war to one whose main aspect was that between socialism and imperialism" as claimed by Stalin and Comintern. Bob Avakian believes that even after the invasion of the Soviet-Union by Germany, the nature of war remained "mainly an inter-imperialist war" (*Revolution*, June, 1981, pp. 5-6). According to him, it was wrong to give priority to the policy of the defence of the USSR. Bob Avakian held the view that all the policies and steps of Stalin about war were taken "as expression of fundamental departures from Marxism-Leninism" (Ibid., p. 6). It made him (Stalin) "seriously deviated" from "correct Leninist analyses of imperialism and imperialist war and from the Marxist-Leninist stand on the nature of the state" (Ibid., p. 8).

According to Bob, Marx and Engels were in "some confusion" on the "question of the nation" and whether or not it was correct to view the working class "as being the inheritors and their best carrying forward the tradition, the best tradition of the nation". While "in their summation of the Commune, as well as in the practice of around Commune itself", they were "obviously outstanding supporters and promoters of proletariat internationalism". But on the "question of summation of the French nation", they expressed a "narrow point of view" and "there is that confusion" (*Revolution*, Special Issue, No. 50., p. 3).

In the view of Bob Avakian, "in Lenin himself ..... There is a wrong view contrary to a certain degree to Leninism". Formerly, he had taken the "correct position, for example, in *Left-Wing Communism* and advised the German communists not to put themselves in a position of allowing the bourgeoisie to corner them into coming out and saying they were against the Versailles Treaty and should determine their attitude towards the Versailles Treaty on the basis of interests of the international proletariat and the world revolution." But later there began "to creep in the view, even somewhat appearing in Lenin and certainly carried towards after him, of pushing the communists in Germany in bits ... to raise the national banner in Germany against the Versailles Treaty and against the victors at the expense of Germany" (Ibid., p. 16). Such a view on the part of Lenin was regarded as "contrary to a certain degree to Leninism and in fact" "internationalism".

The RCP, USA raised high the banner of Mao Tse-tung Thought and later upgraded it into Maoism. They went even to the extent of elevating the era of Lenin into that of Mao. But in his article, "Conquer the World-International Proletariat Must and Will" Bob Avakian has " linked to the general erroneous tendencies in Mao–too much of a country by country perspective, the tendency to see things too much in terms of nations and national struggle–something else that should be reviewed here briefly is confusion, and some of Mao's errors on the question of internal and external, and in particular the internal basis of change and the external condition of change, and how this applies to the relationship between revolutions in particular countries, on the one hand, and the overall world struggle and the world situation, on the other. Even in Mao, despite some contradictions to his contributions, and development of materialist dialectics there were some metaphysical tendencies which interpenetrated with nationalist tendencies on this question" (Ibid., p. 34). Bob, regarded such views of Mao as "erroneous" or "metaphysical" tendencies.

Such a criticism of Mao was based on his premises that the question of revolution should be taken "on a world scale" only. The concept of Mao to take China as internal and the rest of the world as external did not agree with the concept of "viewing the process of world historic advance from the bourgeois epoch to the communist epoch as something which in fact takes place in an overall sense on a world scale." He further writes, "the fundamental contradiction of capitalism which, with the advent of imperialism, has become the fundamental contradiction of this process on a world scale. This was something that Lenin began to stress with his analysis of imperialism", but it was not fully developed by Lenin, at least in an all around way and specifically in a philosophical sense; and it was gotten away from very sharply by the ICM after Lenin, and here again it was a case where there was not radical rupture in a thorough going way on the part of Mao". (Ibid., p. 35). Bob Avakian criticizes Mao for it that he in the place of fulfilling the task left undone by Lenin, incorporates to take revolution by "country to country perspective." The tendency "to see things too much in terms of national struggle" was termed as the "metaphysical one" of Mao.

Bob Avakian also criticized the "absolute, mechanical, metaphysical view" of taking "two types of countries in the world" in which one of them has "one-stage revolutions and the other has two-stage revolutions". A two-stage revolution was the way that was done in China. That was "new democracy as programme". The policy "to go to the countryside, surround the cities, wage protracted people's war and eventually capture power, was also criticized. In the opinion of Bob, the programme of "new democracy", the concepts of to "surround the cities" from the countryside, "wage protracted war" and "eventually capture power" were "absolute, mechanical, metaphysical" mistakes of Mao. Similarly "the specific criticism" had been made of Mao for his view expressed in "On policy" and General Line Polemic "to see US imperialism as the "main enemy" (Ibid., p. 35).

The main thrust of Bob Avakian and leaders of the RCP, USA was on Stalin. While making an attack on him, they went to the extent of criticizing Stalin as such, "Stalin did what he could do (and in some cases it wasn't insignificant) to kill the revolutionary struggle of the masses in order not to bring down the wrath of US imperialism" (Ibid., p. 28).

3

The conference lasted for about one month and I constantly raised many questions mentioned in the Resolution. The parties of Sri Lanka, Turkey, Greece, and Peru and to some extent CRC (CPI-India) also differed on many conceptions of the RCP, USA in one or other way, mainly on the question of principal contradiction and Stalin.

The Resolution vehemently challenges the criticism made against Stalin. The Resolution states: "Today, while evaluating the history and experience of the international communist movement, the tendency of attacking Stalin on the part of many Marxist-Leninist parties of the world is increasing. ... On the basis of all these criticisms they declare that in many questions Stalin had fundamentally deviated from the Marxism-Leninism, and he had no dialectical outlook, and was an opponent of proletarian internationalism and was chauvinist, reformist and rightist."

The Resolution further writes: "Some of Stalin's analyses and conclusions have been proven wrong and it also cannot be denied that he made some tactical mistakes too. But .... such mistakes and weaknesses of Stalin are secondary aspects of his life. The principal aspects of him are that basically he was a great Marxist-Leninist, a proletarian internationalist, and he had made invaluable historical contributions for the advancement of the communist movement and the world socialist revolution. It will not be possible to lead the party and revolution in the right direction in future by negating his great revolutionary aspects, but will lead to another erroneous deviation clearly towards Trotskyism (*Revolutionary Perspectives* ... pp. 13-15) "In such a background what should be the responsibility of the Marxist-Leninist parties and organizations of the world? The answer of Resolution is: "Today, the new kind of public controversy on Stalin among the communists tempered by the long struggle against Khrushchevite revisionism to Teng's renegation is bound to exert in a fathomable negative impact on the communists who are in the process of forging a new international solidarity after the counter revolution in China. Nevertheless, we have to make a correct assessment of this Neo-Trotskyites danger in the new guise and strengthen the unity and organization of true Marxist-Leninists at the international level by waging two-line struggle against the numerous erroneous conceptions surfacing in the international communist movement" (Ibid., pp. 29-31).

At the end of the meeting I presented a Note of Dissent (ND) beginning with the following passage:

"I, on behalf of the Communist Party of Nepal (Mashal) seriously take note of the fact that tendency of a kind of deviation on the question of nationalism and national revolutionary movements, to some extent on the question of New Democratic Revolution too, has taken place in a series of articles, documents of the RCP, USA and in its draft document presented here" (*Two-Line*... p. 135). In the Resolution the New Trotskyite trend of RCP, was criticized in general. But the ND criticized such a line of RCP, USA explicitly. The ND states: "First of all it seems that RCP, USA is trying to weaken the very ideological foundations of nationalism and the national revolutionary movement. For this purpose, Marx, Engels and Lenin are interpreted in a confusing way, and Stalin is opposed in an antagonistic way, Mao is criticized in a friendly way and the history of the Second World War period is evaluated in a wrong way." (Ibid., p. 136). In later decades, it became clear that their attack on the communist.movement and it's ideology as a whole was many times more than indicated in the ND.

In the articles, published in *Revolution*, it is claimed that on the question of nationalism Marx and Engels were in "some confusion", Lenin "went against Leninism", Stalin's policies were "fundamental departure from Marxism-Leninism", and Mao showed up the tendency of "seeing things in terms of nationalism and national struggle" (Ibid., p. 135).

Analysing the metaphysical way of thinking of RCP, USA the ND concludes that "criticism of Marx, Engels, Lenin, Stalin and Mao is an example of observing things in a metaphysical way. It is because of such an outlook that they are seeing only absolute, but not relative; only general, but not particular; only external; but not internal; only whole, but not part; only subjective, but not objective, only world, but not country; only world revolution, but not national revolution; only internationalism, but not nationalism. Their metaphysical approach is manifested on many ideological and political questions and because of an anti-Marxist outlook of seeing the world they have not been able to grasp the dialectical relationship existing between internationalism and nationalism and concluded that on this question Marx did not fully grasp the meaning and implications of even what he himself had commented on earlier" (Ibid., p. 135). It is because of such a metaphysical view of the RCP, USA that, they "see a kind of antagonistic contradiction between the defence of the USSR and the interest of the world proletarian revolution. At a time when there was a serious danger to the first socialist republic of the world, which was a great historical achievement of the whole world, it had become a primary duty of the proletariat and oppressed people of the world to fight to defend it, the base of the world at that time" (*Two-Line...*, p. 136).

It was because of such an erroneous view that the RCP, USA "has not been able to evaluate the history of ICM correctly during the Second World War period and afterwards." The approach of RCP, USA on the question of nationalism, on the national question as a whole is misleading and is against the principles laid down by Marxism-Leninism. According to the draft document presented by CRC (CPI-ML), India, (only CRC hereafter) "the national question has been generally solved in all the imperialist countries and nationalism as such generally does not have a progressive role there. 'Generally' it means that even in these countries nationalism can have a progressive role to some extent. This stand is correct." (Ibid., p. 137). Such a correct approach can be applied to the "pride" Lenin has expressed in the "language", "progressive cultural heritage and revolutionary movement" of Russia. It is not difficult to conceive that by repulsing patriotism or nationalism in totality in imperialist countries RCP, USA "in fact has gone against Leninism." The "national chauvinism representing reactionary interests" of the oppressed country so cannot be supported. Similarly, in the imperialist countries too as long as nationalism represents the sentiments, interests and movement of the working class it cannot and must not be opposed. Such nationalism is always part of internationalism and the world revolution and always must be supported" (Ibid.).

The incorrect approach of the RCP, USA on nationalism and the national struggle made them "criticize" the Dimitroff Report to the Seventh Congress of the Comintern, General Line, Mao and CPC too. It was because of their mechanical and metaphysical approach, which made them see "confusion" in Marx and Engles, or to conclude that "Lenin has gone against Leninism" (Ibid.). From the criticism they have made of Mao on the question of nations and national struggle, it is crystal clear that they are against the national movement of oppressed countries. In fact, their trend was to belittle the national revolutionary movement of Asia, Africa and Latin America as a whole.

4

To put aside the national revolutionary movement, the CoRIM and RCP, USA took the theoretical proposition that "at present in the international situation the inter-imperialist contradiction particularly contradiction between the two superpowers has become principal and war has become the main trend in the world. This conclusion is quite different from the General Line of CPC in 1963, which maintained that the contradiction between oppressed nations and imperialism is the principal one and revolution is the main trend of the world. It clearly said that the countries of Asia, Africa and Latin America are the main revolutionary centres" (Ibid., pp. 137-38).

Unlike such a line of RCP, the Resolution took a clear and firm stand on this point: "The contradiction between the oppressed nations and imperialism is the principal contradiction even today" (*Revolutionary Perspectives*... p. 8). In fact, the majority parties and organizations firmly stood against the proposition of the RCP, USA on the principal contradiction. At the time it seemed that the Conference would break because of that controversy. But later a compromise was reached and this proposal was accepted and was included in the declaration of CoRIM, "all the major contradictions of the world imperialist system are rapidly accentuating: the contradictions between various imperialist powers, the contradiction between imperialism and the oppressed peoples and nations, and the contradiction between the bourgeoisie and the proletariat in the imperialist countries are growing. All these contradictions have a common origin in the capitalist mode of production and its fundamental contradiction. The rivalry between the two blocs of imperialist powers led by the US and the USSR respectively is bound to lead to war unless revolution prevents it and this rivalry is greatly affecting world events" (*Two-Line*... p. 192).

The Declaration speaks only of "all the major contradictions of the world imperialist system without pointing out any of them as a principal" one. However, the attempt on the part of RCP, USA to propose the inter-imperialist contradiction as the principal one and to put aside the national revolutionary movement of Asia, Africa and Latin America was defeated. That was a partial success of the Conference. But our party did not agree with the compressing formula on the principal contradiction and persistently stood in favour of taking the contradiction among the oppressed nations and imperialism as the principal one. That is evident from the following passage given in the ND.

"The document of the RCP, USA states that, as the situation has changed, the conclusion of the General Line is no longer valid. So, the national revolutionary movement of the world has become secondary, the inter-imperialist rivalry being principal, which determines all other fundamental contradictions and affairs of the present world. The inter-imperialist rivalry is increasing and the danger of the world war is also increasing. But this factor has not reached such an extent as to make the contradiction between the oppressed nations and the imperialism and national revolution a secondary one in the present world ... and they have not been able to give any concrete analysis to justify that the objective situation of the 'general line' period has basically changed" (Ibid., p. 138).

On the question of Stalin too, the house was divided sharply. However, after a prolonged discussion the following passage was included in the Declaration of the RIM:

Firstly, "Today, the Revolutionary Internationalist Movement, together with other Maoist forces, are the inheritors of Marx, Engels, Lenin, Stalin and Mao, and they must firmly base themselves on this heritage."

Secondly, as Mao powerfully expressed, 'I think there are two 'swords': one is Lenin and the other Stalin', once the sword of Stalin has been discarded 'once this gate is opened, by and large Leninism is thrown away" (Ibid., p. 197).

It clearly shows that the attempt on the part of RCP, USA in the Conference to erode Stalin from the scene of the world communist movement failed and that was a great success of the Conference.

At the Conference, we had a differing view with the stand of the CRC and other parties or organizations too on the question whether Stalin used metaphysics in his thinking. In the document presented by the CRC at the Conference, they had criticized Stalin for his "basically metaphysical approach". Many concepts of Stalin, particularly those concerned with the class struggle in the socialist society had been proven wrong by history. He held the view that after the elimination of exploiting classes and private ownership of the means of production the class contradiction also had come to an end in the USSR. Due to such an unrealistic conclusion on his part, he was unable to see the bourgeoisie which was emerging from below, from the side of distribution. As a result, the class struggle and dictatorship of the proletariat were slackened in USSR and that provided an opportunity to the bourgeoisie to move ahead, capture power and restore capitalism there. But while criticizing him for his mistakes, we should not overlook the fact that "the historical limits and objective conditions which made him unable to understand correctly the nature of class struggle in the USSR. It is because of their (CRC's) one-sided approach that they have not been able to understand his weaknesses correctly." (Ibid., p. 139).

Such a mistaken view of the CRC towards Stalin is a reflection of the view expressed by Mao about Stalin. He (Mao) had criticized Stalin by saying, "Stalin had a fair amount of metaphysics in him and taught many people to follow metaphysics", (*Revolutionary Perspectives...*, pp. 24-25). Mashal firmly disagreed with Mao's view. All other the participants of the Conferences followed the criticism of Mao about Stalin and the same was true about CRC as well. So, at the Conference Mashal was the only party to disown the criticism of Mao about Stalin.

Our Party also criticized Mao for not having been able to adopt a correct approach towards the 'centrist' opportunism. The result of such a "weakness of GPCR was that it could not persistently wage the struggle against Chou En-lai, who was clearly a right-wing opportunist in disguise" (*Two-Line...*, p. 131). Not only that, "Mao because of Chou's influence, supported the rehabilitation of Teng and others thrown out in the course of GPCR. The promotion in the leadership of the Centrist, opportunists like Hua Ko-feng, who was once removed from the party leadership of Hunan during the cultural revolution, instead of Chang Chun-chiao, Chiang-ching and others, who were in the forefront in the struggle against right-wing forces during the course of GPCR, was also a mistake of Mao. Latter (Hua) became a source of Chinese counter revolution and thereby; history proved the contention that the act of raising him (Hua-Ko feng) in that way into leadership was wrong" (*Revolutionary Perspectives...* pp. 24-25).

The Resolution further states: "But these mistakes should not imply to mean that Mao's understanding itself towards right-wingers or 'centrist' elements was unduly compromising. Mao had been compelled to make compromises with 'centrist' opportunists only because of united pressure of right-wingers or 'centrist' opportunists and the relatively weaker position of revolutionary Marxist-Leninists. Therefore, those mistakes of Mao were chiefly born of the situation. However, Mao's mistakes are his minor and secondary aspects and the trend of adjudging wrong the fundamental relevance of Mao Tse-tung thought and his great revolutionary struggle, are his principal aspects (Ibid., pp. 25-28).

Finally, the ND concludes: "As it is quite crystal clear, CPN (Mashal) has serious differences with RCP, USA and to some extent with the CRC and other parties and groups too. But we believe in the dynamic nature of the two-line struggle. The dynamics of the two-line struggle is such that the different and unanimous views have the tendency of being changed into opposites (Marxist-Leninists) having unity today may differ later, and vice-versa. The comrades having different views on a question may agree with each other on different questions. Not only that, the party that takes a particular stand at the Conference may have a struggle within its own party in future. They might take the opposite stand than what they have taken today. So, the opinions and views expressed (today) are not final and should not be taken as settled for ever".

"We must never compromise on the question of principles and cause of revolution. But, at the same time, as long as differences are within the limit of Marxism-Leninism-Mao Tse-tung Thought and the cause of communism, we should try to resolve them through the two-line struggle and to strengthen unity on a higher level. We should try to avoid any possibility of our international revolutionary solidarity being broken because of misunderstanding and inability to grasp the theory and apply it correctly" (*Two-Line...*, pp. 139-40).

5

Soon after the International Conference was over, the TKML and CRC, left the RIM. But, in spite of serious differences, we had with the CoRIM, we preferred to remain and continue our two-line struggle. Our two-line struggle with CoRIM reached the climax when on August 21, 1996 CoRIM sent a letter to our Central Committee with an ultimatum either to support Maoism or "voluntarily" resign from the Movement. The main part of the letter is as follows:

> Central Committee
> Communist Party of Nepal (Mashal)
>
> August 21, 1996
>
> Dear Comrades,
>
> On December 26, 1993 on the occasion of the Mao Tse-tung Centenary the Revolutionary Internationalist Movement took the historic step of adopting Marxism-Leninism-Maoism as its ideology. The decision was taken after a long and vigorous debate within the RIM which had gone on over a number of years. In the course of this discussion, your party has repeatedly and vociferously argued against this position of our Movement.
>
> The dispute between RIM and the Mashal is by no means limited to a question of terminology. The debate has revealed that the dispute over Marxism-Leninism-Maoism concentrates on a whole series of political and ideological questions. (Ibid., p. 41)

Yes, after the end of the International Conference, the dispute between the Mashal and the CoRIM, as correctly mentioned in the letter of the CoRIM, had concentrated on "a whole series of political and ideological questions." As has been evident from 'In Resolution and Note of Dissent', at the time of the Conference itself, we had a series of ideological or political differences within the RIM. After the Conference, our differences with the CoRIM grew and were intensified more and more.

The RIM, as clearly written in its Declaration, is an "Embryo Political Centre", or a platform for exchange of views all participants having the right to an independent role to play. That is obvious from the practice of RCP, USA and PCP (Peru Communist Party). They had adopted the ideology of "Maoism", which did not agree with the official line of RIM, Mao Tse-tung Thought and in spite of that they remained in RIM.

CoRIM consistently tried repeatedly to turn it into an authoritative leading centre. But owing to the opposition of most the parties or organizations of the RIM, the effort of the CoRIM or RCP, USA could not succeed to turn RIM a leading centre as Comintern. Such an effort on their part was transgression of the limitation laid down by the Conference. Mashal and many other parties or organizations firmly stood against such an effort. Such a style of work was against the rules and norms of RIM and was a despotic one.

A few years after the Conference, the CoRIM started to take the initiative to replace Mao Tse-tung Thought by "Maoism." Such a move on the part of CoRIM was against the ideological foundation of the RIM. Firstly, only the next conference had the right to amend the principles laid down by the International Conference. So, it was basically a wrong act on the part of the CoRIM to take the initiative to amend the ideological foundation of the RIM. Secondly, before such an amendment was made in the ideology of the RIM, RCP, USA and PCP had adopted Maoism, which was against the ideology of the RIM. But no warning was given to those parties for adopting a principle against Mao Tse-tung Thought. Nor was any letter sent to take disciplinary action against those in charge of adopting a principle against Mao Tse-tung Thought. So, the initiative taken to amend the ideology of Mao Tse-tung Thought and the decision taken in this regard was wrong both from an ideological and organizational point of view.

The letter of August 21, 1996, was not sent to us suddenly. But it had a long background of tough struggle between Mashal and CoRIM for years. The struggle was concentrated mainly on the dispute of Mao-Tse-tung Thought and Maoism. But at the same time, it spread to many new questions such as evaluation of Mao's contributions, armed struggle, tactical line on election, style of work and on many other questions. It was in the background of difference on the "whole series of political and ideological questions" that the letter of 21st August was sent to us.

The resolution 'On Maoism' gives a glimpse of how serious the nature of such a political and ideological struggle was between the CPN (Mashal) and the CoRIM. After a long discussion within CPN (Mashal) and outside also an extended meeting of the Central Organization Committee (COC) of CPN (Mashal) held on September 17-19, 1992 adopted the resolution of Maoism and the era of Mao.

The RCP, USA and CoRIM concluded that the communist movement had reached the third and highest stage of Maoism. Our Party differed with both these concepts: Firstly, Maoism and secondly, the third stage or era of Maoism.

The resolution 'On Maoism' states: The Revolutionary Communist Party of USA in its resolution adopted in 1988 writes: "It is an era of imperialism and socialist revolution and we are not living in any new era". (Ibid., p. 173). The Declaration of the RIM of 1984 had taken the present era as that of Lenin. The Declaration asserts: "Stalin said 'Leninism is Marxism of the era of imperialism and the proletarian revolution.' This is entirely correct. Since Lenin's death, the world's situation has undergone a great change. But the era has not changed. The fundamental principles of Leninism are not outdated; they remain the theoretical basis guiding our thinking today"(Ibid., p. 200).

Later, the CoRIM contrary to the resolution of 1988 of RCP, USA and Declaration of RIM took the stand that the era had changed from that of Lenin to that of Mao and Maoism had become the Marxism-Leninism of the era of Mao. The resolution 'On Maoism' criticized such an ideological turnover of the CoRIM as such: "All political parties supporting the misleading concept of Maoism admit that the present era is an era of imperialism and socialist revolution. But none of them touches the sensitive issue of the Lenin era. They have also not made it clear, whether or not the concept of Leninism still occupies a significant place in the whole period of imperialism and socialist revolution. It indicates that Leninism has become a part of the second stage, and it has been replaced or substituted by Maoism. According to their view, the period of imperialism and socialist revolution still continues, but the period of Leninism has already passed away" (Ibid., p. 174).

'A World to Win', quoting a passage from our resolution 'On Maoism' writes: "A key argument the Mashal raises against Marxism-Leninism-Maoism (MLM) is that Leninism is the Marxism of the era of imperialism and that since the era has not changed, speaking of MLM as a new and higher stage of our science means negating Leninism" (A World to Win, the winter of 1998). They have expressed our views correctly. We formerly held that "Leninism is the Marxism of the era of imperialism" and proletarian revolution, and "speaking of MLM as a new and higher stage of our science means negating Leninism."

The Resolution "On Maoism" concluded: "In sum, what Mao has spoken for the new era is nothing but an era of imperialism and socialist revolution. It is an era of Lenin", the RCP, USA has also correctly pointed out that the 1988 resolution concept of the third stage of Maoism was that of Lin-Piao. Such thinking is conducive to weaken, knowingly or unknowingly, the very basis of Marxism-Leninism-Mao-Tse tung Thought in particular and the world communist movement in general. Therefore, the Mashal strongly proposes that the proposal of the committee on Maoism is a misnomer and there should be outright rejection of such a proposal" (Ibid., p. 185).

On February 16, 1993, a seminar on the subject, "Mao Tse-tung Thought or Maoism" was organized at Kathmandu. In a paper presented by M.B. Singh, the General Secretary of Mashal, had expressed the view that "the concept of Maoism in fact aims to put down Leninism" (*RIM Ra Maobadiharuko Kathit Janaudha* (RIM and Maoists' so-called People's War) by Mohan Bikram Singh, 2002 p. 65). In fact, the concept of Maoism is more based on Trotskyism than on Marxism-Leninism. Lin-piao had put forth the view that "the world enters the New Era of the Mao Tse-tung Thought." (*China Reconstructs*, April 1968 pp. 10-11) M. B. Singh expresses the view that the RCP, USA itself in a resolution passed in 1988 had condemned the era of Mao as a concept of Lin-piao. But later they adopted the same view which they had condemned earlier.

Singh in his paper dealt with various Trotskyite tactical lines and showed how they did not conform to the Marxist-Leninist concepts of strategy and tactics. Such a Trotskyite line emphasized to give up the line of mass struggle, giving up the one-sided emphasis on the armed struggle and rejection of election in all circumstances. Leninism had been the obstacle on the path of such a Trotskyite line. So, it had been compulsory for them to remove Leninism from their path. Leninism always stresses the concrete analysis of concrete situation to determine whether to follow the policy of armed struggle or line of peaceful mass struggle; to adopt the line of boycotting election or use of it. Trotskyites take the question of election strategically and stress boycotting it in all circumstances. Singh in his paper had written: "For Lenin the question of election is a tactical one and taking into consideration of the situation and demand of movement election should be used or boycotted" (*RIM Ra Maobadiharuko...*, p. 70).

The CoRIM and the RCP, USA use Maoism as a weapon to push out Leninism. Considering all these aspects, Singh in his paper has concluded that "Maoism" in the hands of CoRIM and RCP, USA has been turned against both Leninism and Mao Tse-tung Thought (Ibid., p. 65).

At the extended meeting of the CoRIM held in December, 1993 M.B. Singh on behalf of Mashal had presented a resolution "On Stalin". The resolution states: "Stalin was a great Marxist-Leninist" (Ibid., p. 102). The resolutions discussed in detail the charge of metaphysics levelled against Stalin by Mao and Bob. We have already dealt with the criticism made by Mao against Stalin. So, we shall refrain from having any more remarks that Bob Avakian has made against Stalin of minimizing the fundamental law of dialectics, the law of contradiction by putting it in the fourth number in place of the first one. Bob Avakian has expressed the view that the law of contradiction is the first and fundamental law of dialectics and violation of that in any way is metaphysical thinking.

In his "Philosophical Notes", Lenin has written that "In short the dialectics can be defined as the unity of opposite". (Lenin, *Collective Works* Vol. 38, p. 222). Similarly, while describing the law of dialectics, it has not put the 'law of contradiction' or 'law of unity of opposites' as fundamental or first ones. But because of that Bob Avakian has not seen metaphysics according to the outlook of Lenin. He (Lenin) has given emphasized that dialectics should not be understood on the basis of any single law, but in totality taking all laws combined. The defect on the part of Bob Avakian is that he analyses Stalin to pieces, instead of considering his ideas and works in totality, which is a metaphysical way of thinking. Because of such a defect in Bob's thinking, he views Stalin from a metaphysical point of view taking all things concerned with him in pieces. So, he has been unable to grasp the dialectical practices of Stalin. But when we consider all ideas and practices concerned with him in totality, there is "no doubt" that he possessed a "highly developed outlook to see things and contradictions contained in them" (*RIM Ra Maobadiharuko...* p. 131).

Notably, the resolution "on Stalin" was rejected by the extended meeting of the RIM.

6

About seven months after the extended meeting of the RIM took the decision on Maoism, a high level representative of the CoRIM came to Nepal to meet us. Our discussion with the representative of the CoRIM was mainly concerned with the difference both of us had on Mao Tse-tung Thought and Maoism. He emphasized that the difference among us on the question of Maoism had reached the stage where it had been necessary to finalize that by two-line struggle or any "other method". The other method meant the organizational method which implied disciplinary action. At that time, he said that in case we continued to oppose Maoism publicly, they would degrade our membership of the RIM to that of candidate member. We put our position clearly that we would make our position clear when any organizational action would be taken against us.

It is worth mentioning here that no action was taken against RCP, USA or PCP when they publicly adopted an ideology, Maoism, which was against the official line of the RIM, the Mao Tse-tung Thought. The answer of the

Representative was: "That was another thing." Thus they had applied double standards–one method in case of RCP, USA and PCP formerly and another method in case of Mashal. We firmly rejected to bow down before such an unequal and unjust method. The representative of RIM also expressed his dissatisfaction for criticizing RIM publicly. When we raised the question why no such objection was raised against RCP, USA and Bob Avakian when they criticized Stalin by name publicly, their answer was: "That was another thing."

At the meeting we also discussed the Naxalite movement of India. The representative of RIM expressed the view that the line of Comrade Charu was correct and a revolutionary one. But we held the view that in spite of his contributions to the struggle against the right deviation, the Soviet revisionism, and national chauvinism or support to Mao Tse-tung Thought and GPCR, basically their line was ultra "leftist" and wrong.

Two years after our meeting with the representative of the RIM, the CoRIM on August 21, 1996 sent us a letter warning either to support Maoism or "voluntarily resign" from the RIM within "three months". On October 24, 1996 the meeting of the Central Committee of Mashal was held to discuss the letter sent by the RIM and adopted the "Resolution on the Letter of CoRIM" (*Two-Line...* pp. 143-153). The resolution concluded that the letter of CoRIM was "unjustified, arbitrary, unprincipled, splittist, sectarian, and even against the norms and tradition of RIM itself." The CC meeting specially called to discuss the letter of CoRIM and decided unanimously, unlike suggestions of the Committee, to continue its stand on Mao Tse-tung Thought and not respond with 'voluntary' (forced?) resignation 'within three months' from RIM and continue to maintain opposition to Maoism"(Ibid., p. 143).

The CC in its Resolution on the letter of the CoRIM made clear that the RIM "is not an authoritative organization as the Communist International was. It is only a platform or forum for exchange of views, experiences and for consultation. According to the Declaration, the RIM is an 'embryonic political centre' of the international communist movement. ... So the Committee has no power more than a consultative one and any policy or decision of Committee is subject to approval of respective parties (Ibid., p. 143). There are ample proofs in the history of the RIM to justify our position regarding such a nature of the RIM. It was due to such a nature of the RIM that the PCP or the RCP, USA were never questioned for their stand on 'Maoism' against the official ideology of the Declaration of the RIM, Marxism-Leninism-Mao Tse-tung Thought, nor was any clarification asked from parties, or organizations of the RIM opposing Mao Tse-tung Thought, nor was any objection raised from any of them on their decisions to adopt 'Maoism'. This single fact is enough to indicate that the letter of the Committee to Mashal to threaten to expel in case if it continues to support Mao Tse-tung Thought is palpable violation and against the norms and practice of the RIM.

The letter of the RIM says, "In our view, it is necessary to conclude this period of clarification and debate between your party and our movement, which has lasted over two years. This is all the more important and urgent given that your opinion of Marxism-Leninism-Maoism has led to the most serious political consequences, including denunciation of the launching of the people's war in your country (Ibid). On the charge of "denunciation of the people's war" in Nepal, the Resolution states: "The 'people's war' referred by the CoRIM, in fact is an ultra 'left' deviation" (Ibid., p. 154). So, in our view it was correct to criticize that.

Finally the resolution writes: "At last Mashal sincerely longs for fraternal relation and solidarity with all the Marxist-Leninist parties and organizations of the world within and outside RIM on the basis of the revolutionary proletarian ideology, equality, proletarian antinationalism and principled two-lined struggle. Workers of the World Unite!" (Ibid., p. 153).

Mashal was expelled from the RIM about two years after the Mashal had sent its response to the letter of the CoRIM, in the first half of 1988. In a long article published by the CoRIM, it is explicitly written: "The Committee has come to the grave decision to propose to the participating parties and organizations the expulsion of the Mashal from the ranks of our Movement". Concluding the article writes, "We call on the rank-and-file of the Mashal to dissociate themselves from M. B. Singh's attacks against the revolution and join the proud ranks of the People's War in Nepal in the advancing battle for a world free of exploitation and oppression." (Ibid., p. 171)

Thus, after 14 years, our relations with the RIM came to an end.

M. B. Singh in an article published in the book *People's War in Nepal : Left Perspectives* edited by Arjun Karki and David Seddon in 2003, Delhi has written: "The period from 1984 to 1998 was ... a period in which the RCP, USA was trying to change the RIM into a pro-Trotsky organization, whereas the Marxist-Leninists tried to struggle against this pressure. During the conference of 1984, and after it, the communist parties of Sri Lanka, Turkey, Greece, India and Nepal struggled against this direction. But soon they resigned or left the RIM, due to their differences with the CoRIM, or they were liquidated in their respective countries. Only the CPN (Mashal) continued their single-handed struggle within the RIM against the attempt of RCP, USA to turn it into a Trotskyite organization" (Ibid., p. 189).

The objective behind 'expulsion' of Mashal was a part of their strategy to turn the RIM into a Trotskyite organization. But the gun backfired. As a result of their anti-Marxist-Leninist principles, organizational methods and style of work made the RIM itself liquidated. A few years after the expulsion of Mashal serious political and ideological differences emerged as written in a letter of the Communist Party of Nepal (Maoist) in June 2006 to the RCP. The letter had "raised serious criticism on the ideological and political line and tactices" (Ibid., p. 80). The CPN (Maoist) also could not remain there longer. Soon, the CPN (Maoist) came out of the RIM. Many other participants of the RIM also in one or another way left the organization. Soon after it was found that the aim of Bob Avakian was to attack the communist movement as a whole and get rid of that, as revealed from the newly developed theory of Bob, NSC. The muddle they had started with Maoism has come to a conclusion with NSC. It is a welcome development that Comrade Dhakal has made a thorough ideological analysis of the theory put forth by Bob, and it is certain that his work will enable Marxist-Leninists to fight opportunism which appear in various new forms.

Comrade Dhakal has a had long history of ideological struggle against Bob's Trotskyite line. It is worth mentioning here that in the long history of the struggle of CPN (Mashal) against the revisionist line of the RCP, USA and Bob, he (Comrade Dhakal) always stood firmly in the struggle against the Neo-Trotskyite line of Bob, and he has contributed much from the very beginning for that. Bob Avakian has succeeded to create an illusion among the Maoists all over the world. In spite of that, Comrade Dhakal, a Central Committee member CPN-Maoist, has not lagged behind to take a clear and firm ideological line against the illusion created by Bob. I thank him very much for the valuable ideological contribution he has made in this regard.

May 18, 2015

Mohan Bikram Singh
General Secretary
Communist Party of Nepal (Mashal)

Part I

Serious Differences with the Revolutionary Communist Party of the USA

The international communist movement has been facing an unprecedented crisis after the death of Mao Tse-tung. The degeneration of the socialist system in the Soviet Union, China and other countries has created a need for investigating the history of the international communist movement among the parties, organizations and individuals active in the international communist movement to find the reasons behind the degeneration of the socialist system.

In the evaluation of the international communist movement, the Revolutionary Communist Party of the USA (RCP, USA), has concluded that the lines of Comintern and Stalin during the Second World War were completely wrong. It says the degeneration of the socialist system all over the world is founded upon Stalin and the Comintern's "wrong" policy. We think the conclusion is totally wrong, and it is creating a 'new' deviation within the international communist movement.

Apart from the RCP, USA, some other parties and organizations in the international communist movement also hold this view. These differences on the following questions do not exist only between the RCP, USA, and us, but exist also within the whole international communist movement. Our differences with RCP, USA can be summed up as follows:

1
Single Country Advancing Towards Communism

On the basis of the development of the socialistic production system about twenty years and the living experience gained from the development, Stalin had said at the Eighteenth Party Congress of the CPSU that the Soviet Union was "moving ahead, towards communism."[1] Completely refuting Stalin's statement, the RCP, USA points out that "moving ahead, towards communism" is not possible in one country alone, and that this view was the source of Stalin and the Comintern's mistakes in the period of the Second World War. As Bob Avakain, Chairman of the RCP, USA has said:

> At that time Stalin drew a distinction between the victory of socialism in one country and the *final victory* of socialism–which he said could not be accomplished in one country alone–already there were within his line at that time erroneous tendencies that would further develop in the future; and within the international communist movement (before as well as after Stalin's influence became dominant in the Comintern) there were already developing economist, reformist and bourgeois-democratic deviations, rationalized in particular on the basis that the movement was in general in a period of "the defensive"[2]

The living experience of a long socialist production system in the Soviet Union had made Stalin conclude that "moving ahead, towards communism" was possible in a single country. While analysing the development of the production system in the Soviet Union during the period, it could be concluded that the Soviet Union was advancing on the road to communism. The development of industries, agriculture and culture in about two decades took place on an unprecedented scale. The gap between physical labour and mental labour, and the gap between the city and countryside was rapidly narrowing down. The transformation of private property into public property was intensifying. Are all these not the living proofs of "moving ahead, towards communism"?

Stalin's principle of "moving ahead, towards communism", based on the statement that the USSR "no longer contains antagonistic, hostile classes; that the exploiting classes have been eliminated"[3] may create a lot of

---

1 J. V. Stalin, "Report to the Eighteenth Congress of the CPSU (B.) On the Work of the Central Committee", March 10, 1939, *Problems of Leninism*, Foreign Language Press, Peking, First ed., 1976, p. 935.

2 Bob Avakian, "Outline of Views on the Historical Experience of the International Communist Movement and the Lessons for Today", *Revolution,* June 1981, p. 5.

3 J. V. Stalin, "Report to the Eighteenth Congress of the CPSU (B) On the Work of the Central Committee", March 10, 1939, *Problems of Leninism*, Foreign Language Press, Peking, First ed., 1976, p. 912.

confusion among the Marxist-Leninists of the world. But when we criticize Stalin's wrong understanding on the question of class struggle in the period of socialism, we must not make the mistake of opposing also the correct principle about the possibility of moving ahead towards communism in a single country. If we practise that method, we will fall prey to another wrong understanding while criticizing one wrong understanding. We should explain the hypothesis that even in a single country, it is possible to advance towards communism on the basis of the existence of classes and class struggles within socialism. Only then we can give this issue a scientific form. Since classes and class struggles continue to exist in the whole period of socialism, the ruling proletariat can advance towards communism only by grasping the theory of class struggle as the principal key.

Communism is the ultimate goal of the proletariat. To achieve that goal, the ruling proletariat of each country should adopt the revolutionary step for the building of socialism and communism. For this, the proletariat should mainly focus on the two points. The first is the consolidation of the dictatorship of the proletariat. After the proletarian revolution, the proletariat should consolidate the dictatorship of its class as the central task. For this, the proletariat has to follow the theory of continuing revolution for the whole duration of socialism. The possibility of the restoration of capitalism remains throughout the whole socialist period (first phase of communism). The restoration of capitalism in the Soviet Union, China and other former socialist countries has made this clear that in a country, the danger of capitalist restoration remains even after building socialism for a long period. In China, the restoration of capitalism has taken place in spite of Mao's grasp of the class struggle as the principal key in the socialist period, and even while he warned all the Marxist-Leninists of the world to grasp the question of class struggle, during the socialist period even more firmly.

The proletarian class, while consolidating its dictatorship, should not make the mistake of limiting it within its own country. It should support also the new democratic, socialist and all types of just movements of other countries, and should assist in all ways possible, directly or indirectly, politically or materially, for the establishment of the democratic and proletarian dictatorship in those countries, mainly it should advance the world socialist revolution. Second, after the proletarian revolution, the proletariat should adopt revolutionary measures for the development of a socialist and communist production system in the country. If the proletariat concentrates only on the political questions and neglects or forgets the issue of the development of a socialist and communist production system, then the attempt at consolidating the dictatorship of the proletariat will definitely fail. For this, it has to develop a socialist and communist production system.

To be more clear on this question, we should study the two main rules distinguishing socialism and communism; the first is "from each according to his ability and to each according to his work", and the second is "from each according to his ability and to each according to his needs." "From each according to his ability and to each according to his work" is the slogan of socialism. Why is it necessary to adopt this slogan under socialism ?

Firstly, in socialism the level of culture and the technical level of production is not very high. Secondly, there still exists a difference between manual and mental labour. The process of the transformation of private property into public property is also in process. The process of socialization of industry and agriculture is also an unfinished process. Because of these reasons, the state cannot provide the citizens all the benefits as per their needs by making them work according to their abilities. This is why the slogan "from each according to his ability and to each according to his work" has been adopted for socialism.

In communism, the second phase, is the developed stage of socialism, and in communism, the rule "from each according to his ability and to each according to his needs" is applied. In communism the cultural level of the people as well as the technical and production level is very high. No difference exists between mental and manual labour, and between the city and countryside, and the transformation of private ownership to public ownership will be completed. There is a high level of development of industry and agriculture. Because of these reasons, during communism, the rule "from each according to his ability and to each according to his needs" applies.

If any socialist country takes steps in raising the level of culture, technology and production, in narrowing down the gap between mental and physical labour and between the city and countryside, in transforming private ownership into public ownership, and in maximizing the development of industry and agriculture, should we stop this process because such steps will be definitely "advancing towards communism" (in a single country)? In the name of building communism throughout the world at the same time, should we oppose those revolutionary lines and policies adopted by socialist countries? No, we can never do it. If the communists themselves are not confident about the possibility of gradual transformation from socialism to communism, from the first phase to second phase, how can they build socialism in their country? When will a socialist world be built in this way? Certainly, we cannot advise the ruling proletariat of a country not to adopt those revolutionary practical measures until the whole world is under socialism.

2
United Front Against Fascism

Intense debate grew in the international proletarian movement over the issue of the distinction of the imperialists into a fascist camp and an anti-fascist camp by the Seventh Congress of the Comintern in 1935. At the moment the RCP, USA was arguing for this view within the international communist movement. According to the RCP, USA, the policy of the Soviet Union to form a united front with America, Britain and France against the fascist axis of Germany, Italy and Japan during the Second World·War was the adoption of a "bourgeois and nationalist banner of defending (an imperialist) country." Comrade Avakian has called the line of Stalin and the Comintern of forming an anti-fascist united front "absolutely wrong in principle".

> Openly rightist deviations, of a fundamental nature, become predominant–the promotion of nationalism, reformism and bourgeois democracy, the subordination of everything to the defence of the Soviet Union, etc., in a qualitatively greater way than before. While the line represented by the writings of Dutt during this general period were a part of this overall development, all this was concentrated in the Dimitroff Report to the 7th World Congress of the Comintern (1935) and the implementation and further development of this line–which, as we know, involved, among other things, as one of its key ingredients, the basic repudiation of the Leninist position on "defence of the fatherland". This whole line was in its essence erroneous.
>
> The Line(s) of the Soviet and Comintern leadership in relation to WWII overall (that is, during the period leading up to the war, from the mid-1930s on, and during the different phases of the war itself) was *basically wrong*. The point is not that particular policies and tactical manoeuvres of the Soviet Union, in dealing with different imperialists and making use of contradictions among them, were absolutely wrong in principle, taken by themselves; the point is that the overall line guiding this was incorrect.[4]

Since the very beginning of the 1930s, the danger from fascism was clearly seen in world. A deep crisis in the world peace appeared after the rise of Hitler in Germany. A new situation of tension emerged in eastern and western Europe. Germany acted as a common enemy for both the East as well as the West. Because of this, new possibilities emerged in the relationship between the Soviet Union and various capitalist countries. Moscow and Paris established a relation in 1933. Similarly, contact increased between America and the Soviet Union too. In view of the growing danger

---

4 Bob Avakian, "Outline of Views on the Historical Experience of the International Communist Movement and the Lessons for Today", *Revolution*, June 1981, p. 5.

from fascism in the world and the corresponding danger to the existence of the Soviet Union, the Soviet Union became a member of the League of Nations in September 1934. Considering the growing danger from fascism in the world, in 1935 the Comintern adopted a tactical line of using the American camp against the fascist camp, by dividing world imperialism into two camps.

In 1936, Germany and Italy launched a joint military attack against Spain. In 1937, Japan annexed Manchuria and then attacked North and Central China, Peking, Tienstin and Shanghai. In 1938, Germany annexed Austria and the Sabten state of Czechoslovakia. Similarly, Japan annexed Canton in 1938. In 1938, Japan annexed Hainan Island. Thus the fascist danger in the world was increasing everyday. In such a situation, to save the world from the danger of fascism, Stalin and the Comintern had no other alternative except to form an anti-fascist camp.

The work of Stalin and the Comintern during the Second World War in dividing the world imperialism into two camps and calling to form an anti-fascist united front was not anything outside Leninism. In reality, the line of Stalin and the Comintern should be considered as an important step. This line was completely based on the teachings of Lenin. Lenin says on this question:

> We must take advantage of the antagonisms and the contradictions that exist between the two imperialisms, the two groups of capitalist states, and play them off against each other. Until we have conquered the whole world, and as long as we are economically and militarily weaker than the capitalist world, we must stick to the rule that we must be able to take advantage of the antagonisms and contradictions existing among the imperialists.[5]

Lenin mentioned that depending on the situation, time and needs, a socialist country can even form a military alliance with one camp of the world imperialism against the other. He writes:

> Although we do not in general reject military agreements with one of the imperialist coalitions against the other in those cases in which such an agreement could, without undermining the basis of Soviet power, strengthen its position and paralyze the attacks of any imperialist power.[6]

The line of a united front against fascism was a line to safeguard world peace, to consolidate the base of the Soviet Union, the vanguard of the world proletarian movement, and to defeat the fascist camp and prevent a reign of fascist oppression over the world. Such tactics was totally accepted

5 V. I. Lenin, "Speech Delivered at a Meeting of Activists of the Moscow Organization of the RCP (B)", December 6, 1920, *Collected Works*, Eng. ed., Progress Publishers, Moscow, Third Printing, 1977, Vol. 31, pp. 438-39.

6 V. I. Lenin, "Theses on the Present Political Situation", *Collected Works*, Eng. ed., Progress Publishers, Moscow, Third Printing, 1977, Vol. 27, p. 361.

by Lenin. Then it is surprising as to why Comrade Avakian says that such tactics are deviations from Leninism. How necessary, timely and justified the formation of an anti-fascist united front at that time is made very clear by the following statement of Mao Tse-tung:

> For Communists throughout the world the task now is to mobilize the people of all countries and organize an international united front to fight fascism and defend the Soviet Union, defend China, and defend the freedom and independence of all nations. In the present period, every effort must be concentrated on combating fascist enslavement.[7]

The united front policy forwarded by Stalin and the Comintern, and supported by Mao Tse-tung, would not keep the working class of the capitalist world away from the class struggle. As Mao Tse-tung writes: "Such compromise does not require the people in the countries of the capitalist world to follow suit and make compromises at home. The people in those countries will continue to wage different struggles in accordance with their different conditions."[8]

Despite this truth, the RCP, USA has said that this anti-fascist united front policy of Stalin and the Comintern was the "class capitulation in the face of war". As Avakian says:

> Especially as the threat of world war mounts, the temptation to make communism more "acceptable" by dressing it up in the national flag mounts. But in the imperialist countries, to do so ultimately means being acceptable to the imperialist bourgeoisie. It means assisting them in throwing dust in the eyes of the workers, who in such times more than ever need to have their eyes firmly fixed on the red flag, on their internationalist *class* interests, on the revolutionary way forward." "Leninism stands opposed to all such capitulation, no matter how refined or well-intended.[9]

The RCP, USA's view is that due to this united front policy, the proletarian class in many countries abandoned the class struggle against the reactionary states of their countries, and took a line of class capitulation after the war, is also wrong. It is true that any tactical unity should not be at the cost of the fundamental principles of Marxism-Leninism and revolutionary goal. In the process of building an anti-fascist united front, it was necessary for all the communist parties of the world to adopt the Marxist-Leninist line of struggle-unity-struggle with the reactionary states of their own. But many parties adopted the line of a united front in a wrong way, and thus

7 Mao Tse-tung, "On the International United Front Against Fascism", June 23, 1941, *Selected Works*, Eng. ed., Foreign Language Press, Peking, Second Printing, 1967, Vol. 3, p. 29.

8 Mao Tse-tung, "Some Points in Appraisal of the Present International Situation", April 1946, *Selected Works*, Eng. ed., Foreign Language Press, Peking, First ed., 1961, Vol. 4, p. 87.

9 "On the So-Called 'National Nihilism', You Can't Beat the Enemy While Raising His Flag", *Revolution,* June 1981, pp. 26-27.

they took a line of weakening the class struggle against the bourgeoisie of their countries and of class capitulation. While we form our view about the necessity and timeliness of the anti-fascist united front of Stalin and the Comintern, we should analyse to what extent Stalin and the Comintern themselves had practised the Marxist-Leninist line.

We should not base our judgments on the wrong lines practised by the parties of many countries under the pretext of a united front. In fact, during the course of the united front, Stalin and the Comintern had emphasized that the proletariat need to establish the dictatorship of their class in each country by firmly grasping the theory of class struggle. They paid attention to this question, while deciding on the formation of the anti-fascist united front. The Comintern made clear the necessity of "*Complete independence from the bourgeoisie and complete rupture of the bloc of Social-Democracy with the bourgeoisie.*" ... "The *revolutionary overthrow of the rule of the bourgeoisie* and establishment of the *dictatorship of the proletariat*", "Support one's own bourgeoisie *in imperialist war*", and to build the party on the basis of *democratic-centralism.*"

Responding to the question "what is and ought to be the basic context of the united front at the present stage?" The Comintern (Seventh Congress) writes: "The defence of the immediate economic and political interests of the working class, the defence of the working class against fascism, must form the *starting point and main content* of the united front in all capitalist countries."

Regarding the realization of the unity of action of the proletariat in the individual countries throughout the world, the Comintern wrote: "The Communist International *puts no conditions for unity of action except one, and at that an elementary condition acceptable for all workers, viz. that the unity of action be directed against fascism, against the offensive of capital, against the threat of war, against the class enemy*, this is our condition."[10]

It is true that during the Second World War, many communist parties of the world had abandoned the theory of class struggle and practised the line of class collaboration while working under the anti-fascist front. The comrades of the RCP, USA, see Stalin and Comintern's line as the responsible factor for the degeneration of these parties. This is because of their wrong view that the revolutionary advancement of class and national struggle in a country is "more determined by what's happening in the world as a whole than it is by what's happening in one country." As Avakian has said:

> If we want to look to see what is the underlying and main driving force in terms of the development of revolutionary situations in particular countries

10 Georgi Dimitrov, "Report to the 7th Congress of the Communist International 1935", Red Star Press Ltd., London, 1975. *For the Unity of The Working Class Against Fascism,* pp. 115, 67, 62.

> at particular times, then too we have to look to the overall development of contradictions on a world scale, flowing out of and ultimately determined by this fundamental contradiction and not mainly to the development of the contradictions within a particular country, because that country and the process there is integrated in an overall way into this larger world process. It's not simply as it was in the feudal era or the beginning of the bourgeois era where you had separate countries more or less separately developing with interpenetration between them; now they've been integrated into this large process.[11]

Materialist dialectics holds the view that the cause of changes in nature, society and human thinking is mainly due to the development of internal contradiction. The external causes are the condition of change. But the comrades of the RCP, USA are trying to reverse these basics of Marxist philosophy. Without the existence of internal causes, external causes cannot be activated. Mao has correctly said: "External causes are the condition of change and internal causes are the basis of change, and the external causes become operative through internal causes." As a doctor can save a patient only to the extent of how long the life-process exists in the patient himself. Likewise, in the present world context, where capitalism has become globalized, there cannot be a socialist revolution in all countries because in most countries, the development of capitalism is still in its initial stage. So, it is necessary for these countries to pass through the stage of capitalism. Does that not make it clear that the revolutionary advancement of class struggle and national struggle in a country is determined more by the development in the particular country than by developments in the whole world as said by Mao:

> According to materialist dialectics, changes in nature are due chiefly to the development of the internal contradictions in nature. Changes in society are due chiefly to the development of the internal contradictions in society, that is, the contradiction between the productive forces and the relations of production, the contradiction between classes and the contradiction between the old and the new; it is the development of these contradictions that pushes society forward and gives the impetus for the suppression of the old society by the new. ... In the era of capitalism, and especially in the era of imperialism and proletarian revolution, the interaction and mutual impact of different countries in the political, economic and cultural spheres are extremely great. The October Socialist Revolution ushered in a new epoch in world history as well as in Russian history. It exerted influence on internal changes in the other countries in the world and, similarly and in a particularly profound way, on internal changes in China. These changes, however, were effected through the inner laws of development of these countries, China included.[12]

---

11 Bob Avakian, "Conquer the World? The International Proletariat Must and Will", *Revolution,* Special Issue, Number 50, pp. 34-35.

12 Mao Tse-tung, "On Contradiction", *Selected Works,* Foreign Language Press, Peking, Vol. 1, p. 314.

Criticizing Mao's above view about class struggle and national struggle, Avakian writes:

> Also linked to the general erroneous tendencies in Mao–to much of a country by country perspective, the tendency to see things too much in terms of nations and national struggle–something else that should be reviewed here briefly is confusion and some of Mao's errors on the question of internal and external, and in particular the internal basis of change and the external conditions of change and how this applies in the relationship between revolutions in particular countries, on the one hand, and the overall world struggle and the world situation, on the other ... even in Mao, despite and in contradiction to his contributions to and development of materialist dialectics, there were some metaphysical tendencies which interpenetrated with nationalist tendencies on this question...
>
> For example in "On Contradiction" the way it's presented is that China is the internal and the rest of the world is the external. And what we have emphasized in opposition to this is viewing the process of the world historic advance from the bourgeois epoch to the communist epoch as something which in fact takes place in an overall sense on a world scale, is a world process and both arises out of and is ultimately determined by the fundamental contradiction of capitalism which, with the advent of imperialism, has become the fundamental contradiction of this process on a world scale.[13]

It is not correct to hold Stalin and the Comintern responsible for the abandonment of the theory of class struggle and the acceptance of class collaboration by the communist parties of most of the countries during the period of the anti-fascist united front. To the contrary, right-wing opportunism developing for long within these parties was responsible for their ideological and political dissolution after the Second World War. It was just a pretext to blame Stalin and the Comintern's united front against fascism in order to expose their right-wing opportunism which had reached its peak. Undoubtedly, even if Stalin and the Comintern had not adopted, the anti-fascist united front policy, sooner or later their opportunism would have certainly come out openly. In essence, it is a question related to the development of opportunism. Opportunism always sacrifices the basic interests for temporary and partial achievements. Most communist parties did that at the time. Stalin had severely criticized the other communist parties for not taking class struggle as a central question by most of the parties during the anti-fascist united front. In this context, Stalin's strong criticism of the communist parties of France, Italy, etc.,at the first meeting of COMINFORM is especially notable here.

---

13 Bob Avakian, "Conquer the World? The International Proletariat Must and Will", *Revolution,* Special Issue, Number 50, p. 34.

3
Civil War in Spain

The RCP, USA has criticized Stalin for not acting according to the lines of proletarian internationalism in the revolutionary civil war of Spain. Avakiar writes:

> Despite the awesome achievements of the masses in the war, it is simply a fact that even had the Republic somehow defeated Franco's forces militarily, the war as a whole would have resulted in a setback for the proletariat anyway: the revolutionary leadership, the Comintern and the Communist Party of Spain (PCE), had capitulated politically well in advance of the military defeat.
>
> How did this happen?
>
> At the root of it was the Comintern's entirely wrong–and disastrous–view of the kind of historic conjucture into which the world was heading at that time. In Spain, to be blunt, the possibilities for big revolutionary advances in that country and worldwide were scarified to the defence–on a state-to-state level–of the Soviet Union.

The Chairman of the RCP, USA Bob Avakian has even gone to the extent of saying:

> It is precisely the bringing to a head of the contradictions on a world scale–the approach of the resolution of a major spiral, with the imminent prospect of world war–that at one and the same time creates the very great likelihood that the socialist country will face all-out attack by an imperialist power or powers, sharpens, brings into being, or brings closer, the objective conditions necessary for revolution in many countries, perhaps even including the imperialist powers themselves. This raises the contradiction between defending the socialist country and assisting, supporting and accelerating the revolutionary struggle in the other countries to a much intensified level. How have the socialist countries and the international communist movement handled this so far? Not too well. In general, as we know, the overwhelming tendency has been to subordinate everything to the defence of the socialist country ...[14]

In 1936, Germany and Italy jointly launched the military attack on Spain, Morocco. After the rise of Hitler in Germany, the danger from fascism had grown rapidly throughout the world. The Soviet Union had been trying its best to checkmate such a danger. In that context, military intervention, in the name of socialist aid, by the Soviet Union in Spain's civil war could have been suicidal.

---

14 Bob Avakian, "The Prospects for Revolution and the Urgent Tasks in the Decade Ahead", *Revolution*, Vol. 4, No. 10-11, p. 16.

The defeat of the revolutionary civil war in Spain was a great loss and concern for the world revolution. We should not base ourselves only on one aspect of the event if we are to arrive at a correct conclusion about the event. We should rather try to study the event in a concrete way. If we analyse a problem by taking the question of proletarian internationalism in an absolute way, this will lead us to an absolute view. Because of the absolute and subjective approach to understanding the question of proletarian internationalism, the RCP, USA concluded that Stalin and the Comintern did not act according to the line of proletarian internationalism in the revolutionary civil war of Spain. Hitler and Mussolini were providing direct and open assistance to Franco to suppress the revolutionary civil war of Spain and to establish a fascist government. On the other, the Soviet Union under the leadership of Stalin, was also providing all possible assistance to the revolutionary civil war as far as possible. The following facts make it very clear:

> The Soviet Government declared on October 7, 1936 that it considered itself free from obligation under the agreement of so-called "non-intervention". At the same time the Government of the USSR declared its intention of helping the Republican Government and the Spanish people in their heroic resistance to fascist aggression.[15]

In his telegram addressed to Jose Diaz on October 16, Comrade Stalin had mentioned that the Soviet Union would assist the revolutionary people of Spain as much as possible:

> The workers of the Soviet Union are merely carrying out their duty in giving help within their power to the revolutionary masses of Spain. They are aware that the liberation of Spain from the yoke of fascist reactionaries is not a private affair of the Spanish people but the common cause of the whole of advanced and progressive mankind.[16]

It will be appropriate to cite the following excerpt from the book entitled *The Only Way* to have an idea about to what extent the Soviet Union was assisting the revolutionary civil war of Spain.

> The Spanish people will never forget the generous and disinterested aid which they received at that dramatic moment form the Soviet Union. In all fields, wherever it was possible to defend the cause of republican Spain, be it in politics, diplomacy, a meeting of the Non-Intervention Committee or a League of Nations session, the Soviet representatives firmly and persistently

15 The "Soviet People's Warm-Hearted Fraternal Solidarity with Fighting Spain", *The Only Way*, Taken from Marxism-Leninism on Proletarian Internationalism, Progress Publishers, Moscow, First Printing, 1972, p. 274.

16 J. V. Stalin, "Telegram from the Central Committee of the CPSU (B) to the Central Committee of the Communist Party of Spain", *J. V. Stalin's Works*, Vol. 14, 1934-1940, Red Star Press Ltd., London, 1978, p. 149.

> upheld the right of the Spanish people and the government to receive aid in their noble and glorious cause–that of arresting the advance of fascism in Europe, setting a barrier to the incendiaries of war.[17]

While studying the world situation at that time, we can see that the assistance provided by the Soviet Union to the revolutionary people of Spain was in line with the proletarian internationalism. If we say that the assistance provided by the Soviet Union to the people of Spain was still lacking in the responsibility of proletarian internationalism, it leads us to the conclusion that the Soviet Union should have declared war against Germany and Italy and that only such an "assistance" would be fulfilling the duty of proletarian internationalism. In fact, if the Soviet Union had opted for such an "assistance", it was very likely that world imperialism would destroy the very existence of the Soviet Union. Clearly, it would be wrong to accept such a possible outcome.

How much attention should we pay in defence of the existence of a country where the proletarian class has come to power, where socialism is being built, and which remains as a vanguard of the world proletarian revolution, can be understood more clearly by the view expressed by Lenin on the Brest-Litovsk Peace Treaty. Lenin writes:

> If we had not concluded the Brest-Litovsk Peace Treaty, we would at once have surrendered power to the Russian bourgeoisie and thus have done untold damage to the world socialist revolution ... at the cost of *national* sacrifices, we preserved such an *international* revolutionary influence...

Lenin's statement clarifies how the question of existence of a country where a dictatorship of proletariat is established, is interrelated to the question of world socialist revolution. Lenin was clear that it was in the interest of the world revolution to defend the dictatorship of the proletariat even at the cost of conceding some small part of the country to the imperialists. If the Brest-Treaty was not reached at, it was likely that the existence of the Soviet Union would be finished and according to Lenin, this would do an "untold damage to the world socialist revolution." If we study the world situation of that time, there remains no doubt that, if in the name of proletarian internationalism, Stalin had taken a line of military confrontation with the fascist camp in Spain, the confrontation would have led to the fall of the Soviet Union.

The event of June 22, 1941 illustrates the consequences of a confrontation of the Soviet Union with the fascist camp. On that day, fascist Germany attacked the Soviet Union. In spite of the fact that the anti-fascist

17 The "Soviet People's Warm-Hearted Fraternal Solidarity with Fighting Spain", *Marxism-Leninism on Proletarian Internationalism*, Progress Publishers, Moscow, First Printing, 1972, pp. 274, 276.

war was advancing in the countries already defeated by fascism and despite the support for the Soviet Union from people of other countries engaged in the anti-fascist war, the Soviet Union had to lose some parts of its territory, and only after the formation of an anti-fascist camp could the anti-fascist popular war claim victory. If Stalin had taken a line of confrontation with the fascist camp in the name of supporting the revolutionary civil war of Spain, it would be impossible for the Soviet Union to get such a high level of support. During the time of the Spanish civil war, on the one hand the question of the anti-fascist movement had not yet become a question of immediate necessity, and on the other, the anti-fascist camp was not yet built. Because of this reason, had the Soviet Union attempted to confront the fascist camp, it would not have received anything except the moral support from the justice-loving people of the world, and thus its existence would itself have been in jeopardy.

The fact that the Western countries ignored Stalin's request to launch a joint action against the naked invasion of Hitler and Mussolini on the revolutionary civil war of Spain also made it clear that had there been an open confrontation of the Soviet Union with the fascist camp, those countries would not support the Soviet Union because by that time there was no clarity among the Western countries regarding which was the main enemy worldwide, which clarifies that it was not feasible to use America, France and Britain against the attack on Spain. At the time, if Stalin had not been successful in implementing this line, if he had decided to provide more direct assistance to Spain, this would mean that Hitler and Mussolini would wage open war against the Soviet Union, and the othe. Western countries, including France, Britain and America would silently watch this war, waiting for their turn to attack both the countries from all sides after they became weak from the war. Thus the existence of the Soviet Union would itself be destroyed.

Any proletarian revolution being launched inside a country should be a part of the world socialist revolution. According to Leninism, if it benefits the revolutionary cause of the international proletariat, then we should be prepared for any big national sacrifice. Lenin reflected on the question of the loss of the Ukraine: "We, however, say that while the loss of the Ukraine was a grave national sacrifice, it helped to steel and *strengthen* the workers and poor peasants of the Ukraine as revolutionary fighters for the world workers' revolution. The Ukraine's suffering was the world revolution's gain."[18]

In fact the Soviet Union's refusal provided direct military assistance to the revolutionary government of Spain and the Communist Party of Spain accepting this line was an adherence to the Leninist teaching, for

18 V. I. Lenin, "Proletarian Revolution and Renegade Kautsky", *Collected Works*, Eng. ed., Progress Publishers, Moscow, Third Printing, 1981, Vol. 28, p. 112.

national sacrifice to advance the international working class movement. The Second World War and the consequences after that, such as the defeat of the fascist camp and then the rise of the national liberation movement and the consolidation of the socialist camp have made it clear that Stalin's line was a true proletarian internationalist line. The Soviet Union had played a decisive role in defeating the fascist camp in the Second World War in providing inspiration to the national liberation movements and in the formation of the world socialist camp. Unlike the assessment of the RCP, USA, the line of Stalin and the Comintern of not providing direct and open military assistance to the revolutionary civil war of Spain was not a line separate from the proletarian internationalism. Stalin's line was a correct one, which did not lead the direction and motion of the world revolution onto a wrong track in the name of solving an immediate issue across the world revolutionary movement.

4
The Soviet Union's Involvement in the 1941 War

After the invasion of the Soviet Union by fascist Germany on June 22, 1941, Stalin and the Comintern called for a defensive war. The aim behind the joint military attack from the fascist camp was to destroy the existence of the great socialist country, the Soviet Union, when even a small mistake could lead to the fall of the Soviet Union, the centre of the world proletarian movement. This would inflict a heavy loss on the world socialist revolution. At that time, Stalin and the Comintern had no other choice except to integrate internationalism with patriotism. In reality, the war for defence was the practical form of proletarian internationalism.

The invasion of fascist Germany on the Soviet Union was an attack against the freedom and liberty of all the nations of the world too. The consequence of the war would determine the future of the Soviet Union and play a decisive role in determining the direction and motion of the world revolution too. Emphasizing the timeliness and justification of Stalin's line and the Comintern Mao writes:

> On June 22 the fascist rulers of Germany attacked the Soviet Union. This is a perfidious crime of aggression not only against the Soviet Union but against the freedom and independence of all nations. The Soviet Union's sacred war of resistance against fascist aggression is being waged not only in its own defence but in defence of all the nations struggling to liberate themselves from fascist enslavement.[19]

19 Mao Tse-tung, "On the International United Front Against Fascism", June 23, 1941, *Selected Works*, Foreign Language Press, Peking, Second Printing, Vol. 3, p. 29.

The above line of Stalin and the Comintern was not against the worldwide interest of advancing revolution. It was the correct form of true proletarian internationalism. However, Comrade Avakian, Chairman of the RCP, USA writes differently:

> It has to be said that with the further development of the Soviet Union, of the beginning of the socialist transformation in the Soviet Union with the leadership of Stalin, this erroneous idea became more pronounced, while at the same time the fact that things would not develop that way became more pronounced. And, at the same time the tendency to say that there was an absolute identity of interests between the Soviet Republic as a proletarian state and the overall advance of world revolution became more pronounced, more marked and tended to a large degree, particularly in the late 1930s to turn rather sharply towards and into its opposite.
>
> The fact that there was indeed a contradiction, as I said, at times a very acute and potentially antagonistic contradiction between the maintaining of power in one socialist state and the advance of the world revolution overall, could in a certain sense be mitigated and buried under the fact that the Soviet national interests, or the national interests, if you will, of the proletariat in power in the Soviet Union went parallel with world revolution at that time and the policies that were being adopted by the Soviet state did not come sharply into conflict with the overall revolutionary struggle in other parts of the world. Yes, it came into conflict here and there but as a secondary matter. Nevertheless, even though the world revolution was promoted overall and the attempt was made to support and advance it, things were presented in terms of an absolute identity of interests and at the same time it was already beginning to be said–and this became much more fully the line later and has been maintained and deepened as the line down to today–that the leading edge, or the cutting edge, of the world revolution was first the building and then the defence of socialism (real or alleged) in the Soviet Union (that is, the socialist road really being embarked on and advanced on for a certain period and then only being alleged and "socialism" being used as a cover for capitalist restoration and imperialism later on).[20]

Avakian has even gone to the extent of saying "anti-Leninist positions ... fundamental departures from Marxism-Leninism." As he says:

> All this was concentrated in the Dimitroff Report to the 7th World Congress of the Comintern (1935) and the implementation and further development of this line–which, as we know, involved, among other things, as one of its key ingredients, the basic repudiation of the Leninist position on "defence of the fatherland". This whole line was in its essence erroneous ...[21]

---

20 Bob Avakian, "Conquer the World? The International Proletariat Must and Will", *Revolution*, Special Issue, Number 50, pp. 18, 19.

21 Bob Avakian, "Outline of Views on the Historical Experience of the International Communist Movement and the Lessons for Today", *Revolution*, June 1981, pp. 5, 6.

It reveals Comrade Avakian's absolute approach of viewing war and world revolution. A war being waged by any country and the world revolution should not be viewed only in terms of absolute and general principles, but it should be viewed on a concrete historic basis. War is a concrete historic phenomenon. On the question of national liberation, whether before the proletarian revolution or during consolidation of socialism, the defence of the fatherland is essential. As Mao writes:

> The specific content of patriotism is determined by historical conditions. There is the "patriotism" of the Japanese aggressors and of Hitler, and there is our patriotism ... China's case is different, because she is the victim of aggression. Chinese Communists must therefore combine patriotism with internationalism. We are at once internationalists and patriots, and our slogan is, "Fight to defend the motherland against the aggressors". For us defeatism is a crime and to strive for victory in the War of Resistance is an inescapable duty ... Only those who are politically muddle-headed or have ulterior motives talk nonsense about our having made a mistake and abandoned internationalism.[22]

It is unfortunate that Comrade Avakian considers putting Mao's views forward means "significant departures from the Leninism" to some extent.[23]

When we talk about defending a country, we should not always think that it goes against the world socialist revolution. Without distinguishing between various kinds of defence, if we think that it is always against world revolution, this will mean a fundamental deviation from the Marxism-Leninism on the question of war and revolution. Every defensive war is not reactionary in an absolute way. It can be progressive too. Such a defensive war does not have an antagonistic contradiction with the interest of the world revolution, and plays a supplementary role for later. This is the only correct approach with which to approach the problem of the defensive war. Lenin clarifies further: "The character of the war (whether it is reactionary or revolutionary) does not depend on who the attacker was, or in whose country the 'enemy' is stationed; it depends on *what class* is waging the war, and on what politics this war is a continuation of."[24]

On the question of war, we can sum up the Leninism as given below:

a. War has a class and national character. We should analyse every war on the basis of class and national independence, and we should support, or oppose a war on the basis of this fundamental point;

---

22 Mao Tse-tung, "The Role of the Communist Party of China in the National War", *Selected Works*, Foreign Language Press, Peking, First ed., 1965, Vol. 2, pp. 196-97.

23 Bob Avakian, "Outline of Views on the Historical Experience of the International Communist Movement and the Lessons for Today", *Revolution,* June 1981, p. 5.

24 V. I. Lenin, "Proletarian Revolution and Renegade Kautsky", *Collected Works*, Eng. ed., Progress Publishers, Moscow, Third Printing, 1981, Vol. 28, p. 286.

b. After analysing the character of the war, if it is waged by the exploiting class for looting and exploitation, we should resolutely oppose it, and if it is waged for class emancipation or for national liberation or for defence of socialist motherland, we should support it; and,

c. To follow any other road, except this road, is to deviate from Marxism-Leninism on the question.

Even Marx and Engels had themselves called for a national war many times. For instance, in 1848, Marx, and in 1859 Engels, had called on Germans for national war. Similarly in 1891, Engels had accepted the "defence of the Fatherland" for Germany. We can also find such support for bourgeois nationalism in the writings of Lenin.

Unlike the position of the RCP, USA, the proletarian class struggle has to follow the line of safeguarding its dictatorship and the socialist state. Undoubtedly, it should be defensive for the whole period of socialist revolution. As long as there is imperialist enclosure, it is wrong for the proletariat to forget or to neglect the question of safeguarding and strengthening its dictatorship and socialist state.

After the joint aggression launched by the imperialists and other capitalist countries against the newly established Soviet Union, Lenin in his writings had given the slogan *"The Socialist fatherland is in danger! Long live the socialist fatherland! Long live the international socialist revolution!"* He had further said that "It is the sacred duty of the workers and peasants of Russia devotedly to defend the Republic of Soviets against the hordes of bourgeois-imperialist Germany."[25] We should always stand firm in favour of a defensive war, which strengthens the power of the oppressed class and does not weaken it, and which consolidates the base of socialism, but does not weaken it. The war waged by the Soviet Union in 1941 was a war for the defence of the proletarian state, for liberation and freedom from fascist enslavement, and to be precise it was a war waged for liberation from fascist oppression and for safeguarding the struggling nations. How does Comrade Avakian see such a war as having an "antagonistic contradiction" with the interest of "advancing revolution worldwide"? In Lenin's words, Comrade Avakian could not understand "Why and when "defencism" is abominable." Answering "Left communists", Lenin had said:

> I shall enlighten you , my amiable friends, as to why such disaster overtook you. It is because you devote more effort to learning by heart and committing to memory revolutionary slogans than to thinking them out. This leads you to write "the defence of the socialist fatherland" in quotation marks, which are probably meant to signify your attempts at

25 V. I. Lenin, "The Socialist Fatherland is in Danger", *Collected Works*, Eng. ed., Progress Publishers, Moscow, Third Printing, 1977, Vol. 27, pp. 33, 30.

being ironical, but which really prove that you are muddleheads. You are accustomed to regard "defencism" as something base and despicable; you have learned this and committed it to memory. You have learned this by heart so thoroughly that some of you have begun talking nonsense to the effect that defence of the fatherland in an imperialist *epoch* is impermissible (as a matter of fact, it is impermissible only in an imperialist, reactionary war, waged by the bourgeoisie). But you have not thought out why and when "defencism" is abominable.

To recognize defence of the fatherland means recognizing the legitimacy and justice of war. Legitimacy and justice from what point of view? Only from the point of view of the socialist proletariat and its struggle for its emancipation. We do not recognize any other point of view. If war is waged by the exploiting class with the object of strengthening its rule as a class, such a war is a criminal war, and "defencism" in *such* a war is a base betrayal of socialism. If war is waged by the proletariat after it has conquered the bourgeoisie in its own country, and is waged with the object of strengthening and developing socialism, such a war is legitimate and "holy".

We have been "defencists" since October 25, 1917. I have said this more than once very definitely, and you dare not deny this. It is precisely in the interests of "strengthening the connection" with international socialism that we *are in duty bound* to defend our *socialist* fatherland. Those who treat frivolously the defence of the country in which the proletariat has already achieved victory are the ones who destroy the connection with international socialism. When we were the representatives of an oppressed class we did not adopt a frivolous attitude towards defence of the fatherland in an imperialist war. We opposed such defence on principle. Now that we have become representatives of the ruling class, which has begun to organize socialism, we demand that everybody adopt a *serious* attitude towards defence of the country.

When we were opposed to defencism on principle we were justified in holding up to ridicule those who wanted to "save" their fatherland, ostensibly in the interests of socialism. When we gained the right to be proletarian defencists the whole question was radically altered.[26]

The war waged by the Soviet Union in 1941 was the war for the proletariat and its liberation; it was a war waged by the proletariat to safeguard its dictatorship, it was a war fought by the proletariat to develop and strengthen socialism in the country. So, that was a "holy" war. Those who say that this war waged by the Soviet Union is criminal, abominable and betrayal to the world revolution should be asked the following question: Was this a war waged "by the exploiting class to strengthen its class rule" which is termed by Lenin as "abominable" and "betrayal to socialism"?

---

26 V.I.Lenin, "The Socialist Fatherland is in Danger", *Collected Works*, Eng. ed., Progress Publishers, Moscow, Third Printing, 1977, Vol. 27, pp. 331-32.

Stalin and the Comintern were not against working in the interest of the world socialist revolution. Instead, by opposing the war of 1941 waged by the Soviet Union, the then vanguard of the world proletarian revolution where the proletariat was in power and was under the socialist construction, the RCP, USA actually abandoned working in the interest of the world socialist revolution and the victory of socialism in Russia.

Stalin and the Comintern raised the slogan for countering the joint fascist attack to safeguard the Soviet Union and the freedom and independence of all nations. The defensive war of 1941 was definitely a concrete step in advancing the world socialist revolution. This has been proved by the safeguarding of the socialist Soviet Union and the formation of the socialist camp after the war. The General Secretary of the Communist Party of Sri Lanka, Comrade N. Sanmugathasan, has rightly said that the war of the Soviet Union was a "glorious and successful struggle of the CPSU against the counter revolution and world fascism."[27] The war waged by the Soviet Union did not have any "antagonistic contradiction" with the world socialist revolution. Only people either politically muddleheaded, or having ulterior motives, can think in this way.

5
Character of the Second World War

Was the character of the war for the whole duration of the Second World War only inter-imperialist or was there a change in its character soon after the launch of war, mainly after June 22, 1941? It is a subject of serious differences within the world proletarian movement. If we look at the reason behind the breaking out of the Second World War and the development afterwards, we find that two kinds of characters were prevalent in the war: the inter-imperialist war for the first two years of the war, and then a war between the fascist camp and the liberation movement after the German invasion on the Soviet Union on June 22, 1941.

The First World War did have the same character of an inter-imperialist war from the beginning to the end. The world situation during the Second World War had its own historical characteristics. They represent different concrete historical stages. At the time of the First World War, no socialist country was in existence in a strong condition in the world. If we look at the whole character of the First World War, the camp opposing the war since the very beginning was very weak. At that time, there was no

27 N. Sanmugathasan, "Stalin: The Great Marxist-Leninist", *International Revolutionary Digest*, September 1984, No. 1, p. 41.

favourable objective situation for using tactics of one imperialist camp against the other. The capitalist world itself was not aware of the consequences of the war. Even the bourgeoisie themselves had no experience of the devastating consequences of the war. Rightist opportunism was dominant over the world communist movement. The First World War was waged by the two world groups of the imperialist, rapacious predatory, reactionary bourgeoisie. It was waged by the exploiting classes with the distinct objective of strengthening its rule as a class. It was a war waged by the two imperialist groups for the division of the world, for the division of the looted goods, and to subjugate and bring the weak and small nations under their lynching feet.

However, the situation at the time of the Second World War was fundamentally different. There was the existence of a great powerful socialist country like the Soviet Union at that time. The revolutionary line emerged victorious in the international communist movement. After the Soviet Union joined the war, one camp of imperialism was used against the fascist camp, a united military front of the Soviet Union, the USA, France and Britain against the fascist camp, and these countries had passed important policies supporting the war of the Soviet Union. In sum, an anti-fascist united front had been formed at the war after fascist Germany invaded the Soviet Union. On the fundamental difference of the situation between the First and Second World Wars, Mao writes: "This new situation is very different from that in First World War. The Soviet Union was not yet in existence then and the people were not politically awakened as they are in many countries today. The two world wars represent two entirely different epochs."[28]

After fascist Germany invaded the Soviet Union on June 22, 1941, the war of defence waged by the Soviet Union in the face of such an attack against its freedom and independence was seen as not merely a war for self-defence, but a war to liberate all the struggling countries from the clutches of fascism:

> This is a perfidious crime of aggression not only against the Soviet Union but against the freedom and independence of all nations. The Soviet Union's sacred war of resistance against fascist aggression is being waged not only in its own defence but in defence of all the nations struggling to liberate themselves from fascist enslavement.[29]

As a result, the war which was taking the form of an inter-imperialist war until June 21, 1941, it changed its form to a war between fascism and the activists of the liberation movement. Comrade John B. Tyles is correct

28 Mao Tse-tung, "On Coalition Government", *Selected Works*, Foreign Language Press, Peking, Second Printing, 1967, Vol. 3, p. 207.

29 Mao Tse-tung, "On the International United Front Against Fascism", June 23, 1941, *Selected Works*, Foreign Language Press, Peking, Second Printing, Vol. 3, p. 29.

when he says, "Second World War changed in character overnight with the invasion of the Soviet Union which changed the objective situation, the necessity, and thus the opportunities for advancing the struggle of the working class."

It was not argued individually by Comrade Tyles within the RCP, USA, but the RCP, USA itself had such a view at a certain time. This fact is clear from these words of the *Programme* of the RCP, USA.

> So, with the German invasion of the USSR in 1941, WWII changed. It was no longer just a battle for the spoils among the imperialists. It became a battle for the defence of the future, as it was already being realized by the Soviet working people in building socialism. Millions of workers and other oppressed people around the world fought, and died to defeat the fascist axis in order to defend socialism and to advance their own march towards socialist revolution.[30]

In spite of the previous position, the RCP, USA says:

> The Second World War, from beginning to end, was the second world *inter-imperialist* war–this was its principal aspect and overall character even after the Soviet Union was invaded and became involved in the war. ... The aspect of socialism vs. imperialism, and more generally of progressive struggle (warfare) against imperialism, was far greater in this Second World War than in the first, but it was not the principal aspect and did not determine the character of the war as a whole (which remained inter-imperialist). Summing this up and analysing the errors on this of the leaders of the USSR (and the Comintern)–much more deeply–is crucial in order to strike more penetratingly and powerfully at the roots of revisionism in the international communist movement".

The RCP, USA comments on the view that the character of the Second World War changed after the fascist invasion on the Soviet Union in this way:

> This was actually a line of *incorrectly* subordinating everything to the defence of the Soviet Union and *along with that* downplaying or even denying the need to advance revolutionary struggles elsewhere that conflicted with this narrowly (and overall erroneously) conceived defence of the USSR, and it seriously deviated from the correct, Leninist analysis of imperialism and imperialist war and from the Marxist-Leninist stand on the nature of the state ... and other cardinal question.

The RCP, USA has given the following arguments to support its view that no change in the characteristic of the war took place even after the German invasion on the Soviet Union: the first argument of the RCP, USA is that even after the Soviet Union entered the war, "not to such an extent

30 Johan B. Tyles, "On the Character of World War 2", *The Communist*, Theoretical Journal of the Central Committee of the Revolutionary Communist Party, USA, Vol. 1, No. 1, p. 108.

or in such a way that their pursuit of their imperialist interests–and the opposition between them and interests and aims of the rival imperialist group–was relegated to a secondary position."

This argument does not fit with the reality as after Germany invaded the Soviet Union, one camp of imperialism was definitely used against the fascist camp by making its expansion a secondary one for a while. Not only that since the fascist danger was escalating in the European countries too, they had also adopted important policies against the fascist camp, by supporting the war of the Soviet Union. Once a camp of the imperialist countries made their expansionist and imperialist interests secondary after entering into the war of the Soviet Union, it was possible to advance the war against the fascist camp from two fronts. If it was not possible to wage war, it was not certain that the Soviet Union and all the oppressed countries would have been victorious over the fascist camp. Britain had agreed to work jointly with the Soviet Union against Germany within a few weeks after Germany initiated war against the Soviet Union. Ten months after the German invasion of the Soviet Union, during the visit of Moltov to Britain, Britain signed a treaty of friendship on May 26, 1942 to fight against Hitler's Germany and its allies. Similarly, in June 1942, during the visit of Moltov to America, America had agreed to a joint cooperation with the Soviet Union against Germany and its backers. Also in the latter days, America, Britain and the European countries went on maintaining better relations with the Soviet Union. The Tehran and Yalta Conferences are clear examples in this regard.

The second argument of the RCP, USA is that even though the Soviet Union had a major and decisive role in defeating fascist Germany, "that does not change the fact that the main opposition being struggled out through the course of the entire war was that between the two groups of imperialists."[31] The RCP, USA has assessed the Soviet Union's role in the Second World War in a very light, subjective and absolutist way. It is a subjectivist, absolutist and wrong understanding of the proposition of Lenin that the war of redivision is inevitable in imperialism, in which two camps of imperialism divide the whole world into two parts. It is the reason behind their wrong evaluation of the Second World War.

For all these reasons, the RCP, USA views that though the Soviet Union had a major and decisive role in defeating fascist Germany, that did not make any change in the character of the inter-imperialist war. It has absolutely refused to accept that in a war of redivision in the imperialist era, the character of the war can be changed from an inter-imperialist war to a war between one group of world imperialism and the activists of the

31 Bob Avakian, "Addendum on the Character of WWII ... and Why it Did Not Change", *Revolution,* June 1981, pp. 8-9.

liberation movement. The thing to pay attention is that this is an entirely different epoch from the epoch of the First World War. This war had two characteristics, i.e. the inter-imperialist war for the first two years of the war and then a war between the fascist camp and the activists of the liberation movement after the German invasion of the Soviet Union on June 22, 1941. To deny this fact is to refuse to see that the First World War and the Second World War were fought in two different contexts.

6
Dissolution of the Comintern

Now, some communist parties are saying that the decision taken by the Presidium of the Comintern in 1943 to dissolve the Comintern was completely wrong. This view is forwarded by the RCP, USA. According to Chairman Avakain, Stalin's only aim behind such a decision was the "defence of the Soviet Union"[32]. In the wake of the breaking out of the Second World War, it was necessary to push forward the joint attack of independent lovers against the common enemy "Hitlerism" to forge a solidarity of all liberation lovers progressive forces without any racial or religious discrimination for the national independence while opposing the world hegemony of Hitler and also to make an alliance of friendship for the future based on equality as a base to galvanize all justice lovers, and to assist patriotic forces. So, it would have been inappropriate to continue the existence of an international level centralized organization like the Comintern for fulfilling the above mentioned objective. America, Britain, France and other bourgeois forces, aligned with the anti-fascist camp, were demanding the Comintern be dissolved. At the time, the war against Hitler's Germany and its allies at the world level was most needed. We think that in the context, the dissolution of the Comintern was quite correct. Stalin himself has thrown light on the necessity to dissolve the Comintern at that time and its timeliness. He writes:

> The dissolution of the Communist International is proper and timely because it facilitates the organization of the common onslaught of all freedom-loving nations against the common enemy–Hitlerism. The dissolution of the Communist International is proper because:
>
> (a) It exposes the lie of the Hitlerites to the effect that "Moscow" allegedly intends to intervene in the life of other nations and to "Bolshevise" them. An end is now being put to this lie.
>
> (b) It exposes the calumny of the adversaries of Communism within the Labour movement to the effect that the Communist Parties in various

32 Bob Avakian, "Outline of Views on the Historical Experience of the International Communist Movement and the Lessons for Today", *Revolution,* June 1981, p. 6.

countries are allegedly acting not in the interests of their people but on orders from outside. An end is now being put to this calumny too.

(c) It facilitates the work of patriots of all countries for uniting the progressive forces of their respective countries, regardless of party or religious faith, into a single camp of national liberation for unfolding the struggle against fascism.

(d) It facilitates the work of patriots of all countries for uniting all freedom-loving peoples into a single international camp for the fight against the menace of world domination by Hitlerism, thus clearing the way to the future organization of a companionship of nations based on their equality.

I think that all these circumstances taken together will result in a further strengthening of the United Front of the Allies and other united nations in their fight for victory over Hitlerite tyranny. I feel that the dissolution of the Communist International is perfectly timely–because it is exactly now, when the fascist beast is exerting its last strength, that it is necessary to organize the common onslaught of freedom-loving countries to finish off this beast and to deliver the people from fascist oppression.[33]

The Comintern had played an important role in the tide of communist and liberation movements after the First World War. It contributed to the international communists by giving suggestions and instructions to the formation of the revolutionary communist party, developing a tactical and strategic plan as well as by warning to prevent mistakes from ultra leftist deviation or tilt to the right-wing revisionism. Likewise, it was always conscious that the liberation movement should not be transformed into a means for transferring power from one reactionary class to the other. The Comintern used to send suggestions and advice to the struggling just and patriotic people so that their movements did not take a wrong direction and it also used to provide suggestions on what form of government should be established after the revolution.

The establishment of the Comintern as the leading organization of the world proletarian movement was a historic necessity and since history is of the dynamic character of social existence, it was certain from the very beginning that this leading body inherited in it the possibility of change in its form, or its dissolution after a certain time. Revolutionary organizations, associations, thoughts and counter thoughts are not absolute things. Concrete historic necessity leads to creation or end of them. The history includes the process of their dissolution as soon as these are created. The form of an organization at a particular time and the change it undergoes depends fully on the change in the balance concerning the class power taking place in the world level, or in any country.

33 *The Communist International 1919-1943 Documents,* Selected and Edited by Jane Degras, Vol. III, 1929-1943, pp. 476-77.

Revolution is the ideological reflection representing the special situation and level of the objective character of the whole world and of any particular country. Therefore, for anything under consideration, as long as it represents the interests for the particular changes at a time, this becomes a thing of historic necessity. On the other, if it cannot represent the interest of the changed objective situation, then its dissolution becomes inevitable. If we criticize Stalin for dissolving the Comintern in the changed situation, then why should we not blame Marx for dissolving the First International?

If we blame the dissolution of the Comintern responsible for the rise of American imperialism and birth of modern revisionism after the Second World War, this is unfair because the imperialism and revisionism had emerged in the period of the Second International. During the same period Bernsteinism too had emerged. Therefore, the rise of American imperialism and the birth of modern revisionism after the Second World War is not related to the establishment and dissolution of an organization. These are the developments which depend on the general and specific laws of class struggle, and contradiction between productive forces and relations of production in society. This is the natural consequence of the development of imperialism. Therefore, to blame Stalin's decision to dissolve the Comintern and for the rise of American imperialism and birth of modern revisionism after the Second World War is to hold a subjective view about the revolution and counter-revolution.

It is clear that the real reasons behind the rise of American imperialism are the devastating attacks on Britain and France by fascist Germany, the inhuman attack against Japan by America and the humiliating defeat of Germany in the Second World War. Because of this, American imperialism, which had been preserving its power during and after the Second World War, could put itself forward as a superpower. As for the emergence of modern revisionism, the dominance of bourgeois agents like Khrushchev in the CPSU and the influence of the revisionist line of the renegade Tito at the international level are the reasons behind this. For this, theoretically and objectively the main thing is the uneven development of capitalism.

Apart from this, the RCP, USA states that the dissolution of the Comintern by Stalin was not a part of any tactical plan. He adds that if it were so, he would pay attention to form a Communist International after the war. But this charge is not based on fact. The establishment of the COMINFORM in 1947 can be taken as a concrete example of this. Stalin's plan was to organize COMINFORM in the form of a Communist International. But this aim could not succeed because of the split in the international communist movement and the dominance of Khrushchev in the CPSU after the demise of Stalin.

7
Proletarian Internationalism and Patriotism

Proletarian internationalism and patriotism are interrelated to each other. We should not separate these two from one another, but we should rather integrate them intimately. It is a big mistake to think that patriotism is always opposed to internationalism. In the name of being internationalist, communists should not give up patriotism. In replying to the question "Can a communist, who is an internationalist, at the same time be a patriot?" Mao Tse-tung says: "We hold that he not only can be but must be."[34]

Internationalism is the essence and it expresses itself in the form of true patriotism. Essence and form are interrelated. To forget the dialectical unity between them means following the metaphysical line of thinking. Marxist-Leninist dialectics not only stresses the decisiveness of the essence, but further adds that form has an active role over the essence and the essence cannot be looked at by separating it from the form. Therefore, we should always view internationalism and patriotism by linking them with each other, not by separating them. To have a correct knowledge about proletarian internationalism and patriotism, it is not enough to know only about the interrelationship between them. For this, we should also understand that proletarian internationalism and patriotism can change from one to another depending on time and necessity. Communists, on the one hand, should be able to perceive the correct reflection of the change in their objective situation, and on the other, they should apply them concretely as necessary. According to Mao, proletarian internationalism integrates with the wars of national liberation, and is necessary to integrate with a socialist country too. As he writes concerning the second part of the subject: "The socialist countries are of an entirely new type in which the exploiting classes are overthrown and the working people are in power. The principle of integrating internationalism with patriotism has been practised in the relations between these countries."[35]

The above proposition of Mao Tse-tung is an excellent example of the truth that proletarian internationalism and patriotism can change from one to another depending on the situation, time and necessity. In the present-day world proletarian movement, a wrong tendency of fully abandoning the question of patriotism by taking the statement "working men have no country" from the *Manifesto of the Communist Party* is intensely

---

34 Mao Tse-tung, "The Role of the Communist Party of China in the National War", *Selected Works*, Foreign Language Press, Peking, First ed., 1965, Vol. 2, p. 196.

35 Mao Tse-tung, "Speech at Moscow Celebrating Meeting, November, 1957", *Selected Works*, Kranti Publications, Secunderabad, India, First ed., 1991, Vol. 7, p. 418.

developing in an absolute sense. On the basis of the fact that the character of the proletariat is international in essence, the RCP, USA speaks as if the proletariat does not have a national character, even in form. In the context of such a partial and wrong understanding of the RCP, USA about the *Communist Manifesto*, it will be appropriate to put forth the following statement of Lenin:

> In the *Communist Manifesto* it is said that the working men have no country. Correct. But *not only* this is stated there. It is stated there also that when national states are being formed the role of the proletariat is somewhat special. To take the first proposition (the working men have no country) and *forget* its *connection* with the second (the workers are constituted as a class nationally, though not in the same sense as the bourgeoisie) will be exceptionally incorrect.[36]

Anyone (including comrades of the RCP, USA) can say that Lenin's above view is related with national questions, not with the socialist countries in which the exploiting classes have been overthrown and the working people are in power. Certainly, Lenin was using the term concerning a national question. It is not correct on this basis that Lenin was against the defence of the socialist fatherland. This concept covers the moments of struggle for the overthrow of national oppression, and the struggle for the overthrow of the international capital. At the beginning, the struggle of the proletariat against the bourgeoisie–though not in essence–is certainly a national struggle in form. Certainly, the proletariat of each country has to destroy the class of bourgeoisie of its own country first.

As the *Communist Manifesto* clarifies:

> The working men have no country. We cannot take from them what they have not got. Since the proletariat must first of all acquire political supremacy, must rise to be the leading class of the nation, must constitute itself *the* nation, it is, so far, itself national, though not in the bourgeois sense of the world.[37]

At one place, while attacking patriotism and nationality, Comrade Avakian writes that he does "not believe that in a fundamental sense there is for a communist such a thing as national pride", and he does "not believe that *ideologically* there is such a thing as national pride nor national nihilism."[38]

This view has not any relation with Leninism, so it is against Leninism. National pride has two forms, one is reactionary and the other is progressive.

---

36 V. I. Lenin, "To Innessa Armand", *Collected Works*, Eng. ed., Progress Publishers, Moscow, Fourth Printing, 1980, Vol. 35, p. 251.

37 Karl Marx and Frederick Engels, "Manifesto of the Communist Party", *Karl Marx and Frederick Engels Selected Works*, Progress Publishers, Moscow, Fourth Printing, 1977, Vol. 1, p. 124.

38 Bob Avakian, Taken from "On the Question of So-Called 'National Nihilism' ", *Revolution,* June 1981, p. 22.

Communists must always oppose the first type of, i.e. reactionary, "national pride" and must welcome the healthy second type of, i.e. progressive national pride. On the importance of "national pride" for communists, Lenin writes:

> Is a sense of national pride alien to us, Great-Russian class conscious proletarians? Certainly not! We love our language and our country, and we are doing our very utmost to raise *her* toiling masses (i.e. nine-tenths of *her* population) to the level of a democratic and socialist consciousness. To us it is most painful to see and feel the outrages, the oppression and humiliation our fair country suffers at the hands of the tsar's butchers, the nobles and the capitalists. We take pride in the resistance to these outrages put up from our midst, from the Great Russians; in *that* midst, having produced Radishchev, the Decembrists and the revolutionary commoners of the seventies ... We are full of national pride because the Great-Russian nation, *too*, has created a revolutionary class, because it, *too*, has proved capable of providing mankind with great models of the struggle for freedom and socialism. ... We are full of a sense of national pride.[39]

The RCP, USA seems to have an allergy against the word patriotism. According to the RCP, USA, patriotism has no class character. The existence of the state which emerged as a result of the existence of classes and class struggle can cease only after the termination of classes and struggle between them. Of course, the form of the state can change according to the situation, time and necessity. The form of nation and patriotism can be changed according to the situation, time and necessity. The proletarian state is also nothing more than the changed form of the state. The concept of the proletarian state does not signify the negation of patriotism, but it signifies their special form. The proletarian state is a fundamentally different kind of state compared to the bourgeois state. This is the final form of the existence of the state. The existence of the proletarian state is for the withering away of the state itself. Likewise, the existence of the proletarian nation and patriotism is for wither out. But as long as the social bases of its existence does not completely wither out, we should keep on adopting their various forms depending on the situation.

Based on the "working men have no country" from the *Communist Manifesto*, and that the class character is not national, but international in essence, Avakian has concluded that "do not believe that ideologically there is such a thing as national pride nor national nihilism." Comrade Avakian has accepted patriotism on the question of colonial countries. But by many instances, especially on the question of socialist countries, it is clear that he has fully abandoned patriotism. Communists accept the importance of patriotism to a certain extent and cannot refute the danger of national

39 V. L. Lenin, "On the National Pride of the Great Russians", *Collected Works*, Third Printing, 1980, Vol. 21, pp. 103-04.

nihilism within the movement. However, Avakian seems to have ignored this risk. As long as there is any value of patriotism for the communists there always exists the danger of national nihilism. These objective facts clearly show that the RCP, USA itself is supporting national nihilism. If it does not take proper steps in safeguarding itself from such deviations, it is certain that it will give rise to another wrong line in the international communist movement. We hope and wish that such a thing will not occur.

We think that by using this phrase Dimitrov was emphasizing the defence of the national sentiments of the broad toiling masses and of the defence of the socialist mother (father) land. At the time, by using this phrase, he was not advocating national chauvinism, he was not abandoning proletarian internationalism as the comrades of the RCP, USA have argued.

Comrade Avakian has raised some questions on the phrase 'national nihilism', used by Comrade Dimitrov, then General Secretary of the Comintern in its Seventh Congress:

> We communists are the *irreconcilable opponents, on principle,* of bourgeois nationalism in all its forms. But we *are not supporters of national nihilism*, and should never act as such. The task of educating the workers and all working people in the spirit of proletarian internationalism is one of the fundamental tasks of every communist party. But anyone who thinks that this permits him, or even compels him, to sneer at all the national sentiments of the wide masses of working people is far from being a genuine Bolshevik, and has understood nothing of the teaching of Lenin and Stalin on the national question.

Finally, in this context, it will be appropriate to cite the following statement made by Dimitrov, the then General Secretary of the Comintern, in the Seventh World Congress:

> Proletarian internationalism must, so to speak, "acclimatize itself" in each country in order to sink deep roots in its native land. *National forms* of the proletarian class struggle and of the labour movement in the individual countries are in no contradiction to proletarian internationalism; on the contrary, it is precisely in these forms that the *international interests* of the proletariat can be successfully defended."
>
> Proletarian internationalism not only is not in contradiction to this struggle of the working people of the individual countries for national, social and cultural freedom, but, thanks to international proletarian solidarity and fighting unity, assures the *support* that is necessary for victory in this struggle. The working class in the capitalist countries can triumph *only in closest alliance* with the victorious proletariat of the great Soviet Union. *Only* by struggling hand in hand with the proletariat of the imperialist countries can the colonial peoples and oppressed national minorities achieve their freedom. The sole road to victory for the proletarian revolution in the imperialist

countries lies through the revolutionary alliance of the working class of the imperialist countries with the national liberation movement in the colonies and dependent countries, because, as Marx taught us, "no nation can be free if it oppresses other nations."

Communists belonging to an oppressed, dependent nation cannot combat chauvinism successfully among the people of their own nation if they *do not at the same time show* in practice, in the mass movement, that they actually struggle for the liberation of their nation from the alien yoke. And again, on the other hand, the communists of an oppressing nation cannot do what is necessary to educate the working masses of their nation in the spirit of internationalism *without waging* a resolute struggle against the oppressor policy of their "own" bourgeoisie, for the right of complete self-determination for the nations kept in bondage by it. If they do not do this, they likewise do not make it easier for the working people of the oppressed nation to overcome their nationalist prejudices.[40]

8
Principal Contradiction in the Present World

Identifying the principal contradiction correctly, out of the many fundamental contradictions inherent in the complex process of development of the world today, is of an immense and far-reaching importance. The principal contradiction plays a leading and decisive role in the complex process of the world. As long as a correct approach is not taken in this regard, the contradiction inherent in the complex process of development of the world cannot be solved. Today it is necessary for all the Marxist-Leninists of the world to think on this question in a very sober and historical materialistic way.

At present, the RCP, USA and some other parties hold the view that the analysis on the principal world contradiction made by the Communist Party of China (CPC) under the leadership of Mao in 1963 is no more valid. On the other, the CPN (Mashal) and some other parties hold that this analysis is still valid and correct at present too.

In 1963, the CPC under the leadership of Mao made it clear that the following were the fundamental contradictions in the complex process of development of the contemporary world: "The contradiction between the socialist camp and the imperialist camp; the contradiction between the proletariat and the bourgeoisie in the capitalist countries; the contradiction

40 Georgi Dimitrov, "Report to the Seventh Congress of the Communist International 1935", *For the Unity of the Working Class Against Fascism,* Red Star Press Ltd., London, 1975, pp. 105-06, 109.

between the oppressed nations and imperialism; and the contradictions among imperialist countries and among monopoly capitalist groups."[41]

Among the fundamental contradictions listed above, the first one, "The contradiction between the socialist camp and the imperialist camp" is a contradiction between two fundamentally different social systems. Since there is no socialist system anywhere in the world today, this contradiction also does not exist any more. In this situation, the only remaining three contradictions from the above list are in existence. Among those fundamental contradictions, the CPC under the leadership of Mao had analysed that "The contradiction between the oppressed nations and imperialism" was the principal world contradiction at that time.

The principal world contradiction is related to time, and it represents the specificity of the complex process of the development of things. The above analysis of the CPC on the principal world contradiction is also related to time, and it represents the specific situation of the complex process of development of the world. The above analysis of the CPC will also change in other specific situations of the development of the world and at some time in future any of the other contradictions can take place. For instance, in future, the other centres of world revolution can be capitalist and imperialist countries, or the socialist camp (after the socialist camp has been built and expanded in future); in future, the main trend of the world can be imperialist war, instead of being revolution and so on.

Thus, in future, the principal world contradiction can be changed. The problem with the international communist movement today is not whether the principal world contradiction will change, or not in future, but it is about deciding on what is the specificity of the complex process of development of the present-day world? On this very question, as we have written, we have serious differences with the RCP, USA in the form of differences on the principal world contradiction. We hold the view that the specific feature of the complex process of development of the world has remained generally the same since 1963, and no basic change has taken place in this situation. Just like in or around 1963, even today the principal contradiction of the world is concentrated in Asia, Africa and Latin America. These regions are still being oppressed by the world imperialism and the people there are fighting liberation movements of worldwide significance against the imperialist oppression. These regions still remain as storm centres of world revolution. The struggles between capital and labour taking place in the capitalist countries are also influenced by the national liberation movements of Asia, Africa and Latin America. Today

41 "A Proposal Concerning the General Line of the International Communist Movement", *The Great Debate*, Mass Line Publications, Kerala, India 1994, pp. 4-5.

the struggle of the proletariat against the capital in the capitalist countries cannot become the principal form of struggle at the world level. The proletariat of these countries should practise proletarian internationalism and support the national liberation movements of Asia, Africa and Latin America, since the struggle of the oppressed countries in these continents is the decisive force in the struggle against the imperialism. The storm centres of world revolution are also the oppressed regions, not the capitalist countries.

There are two aspects of the present-day world proletarian movement. The first is the national and democratic movement, or the liberation movement taking place in the oppressed nations of Asia, Africa and Latin America. The second is the proletarian movement in the capitalist countries. These two aspects of the movement cannot be viewed by separating them from one another. In fact, the liberation movement in the oppressed nations of Asia, Africa and Latin America is the inseparable part of the world proletarian revolution. The communist parties of these countries need to lead the liberation movement against imperialism and its stooges and thus lead the movement towards socialism and communism.

There exists a serious problem before us in relation to the liberation movements in Asia, Africa and Latin America. It is the lack of revolutionary communist leadership in those movements. The result of these movements not being led by true Marxist-Leninists has been such that these movements have ended up in being manipulated and led by one or another superpower. Instead of being an inseparable part of the world proletarian movement, these liberation movements have ended up in tallying behind world imperialism. Superficially, it appears that rather than being storm centres of world revolution, Asia, Africa and Latin America have been the site for the showing of power and for the fulfilment of the interests of the world imperialism. This situation of these regions at present is true only in the subjective form, but not in objective form. In an objective form, in these regions the situation is favourable for the revolutionary liberation movement which can be directly transformed to socialism and communism. The views expressed by Mao about these regions still hold true. Indeed, still in these regions, nations want freedom, countries want liberation and the people there want revolution. The present weak subjective situation of these regions has not lowered in any way epochally, their role and importance as storm centres of the world revolution. Objectively, the situation in these regions, the situation of the storm centre of world revolution is very strong. It is the duty of genuine communists to overcome the subjective shortcomings and make use of the ripe objective situation, and they have to take more initiative than ever in achieving this goal.

A dangerous trend, of denying such an objective situation existing in the world and understanding it only in a subjective way has developed in the present world proletarian movement. Assessing the present international situation, the RCP, Chile and the RCP, USA write:

> The most salient feature of the international situation today is the heightening rivalry between two imperialist blocs, one headed by the US and the other by the Soviet Union, and their feverish preparation for world war. For the US imperialists and their bloc today it is the contest with the rival, Soviet-led bloc–the preparation for and then the carrying out of a global military confrontation–that is their immediate, greatest concern. It is the pivot on which their actions are now hanging.[42]

Such an assessment of the present international situation by the RCP, Chile and the RCP, USA does not match with the objective reality. On the one hand, their view overestimates the power of imperialists and on the other, it underestimates the power of the oppressed nations of Asia, Africa and Latin America, and the people of the world as a whole. Such an assessment of the world situation has given birth to the pessimistic and mechanical materialistic view that the oppressed nations of Asia, Africa and Latin America and the people of the world cannot launch a struggle against the world imperialism.

It is true that the contradiction and struggle between the imperialists has grown manifold compared to the past as evident from the growing contradictions between the USA and Japan, USA and the countries of the common market, America and the countries of West Europe, Soviet social-imperialism and the imperialist powers of West Europe, especially the contradiction between US imperialism and Soviet social-imperialism and so on.

Even though the contradictions between imperialist countries have increased many fold, their former policy of the division of territories of the world still remains. It is clear that in a particular place after one imperialist country establishes its domain, another imperialist power does not move into the same place to snatch it, rather it looks for a new place to establish its dominance. Such a conciliatory policy of division of the world followed by them makes it clear that the contradiction between them has not developed to the highest peak. While assessing any event, we should base ourselves on quality and not on the quantity, on essence and not on the form. Even though the growing contradiction between the imperialists increases the discontent and struggle between them quantitatively, it cannot influence, or determine

42 *Basic Principles for the Unity of the Marxist-Leninists and for the Line of the International Communist Movement*, A Draft Paper for Discussion Prepared by the Revolutionary Communist Party of Chile and the Revolutionary Communist Party, USA, January 1, 1981, pp. 2-3.

the other fundamental contradictions of the world. It has not brought about any change in the main trend of the world, which is revolution.

Even after the RCP, Chile and the RCP, USA have said the inter-imperialist contradiction is the principal one, the world events have been taking place in the same direction as before with the principal and decisive contradiction between the imperialism and the oppressed nations of Asia, Africa and Latin America. The armed struggles of the people in countries like the Falklands, the Middle East, Afghanistan, Palestine, South-West Africa, South-East African countries, Kampuchea, Latin America, Zimbabwe, Namibia, and the armed struggled under the leadership of Marxist-Leninist parties in Peru, Philippines, Iran, Turkey and India, can be taken as living examples in this regard. The glorious struggle against the domestic reaction and the world imperialism, particularly American imperialism, being waged by the Communist Party of Peru since 1980 with Marxism-Leninism-Mao Tse-tung Thought as guiding principles, is a matter of great pride for communists. Thus, the just struggle and the new democratic revolution taking place in the countries of Asia, Africa and Latin America makes it very clear that still the main trend of the world is revolution, not the inter-imperialist war.

9
Conclusion

Today, the world communist movement is passing through a situation of unprecedented crisis in two ways:

The first is the worldwide danger from the rightist revisionism, which is the main problem of the present world communist movement. Modern revisionism first surfaced in the USA and in Yugoslavia, and is spreading like a disease. Now it dominates the communist movement throughout the world. The Yugoslavian rightist revisionism took an official form in the Twentieth Party Congress of the CPSU (CPSU). After that, right revisionism expanded and developed intensely and widely. It appeared in the form of the extreme rightist Euro-communism, Korean national communism, and after the restoration of capitalism in China, it has covered the whole world.

The second is the lack of leadership in the struggle against rightist opportunism. When the rightist revisionism was being born in the USA and Yugoslavia at that time, the position of revolutionary Marxism at the world level was very strong. Under the revolutionary leadership of Stalin, the CPSU had advanced the struggle against the USA and Yugoslavian, i.e. Browderite and Titoite right revisionism decisively. Even after the death of Stalin, the renegade Khrushchev was able to give modern revisionism an official stamp in the Twentieth Party Congress, there was no lack of leadership to advance the struggle against revisionism in a dynamic and decisive way at the world level. Under the leadership of Mao Tse-tung, the CPC launched the struggle against modern revisionism decisively. But today, after the restoration of capitalism in China, it has not been possible to launch a decisive struggle against it as in the past. Unlike in the past, the main reason for not being able to advance the struggle against revisionism in a correct and decisive way is the lack of a leadership recognized at the world level. How can we launch the struggle against world revisionism in this context? Thus, at a time when there is no recognized leadership at the world level for advancing a struggle against revisionism effectively, there is no other alternative except through the joint efforts of all the genuine Marxist-Leninists of the world. The International Conferences of 1980 and 1984, and the formation of the Revolutionary Internationalist Movement (RIM) are right steps in this direction.

The rightist revisionism is not the only problem of the present world communist movement. In spite of it being the main problem, the communist movement is also facing a crisis from dogmato-revisionism. The attack against Mao Tse-tung Thought by the Albanian "dogmatism and sectarianism" and the attack against Stalin by neo-Trotskyites is the revisionism of the second kind. The "leftists" attack against Stalin and Mao Tse-tung does not have any theoretical significance; however, it has emerged as a problem after the degeneration of the socialist system and the restoration of capitalism in the former socialist countries like the Soviet Union and China, arousing the possibility of renewed "leftist" attack against Stalin and Mao by the Marxist-Leninists too.

When the genuine Marxist-Leninists begin to study the history of the world communist movement in the process of finding out the causes of degeneration of the socialist system, then the possibility cannot be denied that (some of them) they may be influenced by the charges against Stalin and Mao Tse-tung made by the "leftists" in the past, and this may again present Soviet revisionism in another form and colour. When we study the differences arising in the world communist movement today, it can be seen that the charges labelled against Stalin and Mao Tse-tung by "leftists" in the past are being renewed by some parties and organizations. Whether this renewed attack on Stalin and Mao will degenerate the movement into revisionism, or if it is corrected to a revolutionary line is a matter that can only be verified in future.

Today, the world communist movement is not only being attacked by deviations from the communist principle, or taking the road to liquidationism, it is also being attacked by the capitalist propaganda at an unprecedented level. Taking the issue of the degeneration of the world socialist camp, the capitalists are saying that scientific socialism is completely utopian, impractical and wrong. While exploring the reasons behind the degeneration of the socialist system, the possibility cannot be denied that the communists (some of them) themselves can be influenced by such bourgeois views and, though not fully denying scientific socialism, they may think many of its views on philosophical, political, economic and social matters to be utopian, impractical and wrong. This is so because the two-line struggle within the world communist movement cannot be separated from the existing class struggle in society.

Revisionism might appear powerful today compared to revolutionary Marxism at the world level, but this situation cannot continue forever. The situation of revolutionary Marxism, or revisionism, or broadly speaking, anything that exists in this world, does not remain the same forever. For everything, including revolutionary Marxism and revisionism, sometimes the situation is favourable and at other times it is just the reverse. Indeed, nothing in the world remains in the same form and situation. Things always keep moving from today to tomorrow, from the present to the future. The history of the world communist movement to date also shows the same thing. In the past, after the emergence of Marxism, many times the position of revolutionary Marxism was strong and that of revisionism was weak. Similarly, there were also times when the position of revisionism was strong and that of revolutionary Marxism was weak. But the same situation did not exist for ever for either revisionism or Marxism. In the process of development many times the strong position of revolutionary Marxism changed into a weak position and the weak position of the revisionism changed into a strong position. This also happened the other way round.

Today, the state of revolutionary Marxism in the world is weak at an unprecedented level, and the state of revisionism is just in the opposite state. The nature of the development of society is dialectical and it passes through the law of negation. Today, we are living in a class society. This class society came into existence after the negation of the primitive society. In the classless society, the primitive age, there were no classes representing antagonistic interests. Neither was there any class struggle nor was there any question of change taking place in the relative position of antagonistic classes. Since the time of the slave system in the history of society, because of the existence of two classes representing mutually opposite interests, the existence of class struggle and the form of class struggle and the relative position of the two classes has been changing. In a class society the strong or weak position of any class is not absolute, but relative. Socialist society does not completely negate the existing class society, since there is the existence of two classes representing mutually opposite interests, so the possibility remains for the change in the position in terms of win-lose situation, or the relative strength of these classes. We see today, revolutionary Marxism in a weak position but the revisionism in a strong position, but it also suffers according to the same general law. There is no doubt that according to the same general law of the class society, the present situation will change, and eventually the revolutionary Marxism will be strengthened while revisionism will be weakened. But the victory of revolutionary Marxism over revisionism will not be absolute, it will be only relative for long. In fact, the possibility of change in the struggle between revolutionary Marxism and revisionism and their situations will continue to exist until the scientific communism is attained worldwide.

A tendency of viewing the question of the degeneration of the socialist system by separating it from the general law of class struggle is also seen in some communist parties and organizations of the world. These parties and organizations are basing the question of the degeneration of the socialist system not on the objective realities, but mainly on subjective grounds. These parties and organizations are, thus, holding Stalin responsible for the degeneration of the socialist system in the world.

They are also refuting the contributions of Stalin already proven correct by history. They are focusing their attack against him by criticizing his point that a single country could also advance towards communism and his policies during the Second World War. They have even gone to the extent of declaring him as an anti-Marxist-Leninist on the above ground.

Today, the parties and organizations, who are saying that Stalin fully deviated from Marxism-Leninism after 1928, are taking Mao Tse-tung Thought as the developed form of Marxism-Leninism. It is noteworthy that the points which are being used by these parties and organizations in the accusation of Stalin of being anti-Marxist-Leninist after 1928 are almost the same points on which Mao Tse-tung had supported the policies and stands of Stalin. It can be seen from the works of Mao Tse-tung that except for a few issues, he has never labelled the line of Stalin after 1928 as deviating from the Marxism-Leninism, rather he supported them. On the one hand, these parties and organizations are reversing Mao's analysis on Stalin, that despite certain shortcomings Stalin was a great Marxist-Leninist.

Dialectical materialism says that the internal factor is the basis of the development or destruction of anything and the external factor is the condition in the development, or destruction. For dialectical materialism, it is also equally true that depending on the time and situation, the external factor acts as the main driving force in the development of thing. But even then we should not forget that the primary role of the external factor, which appears in the particular situation and time in the development of things, is also borne out of the internal factors. To illustrate this point, let us take the example of an egg, which Mao refers to very often. A fertile egg is sufficient enough internally for the birth of a chicken. But if the egg does not receive the required temperature, the birth of the chicken does not take place. In this phase, the role of the external factor, that are the temperature and protection, is primary. The primary role of the external factor in the latter stage does not make any difference in the fact that the main reason for the development of the thing is within itself and that the inspiring element for the development or destruction of the thing is internal. Because that role of the external causes become operative through the internal causes.

According to the dialectical materialist view, the main reason behind the degeneration of the socialist system in the world is also internal. This internal reason is the state of antagonistic classes and the struggle between them on the national and international level. Today, by holding Stalin's policies primarily responsible for the degeneration of the socialist system, some communist parties and organizations of the world are trying to hatch a chicken out of an infertile egg (by providing it with higher temperature and protection). It is true that to a certain extent, the mistakes of Stalin and Mao Tse-tung are also responsible for the degeneration of the socialist system. To deny the class struggle after the completion of the socialist transformation of the means of instruments and the means of production was Stalin's mistake. Such a thinking on his part overlooked the possibility of the existence of national and international bases that could give birth to a new exploiting class and the possibility of laying trap by the capitalists in the party, government and other sectors of structure, which could trigger the danger of restoration of capitalism in future even after having passed through the period of socialist transformation of the means of instruments and the means of production. This mistake, to a certain extent, allowed for the restoration of capitalism in the Soviet Union. But, if we hold this line of Stalin primarily responsible for the degeneration of socialism in the Soviet Union, then how did the socialist system degenerate in China even when Mao Tse-tung correctly followed the theory of class struggle? In the process of building socialism, certainly, Mao Tse-tung had also made some mistakes. Not only Stalin and Mao Tse-tung, Marx, Engels and Lenin too committed many mistakes due to the lack of objective knowledge. Today, history has put the responsibility upon the revolutionaries to solve this serious crisis in the world communist movement and this can be fulfilled only through a long and relentless struggle.

Gorakhpur, India
December, 1985

Part II

Hoxha on Mao Tse-tung Thought

The international communist movement is passing through an unprecedented crisis after the death of Mao Tse-tung and the restoration of capitalism in China. In the international communist movement, this crisis comes mainly from the right-wing opportunism today as in the past. In other words, right-wing opportunism is the main danger to the present international communist movement. Marxist-Leninists worldwide need to centralize a struggle against it. This does not mean that the international communist movement is plagued only from right-wing opportunist thinking, notion and method. Several problems have appeared in the world communist movement from the "left-wing" opportunist (including dogmatism and sectarianism) thinking, notion and method too. This type of thinking is marked mainly in two forms. The first is neo-Trotskyites thinking. They say that Stalin and Mao were anti-Marxist. The second is the thinking that identifies Mao to be a non-Marxist-Leninist, though such a thought strongly supports Stalin. They attack Mao from a "Left" direction and declare him a"rightist." The Labour Party of Albania represents this line. Struggle against the above two is not that of a two-line struggle, but is an outside question and the nature of our struggle against it is determined accordingly.

While talking about "left-wing" opportunism (including dogmatism and sectarianism) and the harm that it has caused to the world communist movement, one more fact is necessary to be mentioned, and that is the effect of the thinking of the "left-wing" (including dogmatism and sectarianism) on different forms and standards in the world proletariat movement itself. Many communist parties and organizations that have been struggling against the wrong thinking on Stalin and Mao have clarified it ("left-wing" sectarianism) through their currently published authorized documents. It is true that such a thinking in the world proletarian movement is only in the initial stage (childhood) and it has not yet developed as "left-wing" opportunism. But, when attention is directed to possible dangers from them, it becomes clear that the struggle against them should not be neglected. However, on the question of the struggle against that type of thinking, unlike neo-Trotskyism and Albanian "left-wing" opportunism, will be friendly. That struggle will be the two-line struggle among true Marxist-Leninists.

The intention of this article is not to refute all types of opportunist thinking, but to expose the Albanian sectarianism, a type of "left" opportunism. After the death of Mao, true Marxist-Leninists of the world started looking at the leader of the Labour Party of Albania, Enver Hoxha. In spite of his many weaknesses and defects, while witnessing his leading role in the course of struggle against modern revisionism, it was natural to think that he would be dedicated against the Chinese revisionism that was simply a form of Soviet revisionism. It was also natural that Hoxha supported the CPC and socialist system under the leadership of Mao. But the result was not found as expected. Certainly , Hoxha tried to take leadership of the world communist movement after Mao. But he tried to do this not by defending Mao Tse-tung Thought, but by declaring it completely non-Marxist-Leninist.

A few years ago, *Imperialism and Revolution*, written by Hoxha was distributed for discussion (April 1978) within the party. After it was passed by the party, it was made public as the party line. Therefore, this book carries not only the views of an individual (Enver Hoxha), but also the views of the party. In the third chapter of the book, Hoxha criticized Mao Tse-tung Thought and the Chinese Communist Party. The questions he raised are:

1. Communist Party and its Role

Hoxha says that as Mao himself was never in favour of a leading role for the communist party, and he did not organize a Leninist party. Hoxha considers Mao's thinking and practice on the question of communist party and its role:

> Mao pretended to be for the application of the Leninist principles on the party, but if his ideas on the party and, especially, the practice of the life of the party are analysed concretely, it becomes evident that he has replaced the Leninist principles and norms with revisionist theses.

> Mao Tse-tung has not organized the CPC on the basis of the principles of Marx, Engels, Lenin and Stalin. He has not worked to make it a party of the Leninist type, a Bolsheviks party. Mao Tse-tung was not for a proletarian class party, but for a party without class restrictions. He has used the slogan of giving the party a mass character in order to wipe out the distinction between the party and the class. As a result, anybody could enter or leave this party whenever he liked. On this question "Mao Tse-tung thought" is identical with the views of the Yugoslav revisionists and the "Eurocommunists".
>
> Besides this, Mao Tse-tung has always made the building of the party, its principles and norms dependent on his political stands and interests, dependent on his opportunist, sometimes rightist and sometimes leftist, adventurist policy, the struggle among factions, etc. ... There has been and there is no true Marxist-Leninist unity of thought and action in the CPC.
>
> Mao Tse-tung, however, conceives the party as a union of classes with contradictory interests, as an organization in which two forces, the proletariat and the bourgeoisie, the "proletarian staff" and the "bourgeois staff," which must have their representatives from the grassroots to the highest leading organs of the party, confront and struggle against each other.
>
> The CPC has never been and never could be a Marxist-Leninist party.

Further he writes:

> The anti-Marxist essence of "Mao Tse-tung thought" on the party and its role is also apparent in the way the relations between the party and the army were conceived in theory and applied in practice.[1]

Whoever devaluates or rejects the leading role of the communist party in a revolutionary movement, can never be a true communist. Marxism-Leninism believes in the leading role of the communist party in revolution. Mao's thinking on this is completely Marxist-Leninist. It is clear that throughout his life he worked in favour of a leading role of the communist party. He emphasized not only the leading role of a communist party in general, but also he added that only a party based on Marxist-Leninist principles can fulfil the responsibility in a revolutionary movement. For example, he says:

> If there is to be revolution, there must be a revolutionary party. Without a revolutionary party, without a party built on the Marxist-Leninist revolutionary theory and in the Marxist-Leninist style, it is impossible to lead the working class and the broad masses of the people to defeat imperialism and its running dogs.[2]

---

1 Enver Hoxha, "Mao Tse-tung Thought: An Anti-Marxist Theory", *Imperialism and the Revolution*, Re-printed by: Norman Bethune Institute, Toronto, 1979, pp. 398-99, 401, 405-06.

2 Mao Tse-tung, "Revolutionary Forces of the World Unite", *Selected Works*, First Eng. ed., Foreign Language Press, Peking, 1961, Vol. 4, p. 284.

Certainly, Mao believed in organizing a broad united front of patriotic and democratic forces and the people's army was essential to complete the new democratic revolution. But, it does not mean that Mao considered having their equal role in revolution. He has clarified that there must be the leading role of the communist party and complementary role of the other two. As he says:

> A well-disciplined Party armed with the theory of Marxism-Leninism, using the method of self-criticism and linked with the masses of the people; an army under the leadership of such a party; a united front of all revolutionary classes and all revolutionary groups under the leadership of such a Party–these are the three main weapons with which we have defeated the enemy.[3]

What a great emphasis Mao gave to the leading role of the communist party becomes clear from his thinking during his struggle against the modern revisionists and from his views during the Great Proletarian Cultural Revolution. The difference of Mao to the principle of the "national democracy" of Khrushchev was over the leadership of a communist party. Contradicting the Khrushchev line that a bourgeois party can lead a bourgeois-democratic revolution in the era of imperialism, Mao emphasized the leadership of the communist party in that period. In the period of the Great Proletariat Cultural Revolution, the role of the communist party was seen as secondary and that of the commune was seen more important. Mao criticized that type of thinking. He emphasized that the commune could not take the position of the communist party. That type of thinking appeared because of the wrong understanding about the Cultural Revolution in China. At that time, the masses revolted against some party committees. Many people took it absolutely and mechanically. They took it as a revolt against the leading role of the communist party. In fact, that revolt did not mean that there was no need for a communist party or its leading role. That revolt was not against the communist party, but the opportunists who had captured party and government bodies. This gives the only conclusion that the revolt did not minimize the leading role of the party, rather it enhanced the role.

Hoxha has denoted the above expressions of Mao on party (thinking that it has a leading role in revolution) to be not real, but simply "slogans". For this he quotes from his book a statement of Mao:

> All army cadres should learn how to take over and administer cities. In urban work they should learn how to be good at dealing with the imperialists and Kuomintang reactionaries, good at dealing with the bourgeoisie, good at leading the workers and organizing trade unions, good at mobilizing and

---

3 Mao Tse-tung, "On the People's Democratic Dictatorship", *Selected Works,* First Eng. ed., Foreign Language Press, Peking, 1961, Vol. 4, p. 422.

> organizing the youth, good at uniting with and training cadres in the new Liberated Areas, good at managing industry and commerce, good at running schools, newspapers, news agencies and broadcasting stations, good at handling foreign affairs, good at handing problems relating to the democratic parties and people's organizations, good at adjusting the relations between the cities and the rural areas and solving the problems of food, coal and other necessities, and good at handling monetary and financial problems.[4]

Hoxha says that this statement proves that Mao was in favour of gun over party and not party over gun. On the basis of the above statement Hoxha concludes that in China "army was above the party, above the state organ, above everything". But, Mao always believed that the party is above army and politics should dictate the gun. The quoted statement does not abandon the conviction of leadership of the party above army and of party above gun. Mao gave this guidance to the People's Liberation Army when a long chain of battle at Liaohsi-Shenyang, Huai-Hai and, Peiping-Tientsin had just finished. In that situation, there was the need to designate the future responsibility of the People's Liberation Army. Reactionaries utilise the army only at the time of fighting. Contrary to this, communists believe that the army's responsibilities to be not only as tool of fighting but to carry the role of a working force. In this situation (when role of massive fighting is over), the CPC was obliged to send guidance for one of the two accountabilities. In this situation, it could be a either parasitic life or working force. There was no other alternative. The CPC carried on the Marxist-Leninist spirit by sending guidance for the second type. The guidance certainly proves the arguments such as "army dictates the party" or "the gun dictates politics" to be irrational or absurd. The liberation army received the responsibility from the Communist Party and its Chairman Mao. On the one hand, many of the fighters themselves were members of the communist party and they were obliged to regulate the party line in the army sector, on the other the People's Liberation Army continuously performed its activities under the supervision and guidance of the centre and local committees of the party in different parts of the country. So, the above arguments prove to be absurd.

Mao's earlier position on subject matter sheds light on his Marxist-Leninist view on military affairs and politics. As he says:

> They do not understand that the Chinese Red Army is an armed body for carrying out the political tasks of the revolution. Especially at present, the Red Army should certainly not confine itself to fighting; besides fighting to destroy the enemy's military strength, it should shoulder such important

4 Mao Tse-tung, "Turn the Army into a Working Forces", *Selected Military Writings*, Foreign Language Press, Peking, 1967, p. 393.

> tasks as doing propaganda among the masses, organizing the masses, arming them, helping them to establish revolutionary political power and setting up Party organizations. The Red Army fights not merely for the sake of fighting but in order to conduct propaganda among the masses, organize them, arm them, and help them to establish revolutionary political power. Without these objectives, fighting loses its meaning and the Red Army loses the reason for its existence.

Various non-proletarian ideas such as in the Fourth Red Army in the Communist Party organizations were seen. Some comrades within these organizations regarded military affairs and politics as opposed to each and refused to recognize that military affairs were only one means of accomplishing political tasks. Mao uncompromisingly criticized those anti-Marxist-Leninist views on military affairs and politics very clearly. Pointing out the manifestations of various non-Marxist-Leninist ideas in the Communist Party and organizations in the Fourth Red Army, Mao says:

> These comrades regard military affairs and politics as opposed to each other and refuse to recognize that military affairs are only one means of accomplishing political tasks. Some even say, "If you are good militarily, naturally you are good politically; if you are not good militarily, you cannot be any good politically"–this is to go a step further and give military affairs a leading position over politics.
>
> Organizationally, these comrades subordinate the departments of the Red Army doing political work to those doing military work, and put forward the slogan, "Let Army Headquarters handle outside matters." If allowed to develop, this idea would involve the danger of estrangement from the masses, control of the government by the army and departure from proletarian leadership–it would be to take the path of warlordism like the Kuomintang army.
>
> How can such type of views be corrected?

Mao has suggested so many methods to correct them, but I want to note two points amongst them. As he says:

> The party must actively attend to and discuss military work. All the work must be discussed and decided upon by the party before being carried out by the rank and file. Draw up Red Army rules and regulations which clearly define its tasks, the relationship between its military and its political apparatus, the relationship between the Red Army and the masses of the people, and the powers and functions of the soldiers' committees and their relationship with the military and political organizations.[5]

5 Mao Tse-tung, "On Correcting Mistaken Ideas in the Party", *Selected Works*, Foreign Language Press, Peking, 1975, Vol. 1, pp. 106, 108.

2. Two-Line Struggle Within the Party

Just as with Lenin, Mao believed in the unity of opposites to be the basic law of dialectics. His conviction in the communist party as well was determined by this very basic consideration. He writes:

> Opposition and struggle between ideas of different kinds constantly occur within the Party; this is a reflection within the Party of contradictions between classes and between the new and the old in society. If there were no contradictions in the Party and no ideological struggles to resolve them, the party's life would come to an end.[6]

Hoxha explains Mao's thinking in this way: "Diametrically opposed to the Leninist teachings on the Communist Party as an organized vanguard detachment which must have a single line and steel unity of thought and action."

Further he says:

> The class struggle in the ranks of the party, as a reflection of the class struggle going on outside the party, has nothing in common with Mao Tse-tung's concepts on the "two lines in the party." The party is not an arena of classes and the struggle between antagonistic classes, it is not a gathering of people with contradictory aims. The genuine Marxist-Leninist party is the party of the working class only and bases itself on the interests of this class."[7]

Hoxa has termed Mao's view within the party as a thinking against "a single line and steel unity of thought and action". This kind of thinking is non-Marxist-Leninist. The issue of opposition and struggle in thinking within the party and party line, i.e. a single line and steel unity of thought and action are two different things. Hoxha has amalgamated the two different things in one. Firstly, as far as the issue of contradiction in the party is concerned, that is absolute. Secondly, there remains the situation of contradiction in the development process of the party from the beginning to the end. The communist party cannot be an exception of the universality of contradiction. The communist party is in motion and according to Engels "motion itself is a contradiction."[8] In reality, Hoxha has come to adopt a non-materialistic dialectical point of view by refuting the objective aspect of contradiction within the party. Steel unity between the party line and action can be achieved by the correct use of democratic-centralism regarding the differing views and struggle within the party. These two things (struggle

6 Mao Tse-tung, "On Contradiction" *Selected Works,* Foreign Language Press, Peking, 1975, Vol. 1, p. 317.

7 Enver Hoxha, "Mao Tse-tung Thought: An Anti-Marxist Theory", *Imperialism and the Revolution*, Re-printed by: Norman Bethune Institute, Toronto, 1979, p. 400.

8 Frederick Engels, "Ch.XII: Dialectic. Quantity and Quality", *Karl Marx and Frederick Engels Collected Works*, Progress Publishers, Moscow, Vol. 25, p. 111.

between differing views within the party and maintaining steel unity between the party line and action in that situation) are two sides of the same thing. The right and honest use of democratic-centralism enable it to maintain a steel unity between different thoughts and actions. If there is no situation of opposition and struggle between different thinking within the party, the organizational principle of democratic-centralism also becomes redundant. Hoxha's denial of the objectivity of the contradictory condition within the party naturally makes the principle of democratic-centralism redundant. It will be appropriate to talk on the thinking of Hoxha expressed against the thinking that there remains the situation of opposition and struggle between different thinking within the party. For example, he says, "The party is not an arena of classes and the struggle between antagonistic classes; it is not a gathering of people with contradictory aims."

He adds:

> By preaching the need for the existence of many parties in the leadership of the country, the so-called political pluralism, "Mao Tse-tung Thought" falls into complete opposition to the Marxist-Leninist doctrine on the indivisible role of the communist party in the revolution and socialist construction.
>
> According to "Mao Tse-tung Thought", a new democratic regime can exist and socialism can be built only on the basis of the collaboration of all classes and all parties. Such a concept of socialist democracy, of the socialist political system, which is based on "long-term coexistence and mutual supervision" of all parties, and which is very much like the current preaching of the Italian, French, Spanish and other revisionists, is an open denial of the leading and indivisible role of the Marxist-Leninist party in the revolution and the construction of socialism.
>
> According to Mao Tse-tung, in socialist society, side by side with the proletarian ideology, materialism and atheism, the existence of bourgeois ideology, idealism and religion, the growth of "poisonous weeds" along with "fragrant flowers", etc., must be permitted.[9]

The communist party is a political vanguard of the proletariat, and it moves ahead with the goal of socialism and communism. Questions of this type of characteristic of the communist party and form and nature of different thinking marked within it do not have the same meaning. The first question is related to the maximum goal of an established principle and party, whereas the other is a question of contradiction. That is a question of contradiction between the thinking present within party members and outside people, contradiction between the class origin of party members and the great goal of the Marxist-Leninist principle, contradictions between the party members regarding the proletarian state and the previous class status,

9 Enver Hoxha, "Mao Tse-tung Thought: An Anti-Marxist Theory", *Imperialism and the Revolution*, Re-printed by: Norman Bethune Institute, Toronto, 1979, pp. 408-10.

contradiction between different classes of the society, contradiction between old and new and contradiction between low and high stages of knowledge, contradiction between imperialism and the great goal of Marxism-Leninism, i.e. communism, and contradiction between friendly and hostile oppositions and struggles going on within the party. Accepting the second situation does not mean the party is denying class character or accepting it to a united front of bourgeoisie and proletariat. This thing cannot be denied that a communist party can degenerate into a bourgeois party. But it is not because of being a party or a united front of two antagonistic classes (bourgeoisie and proletariat). But it is because of the victory of the bourgeois line over the proletariat line in the course of the two-line struggle. It is the result of the non-antagonistic form of struggle changed into the antagonistic form.

In the past and at present as well, there was and is a situation of contradiction between levels of consciousness in party members and Marxism-Leninism, and the great goal of communism, and it will go on in future as well. To justify his thinking, Hoxha quotes Stalin: "The communist party is the monolithic party of the proletariat, and not a party of a bloc of elements of different classes."

Mao's view on the two-line struggle within the communist party and Stalin's statement are related to two separate questions. Stalin's statement is related to the first question mentioned above. Certainly, on that, the communist party is a vanguard of the proletariat. But, that reality does not negate the existence of different thinking and of the situation of struggle between them. Here the thing that Hoxha has expressed to show that Stalin did not believe in that situation within the party is totally wrong. Stalin believed that the establishment of the unity of determination among party members and in the full and absolute unity in action between different thinking among party members can be done in course of the struggle itself. He was sure and unwavering that party policy passed through extensive discussion and struggle must be one in the form of party line and that must be taken in practice in full and absolute unity (even in members who have separate thinking from that as well). As he says:

> Iron discipline in the party is inconceivable without unity of will, without complete and absolute unity of action on the part of all members of the party. This does not mean, of course, that the possibility of conflicts of opinion within the party is thereby precluded. On the contrary, iron discipline does not preclude but presupposes criticism and conflict of opinion within the party. Least of all does it mean that discipline must be "blind". On the contrary, iron discipline does not preclude but presupposes conscious and voluntary submission, for only conscious discipline can be truly iron discipline. But after a conflict of opinion has been closed, after criticism has been exhausted and a decision has been arrived at, unity of will and unity

> of action of all party members are the necessary conditions without which neither party unity nor iron discipline in the party is conceivable.

In his book, Hoxha has tried to prove Mao wrong by quoting the expression of Stalin on different groups in the party. These are two separate questions in themselves. If a faction exists in the party, as Stalin says, that situation "leads to the existence of a number of centres, and the existence of a number of centres means the absence of one common centre in the party, the breaking up of unity of will, the weakening and disintegration of discipline, the weakening and disintegration of the dictatorship."

Factions should not be allowed within the party for certain, but it is not correct to think that multi-centres are born essentially as a result of different thinking and struggle in the party. In this situation, there remains one common centre and only a single line too. Only when a particular thinking out of differing views within the party develops a hostile stance, against Marxism-Leninism, and the great goal of communism, the struggle against it takes the form of external struggle. At different times, bourgeois views do appear in the party. The struggle against such views is the same. That type of thinking can appear because of many factors. It can be the result of firstly, ignorance of some party members and secondly, direct or indirect outcome of previous class status. The first type of thinking can be moulded into a proletariat one. But the second type of thinking may not be corrected. Sometimes the first type of thinking may develop hostile relations in the course of a two-line struggle. If it so happens, or the thinking of that type is used by the imperialists and their agents, the struggle against them should be an external one instead of keeping it limited to the inner party struggle. Also, accepting the struggle between different thinking within the party and intolerance to the existence of different groups are not the same things.

Hoxha criticizes Mao's saying that people from different class origins come into a communist party and their thinking, to a certain extent, is determined or influenced by their class origin. About this, Hoxha says that type of thinking makes the "pure" proletariat character of a communist party muddy. But, of course, he is wrong. The proletarian class is not a class descended from the sky, but it is a product of this very society (capitalist society). The present society is its class source. Along with the development of capitalism, intellectuals and a large part of petty capitalist class are getting continuously thrown into the proletarian class. In this situation, it is very natural that the impact of those class origins of the past on the proletarian class, its thinking and working style would be felt more or less and to contradict the great goal of communism and Marxism-Leninism within the communist party. If on this saying (Mao's saying), we criticize Mao, Lenin and Stalin cannot escape from the same criticism too. On the above question, both of them (Lenin and Stalin) had the same type of thinking for which Hoxha criticized Mao. This clarifies that Mao followed the thinking of Lenin and Stalin.

> The proletariat is not an isolated class. It is constantly replenished by the influx of peasants, petty bourgeois and intellectuals proletarianized by the development of capitalism. At the same time the upper stratum of the proletariat, principally trade-union leaders and members of parliament who are fed by the bourgeoisie out of the super-profits extracted from the colonies, is undergoing a process of decay. "This stratum of bourgeoisfied workers, or the 'labour aristocracy' ", says Lenin, "who are quite philistine in their entire mode of life, in the size of their earnings and in their entire outlook, is the principal prop of the Second International, and, in our days, the principal *social* (not military) *prop of the bourgeoisie.* For they are real *agents of the bourgeoisie in the working class* movement, the labour lieutenants of the capitalist class, real channels of reformism and chauvinism."[10]

Lenin too has said that the upper strata of the proletariat related to the workers' organization and communist party grasps a part of excessive profit of the bourgeoisie, and it works as an agent of the bourgeoisie within the workers' movement. In general differing views exist in communist parties, and the struggle and discussion over them are not necessarily friendly as they may take a hostile form, degenerating the party of the proletariat into a bourgeois party.

3. The Communist Party's Policy Towards Democratic Parties in the Socialist Period

Even after the new democratic revolution was over and socialist ownership over the instruments and the means of production was basically established, Mao said that different democratic parties could exist. He took this line under the special objective situation of China. The whole capitalist class of Russia was a reactionary class and the enemy of socialism. But, the case of China was different. One part of the capitalist class, i.e. the national capitalist class was a participating force in the new democratic revolution. Later on, there were different democratic parties and groups in existence. Having adopted the policy to let such parties and groups exist, Mao presented an argument that they could be moulded in favour of socialism. Hoxha has termed such thinking as "so-called political pluralism" thinking.

The question as to whether different democratic parties and groups other than the communist party should be allowed to exist is a question related not to state power, but to the political system. This is an issue to be determined with the role of different parties and groups during the

10 J. V. Stalin, "Foundation of Leninism", *Problems of Leninism*, Foreign Language Press, Peking, 1976, pp. 109-12.

revolutionary period just before that. The policy Mao adopted on this issue in China can neither be taken as a criteria to declare the policy adopted by Lenin and Stalin in Russia to be wrong nor can the policy adopted by Lenin and Stalin in Russia be taken as a criteria on this question to declare the policy of Mao to be wrong. Having declared the policy adopted by Mao in China to be non-Marxist-Leninist, taking the criteria adopted by Lenin and Stalin in Russia as a basis, Hoxha has nullified the difference between form and essence in reality. By doing so, he has amalgamated the issue of state power with state organization and a concrete question with a basic question.

This does not mean that Mao allowed freedom to the enemies of socialism to get organized in political parties in socialism. To allow enemies of socialism to be organized like this, is to establish an organization that does not agree with the socialist state power. Marxism-Leninism does not allow establishing a political system that does not agree with the socialist state power and above that, the political system that has a completely hostile attitude to that power. Mao was completely opposed to that type of non-Marxist-Leninist working direction. That is clear from the glorious struggle against modern revisionism and the Great Proletariat Cultural Revolution of China. Therefore, this explanation of Hoxha suggests his complete theoretical bankruptcy to compare the thinking of Mao on that question with the "so-called political pluralism" of that Euro-communism that advocates extreme rightist opportunism.

4. Struggle and Unity with Different Thinking in the Socialist Period

Mao has said that different thinking that appears in the course of socialist transformation should not be crushed by force, they should be allowed to compete, and only then it becomes easy for people to identify which one is right or wrong. With this reference, Hoxha has criticized the thinking of Mao's saying "Let a hundred flowers blossom; let a hundred schools of thought contend." According to him, this saying abandons Marxist-Leninist principles related to class struggle.

As argued by Hoxha, Mao's thinking does not abandon Marxist-Leninist teaching in the class struggle. He observed that strengthening the proletarian dictatorship was the highest form of class struggle. The meaning of his saying "Let a hundred flowers blossom, let a hundred schools of thought contend" is not to let those flowers and thinking blossom and contend that are harmful and likely to weaken the role of leadership of the communist party, but those flowers and thinking that contribute to socialist transformation, and strengthen the role of the leadership of the communist party. Relationship of "Let a hundred flowers blossom, let a hundred schools of thought contend" goes with right mobilization of contradiction in the period of socialism. Mao was totally against letting counter-revolutionary flowers blossom and counter-revolutionary thinking contend. The nature of the struggle against the thinking that comes on the part of people in the period of socialist formation and socialist transformation is friendly. The party must follow the policy of unity-struggle-transformation with the concerned. But the nature of struggle against the thinking that comes from counter-revolutionaries is antagonistic. Not unity but struggle is the main aspect in that regard. The dialectical thinking of Mao in relation to the solution of complicated contradictions present in the socialist period becomes fully clear from his statements given below:

> What should our policy be towards non-Marxist ideas? As far as unmistakable counter-revolutionaries and saboteurs of the socialist cause are concerned, the matter is easy, we simply deprive them of their freedom of speech. But incorrect ideas among the people are quite a different matter. Will it do to ban such ideas and deny them any opportunity for expression? Certainly not. It is not only futile but very harmful to use crude methods in dealing with ideological questions among the people, with questions about man's mental world. You may ban the expression of wrong ideas, but the ideas will still be there. On the other hand, if correct ideas are pampered in hothouses and never exposed to the elements and immunized against disease, they will not win out against erroneous ones. Therefore, it is only by employing the method of discussion, criticism and reasoning that we can really foster correct ideas and overcome wrong ones, and that we can really settle issues.[11]

The above statement proves Hoxha's baseless and prejudiced allegation against Mao. Another criticism of Mao made by Hoxha is related to a view on the relationship between communist thinking and non-communist thinking. Mao was in favour of giving people permission to contact wrong thinking, even hostile thinking. He believed that it would be mental bankruptcy to deny that type of right of contact. Mao has said:

> Truth stands in contrast to falsehood and develops in the struggle with it. The beautiful stands in contrast to the ugly and develops in the struggle with it. The same holds true of good and bad, that is, good deeds and good people stand in contrast to bad deeds and bad people and develop in the struggle with them. In short, fragrant flowers stand in contrast to poisonous weeds and develop in the struggle with them. It is a dangerous policy to prohibit people from coming into contact with the false, the ugly and the hostile, with idealism and metaphysics and with the twaddle of Confucius, Lao Tzu and Chiang Kai-shek. It will lead to mental deterioration, one-track minds, and unpreparedness to face the world and meet challenges.[12]

11 Mao Tse-tung, "Correct Handling of Contradictions Among the People", *Selected Works*, Foreign Language Press, Peking, 1977, Vol. 5, pp. 410-11.

12 Mao Tse-tung, "Talks At Conference of Party Committee Secretaries", *Selected Works* Foreign Language Press, Peking, 1977, Vol. 5, p. 366.

Contrary to Mao's above view, Hoxha believes that by permitting people to come in contact with other thinking will be harmful.

Stopping contact of people with other thinking is out of the capacity of communists, and people will be influenced by such thinking in the course of contact is only one aspect of the issue. The other aspect is that in the course of contact with such people, they will get the opportunity to understand in a flash the reality of communist thinking and adopt it as rational. Facts refute the thinking of Hoxha. Marx, Engels, Lenin, Stalin and the whole of Marxism as the best examples to this. Marxism is not a thing that appeared from the sky nor did Marx, Engels, Lenin and Stalin. They are the products of this very society. That (Marxism) is born by the dint of living contact of Marx and Engels with German philosophy, economics of England and French socialism. If a person had to be influenced absolutely because of contact with a bad thing, Marx and Engels would have become Hegelians. Later on, they came into close contact with Feurbach and only after that did they propound the scientific philosophy (dialectical and historical materialism). Scientific economics and socialist thinking are not the thinking of Adam Smith, David Ricardo and Saint Simon. But, they are born in the course of living contact of Marx and Engels with their thinking. The refutation of idealism, metaphysical thinking or any other wrong thinking is possible by their deep study, not by staying away from them. Marx's *The Capital* and the scientific analysis of Lenin's imperialism were results of their close contacts with the different stages of capitalism (competitive and monopoly). Are these facts not enough to refute the wrong thinking of Hoxha? Whether it is related to the relation of a communist party with different democratic parties and groups or whether it is a question of struggle and unity between different thinking in the socialist period, Mao's thinking is fully Marxist-Leninist. The policy that he adopted in China in the socialist period was a glorious example of the analysis of class contradictions and the right use of the principle of unity among the opposite elements of the dialectics in their mobilization.

5. Party Discipline

Marxism-Leninism demands to look at any issue not in a mechanical or metaphysical way, but in a dialectical way. It looks at the issue of discipline as well not in the form of stagnation and formulae, but in the dialectics. Hoxha criticizes Mao as one who does not maintain party discipline and thinks himself to be above the party. To prove this, he quotes Mao: "No telegram, no letter, no document, no order could be issued by anybody without first going through Mao Tse-tung's hands and being approved by him."[13]

13 Enver Hoxha, "Mao Tse-tung Thought: An Anti-Marxist Theory", *Imperialism and the Revolution*, Re-printed by: Norman Bethune Institute, Toronto, 1979, p. 404.

Of course, Mao said that, but on that count Hoxha's allegation does not get vindicated. Hoxha has presented that saying quite metaphysically. Presenting anything, an event or any thinking in that manner shows only one side and the judgement taken on that basis is wrong. While evaluating anything, an event or thinking, it is necessary to study all related aspects. In reality, his view on the above question is far from the truth. Here Hoxha has ignored the second method and has internalized the first one. Mao expressed the view in the light of revisionists like Liu Shao-chi and company issuing guidances in the name of the Central Committee of the Party when he was either on an inspection tour of the countryside or had taken leave. Such events occurred many times. Guidance issued by them was against the revolutionary direction and against Marxism-Leninism, and they represented bourgeois thinking and the political line. They were against the party's general line for the transitional period. In that situation, it was necessary to take an instant step to stop that type of activity. That saying of Mao was a step taken in that direction.

Not only the above quoted statement, but also dozens of statements can be found to give a wrong meaning if looked at and understood from the metaphysical angle. Saying like "Bombard the Headquarters", "If opportunists capture the Central Committee, struggle against that by organizing a separate red army", "It is right to rebel", "Students should be allowed to read novels in colleges", "There is nothing to obey the decision of the majority" and working accordingly are some of the examples of that. Many people can take these sayings to fulfil their vested interests. People of that type bring forward the above sayings as strong proofs to prove their thinking and activities to be "true" Marxist-Leninist. It is not that some "left-wing" elements brought forward some particular thinking of Mao to try to justify their non-Marxist-Leninist working direction. Rightist opportunists too try to justify their argument by referring to Mao's views.

The four rules of discipline emphasized by Mao to follow strictly when Chang Ko-thao breached the party discipline and his emphasis on alliance with the Kuomintang while fighting against the Japanese could be nectar for the rightist opportunists. While being in the minority and their opportunist line not being passed, they can use Mao's above mentioned expressions given in the first order as weapons. Likewise, when they muster a majority in the central committee or succeed in getting their opportunist line passed, they (revisionists) use Mao's views regarding the party discipline to silence the revolutionaries. The conclusion that can be derived from this is that the evaluation of any policy or political line should be done by making a concrete analysis of concrete situations. Only by doing so, can they find out the right and wrong correctly. In some situations, Lenin himself also challenged the policy and actions of the Central Committee of the Party.

He has given his consent to revolt in the Central Committee if required and not obeying the decision of the Central Committee on his part only after objectively assessing the contradiction in the changed situation. If his sayings are understood metaphysically, Hoxha will have to criticize Lenin as well as Mao's saying "taking one self above the central committee" and "not maintaining discipline". But that type of thinking is completely wrong. The same is true about Mao.

6. Using Contradictions Amongst Opportunist Trends in the Communist Party

The CPC, under the leadership of Mao, many times, adopted the policy of using contradictions prevalent among different opportunist trends seen in the party and government while waging a struggle against them. Objectively evaluating the possible effects and influences of opportunist thinking and attitudes, the CPC, under the leadership of Mao adopted the policy to ascertain the primacy of struggle. Unity with Lin Piao to defeat Liu Shao-chi and Company, using the disguised opportunist Chou En-lai in the course of leading a struggle against the open opportunists such as Liu Shao-chi, Teng Hsiao-ping, Lin Pio and use of Hua Kuo-feng against Teng Hsiao-ping and others are remarkable examples in this reference.

According to Hoxha, Mao's policy of using contradictions of opportunist trends, i.e. Mao's policy of uniting temporarily with secondary dangers against the main danger in the course of the struggle against opportunism was wrong. He refers to it as Mao's strategy and the abandonment of the theoretical struggle to keep his group in policy safe.

Many types of opportunist thinking and attitudes can be seen in the party and government at the same time. In this situation, it will not be possible for revolutionaries to struggle against them at a time. In such a condition, they have to identify which type of thinking is the greatest challenge to the party and revolution and to ascertain the order of the primary struggle accordingly. In this context, the policy of unity with secondary dangers to struggle against the main danger can be adopted as tactics. This is something within the Leninist strategy and tactics. Mechanically, the policy of struggle against all opportunist thinking and attitudes in general is to face a great defeat. Had Mao adopted that type of policy in the beginning itself (after revolution), it would have been impossible to defeat the Liu Shao-chi and Lin Piao groups. Mao adopted the policy with a strategy of defeating the opportunist headquarters well settled in the party and the government one by one. That is not his policy of compromise with the opportunists as Hoxha says. It was rather the policy of using one opportunist trend to use contradictions present in themselves and according to the situation and need. As Leninism allows adopting this type of policy in the course of struggle against imperialism, and adopting that policy in the course of struggle against opportunism can never be a mistake.

However, in the course of adopting the policy of using contradiction amongst opportunist trends seen in the party and government, there appeared many weaknesses and resulted in a serious outcome. The question of Chou En-lai and Hua Kuo-feng are especially remarkable examples in this relation. Many weaknesses that appeared in this course were caused by situations difficult to escape. Though, some of them could have been avoided. During the two-line struggle within the party, Chou En-lai in disguise was cooperating with the rightist opportunists, but Mao continued the policy of using him. Because of this, he could not bring forward the task of exposing the opportunist character of Chou En-lai openly and making him publicly exposed (as was done about Liu Shao-chi and Lin Piao). As a result, Chou En-lai took advantage of it and was successful in remaining as a close co-worker of Mao till his death, although he was an underground commander of the rightist opportunists. The thing about Hua Kuo-feng is also the same. Hua Kuo-feng was a person who faced action during the Cultural Revolution. Mao adopted the policy of using him around the end of his life. This strengthened the position of Hua. He came forward as a "revolutionary" leader, although he was a "centrist". As revolutionaries can use such types of people, similarly revisionists can also use them. Teng Hsiao-ping and so on as well used him sufficiently in their favour. After the death of Mao, the arrest of the four revolutionary leaders of the Great Proletariat Cultural Revolution under allegation of being the enemy of Mao Tse-tung Thought and socialism under the order of Hua proves this (as used by rightist opportunists).

7. Choosing a Successor and Marxism-Leninism

In China, one or the other person was made successor, time and again. Instead of thinking of its results, the main question underlying it is the view about the system. Since it is a non-Marxist-Leninist system, and we must oppose that. Hoxha's opposition to this question is correct. What many people can argue about is that the CPC and Mao managed that type of "successor" system to defend Marxism-Leninism and socialism. But, the consequences go contrary to the expected result. The persons who the party declared "successors" went in favour of capitalism and not in favour of Marxism-Leninism and socialism. What is proved from this is that the system of successors from the CPC and Mao compromised at particular times with particular opportunists. Certainly, Marxism-Leninism allows the policy of using in some particular stage and situations a particular trend of opportunists against another trend of opportunists in the course of struggle as tactics, but it does not allow the policy of using contradictions present in opportunists to the level of accepting the system of successors of the party leadership. Party leadership is something that emerges in the course of ideological and class struggle in the long run.

8. Action and Reinstatement

Hoxha has criticized Mao, on the issue of the reinstatement of an opportunist against whom, action was taken for a serious mistake. He has raised the question, especially of Teng Hsiao-ping. This is, of course, not a baseless blame on the CPC and Mao.

Let us take the case of Teng Hsiao-ping against whom action was taken during the Cultural Revolution. The charges against Teng at that time were not of a simple type, but they were related to serious mistakes. He had a second position in the Liu group. He accepted it himself that he was not a communist, but a bourgeois. But, the CPC and Mao adopted the policy of reinstating dozens of opportunists who had faced action along with him after the coup attempt by Lin Pio. Although it was because of the unusual case of the inner party two-line struggle and also because of the underground role of Chou En-lai, however, Mao and the CPC are not blameless. Mao and the CPC's, "reinstatement" policy is responsible to a great extent in making Teng's position in Chinese politics so strong in later years.

Hoxha's criticism on three (6,7 and 8) of the above mentioned questions are correct to some extent, but he cannot be free of the charge of being prejudiced in the same way as for other questions. Instead of treating the weaknesses of Mao and the communist party of China in the course of moving ahead for the great goal of communism, he criticized them as a result of Mao's group interest. That is wrong.

9. Process of Social Development

According to Hoxha, though Mao talked about the process of social development, it was "metaphysical", "evolutionism". He writes:

> Mao Tse-tung makes frequent mention of the role of revolutions in the process of the development of society, but in essence he adheres to a metaphysical, evolutionist concept. Contrary to materialist dialectics, which envisages progressive development in the form of a spiral, Mao Tse-tung preaches development in the form of a cycle, going round in a circle, as a process of ebb and flow which goes from equilibrium to disequilibrium and back to equilibrium again, from motion to rest and back to motion again, from rise to fall and from fall to rise, from advance to retreat and to advance again, etc.

Hoxha has levelled a charge against Mao mainly regarding his explanation of socialist society. Mao defines socialist society principally as: Firstly, there is antagonistic class struggle in socialist society. Secondly, because of this situation, capitalism can be restored in any socialist country. Thirdly, communism, in the long run will negate socialist society. Hoxha says that Mao's explanation "does not see socialist revolution as a qualitative change of society in which antagonistic classes and the oppression and exploitation of man by man are abolished". He comments to the extent that this thinking of Mao is "openly revising the Marxist-Leninist concept of socialism and communism, which, in essence, are two phases of the one type of the one socio-economic order, which are distinguished from each other only by the degree of their development and maturity."[14] Reading Marx and Lenin would clarify whether Mao or Hoxha had a correct Marxist-Leninist thinking. The thinking that there is no situation of antagonistic classes and struggle among them does not agree with the thinking of Marxism-Leninism; Marx has defined the socialist period, i.e. first phase, to be the transition period from capitalism to communism. According to him, "between capitalist and communist society lies the period of the revolutionary transformation of the one into the other. Corresponding to this is also a political transition period in which the state can be nothing but *the revolutionary dictatorship of the proletariat.*"[15]

Lenin declares the situation of class struggle remains even after the dictatorship of the proletariat for along. According to him, although the form of class struggle changes for the time being, it becomes further complicated and sharper compared to the previous situation. As he says, "The transition from capitalism to communism takes an entire historical epoch. Till this epoch is over, the exploiters inevitably cherish the hope of restoration, and this *hope* turns into *attempts* at restoration."[16] He has said that the thinking that no classes and class struggles remain after proletarian dictatorship is an imagination of "the vulgar representatives of the old socialism and the old Social-Democracy."[17]

It is necessary to pay special attention to the above expressions of Marx and Lenin. This is and should be the criteria to ascertain whose analysis is correct about the socialist society.

---

14 Enver Hoxha, "Mao Tse-tung Thought: An Anti-Marxist Theory", *Imperialism and the Revolution*, Re-printed by: Norman Bethune Institute, Toronto, 1979, p. 413.

15 Karl Marx, "Critique of the Gotha Programme", *Karl Marx and Frederick Engels Selected Works*, Progress Publishers, Moscow, Fourth Printing, 1977, Vol. 3, p. 26.

16 V. L. Lenin, "Proletariat Revolution and Renegade Kautsky", *Collected Works*, Eng. ed., Progress Publishers, Moscow, Third Printing, 1981, Vol. 28, p. 254.

17 V. I. Lenin, "Greetings to the Hungarian Workers", *Collected Works*, Eng. ed., Third Printing, 1977, Progress Publishers, Moscow, Vol. 29, p. 389.

Mao has further developed the Marxist-Leninist thinking about the class analysis of socialist society. No analyst by then had spoken of antagonistic class existence and possibility of restoration of capitalism in socialism. The above mentioned statements of Marx and Lenin show that dictatorship of the proletariat would not at all have been essential if "antagonistic classes had ended" in socialist society as Hoxha claimed. If no one was to be suppressed, why would revolutionary violence become necessary? On whom has the proletarian class to exercise revolutionary violence and dictatorship? As we discussed, Marx thought that dictatorship of the proletariat was necessary for a transition period to end class distinction. Had the socialist state been the end of class distinctions, where would be the justification of Marx's statement? How could the statement of Lenin "exploiters inevitably cherish the hope of restoration, and this *hope* turns into *attempts* at restoration" be correct? Had the thing been the same, what should be said about the criticism of opportunists of the Second International by Lenin about this? The history of building the world socialist system is decades in front of us. Similarly, the dissolution of the world socialist system is also in front of us. Let us take the Soviet Union itself. Capitalism was restored there after the death of Stalin and the Labour Party of Albania launched a glorious struggle under the leadership of Enver Hoxha. Capitalism was not restored because of army intervention from any imperialist country. The cause of that was the defeat of the proletariat and the victory of the bourgeoisie in the inner party struggle.

Hoxha's criticism of Mao's saying that communism, some day, will negate socialist society also is not correct. We cannot say comprehensively about communism now, but we can say for sure that in the long run of development, even communism will pass through an infinite complex process of negating one stage by another. Mao's view on socialistic society regarding different stages of development is equally applicable to communism too. The only thing is that in communist society there would not be antagonistic classes and struggle between them but struggle between nature and mankind continues. This contradiction would be the driving force of society which gives rise to different stages in communist society.

The facts of communist society negating socialist society will not be sufficient to understand in general. It must be understood more concretely. Mao kept these two things in mind. Socialist society is a society born out of capitalist society. This is a Marxist-Leninist principle that many capitalists remain present in socialism. In this context, the contradictions present in socialist society between town and countryside, the contradiction between physical and mental labour and the situation of class struggle are specifically remarkable. Although just in a transitional stage, socialist society is also a centralized state with army, police, and bureaucracy.

The remains of capitalism cannot be eradicated immediately after the proletarian revolution. A long historical period is needed to eliminate them. The period to be spent to end those types of leftovers are possible under the all-round dictatorship of the proletariat. It is clear that someday, that period will end, i.e. the communist phase will negate the socialist phase. Rejecting the statement that the communist phase negates the socialist phase has three implications:

(1) Basic differences between the two are unmarked,
(2) Non-belief in the discrepancies of capitalism will be finished in future and a wholesome society will be built, and
(3) Understanding socialism not as a state with motion and life, but as stable and stagnant.

It is necessary to pay special attention to the phrase "two phases of the one type, of the one socio-economic order" used in Hoxha's above quoted saying. According to it both phases, socialist phase and communist phase, are not qualitatively different, because they are just two phases of the one socio-economic order. Certainly, both are two phases, lower and higher phase of communism. But as Hoxha argues, socialism and communism are not simply two phases of the same type of socio-economic order. Long experience of the world socialist system explicitly reveals the basic differences between two communist societies. Capitalist leftovers are the particularity of the first phase of communism. To say those discrepancies, i.e. the existence of leftovers of capitalism will disappear in communism means that unique form of the socio-economic system will also end. Those discrepancies and leftovers of capitalism cannot be eliminated by keeping the same socio-economic system intact. The communist phase means a free society from restoration of capitalism. But, the socialist phase is not a society free from danger of the restoration of capitalism. The only meaning is that socialism and communism are not two forms of the same socio-economic order. So far the issue of socialism being the first phase of communism is concerned; it is to mean that socialism prepares the situation for communism by socialist transformation in industry and agriculture under the dictatorship of the proletarian class through the leadership of the communist party. So, socialism is the first phase of communism.

10. Relationship Between Bourgeois-Democratic and Socialist Revolution

Hoxha says that Mao was unsuccessful in creating the correct relation between the bourgeois revolution and the socialist revolution and then, he adopted the point of view of opportunists of the Second International. He writes: "Mao Tse-tung was never able to understand and explain correctly the close links between the bourgeois-democratic revolution and the proletarian revolution."

Further he says:

> On the question of the relationship between the democratic revolution and the socialist revolution, Mao Tse-tung takes the stand point of the chiefs of the Second International, who were the first to attack and distort the Marxist-Leninist theory about the rise of the revolution and came out with the thesis that between the bourgeois-democratic revolution and the socialist revolution, there is a long period, during which the bourgeoisie develops capitalism and creates the conditions for the transition to the proletarian revolution. They regarded the transformation of the bourgeois-democratic revolution into socialist revolution, without giving capitalism the possibility to develop further, as something impossible, as skipping stages.[18]

This is a wrong explanation of the Mao Tse-tung Thought on the relationship between the bourgeois-democratic revolution and the socialist revolution. The credit of launching the democratic revolution and giving it the theoretical fullness of Lenin and Stalin's view goes to Mao. Mao developed the strategy and tactics of revolution in colonial and semi-colonial countries based on the thinking of Lenin and Stalin with a special reference to the Chinese revolution. He said that, in the new world situations, i.e. after the First World War and the Great October Socialist Revolution, the old type of world revolution (world capitalist revolution) would end and the era of new world revolution (world socialist revolution) would start. He further observed that democratic revolution in colonial, semi-colonial countries should be made an integral part of the world socialist revolution. He said that in those countries, communist parties should take their minimum programme for the new type of democratic revolution and the maximum programme for the socialist and communist revolution by playing a leading role. Mao's explanation of the new type of democratic revolution shows that he was clear in relation to the democratic revolution and socialist revolution.

Mao's criticism of Turkey's Kemalist revolution makes it clear that he was against the thinking of distinguishing democratic revolution from socialist revolution in the era of imperialism and proletarian revolution. Mao himself was the first person in world history who transformed the bourgeois-democratic revolution directly into socialist transformation and the advancement towards communism in an imperialist era.

By attacking Mao for his alleged adoption of the line of the Second International in relation to the democratic revolution, Hoxha exposed his political poverty. In no way do Mao's views resemble the thinking of the

18 Enver Hoxha, "Mao Tse-tung Thought: An Anti-Marxist Theory", *Imperialism and the Revolution*, Re-printed by: Norman Bethune Institute, Toronto, 1979, pp. 418-20.

Second International's opportunists on this issue. In Lenin's period there was a serious difference in the world socialist revolution on the point of view related to revolution in colonial and semi-colonial countries. The opportunists of the Second International viewed that capitalist revolution was possible in a "national boundary" before even a changed situation. They said that the type of revolution is an organ of the world capitalist revolution itself and that it could be led by a bourgeois party itself. The Third International, under the leadership of Lenin, exposed the opportunist thinking of the Second International. It emphasized the fact that a capitalist revolution in the new situation can be and should be integrated with the world socialist revolution. Mao's thinking about the democratic revolution represents the thinking of Stalin and the Third International, not the thinking of opportunists of the Second International.

New Delhi, India
October 1986

Part III

Long Live Leninism

The anti-revolutionary essence of 'On Proletarian Democracy' of the former CRC, CPI (ML)

The former Central Reorganization Committee, of the Communist Party of India (Marxist-Leninist), {CRC, CPI (ML) onward} was a member Party of the Committee of Revolutionary Internationalist Movement (CoRIM). It was also a fraternal party of the Communist Party of Nepal (Mashal)(CPN (Mashal)). It had submitted its document *On Proletarian Democracy* for discussion amongst the CoRIM and other fraternal parties. As far as I know, the CoRIM and its member parties found the viewpoint expressed in the *Document* to be alien to Marxism-Leninism and had criticized it accordingly.

The views expressed in the *Document* are mainly related to the proletarian dictatorship, the role of the communist party during the period of proletarian dictatorship, class struggle, proletarian democracy, democratic-centralism and the capitalist restoration. The CRC has criticized the Leninist approach to these issues and has concluded that Lenin, Stalin and Mao Tse-tung are responsible for the disintegration of the world socialist system and for the present-day weak position of the international communist movement as a whole.

My critical comments are given under the following sub-headings:

1. General

A final evaluation of history is not at all possible as it can be evaluated repeatedly. The history of the world communist movement is also not an exception. It is a common fact that when the movement is at its peak, generally either we do not realize the need of the evaluation of its background, or do not realize it adequately. No one felt the need to evaluate the history of the world communist movement when revolutionary tides were sweeping the world. People were forced to take a look at the history only when some unexpected changes created setbacks to the revolutionary movements. Such examinations have given significant help in the correction of the mistakes and weaknesses in the world communist movement in the past.

Revolutionaries worldwide felt the need of examining the history of China under the leadership of Mao, and to pinpoint the cause of the capitalist restoration in the Soviet Union. The policy to focus on the class struggle during the period of socialism and the Great Proletarian Cultural Revolution of China were the fruits of the same objective of an evaluation of history. This evaluation has another aspect as well and it is the possibility of the emerging of deviations during the course of evaluation. We have had several examples of deviations emerging in new forms, proven wrong in the course of evaluating the history of the world communist movement.

The slanders by Trotsky on Stalin and the accusation of modern revisionists on Mao Tse-tung occur repeatedly time and again under different names. These names are noteworthy. More than that, in the process of the evaluation of the world communist movement, we have had plenty of examples of people and parties influenced by the bourgeois slanders and attacks against socialism and by a misleading information campaign and by adopting a path of liquidation away from the communist movement. We need to study this reality carefully and try to escape from this type of effect during the study and evaluation of history.

One of the important aspects in the study of history is its base. No study and evaluation can be without a base. Studies and evaluation in the present world can be based on one of the two bases. The first is the base of ideological, political and organizational base of Marxism-Leninism-Mao Tse-tung Thought. The second is the base of bourgeois ideology, politics and organizational structure. The first one is the foundation of the historical studies of revolutionary communists worldwide, whereas the second is the base of bourgeois historical studies. The weaknesses of the world communist movement and of Marxism-Leninism-Mao Tse-tung Thought can be identified and eliminated only by assimilating the essence of the teachings of scientific communism. In fact, this is the only creative process for the study and evaluation of the history of world socialism. No creativity, but only destructive conclusions will be derived if one attempts to study and evaluate the history (knowingly or unknowingly) on the basis of bourgeois ideology, politics and organizational structure. Many individuals and parties in the past followed this bourgeois process of historical studies and arrived at a false conclusion and then followed the path of liquidation. This is why we have to be careful not to fall prey to the wrong processes during our studies of history to avoid the false conclusions, be it for the present, or future.

It is good that the CRC has stressed the need of studying and evaluating the history in the context of the disintegration of the world socialist system and the weak position of the international communist movement. But the foundation that the CRC has adopted is obviously not a Marxist-Leninist one but a bourgeois one. The views forwarded by the CRC are only those that are already falsified by history. It has forwarded a "new" deviation in the history of the world communist movement again. The CRC has claimed to be 'firm' for communism and its conclusion to push forward communism. We do not mean that they have come out with such a viewpoint as agents of imperialism, or with full dishonesty. But when we analyse their viewpoints as expressed in the *Document* on the issue of proletarian dictatorship, the role of the party, class struggle, proletarian democracy, democratic-centralism, capitalist restoration, are totally wrong.

The CRC has entered into their study room with the object of making an objective evaluation of the history and have come out with the conclusion that all the achievements of the socialist movement, especially after the October Revolution, are wrong. They have concluded that all the proletarian regimes established after the October Revolution were not truly proletarian. By doing so, they have tried to present themselves in favour of "real" proletarian dictatorship, and also, criticized the policies and practices of Lenin, Stalin and Mao on the establishment of all-round dictatorship over the bourgeois class as not in the interests of proletarian dictatorship and analysing everything only by the class reductionist point of view. The CRC has recognized the Paris Commune as the only real form of proletarian regime and has claimed that Lenin, in the period prior to the October Revolution, had accepted this fact but he himself deviated after that. The CRC has criticized Lenin for formation of the regular army and not dissolving the central authority. This viewpoint is close to the anarchism of Proudhon and Bakunin. The old army and central regime born out of the womb of capitalism, can be dissolved in a socialist system but a regular army and the central authority of the proletariat should be constituted. Opposing the proletarian regular army and central authority of the proletariat consequently helps in restoring capitalism. In essence, the CRC viewpoint presented in *Document* shows it is not in favour of real proletarian dictatorship, rather for bourgeois dictatorship.

The CRC has termed the Leninist viewpoint on the role of the party during the period of the proletarian dictatorship to be anti-Marxist. It has said the policy of no direct role of the communist party should have been followed by all the proletarian state powers established in the post-October Revolution by arguing that the party had no direct role in the Paris Commune. The CRC declared that the Leninist 'dictatorship of the proletariat' was in reality the 'dictatorship of party' in the name of the proletariat. The proletarian dictatorship established in different countries in the past was in essence 'party dictatorship' in the view of the CRC. This viewpoint is a natural expression of the non-Marxist approach of analysing the relationship between class, party leadership and the masses. In modern society, the party represents the class. This is true for both the bourgeois and the proletarian classes. Classes establish dictatorship through the leadership of their parties. Party leadership cannot replace class dictatorship. Class dictatorship is wide. Party leadership is, in essence, an important aspect of class dictatorship.

Thus any attempt to look at these terms as synonymous is tantamount to not understanding the essence of the teachings of Marxism-Leninism on the issues of class dictatorship and party leadership. The views of the CRC, while opposing the Leninist viewpoint on the role of the party during the proletarian dictatorship correspond with the viewpoint of the opportunists within the Second International and the modern revisionists too. The opportunists have always opposed the party leadership as they want to disarm the proletarian class and wish for the victory of the bourgeoisie in the struggle. The thinking of CRC does not strengthen the state power of the proletarian class, rather it leads to liquidationism.

The CRC *Document* on issues like class struggle, proletarian democracy, democratic-centralism and capitalist restoration are anti-Marxist as it stresses that Lenin never considered, rather "neglected" the non-class aspect of bourgeois democracy and has severely criticized Lenin for this. Pleading that bourgeois democracy can have a non-class aspect and asking for its defence, it seeks that socialist democracy also must have a non-class aspect and that it should be maintained. The CRC *Document*, accuses Lenin of having a class reductionism approach. Most parts of the *Document* talk about the rights of the 'whole people'. The *Document* has termed the declaration of the Tenth Congress of the Communist Party (1921), banning all factions within the party, to be wrong. It has rejected all the Marxist-Leninist explanations concerning the restoration of capitalism and has concluded that the main cause of it is "bureaucracy". These views of CRC are totally anti-Marxist-Leninist and they will not lead the proletarian class struggle forward, rather they will push it backwards.

To what extent the views expressed in the CRC *Document* are not Marxist-Leninist has been unfolded by the dissolving of the party by its leadership a few months ago. We are not astonished at the dissolving of the party in the light of its vision for some years. The true Marxist-Leninists worldwide should now refute ideologically and expose such erroneous views expressed by the CRC. Since the CRC was a member party of the RIM and the international communist movement is very weak at the moment, it may have some influence on other parties. We need to be careful to refute and expose this. Only the future will determine which party of which country will be at the forefront in refuting and exposing the anti-revolutionary, anti-Marxist-Leninist essence of this *Document* and which party of which country will be influenced by the path chartered in the CRC *Document*.

2. Proletarian Dictatorship

Amongst all the basic tenets of Marxism-Leninism, the issue of proletarian dictatorship is the most complex and difficult as it is also an issue which has been the subject of attack and slanders by the bourgeois intellectuals, and philosophers in a vicious manner. The bourgeoisie and also the opportunists within the communist movement have also consistently tried to distort this issue. The attack of the bourgeoisie or their misinformation campaign against this issue is rather direct and clear, so it does not have much impact on the proletariat and the working class. However, when the attack and misinformation campaign by the opportunists and the revisionists appear in a twisted way, they are bound to have a grave impact since they present this vilification campaign under the pretext of the Marxist-Leninist explanation and analysis. The former CRC has tried once again to turn up and down the basis of proletarian dictatorship by presenting their "new" explanation of this issue. There is a need to analyse in depth the essence of their view since they are presenting their views in the name of true Marxist analysis.

The CRC in their *Document* have declared all the proletarian political regimes, except the Paris Commune, including the Russian October Revolution, as not real proletarian regimes. The *Document* states:

> Our review reveals that the dictatorship of the proletariat practised so far in the former socialist countries since the October Revolution all ended up in the dictatorship of the party instead of developing towards a genuine system of the dictatorship of the proletariat. (8.1)
>
> The absence of any mention of the role of the party in the whole scheme of the dictatorship of the proletariat as explained in *The State and Revolution*

by Lenin is very conspicuous. It may be due to this influence of the political structure of the Paris Commune. But here, unlike in the Paris Commune, the party was going to play the crucial role because by the time of the October Revolution, a party had already been developed as the vanguard representing the class interests of the proletariat. So this was the crucial theoretical question to be resolved during that period. Lenin's total neglect of this question was a serious lapse leading to the basic error in developing the understanding of the dictatorship of the proletariat. (8.5)

The basic point of departure for the system of the dictatorship of the proletariat had already been identified by Marx while summing up the lessons of the Paris Commune–"the re-absorption of state power by society as its own living force." But Lenin did not take up the questions of translating this concept into practice, and thereby making a qualitative break with the hitherto existing understanding on political power. Even though he was talking about Soviet deputies being revocable agents of power and also about creating the new state with the armed people, in practice no concrete steps were taken to realize this. The unavoidable force of circumstances may be pointed out as the factor preventing any advancement in this direction. But we have no evidence to show that Lenin paid any serious attention to this basic question itself. He did not understand the necessity of evolving a qualitatively new political system under the dictatorship of the proletariat. On the other hand, his whole attempt was to achieve this change by changing the leadership of the state, from a bourgeois one into that of the proletariat through its party. (8.8)

Actually the structure of the new proletarian state envisaged by Marx and Engels had nothing to do with the existing structure of the bourgeois state. This is well reflected in the above quoted statement of Marx (re-absorption ...) and in Engels' statement, "The proletariat seizes power and ... then puts an end to itself as proletariat ... and thus also to the state as state." (*Anti-Duhring*, Peking, 1976, p. 362). This is the point of departure–a state which itself becomes the guarantee for the re-absorption of state power by the society, a state which ceases to be a state in the traditional sense. How can the proletariat achieve such a goal which involves deep internal contradictions? Two practical steps taken by the Paris Commune are in front of us–a political system runs through the revocable agents of power and the replacement of the standing army by the armed people. (8.9)

But if we are really to achieve a qualitative break with the existing understanding of political power, we have to go deeper into its dynamics. In a class society, the dominant class wields political power claiming to represent the whole society. This reflects a contradiction between the political will of the ruling class and that of the society as a whole. It is to resolve this contradiction that power is concentrated in the state structure and wielded by the ruling class as its executive power. So this concentration of the political will of the ruling class in the name of the political will of the whole society, in the concrete form of the state, especially in its armed might, is characteristic of the political power so far existing in class society. The proletariat is aiming at qualitatively breaking with this structure. It must initiate a process which makes the society as a whole capable of re-absorbing this concentrated power. And the replacement of the standing army by the armed people is a concrete initial step in this direction. But in the absence of a complete economic, political, social system which guarantees this re-absorption, this alone will not serve the purpose. In the whole process, conditions and structures should be created so that the (political) will of the whole society can get expressed and realized directly without the mediation of a state. It is only then that the proletariat can achieve its goal of a society where the state withers away. If the proletariat cannot put forward such an alternative political system, it cannot make any qualitative break with the existing bourgeois system. (8.10)

It is here that the whole system of the dictatorship of the proletariat so far practised, starting from Lenin and up to Mao, failed. The whole system revolved around the idea of seizing and maintaining the political power through a centralized state structure. It not only did not initiate any process of re-absorption of power but, on the contrary, led to more concentration of power. Of course, during the Cultural Revolution, Mao tried to reverse the direction, but he could not make any qualitative advance since he could not come out of the basic framework already established. Mao had also not grasped the importance of a new political organizational structure. This is what is reflected in his remark that Lenin's Soviets could easily be transformed into Khrushchev's, meaning that the discovery of Soviets was of no significance. (8.11)

The solution of replacing the dictatorship of the bourgeoisie by the dictatorship of the proletariat by simply reversing the dictatorship of the minority over the majority into a dictatorship of the majority over the minority. Hence no qualitative break with the old structure is required. Ultimately, the old structure which concentrates political power in the hands of the state leadership leads to the emergence and strengthening of a new ruling class from among the working class and the ranks and leadership of the party itself. (9.2)

In the light of this evaluation of the basic reason for the grave deviations in the concept and practice of the dictatorship of the proletariat from the time of Lenin onwards, we will have to come to the conclusion that the whole practice of the dictatorship of the proletariat till now and the experience of building socialism was marked by serious deviations. As a new social system, emerging from the old, socialism was bound to suffer from many blemishes. But apart from those caused by circumstances, the line followed by communists from Lenin onwards has also played its part in this. (9.6)[1]

The CRC has grossly devalued the proletarian revolution by evaluating proletarian regimes of the past in this manner. This school of thinking,

1 "On Proletarian Democracy", *A World to Win*, 1992/17, pp. 81-84.

which considers proletarian revolution as nothing more than a change in the leadership of the state, neglects the basic differences between the two types (bourgeoisie and proletariat) of leadership. It will be correct to make such an analysis of the situation when there is a change in inter-class leadership, however, violent it might have been. But to consider the change in the class nature of the regime through the process of a violent revolution as merely a "change in the leadership of the state", is ideological bankruptcy. Marx and Engels laid much importance to establish the proletarian class as the ruling class. They had termed it to be "the first step of revolution". The CRC has neglected such an important issue by describing it as the "change in leadership only."

The CRC is nowhere clear as to which class had taken over the state machinery and for whose interest, when it terms the proletarian regimes of the past merely as the other form of minority dictatorship over the majority. They have totally neglected the basic differences between the capitalist dictatorship of the minority over the majority and the dictatorship of the majority over minority that is established after the proletarian revolution. The minority under the capitalist enforces its dictatorship over the majority to further its vested interests, to promote private property, to institutionalize the continuation of the exploitation of human beings by other human beings and of states by states and for the continual existence of the state power. On the other hand, the majority (the working class under the leadership of the proletariat) after the proletarian revolution exerts its dictatorship over the minority to put an end to all forms of injustice, exploitation, oppression, inequalities and class differentiation from the world once and forever. Thus, any attempt to analyse the dictatorship of the proletariat as merely the other aspect of the dictatorship of the minority is nothing more than a deliberate attempt not to see this fundamental difference.

The CRC has termed the proletarian regimes of the past as "party dictatorship" instead of the true system of proletarian dictatorship. This view rejects the Marxist-Leninist stand that political parties lead their respective classes in class-based societies and considers classes and political parties as contenders. The bourgeoisie itself does not rule as a whole in bourgeois states of whatever type. The bourgeoisie rules through political parties. Let us consider the US, Britain, France, Germany, India, Nepal and other countries. Is the bourgeois class ruling there by itself? Will it be right to term these regimes as the dictatorship of the party, not class dictatorship of the bourgeoisie, merely because these regimes are being run by political parties? All regimes, whether monarchic, republican, aristocratic or liberal democratic are, in essence, class regimes. They may have differences in form, but they are bourgeois dictatorships in essence.

The stand of the CRC to analyse the proletarian regimes of the past as party dictatorships considers monarchy as the dictatorship of the king, republican or parliamentary system as the dictatorship of the ruling party, and military rule as the dictatorship of the military junta. If it were really so, then where did the feudal or the capitalist classes in these countries go?

The development of capitalism has created a favourable environment in which classes could organize into political parties. There is no reason why the classes should not take the benefits from the environment. Lessons from the past have made it clear that classes must be organized into political parties. We have plenty of examples where the progressive forces have failed to take advantage even in more revolutionary situations in history, mainly because of being disorganized beforehand. Today, the capitalist class cannot rule without being organized into political parties. Likewise, the proletarian class cannot execute its historical responsibilities without being organized into a political party. The issue of affiliation of a conscious section of working class with a political organization is the issue related to the leadership of the oppressed and exploited masses. The CRC does not understand this simple and clear issue, and it has presented it as "party dictatorship".

In the *Document*, the CRC shows no "qualitative" distinction between a political organizational structure system under proletarian dictatorship and that of a bourgeois state. It analyses that the political organization structure adopted in those states were non-Marxist. It has severely criticized proletarian regimes of the past for not "re-absorption of state power by society as its own living force" (Karl Marx) as the basic departure point of commune essence.

The CRC, thus, has described the political systems established in the former socialist countries to be contrary to the teaching of Marx. As we have already discussed, the CRC has termed the proletarian regimes in those countries as the reversed form of the dictatorship of the minority over the majority. It has described all systems adopted by countries like the Soviet Union or China, except the Paris Commune, to be contrary to the proletarian class dictatorship. It seems that they have based their conclusion on the analysis of Marx, Engels and Lenin concerning the Paris Commune. The *Document* has stressed that Lenin, prior to the October Revolution, was in favour of such regimes, but later on he backtracked. They have taken the basis of Lenin's high appreciation of the Paris Commune in his masterpiece, *The State and Revolution* where there is no mention of a communist party.

Based on the dissolution of a regular army at the Paris Commune, the CRC advocated to continue such policies under the socialist state organization as well. It is true that Marx, Engels and Lenin have discussed and appreciated the issue of dissolving the regular army and power decentralization as adopted in the Paris Commune. They have said that this puts an end to the state as a state. This does not mean that all the lines of the Paris Commune were correct and must be followed mechanically in all situations and stages of socialist construction. We have to adopt the essence, not the form of any thing, or event. It is applicable to the Soviet, Chinese and Paris Commune. Many policies of the Paris Commune corresponded not to the regimes born out of the womb of capitalism, but conducive to socialism. This lesson from the Paris Commune has made it clear that policies of later days adopted by the socialist system were basically correct from a practical view. We need to adopt the essence of the lessons from the Paris Commune, but it is wrong to argue that Lenin did not adopt the essence. In the context, the CRC slanders Lenin. However, it is necessary to know the essence of the lessons of the Paris Commune before the debate continues.

Its first essence is that the proletarian class cannot establish its regime in the same superstructure of state machinery after it overthrows the bourgeoisie. It has to destroy the old state machinery and build up a qualitatively different state machinery. Its second essence is that the proletarian class can pass the transitional period (socialist phase) only through the leadership of the communist party. The importance of these lessons is proved by the fact that the first aspect of essence is incorporated as one of the basic corrections in the later edition of the *Communist Manifesto*. As Marx and Engels, in the last preface of the New German edition of the *Communist Manifesto*, have stated: "One thing especially was proved by the Commune, viz. that "the working class cannot simply lay hold of the ready-made state machinery, and wield it for its own purposes."[2]

Marx and Engels, thus, took this lesson so seriously that they decided to include this as one of the basic corrections in the *Communist Manifesto*. Can the CRC say that Lenin did not adopt this lesson? The only thing they mean to say is that the new structure built after destroying the old one was not a copy of the Paris Commune. This will certainly mean that Lenin had adopted the essence of the lessons of the Paris Commune. Let us see why it would be inappropriate for many of the policies adopted by the Paris Commune at the primary stage of the socialism.

The CRC has termed the Leninist stand on the leading role of the party in the period of proletarian dictatorship contrary to the lessons of the Paris Commune. This has revealed their dogmatist thinking in understanding the essence of the lessons of the Paris Commune. Marx and Engels, while evaluating the Commune, after its fall criticized the Commune for the

2 Karl Marx and Frederick Engels, "Manifesto of the Communist Party", *Karl Marx and Frederick Engels Selected Works,* Progress Publishers, Moscow, Fourth Printing, 1977, Vol. 1, p. 99.

dissolution of the rights of the Central Committee. Does this criticism not mean the inevitability of the leading role of the party during the period of proletarian dictatorship? A question may arise, if that is one of the essences of the lessons of the Commune, then why had it not been incorporated in the *Communist Manifesto* as the basic correction?

The simple reason is that the *Communist Manifesto* had prominently stressed, even in its preliminary phase of writing, of the leading role of the party in the movement of building a classless society and in the class struggle of the proletariat. This was not the finding of the Commune, rather the Commune simply proved how correct this idea was. In this context, there is no chance to raise the question as to why this did not become the other basic correction in the *Communist Manifesto.* Let us analyse whether many of the policies adopted by the Commune were relevant to be applicable in the preliminary phase of socialism.

The CRC has criticized Lenin for not adopting the line of the Paris Commune in dissolving the standing army. The development of capitalism into imperialism has brought several changes regarding the proletarian revolution. Marx and Engels had predicted that the proletarian revolution would happen concurrently in the most developed countries of the world. They had predicted that capitalist democracy could turn into socialist democracy. During that time the proletarian revolution was understood and presented as an immediate subject. However, such a thinking required a drastic change after the competitive capitalism turned into a monopolist capitalism. Lenin then said that the proletarian revolution could happen not only in most developed countries, but also in relatively less developed capitalist countries. Likewise, he forwarded the view that such a revolution could take place in a country too. He emphasized that the proletarian revolution was the question of long term, not the short term. We should assess objectively, not subjectively, regarding whether the proletarian should build its permanent army after having captured the power.

The socialist regimes established in a few countries in the world are necessarily encircled by imperialism and it tries to destroy a new born proletarian regime through military intervention. The attack of more than a dozen countries on Russia after the October Revolution, the intervention in the revolutionary civil war in Spain in 1936, the attack on the Soviet Union during the Second World War, the US aggression against Vietnam make it clear that a standing and organized army is mandatory to safeguard a socialist regime. In the absence of such a regular and concentrated army, Russia would have been the second Paris Commune.

Imperialist countries not only use direct military intervention to abolish newly existed socialist countries and follow a strategy to create a situation of civil war by using the former position of the bourgeoisie in different spheres of the superstructure. So, to fight against the imperialist direct military intervention, or threat of civil war, socialist countries must build a powerful socialist military force. To oppose the building of such a mighty armed force will mean leaving the socialist regime at the mercy of God.

The CRC views that the standing army should be replaced by the armed people. In principle, it is correct. But is time not needed to complete this process? Is it possible to execute this policy immediately after the proletarian class takes over power? Is a system not needed to complete this process? The CRC says nothing on these issues. In socialism, people are divided into different classes. Everyone cannot be in favour of socialism. In this situation, a section of people goes against socialist transformation. Imperialists and defeated feudal and capitalist elements uses these people for their revival. In this course they provoke organized people to raise arms. So, the demand of replacement of the standing army by armed people is a nonsensical demand in the present world situation. What we demand is the disbandment of the standing army of the bourgeois state after the proletariat revolution. It will be wrong to oppose building a standing army in a new form. In human history, the standing army of the proletariat is only standing and an organized army which works not for its continuity, but for its own disbandment.

The CRC has criticized Lenin for not adopting the universal suffrage line of the Paris Commune. Lenin should not be criticized for this. He never considered the issue of universal suffrage as the general question of proletarian dictatorship. He considered the policy to deprive the exploiters from voting rights that was adopted in Russia under the special conditions. Throwing light on this issue, he writes:

> It should be observed that the question of depriving the exploiters of the franchise is a *purely Russian* question, and not a question of the dictatorship of the proletariat in general.
>
> After the war and the experience of the Russian Revolution it probably will be so; but it is *not absolutely necessary* for the exercise of the dictatorship, it is not an *indispensable* characteristic of the logical concept "dictatorship", it does not enter as an *indispensable* condition in the historical and class concept "dictatorship".[3]

The above statement, thus, clarifies how prejudiced the CRC is in its criticism against Lenin. However, CRC has raised the issue of the Paris Commune with prominence in its document. But it has neglected Marx's "Critique of the Gotha Programme" penned after four or five years

3 V. I. Lenin, "Proletarian Revolution and Renegade Kautsky", *Collected Works*, Eng. ed., Progress Publishers, Moscow, Third Printing, 1981, Vol. 28, pp. 255-56.

after the Commune. They have given no importance to the spirit of the "Critique of the Gotha Programme". Lenin's thinking on the dictatorship of the proletariat is completely based on this *Critique*.

Marx and Engels have criticized the German Socialists for their understanding of communism and socialism in the same spirit and for their similar line on both the phases. They have identified two phases of communism–socialist phase and communist phase. Marx's following statement quoted below proves it:

> What we have to deal with here is a communist society, not as it has *developed* on its own foundations, but, on the contrary, just as it *emerges* from capitalist society; which is thus in every respect, economically, morally and intellectually, still stamped with the birth marks of the old society from whose womb it emerges.

Continuing, Marx says:

> These defects are inevitable in the first phase of communist society as it is when it has just emerged after prolonged birth pangs from capitalist society. Right can never be higher than the economic structure of society and its cultural development conditioned thereby.
>
> In a higher phase of communist society, after the enslaving subordination of the individual to the division of labour, and therewith also the antithesis between mental and physical labour, has vanished; after labour has become not only a means of life but life's prime want; after the productive forces have also increased with the all-round development of the individual, and all the springs of cooperative wealth flow more abundantly–only then can the narrow horizon of bourgeois right be crossed in its entirety and society inscribe on its banners: From each according to his ability, to each according to his needs![4]

These views of Marx make it clear that the same line cannot be adopted in a communist society from the beginning to the end. The document reveals that the CRC does not accept this. The CRC recommends adopting the same line in both the phases of communism. The CRC has concluded that whole power is concentrated in the state structure, so the system of political power adopted by socialist states in the past was neither a real proletarian system nor a qualitatively different system. It says that state power should be mobilized by the society through decentralization of political power. It has supported this viewpoint based on Marx's concept of "society". Many issues need to be cleared in this context. The CRC has raised the issues of centralization and decentralization in socialism in a metaphoric manner. They have raised the question simply centralization or decentralization

4 Karl Marx and Frederick Engels, "Critique of the Gotha Programme", *Karl Marx and Frederick Engels Selected Works*, Eng. ed., Progress Publishers, Moscow, Fourth Printing, 1977, Vol. 3, pp. 17, 19.

could be adopted at the juncture. The CRC has made a grave error not only on an ideological, or political plane but also philosophically by stating that centralization and decentralization cannot coexist. In fact, centralization and decentralization are two sides of the same thing. They are mutually inseparable. When centralization is not needed, there is no justification to raise the issue of decentralization, and vice versa. The CRC has emphasized decentralization stating that centralization is unnecessary.

It is true that the old centralized state power must be eliminated when the proletarian class assumes power. But it does not mean that proletarian centralized state power should not be developed there. Since socialism is born out of the womb of capitalism, the centralized structure is bound to exist there. But this will be a new type of centralized regime in human history which, contrary to the earlier centralized regime, will follow the gradual process of decentralization with the aim of not providing longevity to it but to let it wither away. In the absence of the proletarian centralized regime under socialism, it would not be possible to further the process of decentralization and to get state power to wither away.

Under socialism there exist conditions like small-scale production, old habits of people, bourgeois rights, attempts by the defeated exploiting class to regain their 'paradise', the emergence of a new bourgeoisie, differentiation between city and countryside and between mental and physical labour, and attempts by the world imperialism to eliminate the proletarian regime. In such a situation, the proletarian regime cannot even complete the transitional phase if it decides to follow the policy of decentralization in an absolute manner soon after capturing state power. The CRC has raised the issue of the merging of state power with the whole people. In the situations where conditions identified above exist; there can be no merging of state power with the 'whole people.' This thinking rejects the need to go forward by identifying the general welfare of the public as such conditions exist among the people. This is possible only through a centralized regime. This viewpoint looks at people under socialism on a classless basis. All regimes are instruments of class rule.

Every state power is the means for class oppression. Socialism is a system which establishes working class dictatorship over the exploiting class, and the dictatorship of revolutionaries over the reactionaries. Thus, under socialism the merging of state power should be practised not by the 'whole people'. Rather, it should be practised only by the section of the population in favour of socialist state power. In such a situation as well, central control is necessary. The section of people which favours socialism cannot itself chart the process of moving forward to communism. We have already discussed the internal contradiction even within that section. The programmes and policies formulated by the physical workers may not suit the interests of mental workers and vice versa; the policies formulated by peasants may not serve the needs of the workers and vice versa. Urban programmes and policies may not serve the rural folk and vice versa, programmes and policies formulated by a particular part of the country may not conform to the interests of other parts. In such a situation, a central power is a must to formulate programmes and policies serving their general interests.

The CRC says the thinking against the central power is based on Marx's view. The CRC, on the basis of Marx's stressing the destruction of the old state machineries, concludes that Marx was against the centralism. This is wrong as Marx has stressed the need to destroy the old state machineries (both central and local) after the takeover of power by the proletarian class. He nowhere says that the proletarians should not build up a new central regime. He was in favour of a central regime of the proletarian class, so he emphasized the need to organize national unity, while discussing in the Paris Commune. He says:

> In a rough sketch of national organization which the Commune had no time to develop, it states clearly that the Commune was to be the political form of even the smallest country hamlet, and that in the rural districts the standing army was to be replaced by a national militia, with an extremely short term of service. The rural communes of every district were to administer their common affairs by an assembly of delegates in the central town, and these district assemblies were again to send deputies to the National Delegation in Paris, each delegate to be at any time revocable and bound by the *mandate imperatif* (formal instructions) of his constituents. The few but important functions which would still remain for a central government were not to be suppressed, as has been intentionally misstated, but were to be discharged by Communal, and therefore strictly responsible agents. The unity of the nation was not to be broken, but, on the contrary, to be organized by the Communal Constitution and to become a reality by the destruction of the State power which claimed to be the embodiment of that unity independent of, and superior to, the nation itself, from which it was but a parasitic excrescence.[5]

The above quoted statement reveals that Marx was not against a central regime in general. He was just against the bourgeois, military, bureaucratic centralism which considers itself independent of and superior to the nation. It is clear that Marx was in favour of the conscious, democratic, proletarian centralism and this is possible only in proletarian state power. Different people interpret Marx and Engels' analysis on the Paris Commune in different ways. At one time, Bernstein chose to analyse Marx in his own way to conclude that Marx was against the centralism. Now, the same analysis is made by the CRC. Lenin and Leninists have always interpreted Marx in

5 Karl Marx, "The Civil War in France", *Karl Marx and Fredrick Engels Selected Works*, Eng. ed., Progress Publishers, Moscow, Fourth Printing, 1977, Vol. 2, p. 221.

favour of centralism. Criticizing Bernstein for his wrong interpretation, Lenin says further:

> As though foreseeing that his views might be distorted, Marx expressly emphasized that the charge that the Commune had wanted to destroy national unity, to abolish the central authority, was a deliberate fraud. Marx intentionally used the words: "National unity was ... to be organized", so as to oppose conscious, democratic, proletarian centralism to bourgeois, military, bureaucratic centralism.[6]

The CRC states that Mao raised the issue of a true proletarian political system in the history of the international communist movement, after Marx. The CRC states "actually the masses who developed the new form of struggle, the Cultural Revolution," and by quoting Mao, it has tried to prove that the concept of proletarian central authority and party leadership is wrong and the masses can develop and lead new forms of struggles. It has tried to use Mao's saying as a weapon to establish the validity of its thinking notwithstanding the fact that it has taken a U turn completely out of track to attack Mao with the same logic. The CRC has stated that although Mao was developing the line of thinking during the initial phase of the Cultural Revolution, he did not put them into practice and turned to Leninist thinking. It said: "They tried to establish an all-round dictatorship over the bourgeoisie using the same old framework of the dictatorship of the proletariat." "Mao had also not adopted the importance of the new political organizational structure."

Mao had a great regard for the role of the masses in the socialist construction and he endeavoured to enhance the role of the masses in that campaign. During the Great Cultural Revolution, Mao was successful at raising the initiatives of the masses (only those who were in favour of socialism), not all people to a new height. But it does not mean that Mao, while enhancing the role of the masses under socialism, was against the leadership of the party and the central authority. He was a great Leninist and always remained under the ideological framework of Leninism. The CRC has twisted the objective facts about Mao's stand on Leninism. It has presented Mao's concept on the role of the masses under socialism wrongly. The CRC has distorted Mao's thought. It has observed that people not only developed a new form of struggle during the cultural revolution, but that was the discovery of the people themselves.

China's Great Proletarian Cultural Revolution was not a finding of the masses. Rather it was an invention of the CPC under the leadership of Mao and its frontline leaders. It was run under Mao's direct leadership. The

---

6 V. I. Lenin, "The State and Revolution", *Collected Works*, Eng. ed., Progress Publishers, Moscow, Fourth Printing, 1980, Vol. 25, p. 435.

direction of revolution from start to end was determined by the same section of the party. It is wrong to draw the forms of struggles that appeared in that period as separated from that leadership or to state that they were developed purely by the masses. In essence, different forms of struggles right from the local level up to the central level were determined by the CPC. Struggles against the bourgeoisie in any industrial units, communes, schools, colleges or offices were the result of the efforts of the local units of the party by mobilizing non-party people who were in favour of socialism. It is not possible to develop an absolute demarcation between party members and the masses. Hundreds and thousands of the masses were party members. The concept of separating a section of the party members, by describing the higher form of struggle as developed by the masses is totally wrong. This thinking considers it wrong for any member of the mass to become a party member voluntarily. Under this type of thinking, if any member of the mass becomes a party member voluntarily, he turns into a parasite on the mass and the nation. He stands against the masses. He fails to be in favour of party dictatorship. This type of understanding of the masses by CRC demands party members to turn into the units of the mass and not vice versa because human beings have the natural tendency to be attached by something good to something better.

The CRC's analysis that Mao attempted to establish all-round dictatorship over the bourgeoisie in accordance with the traditional design of proletarian dictatorship is correct. But the CRC has chosen to present this fact in a manner that portrays Mao as anti-Marxist.

Let us turn our attention to its metaphysical and biased viewpoints in its analysis of Marxism. CRC does not make any difference between the policies stressed by Marx to adopt at different phases separately in the course of building socialism. It has totally neglected Marx's "Critique of the Gotha Programme" where he had differentiated two phases of communist society and had suggested that different policies need to be adopted for different phases and had spoken strongly against following the same policies for both the phases. And the CRC has criticized Mao for following proletarian dictatorship, which for Marx, was an essential aspect for the entire transitional period from capitalism to communism. Let us quote Marx from his "Critique of the Gotha Programme" to clear how much importance Marx had accorded to this issue: "Between capitalist and communist society lies the period of the revolutionary transformation of the one into the other. Corresponding to this is also a political transition period in which the state can be nothing but *the revolutionary dictatorship of the proletariat.*"[7]

---

7 Karl Marx, "Critique of the Gotha Programme", *Karl Marx and Frederick Engels Selected Works*, Eng. ed., Progress Publishers, Moscow, Fourth Printing, 1977, Vol. 3, p. 26.

Does this quote not prove that Mao, was a true Marxist in following the "traditional design" and his critique–the CRC anti-Marxist? This quote also clears another issue. The CRC had, in the past, expressed its difference of opinion concerning ruling systems under the proletarian dictatorship. It had termed them wrong. It had criticized Lenin and Leninists by taking into consideration the formal aspect of the proletarian state, but not for its essence. But the way they have criticized Mao on this issue clears that the CRC's difference of opinion on proletarian democracy is not in its form, but in the essence. It considers proletarian dictatorship to be wrong. And it is ironical that it claims to be truly Marxist, socialists and also in favour of communism. Whatever claim it makes to be true Marxists, its opposition to the establishment of an "all-round dictatorship over the bourgeoisie" under socialism has proved that it is the true follower of the Second International and modern revisionists such as Nikita Khrushchev and Teng Hsiao-ping.

The question is what is the yardstick to distinguish Marxist individuals and parties from non-Marxists? Lenin says:

> Only he is a Marxist who *extends* the recognition of the class struggle to the recognition of the *dictatorship of the proletariat.* This is what constitutes the most profound distinction between the Marxist and the ordinary petty (as well as big) bourgeois. This is the touchstone on which the *real* understanding and recognition of Marxism should be tested.".

By accusing Lenin, Stalin and Mao the CRC has claimed that none of them had followed the essence of Marx's teaching concerning the state and has said that none of the socialist countries in the past followed the Marxist norms on the state. What is the basic criteria to know whether a party or individual has followed Marx's concept of the state or not and whether a country is a socialist country in the Marxist sense or not. The basic criterion is the proletarian dictatorship, one that adopts proletarian dictatorship for a transitional period that has endorsed Marx's teachings on the socialist state. If anyone rejects this and thinks it wrong to maintain that, they can be termed to be ignorant of even the ABC of Marx's teaching on the socialist state. Lenin says further:

> The essence of Marx's theory of the state has been mastered only by those who realize that the dictatorship of a *single* class is necessary not only for every class society in general, not only for the *proletariat* which has overthrown the bourgeoisie, but also for the entire *historical period* which separates capitalism from "classless society", from communism. Bourgeois states are most varied in form, but their essence is the same: all these states, whatever their form, in the final analysis are inevitably *the dictatorship of the bourgeoisie.* The transition from capitalism to communism is certainly bound to yield a tremendous abundance and variety of

political forms, but the essence will inevitably be the same: *The dictatorship of the proletariat.*[8]

These facts make it clear that the CRC's criticism of Mao on the socialist state is a direct criticism of not only Lenin and Stalin but of Marx and Engels as well. It is not Mao, Stalin and Lenin who deviated from the essence of Marx's teachings, but it is the CRC itself. Its analysis of socialist state does not bear even the least concern with the Marxist analysis of these issues. State power means an organization that is centralized and is meant for the use of force. It is not a Marxist view to talk of socialist state power and subsequently oppose proletarian central authority and the use of force against the bourgeoisie. Opposition to these two aspects means rejection of the existence of the state power itself. State power is centralized and also the one which needs to use force. If one talks of the socialist state and opposes the use of force on building central power, then the person cannot be called a true Marxist. It means rejecting the existence of the state.

The CRC *Document* has repeatedly raised the issues of the Commune and Soviets and has appreciated Lenin's slogan of power to the Soviets. Stressing these issues is not correct. The CRC itself does not analyse Soviets in this way, rather it pleads that the leading role of the party and emphasis in building centralized power can unknowingly encourage the bureaucracy to emerge, even leading to restoration of capitalism. Can we ignore the possibility of the Communes or Soviets degrading into bourgeois character? We have the history of Russia before us. The Russian Soviets lacked pure character and it was not possible to be so. The control over Soviets in Russia was not only in the hands of the Bolsheviks, at some time the Mensheviks also had control over them. There were times when more Soviets were under the control of Mensheviks. For the time being, the Mensheviks had increased influence on the Soviets, and Lenin repeatedly criticized the Soviets for the existence of petty bourgeoisie organizational elements and for increased bureaucratization and profit motives within the Soviets. Was it possible there, in such a situation, to eliminate the role of the party and the central authority as demanded by the CRC, in the name of the establishment of a "new political system"? Could such a step help socialism survive in the Soviet Union for another thirty years? It will be wrong to reject the need of leadership and centralization on the basis of higher revolutionary sacrifices seen in the people during the revolutionary upsurge. Firstly, we should not try to separate the feeling of higher revolutionary sacrifices of the people during revolutionary upsurges with the leadership; secondly, it must not be thought that such feelings would continue to exist in the same manner in post-revolutionary situations. The feeling of revolutionary sacrifices, in both

8 V. I. Lenin, "The State and Revolution", *Selected Works*, Eng. ed., Progress Publishers, Moscow, Fourth Printing, 1980, Vol. 25, pp. 417-18.

revolutionary and non-revolutionary situations, exists and continues only in revolutionary communist parties.

The CRC *Document* has stated that under a socialist system, people must have only the right to recall leaders as well as to elect them. This viewpoint of the CRC is correct in general when we consider it separately from other viewpoints of CRC, but it is not the only thing. Decisions concerning the validity of our viewpoints need to be solved dialectically and not in a metaphysical way. This viewpoint of the CRC is not more than a bourgeois myth when we analyse it in the background of their attack on the leading role of the communist party and the centralized proletarian system. The masses do not have an absolute revolutionary character under socialism. Any attempt to ignore this reality and advocate unrestricted rights to elect and recall leadership weakens the essence of the revolutionary regime.

The grave deviation of the CRC from the essence of Marx's teachings on the state is best reflected in its policy of stressing the "non-class aspect of democracy" in bourgeois states. They have said that Lenin "ignored" this "aspect" of bourgeois states by stating that this must not be "ignored" and the CRC has tried to say that such "non-class aspect" also exists in the socialist states and the opportunities must be provided for their unhindered growth. In reality, the "non-class aspect" of democracy under the bourgeois state is eventually determined by the class character and it has no consequence in practice. This way of thinking weakens the class aspect of democracy. We will discuss it in greater detail later on too.

Another grave deviation of the CRC from the essence of Marx's teachings on the state is best reflected in its statement that Lenin simply took socialist society as a stage of classes and class struggles and chose to "ignore" the "non-class aspect" of the socialist society which weakens proletarian dictatorship. It leads to disintegration of proletarian dictatorship because the social condition of any society and dictatorship of the country is not the same thing. Dictatorship means the accession of power by a particular class, and the regime follows policies serving the interest of the class that it represents. Bourgeois dictatorship is not a reflection of the society. It is the reflection of a section of a society. This thing is equally true for proletarian dictatorship. The CRC has chosen to present all the people of the whole society and dictatorship as the same thing. This thinking is totally against proletarian dictatorship. It is also against the essence of Marx's teachings on state power.

3. The Communist Party and the Dictatorship of the Proletariat

The CRC in its *Document* has termed the Leninist view on the role of the communist party during the period of the dictatorship of the proletariat wrong. Leninism considers the leading role of the communist party under socialism as indispensable. The role of the communist party was established in all the countries where socialism was established accordingly in the past. The CRC has described this Leninist view as being principally responsible for the disintegration of the world socialist system. It has argued that Lenin's concept on the role of the communist party was "different" from that of Marx and Engels, and the CRC holds Stalin and Mao's "mistake" in following Lenin's concept on this issue basically responsible for the disintegration of the world socialist system. Thus, it has blamed Lenin for all these negative consequences. It has argued that Lenin himself, prior to October 1917, was not in favour of the leading role of the communist party under socialism. Its *Document* states:

> As has already been pointed out, Lenin was fully relying on the experience of the Pairs Commune as narrated and evaluated by Marx and Engels in order to develop the concept and practice of the dictatorship of the proletariat." (8.2)
>
> It was in this background that Lenin raised the most crucial slogan of the October Revolution, "All Power to the Soviets". In his most important theoretical work on the state, *The State and Revolution*, he envisaged the Soviets as the main form of political organ of the proletariat and other sections of the people." (8.3)
>
> The absence of any mention of the role of the party in the whole scheme of the dictatorship of the proletariat as explained in *The State and Revolution* by Lenin is very conspicuous. It may be due to this influence of the political structure of the Paris Commune." (8.5)
>
> What was developed as the new political system was gradually coming under the control of the communist party. Lenin explained the situation thus: "What happens is that the party, shall we say, absorbs the vanguard of the proletariat, and this vanguard exercises the dictatorship of the proletariat. The dictatorship cannot be exercised or the functions of the government performed without a foundation such as the trade unions. These functions, however, have to be performed through the medium of special institutions which are also of a new type, namely the Soviets. ... The whole is like an arrangement of cogwheels. ... It cannot work without a number of 'transmission belts' running from the vanguard to the mass of the advanced class, and from the latter to the mass of the working people." (*LCW*, Vol. 32, p. 20-21) (5.7)
>
> Further, Lenin categorically declared the role of the communist party thus: "After two and a half years of the Soviet power we came out in the Communist International and told the world that the dictatorship of the proletariat would not work except through the communist party". (*LCW*, Vol. 32, p. 199) Now the circle is complete. The practical programme for establishing the dictatorship of the proletariat which started with the attractive slogan, "All power to the Soviets", ended with the reality that the

dictatorship of the proletariat was exercised through the communist party, where the Soviets became mere cogwheels in the machine." (5.8)

Under the pressure of circumstances, in the face of both external and internal threats, the party was forced to play the central role, relegating the Soviets to the background. And Lenin openly admitted this situation and justified it saying that the proletariat can exercise its dictatorship only through the party. In order to justify this new role of the party Lenin even pointed out the degeneration of the working class, making it unable to rule as a class (*LCW*, Vol. 32, p. 21) Moreover, Lenin was not raising this question as a specific problem of Russia, but as a universal problem, thereby making it a principle that only the party can exercise the dictatorship. Hence Lenin had reached a position just opposite to that of Marx." (8.7).

Another tendency encouraged by Lenin's stand on the party's central role in the dictatorship of the proletariat is the dominant thinking in the communist movement which considers that the party determines everything in relation to social revolution. A one-sided subjective approach towards the party, blind faith in the party, etc., gets strengthened as a result of this tendency." (9.7)

The position taken by Lenin in relation to the party and the dictatorship of the proletariat is not very different from the position Stalin adopted and implemented. Stalin argued that the dictatorship of the proletariat is "in essence", the dictatorship of the party. And in exercising this dictatorship, the party uses the Soviets as mere transition belts like the trade unions, Youth League, etc., ("Concerning Questions of Leninism", *Collected Works*, Vol. 8, pp. 14-39) From this position, the nature and course of development of the bureaucratization process and the emergence of new classes can easily be traced. Under such a political structure, the absence of conscious policy to restrict bourgeois right and the increasing reliance on material incentive for promoting production laid the economic foundation for bureaucratic capitalism." (5.9)

Mao's attempt to evolve a healthy ideological and political struggle within the communist party by developing the two-line struggle to a higher level helped in creating a new atmosphere. Also his attempt to build a new democratic state with a broad united front of different classes under the leadership of the working class was a departure and development conforming to the different situation in a semi-colonial condition. (7.1)

In spite of all these major breakthroughs ... after the completion of the revolution in China and the dictatorship of the proletariat which followed did not mark any significant advancement from the basic framework developed by Lenin and Stalin. Since the New Democratic state was formed as a united front of different class forces, some other political parties other than the communist party were also participating in it. But all these parties were accepting the leadership and the authority of the communist party. Therefore, in effect, the situation was not much different from that in a state with single-party rule. (7.2).

> So the basic problems faced by the Soviet Union under Lenin and Stalin, namely the lack of a political system in which the people can directly participate and assert their political will, socialization of the means of production leading to centralization and the accompanying bureaucratization of the whole system, were all manifested in China also. Hence, the same process of capitalist restoration which had already reached an advanced stage in the Soviet Union had started in China as well." (7.3)[9]

The CRC has stated that China, after the New Democratic Revolution, was not different from one party rule since the united front of different classes and parties were established under the policy of all parties accepting the leadership and authority of the communist party. It has said that this policy of Lenin, Stalin and Mao in regard to the party and the dictatorship of the proletariat led to the restoration of capitalism in the Soviet Union and China. Such a viewpoint of the CRC, concerning the party and the dictatorship of the proletariat has raised many questions. We need to make it clear whether Lenin's concept on this issue is in contradiction or in conformity with that of Marx and Engels. Lenin's concept on this issue resembles that of Marx and Engels, does not contradict it as claimed by the CRC. Marx and Engels in the *Communist Manifesto* and throughout their lives have stressed the leadership role of the communist party in the class struggle of the proletariat (both pre and post-dictatorship of the proletariat). They have made it clear on this issue in several paragraphs of the *Communist Manifesto*. The following statement made in 1872 also helps understand this issue:

> In its struggle against the collective power of the possessing classes the proletariat can act as a class only by constituting itself a distinct political party, opposed to all the old parties formed by the possessing classes. ... This constitution of the proletariat into a political party is indispensable to ensure the triumph of the social revolution and of its ultimate goal: the abolition of classes.[10]

They have made it clear that the proletariat, whether they may be the ruling class or struggling to gain state power, must be organized into a political party to work as a class. However, it is clear from the above quotation that Marx and Engels considered the organization of proletariats of this type into a political party as the eventual necessity for the abolition of classes–the ultimate aim of social revolution and not only for the purpose of the establishment of socialist ownership in the instrument and the means of production or until the stage of elevating the proletariat as the rulers as stated by the CRC. How convinced they were on this issue

9 "On Proletarian Democracy", *A World to Win*, 1992/17, pp. 79-82, 84.

10 Karl Marx and Frederick Engels, "From the Resolution of the General Congress Held in the Hague", *Karl Marx and Frederick Engels Selected Works*, Eng. ed., Progress Publishers, Moscow, Fourth Printing, 1977, Vol. 2, p. 291.

is amply demonstrated in the letter Engels wrote to Gerson Trier in 1989. In that letter Engels says: "For the proletariat to be strong enough to win on the decisive day it must–and Marx and I have advocated this ever since 1847–form a separate party distinct from all others and opposed to them, a conscious class party."[11]

The fall of the Paris Commune proved how right Marx and Engels were on this issue. Marx and Engels, in their analysis of the fall of the Commune itself, described the dissolution of the leading role of the Central Committee as one of the two important reasons for its defeat.

The CRC has tried to throw into a dustbin this clear cut and straightforward Marxist explanation on the relation between the proletarian class struggle and the role of the communist party. It has tried to present the Leninist doctrine on proletarian dictatorship being anti-Marxist while vulgarizing Marx's concept on the dictatorship of the proletariat in the same manner as distorted by Kautsky. Marx's concept on the dictatorship of the proletariat was presented by Kautsky, as "rests upon a single word of Karl Marx's", "opportunely recalled the little word", "about the dictatorship of the proletariat which Marx once used in 1875 in a letter." (Taken from *LCW*, Vol. 28, p. 233)

Thus, Kautsky grossly undervalued the essence of the whole of Karl Marx's revolutionary teachings as a "single word". The CRC has followed exactly the same method of the leadership of the party. In its evaluation of the fall of the Commune, its *Documents* never mention the above quoted teachings of Marx and Engels while prominently presenting their criticism on handing over the Central Committe's leading role to the Commune in haste. The Central Committee should have continued its leading role but for how long? Marx and Engels have not written anything on this issue and CRC seems to mean they were not in favour of it for the whole period of socialism. This is sheer idealism. How baseless and biased the logic of the CRC is demonstrated by the above quote with its conviction that is indispensable "to ensure the triumph of the social revolution and of its ultimate goal: the abolition of classes". In this statement the "ultimate goal: the abolition of classes" bears specific importance. Since there are classes in socialism, the proletariat have yet to attain their ultimate goal. They have to wait for a long time, until and unless classes are abolished to attain this victory. This means the proletarian class has to remain organized into a political party for the whole period of this 'first' stage of communist society. There in the Paris Commune, Marx and Engels did not prescribe the duration of the time for the party to continue the leadership, so the same

11 Marx-Engels, *Selected Correspondence*, Progress Publishers, Moscow, Third revised ed., 1975, p. 386.

thing cannot be the base for the role of the party during the proletarian dictatorship of CRC.

The CRC, in this context, terms the organization of the proletariat into a political party and the leadership of the party during the period of the dictatorship of the proletariat as being opposed to each other. It tries to present themselves as 'true' Marxists by arguing that they accept the first term. But this is wrong. When it is said that the proletariat need to be organized into a political party, the natural question is, what for? It needs to be stressed that the organization of any class into a political party in class societies aims primarily for the establishment of class dictatorship in the state power. This is equally true for both the bourgeoisie and the proletariat. If establishment of class dictatorship by any class does not eliminate the need for being politically organized, it means to continue the leading role of the party. When there is no need of the leading role of a party in a society to represent the interest of a particular class then the need to be organized politically for any class will be automatically null and void.

These facts are clear that the attempt of the CRC to attack the Leninist view on this issue with the weapon of 'Marxism' is not more than an attack against Marxism itself in a round about way under the pretext of attacking Leninism. The CRC has raised the issue of proletarian dictatorship and the "dictatorship" of the communist party. It has termed the theory and practice followed by Lenin, Stalin and Mao Tse-tung concerning the leading role of the communist party in socialism as being the policy of "dictatorship" of the communist party. There is no need to feel surprised at such a presentation of this issue by the CRC since the issue of the dictatorship of the proletariat has been presented as the 'dictatorship' of the party in the history of the international communist movement in the same spirit. At different times.

Even in the time of Lenin himself, Kautsky, Rosa Luxemburg and some groups presented this issue in this manner. The CRC has, on this issue, based itself primarily on Rosa Luxemburg's view. Rosa is an immortal name in the history of the world communist movement. She is a great revolutionary and we have to learn important lessons from her. But it does not mean that she had never committed mistakes throughout her revolutionary career. Her views on the rights for self-determination of nations, capital accumulation, and proletarian democracy, proletarian dictatorship and the relationship with the communist party are very important ones. Later, she corrected some of them. Learning from revolutionaries, philosophers or ideologues does not mean to accept their mistakes and weaknesses as well. This is equally true in the case of Rosa Luxemburg, so the CRC's views built on the wrong foundation of Rosa is self-defeating.

This type of view concerning the party and the dictatorship of the proletariat, whether those that emerged during Lenin's time or the present version presented by the CRC, negates the basic facts that in modern societies classes are led by political parties. This concept overlooks that the leading of the proletariat is done by the communist party, whether in struggles to assume state power, or during the socialist construction after the accession of power. We have experiences from bourgeois politics. Even capitalist countries, the capitalists rule through their political parties. In such a situation any attempt to explain the leadership of the communist party as dictatorial, or against the proletarian regime is nothing more than disarming the proletariat while struggling to compete with the armed (politically organized) bourgeoisie.

Marx and Engels have made it clear that scientific socialism is not the consequence of only class struggle. Socialism is the result of class struggles continuing for thousands of years and the tradition of intellectual thinking as well side by side. By rejecting the leading role of the communist party under the dictatorship of the proletariat, the CRC has rejected this Marxist tradition.

This type of the CRC's thinking regarding the relationship between a communist party and the proletarian dictatorship neglects the differences between class-party-leadership and the masses. Differences between them are the result of the existence of the class society. This difference does not get eliminated in socialism as that is born out of the womb of capitalism. There is a need to discover the common interests of the whole working class free from a specific type present in struggles launched in different nations with differences marked in particular (although only in form) even after the establishment of socialism in one or even in more countries. This will be possible only through the leading role of the communist party during the dictatorship of the proletariat. Socialism is not a stage of the end of the class struggle of the proletariat against the bourgeoisie; rather it is a further more complex stage of the struggle. There are conditions of stronger proletarian movements not only to reach state power, but also after the power is captured. There is need to identify its activities and find its satisfactory solutions. The only thing it means is that the leading role of the communist party is present and a must. Only the communist party can do this and understand what it should be, but the CRC document denies this inevitability. It tries to finish all subjectively the instant and future differences that are certain to exist longer among the masses and in the proletarian, trade unions and the communist party.

The CRC has said that Lenin had accepted the Paris Commune as his model of the dictatorship of the proletariat prior to the October Revolution and put forward the slogan of 'all power to the Soviets', but he adopted the policy of imposing the dictatorship of the party after the October Revolution. They have presented Lenin's famous work, *The State and Revolution* as an instance. It is true that Lenin has dealt with the Paris Commune in great detail in this book. He has gone into great detail on these issues like the dissolution of the standing army, equal salary and wages, the election of representatives by the people and their rights to recall them, and on the Commune's supremacy over the bourgeois parliament. But the conclusion developed by the CRC on this basis clearly exposes the fact it was following a metaphysical and not dialectical approach in understanding the book. It is trying to conceal the essence of this book. Lenin has not written anything on the issue of the role of the party in this work. This work was prepared at a time when there was a serious debate within the international communist movement on the nature of the new regime destined to take over from the bourgeois regime. The opportunists within the communist movement, particularly, when the Second International and their leader Kaustsky, were presenting this issue in a distorted manner. In such a situation it was correct and natural for Lenin to focus his analysis on the proletarian state.

The CRC considers Lenin as having accepted the Paris Commune as his model in this work. This conclusion does not grasp the essence of this book. He discussed the rights of the people, but not about the level of the communist society in great detail. In this context, he had relied mainly on the "Critique of the Gotha Programme". Lenin's policy after the October Revolution is fully in conformity with the "Critique of the Gotha Programme" and *The State and Revolution.* It is not true, as the CRC says, that Lenin developed the concept of the leading role of the party under the dictatorship of the proletariat as a post October Revolution phenomenon. This concept is an integral part of Leninism. This fact is very clear from his works such as *What is to be Done?* and so many other articles. The CRC *Document* has spoken of Lenin as imposing dictatorship of the communist party, depriving the Soviets of their power. So many facts refute these charges and prove them to be slanders. Lenin has never said leadership of the communist party is unnecessary while, he talks about 'all power to Soviets'. On the other hand, he had been giving due weight to the reasons found responsible by Marx and Engels for the fall of the Paris Commune while dealing with this issue. He gave this slogan within the structure of leadership of the party. We need to give our due attention to an important reason which surely does not undermine the importance of the dictatorship of the proletariat, although he has not talked much about it in this work. The issue of the leadership of the party (both pre and post-revolution) in the class struggle of the proletariat is an ideological and a basic issue, not something special. It does not mean that its importance has been reduced or that Lenin has dropped it simply because it was not mentioned in a specific time or work.

Lenin's explanation on the mechanism of proletarian dictatorship proves it wrong that Lenin established the "dictatorship" of the communist party in the place of the dictatorship of the proletariat. Lenin has given its detailed and scientific explanation and has said that the dictatorship of the proletariat is formed out of the mechanism of transmission belts, the levers, and the directing force. Lenin considered the communist party as a part (leading part) of the totality of the dictatorship of the proletariat. Any object or a part of the total structure of any event can never represent, whatever important it may be, the whole thing or event. The CRC has, by presenting Lenin's views on the issue of party leadership in opposition to the class dictatorship, fallen victim to a non-Marxist and non-dialectical approach on the relationship between part and totality.

Stalin has ideologically and logically refuted this kind of slander against Lenin in his famous work, *Concerning Questions on Leninism* appropriately to prove that Lenin was fully correct. There is no single instance where Lenin has equated the 'leadership of the party' with the dictatorship of the proletariat, Stalin has claimed that Lenin meant, by this "party holds power alone and that it does not share power with other parties". Lenin has used the term within quotation marks like "in essence" "dictatorship" of party. Stalin describes this in terms of "only a conscious minority can lead them" (Lenin) or in terms of "dictatorship" (... discipline) over the overthrown bourgeoisie trying to regain power, not over the working class. In this context, Stalin has stressed the term "in essence". Lenin has presented this viewpoint not in totality but "in essence", Stalin has argued. Stalin has given the examples of the 'national question' and the 'peasant question' to prove that Lenin's views on this issue is not contrary to Marxism. The national question is in essence a peasant question. But it does not mean that the peasant question and national question are the same thing in their totality. The national question are more extensive than the peasant question. It is equally true about the party and the dictatorship of the proletariat. The dictatorship of the proletariat is extensive while the leading role of the party is only a part (leading part). Stalin has shed light on the differences between these two aspects:

> Although the party carries out the dictatorship of the proletariat, and in this sense the dictatorship of the proletariat is, *in essence*, the "dictatorship" of its party, this does not mean that the "dictatorship of the party" (its leading role) is *identical* with the dictatorship of the proletariat, that the former is *equal* in scope to the latter. There is no need to prove that the dictatorship of the proletariat is wider and richer in its scope than the leading role of the party. The party carries out the dictatorship of the proletariat, but it carries out the

> dictatorship of the *proletariat*, and not any other kind of dictatorship. Whoever identifies the leading role of the party with the dictatorship of the proletariat substitutes "dictatorship" of the party for the dictatorship of the proletariat.

Let us discuss Lenin's polemics with Kautsky while dealing with the charge that Lenin was in favour of 'party dictatorship'. Kuatsky had said that a class can only rule, not govern. Criticizing this view, Lenin said that a class cannot only rule, but also govern. It means the proletarian class is itself governs under the dictatorship of the proletariat. The only thing is that they do so through their vanguard, their party.

Let us present Stalin's criticism of Sorin while discussing the charge that the Leninists are in favour of "party dictatorship". Stalin refuted Sorin's view saying:

> The dictatorship of the proletariat cannot be counterposed to the leadership ("dictatorship") of the party if correct mutual relations exist between the party and the working class, between the vanguard and the masses of the workers. But from this it follows that it is all the more impermissible to identify the party with the working class, the leadership ("dictatorship") of the party with the dictatorship of the working class. *On the ground* that the "dictatorship" of the party cannot be counterposed to the dictatorship of the proletariat, Sorin arrived at the wrong conclusion that "*the dictatorship of the proletariat is the dictatorship of our party*."

The dictatorship of the proletariat and party leadership cannot be the same. If someone thinks along this line, that is not a Marxist thought. Transmission belts or levers are equally important in their places under socialism. Trade unions establish relations between people engaged in productive activities and the party; Soviets establish relations between state machinery and the party; cooperatives relate peasantry with the party; and, the Youth League performs the task of indoctrinating the new generation with socialism. There is no question of the communist party reaching the different strata of the masses and leading them in the great socialist movement without these fronts. They are deeply related to the dictatorship of the proletariat and do represent, as the party, in the respective parts of the dictatorship of the proletariat. There can not be even an imagination of the dictatorship of the proletariat in their absence. Stalin has shed light on the issues: "The levers or transmission belts are those very mass organizations of the proletariat without the aid of which the dictatorship cannot be realized."

Rightly in the same manner, all these organizations need to be directed to the common goal of building socialism and moving towards communism. There exist contradictions, however friendly, between these organizations under socialism as well. At times, these contradictions may turn out to be antagonistic. The leadership of the communist party is indispensable at such times to arrive at common policies representing the interest of all these organizations. In fact, the importance of the role of the communist party in the class struggle of the proletariat (both pre and post-revolution) lies in furthering the interest of the great goal of communism through different mass organizations. Socialism and communism cannot be attained in the absence of such leadership. Stalin says while explaining these aspects:

> There is the *party* of the proletariat, its vanguard. Its strength lies in the fact that it draws into its ranks all the best elements of the proletariat from all the mass organizations of the latter. Its function is to *combine* the work of all the mass organizations of the proletariat without exception and to *direct* their activities towards a single goal, the goal of the emancipation of the proletariat. And it is absolutely necessary to combine and direct them towards a single goal; for otherwise unity in the struggle of the proletariat is impossible, for otherwise the guidance of the proletarian masses in their struggle for power, in their struggle for building socialism, is impossible. But only the vanguard of the proletariat, its party, is capable of combining and directing the work of the mass organizations of the proletariat. Only the party of the proletariat, only the communist party, is capable of fulfilling this role of main leader in the system of the dictatorship of the proletariat.[12]

The views of the CRC on the leadership of the communist party presented in the chapter *The Need for a New Orientation* clearly exposes their lack of clarity. They have termed it necessary to have the leadership of the communist party to abolish the old state machinery and to establish a new state system.

> The vanguard party of the proletariat will have to play the leading role until the new political system starts functioning effectively, by completing the process of the socialization of the means of production and then consolidating the power in the hands of the new ruling classes under the leadership of the proletariat.

The CRC accepts the need of the leadership of the communist party not only for the period prior to the revolution but also for a long duration in the post-revolutionary period (until the new political system functions properly). But its previous viewpoints do not accept this need. The *Document* mentions this while criticizing Stalin and Mao for adopting the Leninist view of party leadership. The same *Document* has criticized Lenin for the decision of the party for the 1917 armed insurrection without any consultations with the Soviets. The views expressed in *New Orientation* and others are contradictory. It is difficult to be clear with which of the two antagonistic views it would feel pleased. The CRC, immediately after the

12 J. V. Stalin, "Concerning Questions of Leninism", *Problems of Leninism,* Foreign Language Press, Peking, 1976, pp. 185-86, 201-202 , 181.

above quote, also says: "Once this is achieved the communist party must give up its monopoly control of the revolutionary transformation and allow the system to function on its own. (10.4)[13]

The view limits the leadership of the communist party in the post-revolutionary periods. According to this view, the party needs to retreat from its leading role once social ownership is established over the instruments and the means of production. Such a situation has been described by the *Document* as the stage of the completion of the "revolutionary transformation" and the stage where "the new political system starts functioning effectively". This is amazing since the CRC had, prior to this statement, preferred to term socialist regimes of the past, where many more things, not simply the social ownership over the instruments and the means of production were achieved, as no different from the bourgeois regimes. But here, they have declared the stage of social ownership of the instruments and the means of production as completion of the "revolutionary transformation" and even "the stage where the new political system starts functioning effectively". This is the extreme example of the CRC's ideological bankruptcy.

It is true that the stage where social ownership is established over the instruments and the means of production, that represents revolutionary transformation. But it is, in no way, as the *Document* suggests, the mature stage required for the dissolution of the active role of the communist party. If it were the stage of the completion of revolutionary transformation, then how could capitalism be restored in the Soviet Union or China where socialist ownership was established? According to the CRC, communist party leadership is necessary for sometime in a socialist state system, and then unnecessary afterwards. It is very difficult to determine for how long it is necessary, and also to identify the stage when it is no more necessary. There is yet another problem as to who is to decide on the break even point? Should it be decided by the communist party itself or by the masses? Since people are still divided into classes in socialism, what is the process of generalization? What is to be done with different processes and logic of reaching the stage propounded by different people? The imperialists may also play their part in creating a situation where people may be provoked to think that the time has come for the leadership of the communist party to go. We have the experience of Russia. During Lenin's time a 'Joint Socialist Forum' was demanded in place of the communist party. But the Bolsheviks Party rejected this. Was it correct to form such a forum and end the leading role of the Bolsheviks Party at that stage? These are a few of the issues which the CRC has preferred to neglect while reaching its conclusions.

13 "On Proletarian Democracy", *A World to Win*, 1992/17, p. 85.

The CRC has asked the proletariat to "assert its authority only politically through bodies elected by the people." It has also said that the communist party must then be an "open party", very democratic accepting even factions, etc. "Its right to govern should be strictly based on the electoral support". Here, the CRC's view on the role of the communist party during the dictatorship of the proletariat is more than clear. This view is nothing but a bourgeois view. They have talked of the need of the communist party to follow the path of "elections" by people and rule. People are divided into different sections under socialism as progressive elements and retrogressive elements. In such a situation the advanced elements try to get majority support for the communist party while the other elements want a non-communist party to attain the majority in the election battle. This means that the CRC also thinks in terms of socialism being governed by non-communist parties. This means that the CRC also thinks the party of the proletariat is a party to be ruled under socialism. This view of CRC has brought forward the notion that the communist party must not only compete with other parties, but also with different internal factions of the communist party itself in elections to rule. This means that the CRC is moving forward to think in terms of more than one party of the proletariat under socialism. It is noteworthy that the CRC, while raising the slogan of electoral competition under socialism, has once in the *Document* expressed in terms of the communist party relinquishing its 'monopoly' after revolutionary transformation is completed. What do they mean by this stage of revolutionary transformation? Is not the CRC describing the presence of different classes and their political parties as the stage of revolutionary transformation? Its stress on the electoral competition compels us not to doubt the fact that it is talking about the stage of revolutionary transformations as nothing different from this one. In reality, the communist party must assert its leadership and not relinquish it as demanded by the CRC for such a stage. If, however, the CRC is not presenting the term revolutionary transformation as something of this stage rather in terms of a stage where classes and their political parties cease to exist, only raising the very issue of electoral competition between political parties is nothing more than ideological and political bankruptcy.

4. Class Struggle

Although the CRC has not explicitly rejected the class struggle, a study of the *Document* in its totality and its views on the socialist state system, communist party leadership, system of government under the dictatorship of the proletariat, and its relation with democracy reveals that the CRC has totally discarded the essence of the teachings of Marxism. By doing so it has assimilated bourgeois thinking, and adopted the policy of 'divide and rule' on this issue just like in other issues. It has placed Lenin against Marx and

Engels. According to the CRC, Lenin discarded the essence of the teaching of Marxism on class struggle and adopted the policy of understanding and looking at everything on a class basis. As we find it written in the *Document*:

> One dominant tendency can be identified as that of a class-reductionist tendency. That is, analysing society only in terms of class and class struggle, thereby neglecting the non-class aspects in the complex phenomenon of society. Lenin's one-sidedness in understanding the complexities of the dictatorship of the proletariat and his total neglect of the need to develop a political system will have to be attributed to this class-reductionist approach, which is still very dominant in the whole communist movement. (9.6)[14]

The CRC has opined that the world communist movement like in the past is still suppressed by the class reductionist tendency. The very first fact in this context is that Lenin had no contradiction and differences with Marxism in understanding and implementing class struggles. Lenin always was a great Marxist on the issue. Secondly, the CRC slanders Lenin by saying that he attempted to look at and understand everything on the basis of class and class struggles. It is designed either at their attempt to prepare the background for discarding class struggle openly, or they do not even know the ABC of Lenin's concept of class struggle. Which of these two arguments is true? Only the future will answer the question. The attempt of the CRC to characterize Lenin as the one who understood and presented everything only in terms of class and class struggles is totally wrong. He has never presented such a viewpoint. Let us examine some facts. It must be well known to the CRC that Lenin was in favour of the right to self-determination of nations. It is not only a question of being in favour; he also developed the concept of Marx and Engels on this issue to a new height. Even today, revolutionary communists all over the world are leading their programmes and activities on the liberation of the oppressed nations on the basis of this Leninist principle. Likewise, we all know the concept of Lenin with regard to the Russian revolution of 1905. That revolution was not a class revolution. It was a bourgeois revolution–a bourgeois revolution of specific characteristics. But Lenin evaluated this revolution highly and used the full force of the party for the revolution. In the same way, Lenin had given the slogan of Constituent Assembly in the bourgeois revolution of 1905 and February 1917. This was not a proletarian slogan. It was simply a bourgeois slogan. Let us take the example of the dictatorship of the proletariat, the higher stage of class struggle. Lenin was against the view that the dictatorship of the proletariat is constituted only of "pure" proletariat. He was of the view that the dictatorship of the proletariat was an alliance of the proletariats with other labouring or exploited masses. He has himself said:

> The dictatorship of the proletariat is a specific form of class alliance between the proletariat, the vanguard of the working people, and the

14 Ibid., p. 84.

> numerous non-proletarian strata of the working people (petty bourgeoisie, small proprietors, the peasantry, the intelligentsia, etc.), or the majority of these strata, an alliance against capital, an alliance whose aim is the complete overthrow of capital, complete suppression of the resistance offered by the bourgeoisie as well as of attempts at restoration on its part, an alliance for the final establishment and consolidation of socialism.[15]

Two things are clear from Lenin's statement. First, the dictatorship of the proletariat is a special alliance of the proletarians. Secondly, it is an alliance designed to completely overthrow the rule of capital and for the establishment and consolidation of the socialism. Thus, Lenin was in favour of extending the limit and essence of class struggle according to the need on the one hand and this extension was meant for promoting the struggle against the capital and for attaining success in such struggles on the other. Lenin's dialectical thinking is also effectively expressed in the following statement that he made during the bourgeois revolution of 1905 in Russia.

> The revolution in our country is one of the whole people, the Social-Democrats say to the proletariat. As the most progressive and the only thoroughly revolutionary class, you should strive to play not merely a most active part in it, but the leading part as well. Therefore, you must not confine yourself within a narrowly conceived framework of the class struggle, understood mainly as the trade union movement; on the contrary, you must strive to extend the framework and the content of your class struggle so as to make it *include* not only *all* the aims of the present, democratic Russian revolution of the whole people, but the aims of the subsequent socialist revolution as well.[16]

In the context of the Leninist being slandered as class reductionist, the struggle launched by Stalin against Trotsky's and Kamanev's attempts to isolate the peasantry by defining the dictatorship of the proletariat on a "pure" class regime, the attempt made by revolutionary communists all around the world to build the anti-fascist united front after the rise of fascism in Germany for decades and its success, the slogan of national struggle given by the CPC under the leadership of Mao during the period of Japanese aggression against China, completion of the new democratic revolution of China under the leadership of Mao in 1949, the vanguard role played by the communist parties in the struggles of liberation by oppressed nationalities and colonialised countries, new democratic revolutions in semi-colonial, semi-feudal countries and the principal contradiction at the international level analysed in 1963 are some noteworthy achievements and that facts prove the bankruptcy of the charges levelled by the CRC against Leninists.

---

15 V. I. Lenin, "Forward to Deception of the People with Slogan", *Collected Works*, Eng. ed., Progress Publishers, Moscow, Third Printing, 1977, Vol. 29, p. 381.

16 V. I. Lenin, "Two Tactics of Social-Democracy in the Democratic Revolution", *Collected Works*, Eng. ed., Progress Publishers, Moscow, Fourth Printing, 1977, Vol. 9, pp. 121-22.

What can be said of the CRC slanders against Lenin and Stalin is that the CRC has differed with Lenin not in the context of the first aspect, i.e. extending the limitation and essence of class struggle, but in the direction of using this extension to overthrow the capitalist regime and be oriented to building socialism. In its view, the first approach is the right one while the latter aim is a class reductionist tendency. The view of the *Document* concerning the dictatorship of the proletariat, leadership of the communist party, political system under the dictatorship of the proletariat and proletarian democracy totally discards this second aspect that is of decisive importance on which Lenin has stressed so much. The thinking of the CRC to oppose the line of Lenin, Stalin and Mao of limiting the class struggle and extending its essence by way of forwarding the goal explicitly for bourgeois state power and building socialism is completely anti-Marxist and revisionist thinking.

Leninism upholds the view that all the issues like the problems of peasantry, nationality, labour problem and many such erupting problem can be and will be solved through class struggles led by the proletariat. An analysis of the *Document* reveals that the CRC has based itself on this analysis while terming the Leninists as class reductionist. This is yet another instance of the CRC's attempt to understand Leninism on different issues in an absolute and mechanical manner. We must not follow absolutism and the mechanical way of thinking but try to understand Leninism in these issues in a dialectical manner. Firstly, Leninism's stress on every issue being solved by the class struggle means that the final and total solution of any issue should be settled through class struggle. So far as solutions or reforms of partial problems are concerned, they are also by-products of class struggle. Secondly, the Leninist concept of the leadership of the proletariat does not reject the role of other classes (peasants, petty bourgeoisie, intellectuals, etc.) in issue settlements, which means the proletarian class is the most revolutionary class in the history of the capitalistic era and this is the only class that can lead all the struggles towards the right direction.

5. Proletarian Democracy

There are serious differences of opinion concerning the proletarian democracy in the international communist movement for long. The issue of proletarian democracy had to face relatively little criticism in the pre-October Revolution period as there was no proletarian dictatorship then. This issue received serious attacks after the Russian October Revolution in 1917. When the proletarian class had to clear its stand from a theoretical stand point, and had also to implement it. Lenin implemented proletarian democracy in Russia in a concrete way. After that the bourgeoisie is interpreting proletarian democracy as a dictatorship and continued to advocate in favour of bourgeois (formal) democracy. Consequently, the entire bourgeoisie worldwide and the opportunists within the communist movement initiated their attack against this. The bourgeois attack on this issue has no specific ideological and political importance. But the opportunists' attack on this issue harms it to a great extent. The attack on this issue by the Second International and its leader Karl Kautsky bears special significance in this context. Kautsky presented the proletarian democracy as a "pure" democracy. He advocated the establishment of proletarian democracy without denying the "democratic" rights to the bourgeoisie. Lenin wrote a book entitled *Proletarian Revolution and Renegade Kautsky* and made it clear that Kautsky's views are anti-proletarian democracy. This exposure of Kautsky's view by Lenin has provided guidance to the revolutionary communists worldwide.

Modern revisionists have presented Kautsky's views on this issue in a "new" manner. This issue has continued to be vulgarised in latter days. Now the CRC has once again brought this issue on a trial or controversy. They have described the democracy practised under socialism in the past as not being proletarian democracy. Like in other issues, they have blamed Lenin for being principally responsible for this 'misuse'. They have concluded that Lenin had gone against the Marxist tenets of proletarian democracy. Why did the CRC reach this wrong conclusion? To know this rightly, once again we need to go back to what Lenin has stated: "The question of the dictatorship of the proletariat is a question of the relation of the proletarian state to the bourgeois state, of proletarian democracy to bourgeois democracy."[17]

We have concluded that the CRC is against the dictatorship of the proletariat It is natural then as Lenin says that its view on proletarian democracy is influenced by its view on the dictatorship of the proletariat We need to discuss CRC's views on proletarian democracy in the light of this fact.

> It is on this basis that Lenin stressed the point: "democracy based on private property or on a struggle for the abolition of private property". Here he is emphasizing the class-dominant aspect of democracy, the rule of private property. But by equating bourgeois democracy to the bourgeois state, he has neglected the non-class aspect of democracy reflected in bourgeois democracy. The recognition of the individual's political role in the political system of a society is actually a historical advance in dealing with the non-class contradiction of individual/society. Bourgeois democracy also reflects this non-class aspect. It is actually a development in the forms of social functioning which was (and is) taking place in the whole process of social development in close relation with the development of class struggle.

17 V. I. Lenin, "Proletarian Revolution and Renegade Kautsky", *Collected Works*, Eng. ed., Progress Publishers, Moscow, Third Printing, 1981, Vol. 28, p. 232

> Even though Lenin talks about the formal equality reflected in bourgeois democracy and its representative nature, he does not demarcate between the class-dominant and non-class aspects of democracy. (9.2)
>
> The development of proletarian democracy will not take place simply by reversing the dictatorship of the minority over the majority. Elimination of private property and socialization of the means of production are certainly crucial steps for establishing the system of proletarian democracy or the genuine dictatorship of the proletariat. But as has already been seen from the experience of the former socialist countries, the mere juridical socialization of the means of production is not going to solve this problem. Rather, that will create concrete conditions for further centralization of political power since the whole means of production get concentrated into a single entity. So the real socialization of the economy, an essential for proletarian democracy, can be achieved only through an effective political system which can ensure genuine democracy by decentralizing the political power, by ensuring the realization of real power by the people directly. So the socialization of the means of production and the development of a political system that ensures proletarian democracy are essential, complementary aspects of the socialist system which must be capable of surviving on its own.(9.3)
>
> Bourgeois democracy will be transcended only by passing through this transitional phase of proletarian democracy which will create a new form for social organization in communism. Here the non-class aspect of democratic functioning will further develop, creating favourable conditions for all-round development of the individual, though within the contradictory relationship between the individual and society.(9.4)
>
> Under the proletarian democratic system, the effectiveness of the new system will be accepted or rejected by the people through an open democratic process in which the whole people will be freely involved through their own political organizations or otherwise. (10.4)[18]

The CRC, thus, the interprets the character of democracy under bourgeois states in terms of both of a class dominating and non-class aspect. It has also argued that even under the proletarian dictatorship this concept of class domination and non-class aspect must continue. Bourgeois states provide more rights to individuals compared to the previous regimes, but the way the CRC has presented this issue and preferred to criticize Lenin for not adopting the view reveals its non-Marxist approach to the relation between individual and social classes. In a classless society, the individual is a member of the society and social production is the combined will of the individuals. But no individuals remains the product of the society as a whole in a class society. He is the product of a special class there. So, the individual in a class society represents a special class interest. Mao has shed some light on this issue: "In a class society everyone lives as a member of a particular

18 "On Proletarian Democracy", *A World to Win*, 1992/17, pp. 83, 85.

class, and every kind of thinking, without exception, is stamped with the brand of a class."[19]

Amazingly, the CRC has quoted Lenin as the Marxist view separating individuals and the society. Quoting a statement of Marx from *German Ideology* tries to prove individual will have no bearing on class basis even in a class society. This view does not conform to Marxism. The CRC has quoted the *German Ideology* in a metaphysical way. A simple reading of a few lines from the part it quoted reveals that Marx and Engels were against what is being professed by the CRC:

> Individuals have always built on themselves, but naturally on themselves within their given historical conditions and relationships, not on the "pure" individual in the sense of the ideologists. But in the course of historical evolution, and precisely through the inevitable fact that within the division of labour social relationships take on an independent existence, there appears a division within the life of each individual, insofar as it is personal and insofar as it is determined by some branch of labour and the conditions pertaining to it. We do not mean it to be understood form this that, for example, the rentier, the capitalist, etc., ceases to be persons; but their personality is conditioned and determined by quite definite class relationships, and the division appears only in their opposition to another class and, for themselves, only when they go bankrupt.[20]

The views expressed by Marx in the *Preface* of his book *Critique of Political Economy* also helps us to understand his views on this issue. He writes:

> In the social production of their life, men enter into definite relations that are indispensable and independent of their will, relations of production which correspond to a definite stage of development of their material productive forces. The sum total of these relations of production constitutes the economic structure of society, the real foundation, on which rises a legal and political superstructure and to which correspond definite forms of social consciousness. The mode of production of material life conditions the social, political and intellectual life process in general. It is not the consciousness of men that determines their being, but, on the contrary, their social being that determines their consciousness.[21]

These quotes from Marx and Engels make it clear how unfounded is the CRC's viewpoint. These quotes also reveal that the CRC views do

19 Mao Tse-tung, "On Practice", *Selected Works*, Eng. ed., Foreign Language Press, Peking, Third Printing, 1975, Vol. 1, p. 296.

20 Karl Marx and Frederick Engels, "Feuerbach. Opposition of Materialistic and Idealistic Outlook", *Karl Marx and Frederick Engels Selected Works*, Eng. ed., Progress Publishers, Moscow, Vol. 1, p. 66.

21 Karl Marx, "A Preface to the Critique of Political Economy", *Karl Marx and Frederick Engels Selected Works*, Progress Publisher, Moscow, Fourth Printing, 1977, Vol. 1, p. 503.

not have even a distant relationship with Marxism. This interpretation of proletarian democracy by the CRC is in no way different from the "pure" democratic interpretation by Kautsky. This is not a Marxist-Leninist, but a bourgeois view on democracy. This is an attempt to replace proletarian democracy by bourgeois democracy.

6. Democratic-Centralism

The CRC has attacked the Leninist principle of democratic-centralism from two sides. First, it has termed wrong the Leninist principle of democratic-centralism within the communist party. It has supported the policy adopted by Lenin in this context until the Tenth Party Congress of CPSU. The Party Congress had banned and dissolved different factions within the Communist Party. The CRC has not criticized Lenin for that decision as being a particular decision in a particular context. However, it has criticized Stalin for allegedly adopting the same specific decision in the form of fundamental policies. The *Document* says:

> The practice under Lenin shows that there was a free and lively atmosphere within the organization to voice different views and opinions and to debate over such differences. In the post-revolutionary situation, groups were allowed to function openly and even to publish their own materials separately. But in the context of growing counter-revolutionary attempts, the Tenth Congress of the Party (in 1921) under Lenin's guidance decided to ban such factions and their separate functioning. Even though it can be seen as a particular decision in a particular context. (11.3)

The *Document* also states:

> Afterwards, the whole concept of the monolithic communist party, propounded by Stalin and solidified during the whole Comintern period and afterwards, was centered around this Tenth Congress decision. And this monolithism naturally gave rise to an atmosphere where centralism was always emphasized, while democracy was belittled or neglected. (11.4)

> After the seizure of power ... the party will have to function rather as an open party. The internal life of the party will also have to be very democratic, even allowing factions, etc., as a matter of principle. (10.5)

The document discusses Mao's attempt in this regard:

> Mao's attempts to develop the two-line struggle within the party was a step to re-establish the style of functioning of democratic-centralism practised by Lenin, in a more systematic manner. ... But as Mao did not openly criticize the above concepts, in effect the two-line struggle, etc., were only some minor steps at rectification within the overall framework established earlier. (11.5)

> The sanctification of the party and the consequent religious attitude towards it developed on the basis of the above concepts. The concepts of revolutionary authority put forward by Stalin by defining Leninism and establishing the authority of Lenin, intensified the negative effects of this religiosity. All views of the opponents of the established authority were considered not only irrelevant but taboos to the communists. For example, while criticizing their ideas, nobody thought it necessary to examine whether any ideas expressed by Kautsky, Rosa Luxemburg, Trotsky, Bukharin, etc., were correct and worthwhile for consideration. Even though Mao's style of open two-line struggle through open debate and polemics created a new atmosphere, we can see that even during the Cultural Revolution the concept of revolutionary authority emerged in a more powerful way, again curtailing the democratic atmosphere. The personality cult, as the follow-up of the concept of revolutionary authority, assumed dangerous dimensions during the Cultural Revolution, especially at the instance of Lin Piao (11.6)[22]

Lenin took democratic-centralism, as on every other issue, not in an absolute and mechanical manner, but in a dialectical way. That is why he used to give prominence to different aspects of democratic-centralism in different situations. Sometimes he stressed more on democracy while at other times he focussed more on centralism. Prior to the Tenth Party Congress there were factions within the communist party and Lenin agreed with their existence. This is an excellent instance of his dialectical thinking on democratic-centralism. As for the CRC's argument that Lenin basically approved the existence of inter-party factions before the Tenth Party Congress was a particular decision in a particular context. The Tenth Party Congress represents the basic thinking of Lenin. Stalin and the Comintern have done a commendable job in executing this decision of the Tenth Party Congress which represents one of the major principles of Leninism.

The CRC has commended Mao for playing a positive role in adopting the pre-Tenth Party Congress line in this issue. It has presented this case as if Mao took Lenin's pre-Tenth Party Congress policy not as a particular decision in a particular context. Mao viewed democratic-centralism, like Lenin, in a dialectical manner. This is why he has presented democratic-centralism differently in different contexts. But in an ultimate analysis, Mao, like Lenin, was in favour of monolithic unity in the communist party for building socialism and to move towards communism he considered inter-party groups could render disharmony and disunity which means that Mao was not opposed to the decision of the Tenth Party Congress. Actually he supported it. The CRC has indicated that it was also dissatisfied with Mao on this issue.

22 "On Proletarian Democracy", *A World to Win*, 1992/17, p. 86.

The facts above make it clear that the CRC disagrees with the general organizational principles of Leninism.

Secondly, the CRC has termed wrong the Leninist approach of democratic-centralism in the political system of socialism. Lenin had applied democratic-centralism in the socialist regime. He had developed the basic organizational principle of the communist party as the basic foundation of the state regime under the dictatorship of the proletariat. The viewpoint expressed by the CRC on the socialist regime under the dictatorship of the proletariat has discarded the Marxist-Leninist concept of democratic-centralism. Their viewpoint that under the dictatorship of the proletariat the communist party should go for competitive elections to govern, based on the dissolution of the standing army, and its opposition to centralization represents acceptance of the bourgeois process, not the Leninist approach for running the socialist state. For communists, democratic-centralism is related to pushing forward class struggles. Leninism in the democratic or socialist system means relations with the proletarian party and the leadership beginning from the top organ of the state organ to the local level in order to push the socialistic line by selecting representatives, calling them back, and suppressing the people opposed to socialism. The CRC calls for replacing the Leninist principle of ruling system with formal democratic process.

7. Capitalist Restoration

The CRC in its *Document* has made its view clear on capitalist restoration. It has stated that the analysis and explanations made so far on this issue have been correct only from the economic point of view. The *Document* states:

> From the angle of the traditional Marxist-Leninist interpretation of capitalist restoration in the former socialist countries, this interpretation is sufficient. The capitalist roaders in the ruling communist parties of these countries transformed the budding socialist economy into a capitalist one by promoting, instead of restricting the bourgeois right and relying on material incentives for promoting production. The resultant bureaucratic capitalism has led to the present crisis in all these countries. This explanation is basically correct in relation to the economic aspect of capitalist restoration. But it is not sufficient to answer the principal political issue raised by the masses in these countries. Their major demand is the dismantling of the existing political system which ensures the monopoly of the communist party. The Marxist-Leninists have correctly pointed out that these parties are not communist and that the political system there represents the dictatorship of a new bourgeoisie, social fascism. But so far as the masses of these countries are concerned, there is no difference between the essential structures of this social fascist political system and those which existed earlier when they were socialist. Even in China, where the Cultural Revolution gave rise to

> a new political situation, the state structure under Deng is not essentially different from the one which existed previously. The distinction is mainly in content, in who leads the state, Marxist-Leninists or revisionists. But the people are not able to see any qualitative difference in the structures of the political system, even though they can recognize the changes in their living conditions. That is why a mere call to re-establish socialism and a genuine dictatorship of the proletariat will not be sufficient. (1.3)

After all what is the 'principal political issue', responsible for capitalist restoration, that has failed to attract the attention of Marxist-Leninists worldwide so far? According to the CRC this political issue is nothing, but the policy of centralization followed on economic and political sectors and the leading role of the communist party under socialism. It has made it clear in its document that bureaucracy developed in socialist countries as a result of these policies and capitalism were restored there as a natural consequence. The *Document* states: "The whole system revolved around the idea of seizing and maintaining the political power through a centralized state structure. It did not only initiate any process of re-absorption of power but, on the contrary, led to more concentration of power."

According to the CRC the fundamental cause of capitalist restorations in the Soviet Union and China is "one party rule". Based on this logic, the CRC concludes: "The whole system of the dictatorship of the proletariat so far practised, starting from Lenin and up to Mao, failed." (8.11)[23]

The CRC has, thus, raised this issue as if never had the history of the world communist movement focused its attention on the problem of bureaucraticism. It seems as if the *Document* has made a major finding, about the disintegration of the socialist system that is the issue of bureaucracy hitherto not known to the revolutionaries, including Lenin, Stalin and Mao. As far as the statement of the CRC in the role of bureaucracy, is concerned both in the party and government, in capitalist restoration is concerned, it is basically correct. But the way the CRC has presented it as the cause is wrong. Bureaucracy is not a cause; it is a consequence. The causes are the existing capitalist maladies in socialism, such as small-scale production, old habits of the people, bourgeois rights, important role of bourgeois experts, difference between urban and rural areas, between physical and mental labour, law of value, commodity production, relation of the defeated bourgeoisie with international capital, and the attempts of the defeated bourgeoisie to regain the lost 'paradise'. This reality of socialism creates an atmosphere where the old bureaucracy is capable of maintaining its influence for a long time. The centralization and communist party leadership are necessary to control these maladies and to lead the country onto the road to socialism. The country cannot move in this direction re-absorbing the state power by the

23 "On Proletarian Democracy", *A World to Win*, 1992/17, pp. 74-75, 83.

'whole people'. The CRC fully supports the Soviets. Even the Soviets are not free from centralization. They have different tiers. Soviets have different levels–from local to centre. The Congress is their highest organ. Again in socialism not the 'whole people' are involved in the great movement of socialism. Even that portion of the 'whole people' who are interested in that movement do not succeed fully due to their own limitation and capabilities. These objective realities make centralization and communist party leadership necessary.

The CRC is confused between causes and effects. It has taken effects for causes. Such a thinking undermines the struggle against the real cause of capitalist restoration. It is clear from what we have quoted above and from the whole *Document* that the CRC takes the centralization and the communist party leadership as the cause of bureaucratization. The CRC has said that it is possible to escape from bureaucracy and its 'natural' consequence of capitalist restoration by dissolving these things and through re-absorption of state power by the 'whole people'. This viewpoint is also incorrect.

Such a thinking fails to understand that the structure and the level of the Communes and Soviets are themselves determined by the socio-economic structure of the new system, which is born out of capitalism. It also neglects historical facts. Bureaucratic tendencies were on a rapid rise after the October Revolution in the Soviets. Does this fact not prove the bankruptcy of the CRC's argument to do away with the bureaucracy through the dissolution of the party leadership and centralization and the re-absorption of state power by the 'whole people'?

Let us now discuss the "new" invention of the CRC. It presents the issue of struggle against bureaucratization as its new finding. Is this issue something totally neglected by the revolutionaries worldwide, including Lenin, Stalin and Mao? It is not actually so. The CRC is not the first party to stress the need of struggle against bureaucracy, it is the CPSU and its leaders Lenin and Stalin. So, the CRC is trying to steal the weapon of Leninism against bureaucracy and attack Leninism by this. Lenin and Stalin were most concerned with the increasing bureaucratic maladies within the Soviet Communist Party and the state power. They had given prominence to the struggle against the maladies. There were many people who advocated an end to these maladies within a night, but Lenin and Stalin stressed the possibility of eliminating it only on the basis of a long-term policy. Their views on this issue reveal the reality. I have presented below a few quotes to make it clear how Lenin thought about this issue:

> We shall be fighting the evils of bureaucracy for many years to come, and whoever thinks otherwise is playing demagogue and cheating, because overcoming the evils of bureaucracy requires hundreds of measures,

> wholesale literacy, culture and participation in the activity of the Workers' and Peasants' Inspection.[24]
>
> We need to understand that the struggle against the evils of bureaucracy is absolutely indispensable, and that it is just as intricate as the fight against the petty-bourgeois element. The bureaucratic practices of our state system have become such a serious malaise that they are dealt with in our party programme, because they are connected with this petty- bourgeois element, which is widely dispersed. This malaise can only be cured by the working people's unity and their ability not only to welcome the decrees of the Workers' and Peasants' Inspection (have you seen many decrees that have not been welcomed?) but to exercise their right through the Inspection, something you don't find either in the villages, the towns, or even the capital cities. Those who shout loudest against the evils of bureaucracy very frequently do not know how to exercise this right. Very great attention needs to be paid to this fact.[25]

After Lenin, Stalin had launched the struggle against bureaucracy within the Soviet State and party uncompromisingly in the Leninist manner. He initiated the correct path of struggle and direction. The article *Organized Criticism from Below* as given below reveals this.

> Bureaucracy is one of the worst enemies of our progress. It exists in all our organizations–Party, YCL, trade-union and economic. When people talk of bureaucrats, they usually point to the old non-party officials, who as a rule are depicted in our cartoons as men wearing spectacles. That is not quite true, comrades. If it were only a question of the old bureaucrats, the fight against bureaucracy would be very easy. The trouble is that it is not a matter of the old bureaucrats. It is a matter of the new bureaucrats, bureaucrats who sympathize with the Soviet government, and finally, communist bureaucrats. The communist bureaucrat is the most dangerous type of bureaucrat. Why? Because he masks his bureaucracy with the title of party member. And, unfortunately, we have quite a number of such communist bureaucrats.

Regarding how to end bureaucracy in these organizations, Stalin says:

> There is only one sole way of doing this, and that is to organize control from below, to organize criticism of the bureaucracy in our institutions, of their shortcomings and their mistakes, by the vast masses of the working class. I know that by rousing the fury of the masses of the working people against the bureaucratic distortions in our organizations, we sometimes have to tread on the toes of some of our comrades who have past services to their credit, but who are now suffering from the disease of bureaucracy. But

---

24 V. I. Lenin, "The Second All-Russia Congress of Miners", *Collected Works*, Eng. ed., Progress Publishers, Moscow, Fourth Printing, 1977, Vol. 32, p. 68.

25 V. I. Lenin, "Tenth Congress of the RCP (B), March 8-16, 1921", *Collected Works*, Eng. ed., Progress Publishers, Moscow, Fourth Printing, 1977, Vol. 32, p. 191.

> ought this to stop our work of organizing control from below? I think that it ought not and must not. For their past services we should take off our hats to them, but for their present blunders and bureaucracy it would be quite in order to give them a good drubbing.
>
> There is talk of criticism from above, criticism by the Workers' and Peasants' Inspection, by the Central Committee of our party and so on. That, of course, is all very good. But it is still far from enough. More, it is by no means the chief thing now. The chief thing now is to start a broad tide of criticism from below against bureaucracy in general, against shortcomings in our work in particular. Only by organizing twofold pressure–from above and from below–and only by shifting the principal stress to criticism from below, can we count on waging a successful struggle against bureaucracy on rooting it out. ... From this follows the immediate task of party: *to wage a ruthless struggle against bureaucracy, to organize mass criticism from below, and to take this criticism into account when adopting practical decisions for eliminating our shortcomings.*[26]

The above given some statements of Lenin and Stalin reveal how they are alert to the tendency of bureaucracy usually seen in the party and government.

Mao raised the struggle against bureaucracy in the communist party and apparatus to a new height. The whole historical period of the socialist transformation in China is an example in itself. It is clear from all the facts that the fall of the world socialist system has not occurred, as the CRC says, as a result of not launching a struggle against bureaucracy, but despite this struggle. It must be a welcome proposal that the struggle against the bureaucracy must be launched with more efficiency under socialism, or that we should learn more from our past experiences. The thinking that the struggle against bureaucracy has attained its height through the deeds of Lenin, Stalin and Mao is not Marxist-Leninist thinking. We must not follow a sectarian view in learning from our past experiences while fighting against the bureaucracy and removing the obstacles of bureaucracy in the socialist order in the future. We can do this within the framework of Marxism-Leninism. To go outside it would be suicidal for waging a successful struggle against bureaucracy and rooting it out. The CRC is now trying to go outside the framework, so, the CRC will not lessen the danger of the bureaucracy on socialist regimes; rather it will sharpen the possibility further.

Bharatpur, Chitawon, Nepal
January-February 1992

26 J. V. Stalin, "Organize Mass Criticism From Below", *The Essential Stalin, Major Theoretical Writings 1905-52*, Edited and with an Introduction by Bruce Franklin, 1973, Re-printed by: Rahul Foundation, First ed., January 2010, pp. 221-23.

Part IV

One Step Forward, Two Steps Back

In the Context of Maoism

1. Introduction

Many of the communist parties that adopted contributions of Mao Tse-tung in the form of 'Mao Tse-tung Thought' in the past have started using the term "Maoism". This term was used, first of all, by the Communist Party of Peru (PCP). The practice of using this term started with the PCP, after the first Congress of the party before the formation of the Revolutionary Internationalist Movement (RIM), passed it in 1988. Likewise, the Revolutionary Communist Party, USA (RCP, USA), after an extended meeting, this term in 1988. Later on, the Communist Party of Nepal (Maoist), the Afghanistan Revolutionary Communist Organization, the Union of Iranian Communists (Sarbedaran), the Revolutionary Communist Group, the Communist Party of Bangladesh and Columbia also presented the proposal of Maoism amongst the member parties for discussion. The supporters of Maoism think that the term 'thought' cannot reflect the contributions of Mao Tse-tung adequately. According to them, only the term 'ism' can represent the contributions of Mao Tse-tung. The first Congress of PCP of 1988 states: "Not to recognize Maoism's character as an 'ism' is to deny that it is universally applicable and, consequently, its character as the third, newest and highest stage of the ideology of the international proletariat: Marxism-Leninism-Maoism, principally Maoism, which we uphold, defend and apply."

On the content of Maoism, the PCP further states:

> *Theory*. Marxism is made up of three component parts: Marxist philosophy, Marxist political economy and scientific socialism. The development of all these gives rise to a great qualitative leap for Marxism as a whole, as a unity, to a higher level, which means a new stage. Consequently, it is essential to point out that Chairman Mao has produced, in theory and in practice, precisely such a great qualitative, leap. In order to better explain we will examine this point by point.
>
> In *Marxist Philosophy* he developed the essence of dialectics, the law of contradiction, establishing it as the only fundamental law; and in addition to his profoundly dialectical understanding of the theory of knowledge, whose essence is the two leaps that make up this law (from practice to knowledge and back to practice, the leap from knowledge back to practice being principal), we must emphasize his masterful application of the law of contradiction to politic; moreover, he took philosophy to the masses, fulfilling the task laid out by Marx.
>
> In *Marxist Political Economy* Chairman Mao applied dialectics to analyse the relationship between the base and superstructure and, in carrying out the struggle of Marxism-Leninism against the revisionist theory of the "productive forces", he concluded that the superstructure, consciousness, can transform the base and with political power develop the productive forces. He developed the Leninist idea that politics is the concentrated expression of economics, and proclaimed that politics must be in command (applicable to all fields) and that political work is the lifeblood of economic work; all this led to a genuine management of the political economy and not just a series of economic policies.
>
> One question that is overlooked, despite its importance especially for those who face new democratic revolutions, is the Maoist theory of bureaucratic capitalism, that is, the capitalism that imperialism develops in the oppressed countries on the basis of different levels of feudalism or other previous systems. This is a crucial problem especially for Asia, Africa and Latin America, since from its understanding flows the correct leadership for the revolution, particularly because the economic basis for advancing the revolution to the second, socialist stage depends on confiscating bureaucrat capital.
>
> But the main thing is that Chairman Mao Tse-tung has developed the political economy of socialism. His criticism of socialist construction in the USSR is extremely important. So too are his theses on how to build socialism in China: taking agriculture as the foundation and industry as the

leading factor, industrialization guided by the relationship between heavy and light industry and agricultural, centring economic construction on heavy industry and simultaneously giving full attention to light industry as well as agriculture. We should highlight the Great Leap Forward and the conditions for its implementation: one, a correct line setting an appropriate and correct course; two, a range of small, medium and large organizational forms in terms of quantitative size; three, a tremendous push, a colossal effort on the part of the masses to set it in motion and finally to win, a leap forward whose results are more appreciated by looking at the process it sets in motion and its historical perspectives than by the immediate results, and at its links to agricultural cooperatives and people's communes. Finally, we must keep in mind his teachings on objectivity and subjectively in understanding and managing the laws of socialism (whose full flowering has not been seen in the short decades of socialism, which likewise has prevented a better understanding of these laws and their specificity), and especially the relationship between revolution and economic development, concentrated in "grasp revolution, promote production." Nevertheless, despite its crucial importance, not much has been said about this development of Marxist political economy.

In *Scientific Socialism,* Chairman Mao developed the theory of classes, analysing them on the economic, political and ideological plane; revolutionary violence as a universal law without exception; revolution as the violent replacement of one class by another, putting forth his theory that "political power grows out of the barrel of a gun," and he solved the problem of the seizure of power in the oppressed nations by indicating the road of encircling the cities from the countryside and establishing its general laws. He brilliantly defined and developed the theory of the class struggle under socialism: that under socialism antagonistic struggle persists between the bourgeoisie and the proletariat, between the capitalist road and the socialist road and between capitalism and socialism, and that it was not yet settled which will win out; it would be resolved over a long period of time, a process of restoration and counter-restoration until the proletariat would finally achieve the definitive consolidation of its political power, the dictatorship of the proletariat. Finally and most importantly he formulated the great historic solution for continuing the revolution under the dictatorship of the proletariat, the Great Proletarian Cultural Revolution.

These basic questions, simply outlined but well known and undeniable, show Chairman Mao's development of the component parts of Marxism and the obvious development of Marxism-Leninism to a new, third and higher stage: Marxism-Leninism-Maoism, principally Maoism."[1]

A quote from an interview of the party Chairman Comrade Gonzalo to the magazine *El Diario* further clarifies the vision of the PCP related to this:

1 Documents from PCP First Congress, "On Marxism-Leninism-Maoism and On Gonzalo Thought", *A World to Win*, 1988/11, pp. 59-61.

> For us, Marxism is a process of development, and this great process has given us a new, third, and higher stage. Why do we say that we are in a new, third, and higher stage, Maoism? We say this because in examining the three component parts of Marxism, it is clearly evident that Chairman Mao Tse-tung has developed each one of these three parts. Let's enumerate them: in Marxist philosophy no one can deny his great contribution to the development of dialectics, focusing on the law of contradiction, establishing that it is the only fundamental law. On political economy, it will suffice to highlight two things. The first, of immediate and concrete importance for us, is bureaucratic capitalism, and second, the development of the political economy of socialism, since in synthesis we can say that it is Mao who really established and developed the political economy of socialism. With regard to scientific socialism, it is enough to point to the People's War, since it is with Chairman Mao Tse-tung that the international proletariat has attained a fully developed military theory, giving us then the military theory of our class, the proletariat, applicable everywhere. We believe that these three questions demonstrate a development of universal character. Looked at in this way what we have is a new stage–and we call it the third one, because Marxism has two preceding stages, that of Marx and that of Lenin, which is why we speak of Marxism-Leninism. A higher stage, because with Maoism the ideology of the worldwide proletariat attains its highest development up to now, its loftiest peak, but with the understanding that Marxism is–if you'll excuse the reiteration–a dialectical unity that develops through great leaps, and that these great leaps are what give rise to stages. So for us, what exists in the word today is Marxism-Leninism-Maoism, and principally Maoism. We think that to be Marxists today, to be Communists, necessarily demands that we be Marxist-Leninist-Maoists and principally Maoists. Otherwise, we could not be genuine communists.[2]

After a self-criticism over its past use of the term Mao Tse-tung Thought, the RCP, USA, in its document passed at the Eighth Plenum Meeting (1988) states that, "today we feel it is even more correct to name the science Marxism-Leninism-Maoism."

> In making this change we believe we are bringing the name in correct relationship to the science as it has been developed by its practitioners and theoreticians since the time of Marx. The theoretical basis for this change is the fact that there have been three milestones in the development of this theory. Marx founded the science and laid out the basic precepts; Lenin developed it to another level; and Mao took it again to another level. Previously, in opposition to a Lin Piaoist conception that we had entered a new era, which Mao Tse-tung Thought was equated with, we were careful to point out that there is not a new era. It remains the case that this is the era of imperialism and proletarian revolution. However, we tended to confuse the notion of *new era* with *new stage* in the development of the science. While there is no *new era*–we are not in a new historical epoch–there have been

2 "Interview with Chairman Gonzalo", *A World to Win*, 1992/18, p. 39.

qualitative developments in the science made by Mao Tse-tung of such importance that we can say there is a new and higher stage in the science. Thus we call our science Marxism-Leninism-Maoism.

By this formulation we mean the same thing as Marxism-Leninism-Mao Tse-tung Thought. Why, then, make the change? Because, whatever the intentions, to use Mao Tse-tung Thought does not give proper weight to the contributions of Mao; It can suggest that these contributions are less important than the contributions of Marx and Lenin. We want to make clear that the contributions of Mao are on the level, of the same magnitude, as those of the other great revolutionary leaders and theoreticians, Marx and Lenin. Secondarily, and as an expression of the principal reason, it is easier and better to popularize the science as Marxism-Leninism-Maoism.[3]

The CPN (Unity Centre) says:

At present, the revisionist Teng group is killing the spirit of Mao's revolutionary lessons by using this term. Presently, on the one hand, this term is being used by revisionists with the meaning of assumption, whereas on the other with meaning of universal principle of communist revolutionaries by using the controversial word "thought" when 'ism' scientifically correct word expressing correct meaning of its weightage is already available.[4]

Many others parties have said that to reject "Maoism" is equal to rejecting Marxism-Leninism". The Committee of RIM (CoRIM) has said, "Today, without Maoism there can be no Marxism-Leninism. Indeed to negate Maoism is to negate Marxism-Leninism itself."[5]

The Union of Iranian Communists (Sarbedaran) has forwarded the same view:

It conforms explicitly that while talking on basic theoretical and political principles of the international proletariat, on the science and thinking of the proletarian class and its highest peak, Marxism-Leninism-Maoism expresses better than any other term (mainly Marxism-Leninism-Mao Tse-tung Thought) that we have been using before. This formulation reflects that contributions of Mao related to theory and use of proletarian revolution and communism are equal-potential to those of Marx and Lenin.[6]

The Revolutionary Communist Group of Columbia writes on Maoism:

Maoism is the third stage of Marxism. By stage we mean all-round development of all three constituent organs of the fundamentals of

3 "Marxism-Leninism-Maoism", New Document from RCP, USA, *A World to Win*, 1988/12, p. 70.

4 Document of the CPN Unity Centre on Maosim, *Long Live Maoism,* p. 6.

5 Long Live Marxism-Leninism-Maoism, *A World to Win*, 1995/20, p. 9.

6 "Our Ideological Guide: Marxism-Leninism-Maoism", A Document Approved by the First Conference of the OCC/MLM, July 1991.

> Marxism. This means that we had Marxism in the time of Marx; we had Marxism-Leninism in the time of Lenin; and we have Marxism-Leninism-Maoism in the time of Mao. Every stage develops under a particular international and national context and at every stage, a particular person consolidates these contexts to centralize and synthesize them. Accepting the 'ism' is the acceptance of universal reality of the contributions of Marx, Lenin and Mao.

Likewise, the organization of the revolutionary communist of Afghanistan asserts:

> Maoism correctly shows that Mao's contribution are as precious and on the same level as those of Marx and Lenin; it clears up any incorrect understanding or underestimation regarding Mao's contributions thus indicates more clearly than the term "Mao Tse-tung Thought" the third stage in the development of the proletariat's science of revolution. So, we consider it correct to use Maoism rather than Mao Tse-tung Thought. Maoism, in our opinion, will sooner or later become generalized among the participants and supporters of RIM, replacing Mao Tse-tung Thought.[7]

Supporters of Maoism believe that new things have been added to the treasury of Marxism-Leninism by Mao. They give examples of the development made by Mao in all three constituent organs of Marxism, namely, new democratic revolution, encircling towns with the countryside, party leadership, the struggle against revisionism, and an uninterrupted revolution to advance socialism towards communism. It is noteworthy that the above mentioned contributions of Mao which used the term 'Mao Tse-tung Thought' was already accepted by those parties. Presently, when the proposal of Maoism is brought forward, nothing is brought new other than those examples mentioned above. The new bases brought by them to validate the justification of Maoism are the arguments that state it is the third and superior stage, difference between era and stage, and the fundamental principles propounded by Mao. The point is that many parties are positive to all those, and then equally accept the contributions of Mao as done by the supporters of Mao Tse-tung Thought, who are still firm in their analysis that in spite of all these contributions, it is not correct to use the term Maoism.

In spite of the acceptance and recognition of all the above mentioned contributions, supporters of Mao Tse-tung Thought reject that these contributions represent a different and third stage in the development of scientific socialism, on par with the contributions made by Marx and Lenin. Supporters of Maoism criticize them for taking Mao's contributions as developed thought within the Leninist era. They believe that such a view underestimates or incorrectly understands Mao's contributions inadequately.

7 "Long Live Marxism-Leninism-Maoism", *A World to Win*, 1991/16, pp. 16, 86.

By criticizing the advocates of Mao Tse-tung Thought, and bringing the proposal of 'ism', the supporters of Maoism have certainly moved a step ahead. But, by doing so, they have devalued Leninism. As they have gone two steps back while walking one step forward. Their thinking pushes back the whole international communist movement. Therefore, we need to launch an uncompromising struggle against this thinking as an immediate task. Some people think that there is no need to make a difference between Maoism and Mao Tse-tung Thought, fearing it will create a conflict. At a cursory glance, it appears so. But, it is never reasonable to reach a decision on such an issue after only a preliminary study.

The question of Maoism and Mao Tse-tung Thought is not a simple or a technical issue; it is a question related to principle, which are:

i. Imperialism and the world proletarian revolution;
ii. Leninism and the characteristics of the present world;
iii. Imperialism and the strategy and tactics of the proletarian revolution;
iv. Solution of the fundamental problem of Leninism, i.e. seizure of power, and consolidating it and moving towards communism;
v. Organizing a new type of party in the era of imperialism and the world proletarian revolution; and
vi. Objective evaluation of contributions of Mao Tse-tung in the international communist movement.

We are compelled to stand at the forefront on this issue immediately because of one more significant factor–the facts and arguments by the supporters of Maoism are subjective and absolutist by nature. Before entering into this controversy, we need to make an enquiry as a prerequisite and to be careful that some non-objective or non-Marxist-Leninist view should not enter into the course of struggle. The fact equally applies in relation to the two-line struggle, presently going on between Maoism and Mao Tse-tung Thought in the international communist movement. It is possible that one or both of the lines concerned, for or against, may bring forward subjective or imaginary arguments to justify their thinking, and thereby take leave of the reality.

The argument and facts given by the supporters of Maoism make it clear that their link with reality is collapsing. Those who accept "Thought" must be careful that they should not devalue the contributions of Mao in an attempt to prove the impropriety of the term 'Maoism'. In the course of this discussion, on the one hand, there is possibility of the devaluation of Leninism by supporters of Maoism as the generalization of something of the past epoch. On the other, there is also the possibility of Mao's devaluation of the creative application of Marxism-Leninism and its development by those who uphold Mao Tse-tung Thought. Neither can there be a correct evaluation of the contributions of Mao by devaluating Leninism, by pointing to it as something of the past epoch, nor can Leninism be defended by denying the developments added by Mao to the treasury of Marxism-Leninism.

The struggle between Maoism and Mao Tse-tung Thought is a question of inner struggle in the international communist movement. So, the criticism of the other side is not antagonistic, but friendly and creative. Antagonistic criticism does not improve the situation, rather it goes faster in the wrong direction with serious mistakes. The problem is of a wrong and non-objective analysis linked indifferently with the tenets of Maoism. Its main cause is that Maoism does not exist in the world objectively; its existence is only subjective. Therefore, the arguments and facts brought forward are not objective, but subjective and automatically wrong too. This should not mean that the proposal is brought forward with a wrong intention. The parties forwarding this proposal have been supporters of Marxism-Leninism-Mao Tse-tung Thought for long. They have been leading the Marxist-Leninist movement with success. The PCP had led a 13-year long People's War. The RCP, USA has played a significant role in analysing the resurgence of capitalism in China after the death of Mao, and they exposed the Chinese revisionism, which needs to be appreciated in spite of many weaknesses in them. Its role was specifically remarkable at the International Conferences of 1980 and 1984, and in the formation of the RIM.

2. Maoism and its "Historical Roots"

Discussing Leninism, Stalin spoke about its historical roots as well. It is the only right and scientific procedure to speak on the foundations first and then later on its products. The PCP also spoke of foundations while talking about Maoism. For example, on international foundations:

> As for the context in which Chairman Mao worked and in which Maoism was forged, on an international level the basis was imperialism, world wars, the worldwide proletarian movement, the national liberation movement, the struggle between Marxism and revisionism and the restoration of capitalism in the USSR[8]

Stalin defined the universal contradictions of imperialism as the historical roots of Leninism. For example, he writes:

> The *first contradiction* is the contradiction between labour and capital. Imperialism is the omnipotence of the monopolist trusts and syndicates, of the banks and the financial oligarchy, in the industrial countries. In the fight against this omnipotence, the customary methods of the working class–trade

8 Documents from the PCP First Congress, "On Marxism-Leninism-Maoism and On Gonzalo Thought", *A World to Win*, 1988/11, p. 60.

unions and cooperatives, parliamentary parties and the parliamentary struggle–have proved to be totally inadequate. Either place yourself at the mercy of capital, eke out a wretched existence as of old and sink lower and lower, or adopt a new weapon–this is the alternative imperialism put before the vast masses of the proletariat. Imperialism brings the working class to revolution.

The *second contradiction* is the contradiction among the various financial groups and imperialist powers in their struggle for sources of raw materials, for foreign territory. Imperialism is the export of capital to the sources of raw materials, the frenzied struggle for monopolist possession of these sources, the struggle for a redivision of the already divided world, a struggle waged with particular fury by new financial groups and powers seeking a "place in the sun" against the old groups and powers, which cling tenaciously to what they have seized. This frenzied struggle among the various groups of capitalists is notable in that it includes as an inevitable element imperialist wars, wars for the annexation of foreign territories. This circumstance, in its turn, is notable in that it leads to the mutual weakening of the imperialists, to the weakening of the position of capitalism in general, to the acceleration of the advent of the proletarian revolution and to the practical necessity of this revolution.

The *third contradiction* is the contradiction between the handful of ruling, "civilized" nations and the hundreds of millions of the colonial and dependent peoples of the world. Imperialism is the most barefaced exploitation and the most inhuman oppression of hundreds of millions of people inhabiting vast colonies and dependent countries. The purpose of this exploitation and of this oppression is to squeeze out super-profits. But in exploiting these countries imperialism is compelled to build their railways, factories and mills, industrial and commercial centres. The appearance of a class of proletarians, the emergence of a native intelligentsia, the awakening of national consciousness, the growth of the liberation movement–such are the inevitable results of this "policy". The growth of the revolutionary movement in all colonies and dependent countries without exception clearly testifies to this fact. This circumstance is of importance for the proletariat inasmuch as it saps radically the position of capitalism by converting the colonies and dependent countries from reserves of imperialism into reserves of the proletarian revolution.

Imperialism carries the contradictions of capitalism to their last bounds, to the extreme limit, beyond which revolution begins.

Stalin believed that the general contradictions of imperialism are the roots of Leninism. Stalin does not take revolution or world war as the roots of Leninism. He accepts them as the result of development of the above contradictions of imperialism up to the last stage–the extreme stage. As he says:

The significance of the imperialist war which broke out 10 years ago lies, among other things, in the fact that it gathered all these contradictions into

> a single knot and threw them on to the scales, thereby accelerating and facilitating the revolutionary battles of the proletariat."[9] In Mao's words, "Stalin analysed the universality of contradiction in imperialism, showing why Leninism is the Marxism of the era of imperialism and proletarian revolution.[10]

While comparing the analysis of the PCP to the analysis of Stalin on the historical roots of Leninism, it becomes clear that the former has failed to make an objective evaluation of the contributions of Mao. According to Stalin and the above statement of Mao, the thinking of Lenin was the Marxism of the era of the imperialism and the proletarian revolution because it stood on the foundation of the universal contradictions of imperialism. The basic contradictions of imperialism present in Mao's period steadily remain the same today. So, the idea that Maoism is the Marxism of the present era now directly disagrees with the thinking of Stalin and Mao that "Leninism is the Marxism of the era of imperialism and proletarian revolution." If imperialism, world war and worldwide proletarian class movement, national liberation movement, the struggle between Marxism and revisionism and resurgence of capitalism in the Soviet Republic are foundations of Maoism, what is the bases and historical root of Leninism? Can the bases of both Leninism and Maoism be the same? On the birthplace of Maoism, the PCP writes:

> Maoism took concrete shape in China, the centre of the world revolution, amidst the most complex convergence of contradictions, intense and bloody class struggle marked by the imperialist powers' attempt to carve up China amongst themselves, the fall of the Manchu empire (1911), the anti-imperialist movement of 1919, the upheaval of the vast peasantry, the 22 years of armed struggle for the democratic revolution, the tremendous struggle to build and develop socialism and the ten years of revolutionary fervour to advance the Cultural Revolution in the midst of the greatest two-line struggle in the CPC, principally against revisionism, with the world situation already described in the background. Four of these historic events are of particularly extraordinary importance: the founding of the CPC in 1921; the 1927 Autumn Harvest Uprising which was the beginning of the path of surrounding the cities from the countryside; the founding of the People's Republic of China in 1949; and the Great Proletarian Cultural Revolution of 1966-1976; in all these Chairman Mao was the leading figure, and, above all, the highest and acknowledged leader of the Chinese Revolution.[11]

So far as Mao worked in the above complicated situation and led the new democratic revolution and socialist revolution successfully is concerned,

9 J. V. Stalin, "Foundations of Leninism", *Problems of Leninism*, Eng. ed., Foreign Language Press, Peking, 1976, pp. 4-6.

10 Mao Tse-tung, "On Contradiction", *Selected Works*, Foreign Language Press, Peking, Third Printing, 1975, Vol. 1, p. 330.

11 Documents from PCP First Congress, "On Marxism-Leninism-Maoism and On Gonzalo Thought", *A World to Win*, 1988/11, p. 60.

it is absolutely commendable. But the thinking that reality raised the works of Mao to the level of an "ism" is not correct. Stalin suggested the objective factor causing the birthplace of Leninism to be Russia because "Russia was the focus of all these contradictions of imperialism."[12] So, Russia became the birthplace of Leninism.

In the words of Mao:

> Stalin, analysed the particularity of tsarist Russian imperialism within the general contradictions, showing why Russia became the birthplace of the theory and tactics of proletarian revolution and how the universality of contradiction is contained in this particularity. Stalin's analysis provides us with a model for understanding the particularity and the universality of contradiction and their interconnection.[13]

What this statement of Mao clarifies is that Russia could become the birthplace of Leninism because the three main contradictions of imperialism as suggested by Stalin were prevalent in Russia. The contradictions in Russian imperialism were the products of the same general contradictions of imperialism. The specific contradictions of China mentioned above by PCP are also the contradictions underlying those general contradictions of imperialism, and not something different from them. We must understand the Chinese situation in the way that the universality of the contradictions of imperialism were underlying the specific contradiction of China.

The contemporary world has seen several revolutionary events such as the Great October Socialist Revolution of 1917, the successful establishment of socialism in Russia, the victory in the struggle against fascism, the emergence of a world socialist system, the New Democratic Revolution in China (1949), the appearance of Asia, Africa and Latin America as the storm centres of the world revolution, and the People's War of Peru moving to success. The present world has been full also of numerous revisionist and counter-revolutionary events such as the treachery of Browder, Tito, Khrushchev, the Euro-Communists, the appearance of the Soviet social-imperialism, the disintegration of the world socialist system, the fall of most of the previous communist parties and the First and Second World War. In brief, the present era is the era of upheaval. But this situation of the world cannot at all be the base of the growth of Maoism. This type of situation of the world with upheavals is the natural outcome of the universal contradictions of imperialism and the ideas for the solution of those contradictions is basically Leninism. In that situation, to take this situation of upheavals to be the base of Maoism is a serious theoretical fallacy.

12 J. V. Stalin, "Foundations of Leninism", *Problems of Leninism*, Eng. ed., Foreign Language Press, Peking, 1976, p. 6.

13 Mao Tse-tung, "On Contradiction", *Selected Works*, Foreign Language Press, Peking, Third Printing, 1975, Vol. 1, p. 330.

From the above facts it becomes clear that Stalin started his analysis with matter, and ended with thinking. But the advocates of Maoism started their analysis with thinking and ended with the matter.

3. Explanation of Maoism on the Bases of Leninism

While explaining Leninism, Stalin explained the specific contributions made by Lenin, specially how he "contributed to the general treasury of Marxism." He mentioned those specific contributions "that are naturally connected with his name." Further, he made very clear that "an exposition of Leninism ought to begin with an exposition of the foundations of Marxism."[14] But, at present, the supporters of Maoism explain that Maoism is fundamentally different from the way Stalin explained Leninism. They have explained Maoism on the bases of Leninism; this may not be their intention or ignorance, rather their helplessness. Lenin filled the treasury of Marxism adding those types of new things which could be named Leninism. But the case of Mao is different. The contributions of Mao are the creative development of the thinking of Leninism. Supporters of Maoism, while explaining Maoism, do not mention any new base other than those "new things" that Lenin added to Marxism. Let us examine some facts related to this.

a. Imperialism and the World Proletarian Revolution

The supporters of Maoism claim that Mao added an impetus to the defination of imperialism and to the world proletarian revolution. They say that Mao "discovered a law of imperialism"[15] and emphasized "the importance of the world revolution understood as a single whole ... revolution is the main trend while imperialism is increasingly falling apart every day"[16] and so on. The principles and tactics of imperialism and proletarian revolution were propounded by Lenin. This principle is thoroughly Lenin's own, which supporters of Maoism accept. They plead that Mao "developed the great principle of Lenin related to imperialism." On the one hand, they claim that Mao established the "law of imperialism", on the other, they accept "the great principle" of Lenin. These two claims do not go together. The other important thing is that Stalin does not say that Lenin developed the "theory and tactics of imperialism and world proletarian revolution" of Marx, and he does not say that the thoughts of Lenin represent the second stage in the process of the development of scientific socialism. Rather, what he said

---

14 J. V. Stalin, "Foundations of Leninism", *Problems of Leninism*, Eng. ed., Foreign Language Press, Peking, 1976, pp. 1-2.

15 "Interview with Chairman Gonzalo", *A World to Win,* 1992/18, p. 39.

16 Documents from PCP First Congress, "On Marxism-Leninism-Maoism and On Gonzalo Thought", *A World to Win*, 1988/11, p. 76.

is that the theory, strategy and tactics of imperialism and world proletarian revolution was a new thing added to the general treasury of Marxism.

The development made by Mao is well-recorded and recognized. But, to use the term Maoism simply because of the development is not correct. After all, Mao and Stalin developed the theory, strategy and tactics of Lenin. Stalin is the first person who applied the principle, strategy and tactics of imperialism and the world proletarian revolution of Lenin in the Soviet Union and internationally for thirty years after Lenin. Had Stalin not understood the theory, strategy and tactics correctly, and had he not applied and developed them creatively in the various international situations for thirty years after the death of Lenin, socialism in the Soviet Union would not have been possible; nor the victory over the fascist Axis powers and the formation of the socialist camp under his leadership would have materialized Actually, the Leninist theory of imperialism and proletarian revolution remains limp in the absence of explanation and application about it by Stalin. However, we do not say that it was the common theory of Lenin and Stalin, simply because it originated with Lenin.

It is a similar case with Mao as well. Even, after a thirty-year long experience of building socialism in the Soviet Union and resurgence of capitalism there; and the living experience of the building of a socialist system in China, Mao raised the Leninist theory of proletarian revolution, and that was a creative development of Lenin's thinking, but not an original one.

b. Revolution in Semi-Colonial and Semi-Feudal Countries

Supporters of Maoism emphasized Mao's ideas on revolution in semi-colonial and semi-feudal countries as an explanation of Maoism. We fully agree with the contributions of Mao in giving a consistent form to ideas of Lenin and Stalin on the revolution in colonial, semi-colonial and semi-feudal countries. But we do not agree with the claim that the development made by Mao raises scientific socialism to the height of "the third stage", thus becoming Maoism. It is known from the principle of dialectical materialism that knowledge always follows an upward movement. By this principle, it becomes clear that Lenin's thought represents a further stage of development from the thinking of Marx and Engels. Lenin's ideas developed at the turning point from the competitive stage of capitalism to a new (imperialist) stage in the development of capitalism. But Mao's theory, strategy and tactics regarding revolution in colonial, semi-colonial and semi-feudal countries should be viewed under the era of imperialism and proletarian revolution. We should not forget this fact that Lenin and Stalin had already clarified that development of capitalism to imperialism had changed the colonial and semi-colonial countries from the reserve force of capitalism to the reserve force of world proletarian revolution. Furthermore, especially Stalin argued that because of imperialism, revolutions in colonial, semi-colonial and semi-feudal countries would be a new type of bourgeois-democratic revolution of the new era which would be an integral part of the world proletarian revolution. Stalin also explained that the main function of the new type of bourgeois-democratic revolution of the new epoch would be to end the power of imperialism and the domestic reaction. Only later, Mao developed the theory of Lenin and Stalin. Mao himself has accepted this.[17]

The problem of revolution in colonial, semi-feudal and semi-colonial countries is one of the important problems of the world proletarian revolution. That is the problem of socialist revolution too. As Leninism is the Marxism of the era of imperialism and the world proletarian revolution, the solution to the problems of the world proletarian revolution is primarily underlined in Leninism itself. Mao's thinking is related to this, i.e. revolution in colonial, semi-colonial and semi-feudal countries. The problem of colonial, semi-colonial and semi-feudal countries is an integral part of the problem of the world proletarian revolution. In this context, to say that Mao's thinking represents a superior stage in the process of development of scientific socialism is contradictory to the proposition of dialectical materialism that claims that knowledge moves forward, and never backward. It is absurd to substitute the fundamental question, proletarian revolution, by the secondary and derived question, i.e. new democratic revolution. What is self-evident here is that the principle of new democratic revolution by Mao answers a new sphere of the general problem of imperialism and proletarian revolution. So, this development has enriched Leninism, but it does not represent the superior stage in the process of development of scientific socialism.

c. Military Line

Supporters of Maoism bring forward Mao's statement that "political power grows out of the barrel of a gun." They talk a lot about the theory, strategy and tactics of Mao, for encircling the cities from the countryside in colonial, semi-colonial and semi-feudal countries, and capturing power through a protracted armed struggle. It is true that Mao had emphasized the need and importance of armed revolution to capture power. He developed the way to capture power in a colonial, semi-colonial and semi-feudal country in the course of revolution in China. Mao's contribution certainly deepened and broadened the Marxist-Leninist thinking on armed struggle. But to use the term Maoism on this ground is not reasonable. Violent revolution is a universal law of proletarian revolution. Lenin has

17 Mao Tse-tung, "On New Democracy", *Selected Works*, Eng. ed., Foreign Language Press, Peking, First ed., 1965, Vol. 2, p. 345.

said that the bourgeois state, "*cannot* be superseded by the proletarian state (the dictatorship of the proletariat) through the process of "withering away", but as a general rule, only through a violent revolution." Actually, the "view of violent revolution lies at the root of the *entire* theory of Marx and Engels."[18]

Likewise, Stalin says: "The dictatorship of the proletariat arises not on the basis of the bourgeois order, but in the process of the breaking of this order, after the overthrow of the bourgeois, in the process of expropriation of the landlords and capitalists, in the process of the socialization of the principal instruments and means of production, in the process of violent proletarian revolution."[19]

Only a few statements quoted above make it clear that the principle of revolution with violence is not an original principle of Mao. So far as the contribution of Mao is concerned, he has further developed it basing himself on the Marxist-Leninist principle related to the violent revolution and taking forward the experience of the proletarian revolution and democratic revolution led by the proletarian class. So far as the problem of the way to revolution in colonial, semi-colonial and semi-feudal countries and the way ascertained by Mao is concerned, it is a question within the era of imperialism and proletarian revolution, and not one of a different social and economic world order. As capital is internationalized in the imperialist epoch, there remains some development of capital in undeveloped and dependent countries, and it brings a proletarian class into existence. Further, the development of capitalism that takes place in imperialism creates two other things. The first is that it highlights the need for revolution in the oppressed countries to be directed against imperialism, and second is the revolution in the oppressed countries that needs to be integrated into the world proletarian revolution. This new situation becomes favourable for the proletarian class in the oppressed countries as it gets organized and leads the movement forward. However, as there is not sufficient development of capitalism in the oppressed countries, such a revolution is not a proletarian revolution, but a peasant revolution. Thus, in the imperialist epoch, the character of revolution in colonial, semi-colonial and semi-feudal countries is peasant revolution, and the internationalization of capital. Such a revolution takes a long time because of the imperative of fighting with the imperialists and the neo-colonialists too. So, revolution starts in the rural areas and spreads towards cities, and the armed revolutions will be of a protracted nature in such countries.

18 V. I. Lenin, "The State and Revolution", *Selected Works*, Eng. ed., Progress Publishers, Moscow, Fourth Printing, 1980, Vol. 25, p. 405.

19 J. V. Stalin, "Foundations of Leninism", *Problems of Leninism*, Eng. ed., Foreign Language Press, Peking, 1976, pp. 43-44.

The greatness of Mao Tse-tung is in understanding the situation and taking the most suitable steps. In the course of the Chinese revolution, Mao argued that capturing power in that type of country was possible only through surrounding the cities from the countryside and through a protracted armed struggle. The success of the great Chinese revolution was possible through Mao's correct analysis of the Chinese society and world situation, and also the political line accordingly. It should be regarded as the development within the era of imperialism and proletarian revolution. It can be considered as the development of the creative application of Lenin and Stalin's theory. However, the particular strategy and tactics that Mao adopted in the course of the Chinese revolution cannot be seen as a universal law of revolution regarding semi (neo)-colonial countries. The only universal law is that of the necessity of revolution with violence in the proletarian and democratic revolution in the present era. Under this universal law of proletarian revolution, according to the national and international situation, the centre of the activities of revolution and the period of armed struggle should be decided. These can only be seen as a creative development in the course of handling a particular problem of revolution.

Let us take Lenin's theory on the proletarian revolution. The proletarian revolution only in one country and the building of socialism are important elements of Leninsm. In the period of Marx and Engels, it was not accepted that the proletarian revolution of that type was possible. It was generally accepted that the proletarian revolution would take place in the developed capitalist countries. This understanding of the proletarian revolution ceased to be correct after capitalism developed into imperialism. Lenin analysed this new situation, which did not exist in the period of Marx and Engels. From this analysis, he puts forward the theory, strategy and tactics of the proletarian revolution. According to Stalin, Lenin's theory of the proletarian revolution consists of "three fundamental theses". Stalin says further:

> (1) "Intensification of the revolutionary crisis within the capitalist countries and growth of the elements of an explosion on the internal, proletarian front in the 'metropolises'." (2) "Intensification of the revolutionary crisis in the colonial countries and growth of the elements of revolt against imperialism on the external, colonial front." (3) "A coalition between the proletarian revolution in Europe and the colonial revolution in the East in a united world front of revolution against the world front of imperialism is inevitable."[20]

Lenin accomplished the strategy and tactics of the proletarian revolution by basing himself above the propositions. He said "because of internationalization and the uneven development of capitalism, proletarian

20 J. V. Stalin, "Foundations of Leninism", *Problems of Leninism*, Eng. ed., Foreign Language Press, Peking, 1976, pp. 24-25.

revolution and building of a socialist system are possible even in only one country even though there has been comparatively little development of capitalism." After a cursory glance at the comments of Stalin, it becomes clear that Mao's ideas of surrounding the cities from the countryside and protracted armed struggle, the whole theory, strategy and tactics of new democratic revolution, etc., are not taking place in the new world situation different from the time of Lenin. Lenin put forward the theory, strategy and tactics of proletarian revolution in a specifically new world situations from the period of Marx and Engels in the process of the development of capitalism. Therefore, the theory, strategy and tactics of Mao regarding the new democratic revolution is simply a creative use and development of Lenin's thinking and not a "new, third and superior stage" in the process of the development of scientific socialism.

d. Communist Party

Supporters of Maoism emphasize the communist party. The PCP states: "Concerning the *Party*, Chairman Mao takes as his starting point the need for a Communist Party, a party of a new type, a party of the proletariat."[21]

Mao's "starting point" that the PCP mentions the communist party is not any other, but the starting point of Leninism. It has explained that Mao took the communist party as the base and starting point. Discussing Leninism, Stalin said that Lenin took the communist party as the base and starting point of Leninism. Stalin included the ideas of Lenin about the communist party because it represented a new and developed stage of struggle between the capitalist class and the proletarian class. Stalin sheds light:

> In the pre-revolutionary period, the period of more or less peaceful development, when the parties of the Second International were the predominant force in the working-class movement and parliamentary forms of struggle were regarded as the principal forms–under these conditions the party neither had nor could have had that great and decisive importance which it acquired afterwards, under conditions of open revolutionary clashes. Defending the Second International against attacks made on it, Kautsky says that the parties of the Second International are an instrument of peace and not of war, and that for this very reason they were powerless to take any important steps during the war, during the period of revolutionary action by the proletariat. That is quite true. But what does it mean? It means that the parties of the Second International are unfit for the revolutionary struggle of the proletariat, that they are not militant parties of the proletariat, leading the workers to power, but

21 Documents from the PCP First Congress, "On Marxism-Leninism-Maoism and On Gonzalo Thought", *A World to Win*, 1988/11, p. 61.

election machines adapted for parliamentary elections and parliamentary struggle. This, in fact, explains why, in the days when the opportunists of the Second International were in the ascendancy, it was not the party but its parliamentary group that was the chief political organization of the proletariat. It is well known that the party at that time was really an appendage and subsidiary of the parliamentary group. It scarcely needs proof that under such circumstances and with such a party at the helm there could be no question of preparing the proletariat for revolution.

But matters have changed radically with the dawn of the new period. The new period is one of open class collisions, of revolutionary action by the proletariat, of proletarian revolution, a period when forces are being directly mustered for the overthrow of imperialism and the seizure of power by the proletariat. In this period the proletariat is confronted with new tasks, the tasks of reorganizing all party work on new, revolutionary lines; of educating the workers in the spirit of revolutionary struggle for power; of preparing and moving up reserves; of establishing an alliance with the proletarians of neighbouring countries; of establishing firm ties with the liberation movement in the colonies and dependent countries, etc. To think that these new tasks can be performed by the old Social-Democratic Parties, brought up as they were in the peaceful conditions of parliamentarism, is to doom oneself to hopeless despair, to inevitable defeat. If, with such tasks to shoulder, the proletariat remained under the leadership of the old parties, it would be completely unarmed. It scarcely needs proof that the proletariat could not consent to such a state of affairs.

Hence the necessity for a new party, a militant party, a revolutionary party, one bold enough to lead the proletarians in the struggle for power, sufficiently experienced to find its bearings amidst the complex conditions of a revolutionary situation, and sufficiently flexible to steer clear of all submerged rocks in the path to its goal.

Without such a party it is useless even to think of overthrowing imperialism, of achieving the dictatorship of the proletariat.

This new party is the party of Leninism.[22]

Mao's thinking about the communist party does not represent a different and developed stage of class struggle as that of the Leninist thinking about the party. Open class confrontations, proletarian revolutionary actions and the proletarian revolutionary era constitute the Leninist era and that brought forward the need for a new type of party. So, Mao's working period falls under the Leninist era. In that situation it is unreasonable to present thinking of Mao on party organization as a base for Maoism. This should not mean that thinking of Mao about party is a lifeless use of the Leninist principles. Basing himself on the Marxist-Leninist principle of party

22 J. V. Stalin, "Foundations of Leninism", *Problems of Leninism*, Eng. ed., Foreign Language Press, Peking, 1976, pp. 97-99.

organization, Mao developed the thinking of Marx, Engels, Lenin and Stalin about party organization on the basis of his experience from democratic revolution, and especially the resurgence of capitalism in the Soviet Union and the transformation of the socialist system in China.

e. Political Power

Another factor that supporters of Maoism emphasize is the question of political power. In response to what the essence of Maoism is, the PCP provides an answer:

> *The essential thing in Maoism is political power.* Political power for the proletariat, power for the dictatorship of the proletariat, power based on an armed force led by the Communist Party. More explicitly: (1) political power under the leadership of the proletariat in the democratic revolution; (2) political power for the dictatorship of the proletariat in the socialist and cultural revolutions; (3) political power based on an armed force led by the Communist Party, seized and defended through people's war.
>
> What is Maoism? Maoism is the raising of Marxism-Leninism to a new third stage in the proletariat's struggle to lead the democratic revolution, the development and building of socialism and continuing the revolution under the dictatorship of the proletariat through the proletarian cultural revolution, at a time when imperialism is increasingly falling apart and revolution has become the main trend in history, in the midst of the greatest and most complex struggles ever seen, along with the inexorable struggle against modern revisionism.[23]

The PCP has presented a completely wrong concept. If the issue is political power, the political power for the proletarian class is the main feature of Maoism, the "essence of Maoism," then what is the main essence of Marxism-Leninism? It is well known that the question of acquiring power and making it stable is the main idea of Marxism-Leninism. It is the essence of it. Just a few quotes of Marx, Engels, Lenin and Stalin make this fact quite clear. They have said repeatedly, explaining the vision of scientific socialism on the issue of political power:

> The first step in the revolution by the working class, is to raise the proletariat to the position of ruling class, to win the battle of democracy. ... The proletariat will use its political supremacy to wrest, by degrees, all capital from the bourgeoisie, to centralize all instruments of production in the hands of the State, i.e. of the proletariat organized as the ruling class; and to increase the total productive forces as rapidly as possible.[24]

---

23 Documents from the PCP First Congress, "On Marxism-Leninism-Maoism and On Gonzalo Thought", *A World to Win*, 1988/11, pp. 76-77.

24 Karl Marx and Frederick Engels, "Manifesto of the Communist Party", *Karl Marx and Frederick Engels Selected Works*, Progress Publishers, Moscow, Fourth Printing, 1977. Vol. 1, p. 126.

This socialism is the *declaration of the permanence of the revolution*, the *class dictatorship* of the proletariat as the necessary transit point to the *abolition of class distinctions generally*, to the abolition of all the relations of production on which they rest, to the abolition of all the social relations that correspond to these relations of production, to the revolutionizing of all the ideas that result from these social relations.[25] ... To conquer political power has therefore become the great duty of the working classes.[26] ... The worker will some day have to win political supremacy in order to organize labour along new lines.[27] ... A revolution is certainly the most authoritarian thing there is.[28]

Clarifying this issue, quoting Lenin, Stalin says:

The proletarian revolution, its movement, its sweep and its achievements acquire flesh and blood only through the dictatorship of the proletariat. The dictatorship of the proletariat is the instrument of the proletarian revolution, its organ, its most important mainstay, brought into being for the purpose of, firstly, crushing the resistance of the overthrown exploiters and consolidating the achievements of the proletarian revolution, and, secondly, carrying the proletarian revolution to its completion, carrying the revolution to the complete victory of socialism. The revolution can defeat the bourgeoisie, can overthrow its power, even without the dictatorship of the proletariat. But the revolution will be unable to crush the resistance of the bourgeoisie, to maintain its victory and to push forward to the final victory of socialism unless, at a certain stage in its development, it creates a special organ in the form of the dictatorship of the proletariat as its principal mainstay.[29]

The fundamental question of every revolution is the question of power". (Lenin) Does this mean that all that is required is to assume power, to seize it? No, it does not. The seizure of power is only the beginning. For many reasons, the bourgeoisie that is overthrown in one country remains for a long time stronger than the proletariat which has overthrown it. Therefore, the whole point is to retain power, to consolidate it, to make it invincible.

Marx-Engels, Lenin and Stalin said clearly that "the main thing", is its "essence" to acquire political power and strengthen it for its final goal. In

25 Karl Marx and Frederick Engels, "The Class Struggle in France", *Karl Marx and Frederick Engels Selected Works*, Progress Publishers, Moscow, Fourth Printing, 1977, Vol. 1, p. 282.

26 Karl Marx and Frederick Engels, "Inaugural Address of the Working Men's International Association, September 28, 1864", *Karl Marx and Frederick Engels Selected Works,* Progress Publishers, Moscow, Fourth Printing, 1977, Vol. 2, p. 17.

27 Karl Marx and Frederick Engels, "The Hague Congress, September 8, 1872", *Karl Marx and Frederick Engels Selected Works,* Progress Publishers, Moscow, Fourth Printing, 1977, Vol. 2, p. 292.

28 Karl Marx and Frederick Engels, "On Authority", *Karl Marx and Frederick Engels Selected Works,* Progress Publishers, Moscow, Fourth Printing, 1977, Vol. 2, p. 379.

29 J. V. Stalin, "Foundations of Leninism", *Problems of Leninism*, Eng. ed., Foreign Language Press, Peking, 1976, pp. 38-39.

so far as Mao's concept of political power is concerned, it is the same as the Marxist-Leninist concept. It is wrong to present the ideas of Mao on state power as a base to establish Maoism as the third and the higher stage.

f. Struggle Against Modern Revisionism

Defenders of Maoism talk of the struggle advanced by Mao against modern revisionism to be an important element of Maoism. So far as it is a question of the struggle against modern revisionism, this has been an important contribution of Mao. He defended Marxist-Leninist principles in the course of the struggle against the modern revisionism and developed them as well. But only on the basis of these facts, it is still not correct to speak of Maoism as a third stage. Revisionism and the struggle against it did not come into existence in the period of Mao. Revisionism is a special characteristic of the era of imperialism and proletarian revolution. Therefore, it is an integral part of Leninism. The struggle against modern revisionism is possible only through the guidance from the struggle conducted by Lenin against the old revisionists (Bernstein, Kautsky, etc.). Mao continued that struggle, marching ahead on the way as guided by Lenin. Mao neither considered the struggle against modern revisionism as any episode different from the Leninist era, nor did he consider any need to establish any other new and original principle to lead the struggle ahead. To understand Mao's view rightly, it will be appropriate to present an extract of expression, expressed in the course of that struggle. Fully supporting Lenin, CPC writes:

> Like the old-line revisionists, the modern revisionists' answer to the description given by Lenin: ... "objectively, they are a political detachment of the bourgeoisie, ... they are transmitters of its influence, its agents in the labour movement." ... The economic basis of the emergence of modern revisionism, like that of old-line revisionism, is in the words of Lenin "an insignificant section of the 'top' of the labour movement". (Lenin, Opportunism and the Collapse of the Second International.)
>
> Modern revisionism is the product of the policies of imperialism and of international monopoly capital. ... We have quoted Khrushchev as well as Bernstein and Kautsky and Lenin's criticism of these two worthies at some length in order to show that Khrushchev's revisionism is modern Bernsteinism and Kautskyism, pure and simple. ... Kautsky and Bernstein have now clearly lost their title to Khrushchev who has set a new world record. Khrushchev, the worthy disciple of Bernstein and Kautsky, has excelled his master. ... Lenin's criticism of Kautsky is an apt portrayal of the present leaders of the CPSU.[30]

30 The Communist Party of China, "The Proletarian Revolution and Khrushchev's Revisionism", *The Great Debate*, Mass Line Publications, Kerala, India, November 1994, pp. 308, 274, 298.

In this situation, the bankruptcy of the thinking is self-evident; to present the struggle that Mao conducted against the modern revisionism as his original contribution in the international communist movement. Action and reaction, i.e. the form and level of the struggle between Marxism-Leninism and the revisionism are not always the same. It constantly marches towards a higher form. What this makes clear is that as more victories Marxism gains, revisionism takes on new forms. The same is true about the victory of Lenin and Stalin over the old revisionism. Modern revisionism is basically a new version of the old revisionism itself, on the criteria of development, it represents a higher form. It is the struggle against the higher form that also should be higher in the form than the struggle conducted by Lenin and Stalin. The struggle against modern revisionism by Mao represents the same but higher form of the struggle.

g. Continuation of Revolution Under the Dictatorship of the Proletariat

The supporters of Maoism place great importance on Mao's ideas related to the continuation of revolution under the dictatorship of the proletariat. It is the essence of Mao's thought. So, it is natural that this question is an extremely important part of Mao's contribution. However, trying to justify Maoism on this basis is incorrect.

Those who argue for using the term Maoism say that Marx propounded the principle of socialism with Engels, and Lenin, put forward the theory, strategy and tactics of imperialism and proletarian revolution, and Mao created the general solution to the problems of the entire period of socialism. According to them, these three stages represent three different stages in the development of scientific socialism. These claims are true regarding Marx and Lenin, but not true regarding Mao. The general problem of the proletarian revolution is a basic problem of Leninism, and this problem is one of the most important problems of Leninism too. The way those who argue for Maoism divide the process of the development of scientific socialism, and do not accept the conditions in what situation proletarian dictatorship can be achieved and in which conditions it can be consolidated is "the fundamental question of Leninism, and its point of departure."[31] They think that only the problem "under which conditions proletarian dictatorship can be achieved" is the basic problem of Leninism and "under which conditions it can be consolidated", is the basic problem of Maoism. For example, revolution should be continued after the proletarian revolution is the other aspect, i.e. "under which conditions, proletarian dictatorship can be consolidated"

31 J. V. Stalin, "Foundations of Leninism", *Problems of Leninism*, Eng. ed., Foreign Language Press, Peking, 1976, p. 52.

is the basic problem of Maoism and is a question related to the Great Proletariat Cultural Revolution. On the contrary, Mao's thinking that revolution should be continued under the proletarian dictatorship is something within Leninism. It is certain that Lenin's thinking on "under which situations dictatorship can be achieved" and "under which conditions proletarian dictatorship can be consolidated" cannot be considered to be perfect. So far as Lenin's thinking on this question is concerned, it is still basic thinking. The paths to the general solution to the problems of "under which conditions proletariat dictatorship can be achieved" and "under which situation it can be consolidated" are directed by Lenin. The general principle is worked out in concrete form through a concrete analysis of the concrete situation. Just as other principles of Marxism-Leninism, this principle as well demands creative work and development. Both Stalin and Mao, and especially Mao, raised understanding on this basic question of Leninism to a new level. Learning from the degeneration of the proletarian dictatorship in the Soviet Union and Yugoslavia, and in China, attempts were being made to replace proletarian dictatorship with the bourgeois dictatorship by the rightists, and Mao developed his ideas of "under which conditions, proletarian dictatorship can be consolidated."

This is the era of imperialism and proletarian revolution and Leninism is Marxism of this era. What does the Marxism of the era of proletarian revolution mean? Is Mao's thinking that revolution should be continued under proletarian dictatorship in any way different thinking than the Leninist era? That is not thinking of any different era other than the Leninist era. This means Mao's thinking on this question is thinking under Leninism itself. If it is agreed that Mao's thinking that revolution should be continued under proletarian dictatorship represents a third stage in the process of the development of scientific socialism, Leninism can neither be accepted as the Marxism of the era of proletarian revolution, nor the question such as "under which conditions it can be consolidated", be accepted as the basic question of Leninism. If the analysis of Stalin and Mao about Leninism is true, then the thinking of Mao on continuing the revolution under proletarian dictatorship should be seen as a creative development under Leninism.

4. Marxist-Leninist Principles, Contributions of Mao Tse-tung and Maoism

Supporters of Maoism try to prove Maoism correct by bringing forward the facts that Mao developed as the three constituents of Marxism and its creative application. This is a natural result of a mechanical and absolute vision. Our way of thinking on this question should be dialectical, not mechanical and absolute. The first thing to be considered is specifically whether the new and higher stage produced during the process of development of scientific socialism is because of the specific changes that appear in the objective conditions. Leninism is a stage produced by the specific changes appearing in the objective conditions. To talk of the new situation and special stage appeared in the objective conditions of capitalism; imperialism is the second and higher stage. We understand that Lenin's thinking produced in the background of specific changes that appeared in this very objective process. The second thing is that except this type of specific change, there appear quantitative changes continuously in objective conditions. Those changes in such conditions generate the need of developing the general principles of Marxism-Leninism accordingly. The third thing is that Marxism-Leninism is a general principle. Regarding its application, the need of working out this universal principle in the concrete national and international conditions of a particular time leads to the continuous development of the scientific socialism. In the course of trying to understand objectively any problem, one may not have correct knowledge. Many great intellectuals at times have got only partially true or wrong information. But such situations cannot exist for long. In the course of practice, sooner or later, this situation essentially gets changed. Mao's contributions in the international communist movement are related not to the first condition, but to the latter condition.

In the Marxist-Leninist principle and communist movement, Mao not only applied Leninism according to the concrete conditions that appeared and also particular changes in the objective situation, but he also developed Marxist-Leninist thinking in the class struggle in the socialist period by eradicating some defects found in the thought of Stalin. He raised the development of Marxism-Leninism to a new height in this regard. But, these achievements in Marxism-Leninism were not out of Leninism. Mao's achievements are gained in the course of creative application of the Marxism-Leninism. They do not represent a fundamentally new and higher stage in the development process of scientific socialism. So, it is not correct to use the term Maoism on that ground.

The role played by Engels and Stalin in the development of the Marxist-Leninist principle and in the international communist movement is with us. Engels played "a certain independent role in laying the foundations of the theory, and more particularly in its elaboration."[32] It is known to everyone who knows the ABC of Marxism that Engels had a very important role in the development of Marxist principle. Lenin

---

32 Frederick Engels, "Feurbach and End of Classical German Philosophy", *Marx and Engels Selected Works*, Eng. ed., Progress Publishers, Moscow, Fourth Printing, 1977, Vol. 3, p. 361.

described Engels and Marx as well as Marx and Engels' theory as "The founders of scientific socialism."[33] The role of Engels in the creation of scientific socialism becomes clear from this fact. Engels is the co-writer of the *Manifesto of the Communist Party*. This is the first document and programme of scientific socialism, and it is a whole and well-organized explanation of the basic principles of Marx and Engels. It has clearly mentioned the development of capitalism and the inevitablity of the victory of the proletarian revolution on the basis of scientific proofs. He has defined this task and the goal of the working class. Engels was not only an "assistant" but to a certain extent, independent of Marx. Engels prepared the draft Programme of the Communist League in the form of *Principles of Communism* on the instructions from the District Committee of the League. He was not satisfied with the Programme drafted in question-answer form. Writing a letter to Marx on November 22-23, he suggested preparing a programme of the League in the form of the *Manifesto of the Communist Party* by changing the form of the programme. He writes in that letter:

> Think over the Confession of Faith a bit. I believe we had better drop the catechism form and call the thing: *Communist Manifesto*. As more or less history has got to be related in it the form it has been in hitherto is quite unsuitable. I shall bring along what I have done here; it is in simple narrative form, but badly formulated, in fearful haste. I begin: What is communism? And then straight to the proletariat–history of its origin, difference from workers in earlier periods, development of the antithesis between the proletariat and bourgeoisie, crises, conclusions. In between this all sorts of secondary matters and in conclusion the party policy of the Communists, in so far as it should be made public. What I have here has not yet all been submitted for endorsement, but, apart from a few quite minor details, I mean to get it through in a form in which there will at least be nothing contrary to our views...[34]

The Second Conference of the Communist League, from 21 November to 8 December, passed the proposal by Marx and Engels (Marx already accepted that suggestion of Engels) and they were given responsibility to prepare the *Communist Manifesto* as the programme of the League. In the *Communist Manifesto* prepared by Marx and Engels, the basic principles of the *Principles of Communism*, first drafted by Engels alone as the programme of the League, are included. It will be reasonable to quote here Lenin's statement about the historical letter written to Marx by Engels about the first draft of the *Communist Manifesto*:

---

33 V. I. Lenin, "Prophetic Words", *Collected Works*, Eng. ed., Progress Publishers, Moscow, Third Printing, 1977, Vol. 27. p. 498.

34 Frderick Engels, *Marx and Engels Selected Correspondence*, Eng. ed., Progress Publishers, Moscow, Third revised ed., 1975, p. 40.

> This historical letter of Engels on the first draft of a work which has travelled all over the world and which to this day is true in all its fundamentals and as actual and topical as though it were written yesterday, clearly proves that Marx and Engels are justly named side by side as the founders of modern socialism.[35]

In spite of this fact, neither Engels nor Marxists after him brought up "Engelsism" forward. The role of Engels is self-evident instantly when Marxism is discussed. Certainly, Engels was not sad when he said that scientific socialism rightly bears Marx's name. Likewise, Stalin has a multi-dimensional and important role in the international communist movement. He developed Marxism-Leninism in the course of building socialism. In many places, Mao speaks of the important role of Stalin in ascertaining the theory, strategy and tactics of proletarian revolution in the era of imperialism. Just as in the relation to the explanation of concrete contradictions of competitive capitalism, Mao has mentioned not only the name of Marx but also of Engels, while speaking on the theory of imperialism. He mentioned the name not only of Lenin, but also of Stalin. He has said in various places: "Marxism-Leninism is held to be true not only because it was so considered when it was scientifically formulated by Marx, Engels, Lenin and Stalin"[36], Dialectical materialism "was further developed by Lenin and Stalin", "the great creators and continuers of Marxism–Marx, Engels, Lenin and Stalin"[37], "Lenin and Stalin integrated the universal truth of Marxism with the concrete practice of the Soviet revolution and thereby developed Marxism"[38]. It will be suitable to quote Mao's statement with a reference to the contribution of Stalin to Marxist-Leninist principles and the international communist movement:

> Comrade Stalin's contribution to our era through his theoretical activities and practice is incalculable. Comrade Stalin represented our entire new age. ... Comrade Stalin developed Marxist-Leninist theory in a comprehensive and epoch-making way and propelled the development of Marxism to a new stage. Comrade Stalin creatively developed Lenin's theory concerning the law of the uneven development of capitalism and the theory that it is possible for socialism to first achieve victory in one country; Comrade Stalin creatively contributed the theory of the general crisis of the capitalist system; he contributed the theory concerning the building of communism in the Soviet Union; he contributed the theory of the fundamental economic

35 V. I. Lenin, "The Marx-Engels Correspondence", *Collected Works*, Eng. ed., Progress Publishers, Moscow, Fifth Printing, 1980, Vol. 19, p. 558.

36 Mao Tse-tung, "On Practice", *Selected Works*, Eng. ed., Foreign Language Press, Peking, Third Printing, 1975, Vol. 1, p. 305.

37 Mao Tse-tung, "On Contradiction", *Selected Works*, Eng. ed., Foreign Language Press, Peking, Third Printing, 1975, Vol. 1, pp. 315-16.

38 Mao Tse-tung, "Reform Our Study", *Selected Works*, Eng. ed., Foreign Language Press, Peking, 1967, Vol. 3, p. 24.

> laws of present-day capitalism and of socialism; he contributed the theory of revolution in colonies and semi-colonies. Comrade Stalin also creatively developed Lenin's theory of party-building. All these creative theories of Comrade Stalin further united the workers throughout the world, further united the oppressed classes and oppressed people throughout the world, thereby enabling the struggle of the world's working class and all oppressed people for liberation and well-being and the victories in this struggle to reach unprecedented proportions.

Further he says:

> All of Comrade Stalin's writings are immortal documents of Marxism. His works, *The Foundations of Leninism*, *The History of the CPSU (Bolsheviks)*, and his last great work, *Economic Problems of Socialism in the USSR*, constitute an encyclopedia of Marxism-Leninism, a synthesis of the experience of the world communist movement of the past hundred years.[39]

Likewise, the CPC has said:

> After Lenin's death Stalin, as the chief leader of the party and the state, creatively applied and developed Marxism-Leninism. In the struggle to defend the legacy of Leninism and against its enemies–the Trotskyites, Zinovievites and other bourgeois agents–Stalin expressed the will and wishes of the people and proved himself to be an outstanding Marxist-Leninist fighter. The reason why Stalin won the support of the Soviet people and played an important role in history was primarily because he, together with the other leaders of the CPSU, defended Lenin's line on the industrialization of the Soviet land and the collectivization of agriculture. By pursuing this line, the CPSU brought about the triumph of socialism in the Soviet Union and created the conditions for the victory of the Soviet Union in the war against Hitler; these victories of the Soviet people conformed to the interests of the working class, of the world and all progressive mankind. It was therefore quite natural for the name of Stalin to be greatly honoured throughout the world.[40]

However, on the basis of these contributions, it is still not correct to speak of "Stalinism". The proposal of "Stalinism" was put forward at the time of Stalin himself. Nikita Khrushchev, then secretary, in 1936, had said that the "Moscow Bolsheviks Organization was the supporter of the Stalinist Central Committee." Likewise, he emphasized the Eighth All Soviets Congress in November 1936 that the new constitution of the Soviet Union should be called a "Stalinist Constitution". In that speech, he declared the constitution of the Soviet Union to be a victory of Marxism-Leninism-

---

39 Mao Tse-tung, "The Greatest Friendship, March 9, 1953", *Selected Works*, Kranti Publications, Secundarabad, India, First ed., 1991, Vol. 7, pp. 220-21.

40 The Communist Party of China, "On the Historical Experience of the Dictatorship of the proletariat", The Documents of the Great Debate (February 1956-June-1963, First ed., Antararashtrya Prakashan, India, December 2005, Vol. 1, p. 276.

Stalinism over one-sixth of the world. But at the time of Stalin and later as well, the term Stalinism was not used in the international communist movement. Quite certainly, the reasons behind not accepting the term of Stalinism are not weaknesses in reference to his works. If 'ism' was not acceptable because of some weaknesses, there would have been no Marxism-Leninism either. There have been some weaknesses in the works of Marx and Lenin. It is true of Mao as well. Many parties that have proposed the use of the term Maoism have severely criticized Mao over different issues. In the course of criticism itself, they have proposed Maoism. In reality, in spite of as many contributions of historical importance by Stalin in Marxist-Leninist principles and in the world communist movement, there can be no Stalinism because the thinking and actions of Stalin took place in the Leninist era.

Many attempts were made in Mao's lifetime too to establish Maoism to describe the developments he made in the Marxist-Leninist principles as "ism" in China. Lin Piao took the lead of that attempt. But, the CPC, under the leadership of Mao, rejected the attempt to establish the thinking of Mao's contributions as Maoism. Lin Piao and his clique led a campaign to bring forward a personality cult of Mao. It was told that "The world has entered into the era of Mao Tse-tung Thought."[41] An extract from the Party Constitution passed by the Ninth Congress of the CPC is especially remarkable. *The Constitution* says: "The CPC takes Marxism-Leninism-Mao Tse-tung Thought as the theoretical basis guiding its thinking. Mao Tse-tung Thought is Marxism-Leninism of the era in which imperialism is heading for total collapse and socialism is advancing to worldwide victory."

In the above statement, the phrase "Mao Tse-tung Thought is Marxism-Leninism of the era in which imperialism is heading for total collapse and socialism is advancing to worldwide victory" needs special attention. Had any individual said this, it would have had a different meaning. But it was something included in the party constitution by the Ninth Congress of the CPC.

Likewise, the Afro-Asian Authors Association, under the influence of the same "new era" declared by the Lin Piao clique in its statement of January 15, 1968 declares:

> In the world today, imperialism is heading for total collapse and socialism is advancing towards worldwide victory ... A completely new historical era has dawned in which Mao Tse-tung's thought has become the most revolutionary ideology guiding the world peoples in their struggle against imperialism, colonialism, reaction and revisionism, and for winning and safeguarding national independence, people's democracy and socialism.[42]

---

41 *China Reconstructs*, April 1968, p. 10.

42 "Statement of the Afro-Asian Writers' Bureau", *Chinese Literature*, No. 3, 1968, p. 142.

Lin Piao denoted "Mao Tse-tung's Thought-Marxism-Leninism at its highest in the present era".[43]

The Lin Piao Clique had a theoretical problem to present Mao's ideas in the form of an 'ism', in the perspective of Leninism being the Marxism of the era of imperialism and proletarian revolution. As a result of attempts to establish Mao's thought as an 'ism' by inventing "new era", they included "imperialism is heading for total collapse and socialism is advancing to worldwide victory" in the constitution of the communist party. In reality, no "new era" was in existence in the world and that type of thinking was completely wrong. After that, the CPC drew that part back at the Tenth Party Congress, and soon after, the phrase stopped appearing any more.

In the course of establishing Mao Tse-tung Thought in the form of 'ism', Lin Piao and Company advocated a "new" era in the world in place of the previous Leninist era. Lin Piao and Company were clear on the question of era; they were clear that talking of Maoism under the era of Lenin himself was a paradox. So, they tried to invent the "new era". But, proposers of Maoism have given no importance to the question of era.

5. Contributions of Mao Tse-tung for a "New, Third and Superior Stage"

Returning to the theme of the introduction, many communist parties have adopted the contributions of Mao as an 'ism' and not as 'thought'. According to them, his contributions represent a different stage, similar as those of Marx and Lenin. They argue that the contributions of Mao represent a "new, third and superior stage" in the process of the development of socialism. Raising the issue of the first and the second stage and objective conditions, there are straight answers. The stages of competitive and the monopoly, in the history of capitalism till today, are in accordance with the concept of historical materialism. However, regarding Mao, the "third stage" does not agree to a change in the objective situations, similar to that of the change from the competitive capitalism to monopoly capitalism. If the contributions of Mao are taken to be the "third stage" of development of scientific socialism, then what "third stage' is present in the world objectively that corresponds to it? The two stages marked in the process of development of scientific socialism are natural products of two marked stages, i.e. competitive stage of capitalism and monopolistic stage. But, those who argue for Maoism talk of the third stage only in regard to thought, without showing the existence of any

43 "Hail the Mass Publication of Chairman Mao's Works", *Chinese Literature*, No. 3, 1968, p. 11.

kind of third stage objectively. This fact proves the proposal for Maoism to be subjective and against historical materialism.

Mao's higher deliberations related to dialectics, shed light on the revolution in colonial, semi-colonial and semi-feudal countries, political economics of socialism, the struggle against modern revisionism, and class struggle in the socialist period. But to say that his thinking represents "the new and third stage" is not understanding the process of the development of scientific socialism from two angles. In other words, it rejects the view that specific changes appear in the objective process of development, which play the main role in the process of the development of scientific socialism, and quantitative changes. The intellectual aspect has a relative role in such a development process of theory. It ignores the active intellectual role and quantitative changes that arise in the process of development.

While talking about the stages that come up in existence during the process of development, we should do it on the objective basis, not on the subjective basis. It means to look at things on the basis of specific contradiction that arise in existence during the long process of emerging contradictions. Mao says that by not to pay attention to the particularity of contradiction in the process of development of a thing, "is tantamount to abandoning dialectics." Certainly this fact compels us to pay attention to particular contradictions. Dogmatists completely neglect the question of studying the particular prominence of contradictions. Mao states that "in studying the particularity of all these contradictions, we must not be subjective and arbitrary but must analyse it concretely."

Completely opposite to Mao to study particular contradictions, the supporters of Maoism have adopted a "subjective and arbitrary" method. Their talk of the "third stage" is the result of this. Lenin and Stalin said that imperialism is the highest and also moribund stage. They have not reached this conclusion in a subjective and anarchic way. They have explained this new stage, i.e. imperialism, by studying the basic contradiction of capitalism and particular contradictions born in the process determined by the basic contradiction. The imperialist stage is not imagination. That is the stage that exists, with the basic contradictions getting more and more intense. For example, Mao writes:

> When the capitalism of the era of free competition developed into imperialism, there was no change in the class nature of the two classes in fundamental contradiction, namely, the proletariat and the bourgeoisie, or in the capitalist essence of society; however, the contradiction between these two classes became intensified, the contradiction between monopoly and non-monopoly capital emerged, the contradiction between the colonial powers and the colonies became intensified, the contradiction among the

capitalist countries resulting from their uneven development manifested itself with particular sharpness, and thus there arose the special stage of capitalism, the stage of imperialism. Leninism is the Marxism of the era of imperialism and proletarian revolution precisely because Lenin and Stalin have correctly explained these contradictions and correctly formulated the theory and tactics of the proletarian revolution for their resolution.[44]

Presenting the world situation of Mao as being different from the world situation of Lenin and Stalin means that contradictions between monopolistic and non-monopolistic capital, between colonial powers and colonies, contradictions amongst the capitalist countries because of uneven development have ended, or have taken a different direction and form in the course of development, distinctively different from the analysis of Lenin. But those arguing for Maoism would not express it like that. It is, therefore, incorrect to attribute to Mao's contribution a "new, third stage" in the process of the development of the scientific socialism.

Comrade Gonzalo used the term a "superior stage" comparing the stages of Marxism-Leninism in the process of the development of scientific socialism. He said that Maoism is a "superior stage". This type of thinking is completely wrong. While explaining Leninism, Stalin said, "it is the Marxism of the era of imperialism and proletarian revolution." In the course of that explanation, instead of comparing it with Marxism and declaring it to be a "superior stage", he understood it as a developed form of Marxism. However, Comrade Gonzalo's declaration of Maoism as a "superior stage" does not follow this way of thinking. Stalin declares Leninism to be nothing other than a developed form of Marxism, while Comrade Gonzalo speaks of a "superior stage" to Marxism-Leninism. However, he does not take Maxism-Leninism-Maoism Thought in the objective sequence of development, but taking each separately. It is a serious theoretical mistake on our part to make comparisons between them in terms of their contributions, with some as superior or inferior. Their contributions must be taken in the context of the concrete historical conditions, but never for comparison in terms of superior and inferior.

6. One Revolution or Two Revolutions

The PCP presents the fact that "Chairman Mao led two of these glorious historic events" as the proof of Maoism being a strong base. It writes:

Three milestones stand out in this century: first, the 1917 October revolution, the dawn of the world proletarian revolution; second, the victory of the Chinese revolution in 1949, changing the correlation of forces in favour of

44 Mao Tse-tung, "On Contradiction", *Selected Works*, Eng. ed., Foreign Language Press, Peking, Third Printing, 1975, Vol. 1, p. 325.

> socialism; third, the Great Proletarian Cultural Revolution initiated in 1966 as a continuation of the revolution under the dictatorship of the proletariat in order to continue on the road to communism. Suffice it is to say that Chairman Mao Led two of these glorious historic events.[45]

To take the fact that Mao led two revolutions to be sufficient to use the term "Maoism" exposes the pitiable position of the claim about Mao. The historical fact of leadership of only one milestone by Lenin is presented here makes the intention of PCP clear, to compare Lenin and Mao and then by assigning primacy to Mao over that of Lenin. If leadership of revolution is taken to be the criteria, it would be wrong to say Marxism, since Marx did not lead any revolution. The main thing is whether the question of leadership is the base for a principle. Revolution may not occur for long. Similarly, there may appear several revolutionary changes based on a theory. So, this thinking devalues not only Engels and Stalin, but Marx too.

7. "Principle of Era" and Invention of "Principle of Stage"

Rejecting the "principle of era", the CPN (Unity Centre) writes:

> Some people say there must be representation of the whole era to be 'ism'. According to them, Marxism is the product of the capitalist era and Leninism is the product of the imperialist era. But, there is no new era of Mao and therefore there cannot be Maoism. If the era itself is talked about from the point of view of development of society, imperialism is also not a new era and rather is the highest and dying stage of capitalism.[46]

What is the difference between an "era" and a "stage"? In Marxist-Leninist literature, there is no clear explanation of the difference between an era and a stage. These words are used interchangeably. Is it reasonable to use the term era or not? Only Stalin and Mao used this term about Leninism. Mao has used the term "era" about the state of competitive capitalism also. The other thing is that they have mentioned imperialism to be the highest and moribund stage capitalism. As far as the word "stage" is concerned, it is used not only to convey the highest and moribund state of the development of capitalism, but also used to mean different states of the qualitative condition such as the capitalist stage of social development, the socialist stage and so on. So far as the reference of this word is used by Stalin and Mao regarding imperialism, they did so because the contradiction between the two classes sharpened as a result of the development of capitalism. Contradiction appeared between monopolistic and non-monopolistic capital and contradiction between colonial powers and colonies. Similarly,

45 Documents from the PCP First Congress, "On Marxism-Leninism-Maoism and On Gonzalo Thought", *A World to Win*, 1988/11, p. 60.

46 Document of the CPN(Unity Centre) On Maoism, *Long Live Maoism*, p. 10.

contradiction sharpened among the capitalist countries as a result of uneven development and the word era is used to mean this very special stage in the process of the development of capitalism. Therefore, the recognition that Leninism is the Marxism of the era of imperialism and proletarian revolution can be understood this way too. There has been no change in the basic contradiction between the class character of the proletariat, or bourgeoisie, because of the development of capitalism in the competitive capitalist era and the contradiction between the monopolistic and the non-monopolistic capitalism led to the contradiction even more between the two classes, and the contradiction amongst the capitalist countries deepened due to the uneven development caused by the contradiction between the colonial powers and colonies in the course of the development of capitalism. Leninism is Marxism of this very special stage, appeared in the development of capitalism.

The statement of the CPN (Unity Centre) quoted suggests that it is not necessary for a thinking to be representative of the era to be established as an 'ism', and that it suffices to be a representative of a stage. Mao's thinking comes under Leninism, not only from the point of view of era but also of stage. The third special stage in the development of capitalism does not exist. So, even the rejection of the principle of era and inventing the principle of stage cannot help them to justify the use of the term of Maoism.

8. Maoism and the Two "Swords" of Mao

The essence of Maoism is that it considers Leninism as a thing of the past, which is wrong. As Stalin says:

> Leninism is Marxism of the era of imperialism and the proletarian revolution. To be more exact, Leninism is the theory and tactics of the proletarian revolution in general, the theory and tactics of the dictatorship of the proletariat in particular. Marx and Engels pursued their activities in the pre-revolutionary period (we have the proletarian revolution in mind), when developed imperialism did not yet exist, in the period of the proletarians' preparation for revolution, in the period when the proletarian revolution was not yet an immediate practical inevitability. But Lenin, the disciple of Marx and Engels, pursued his activities in the period of developed imperialism, in the period of the unfolding proletarian revolution, when the proletarian revolution had already triumphed in one country, had smashed bourgeois democracy and had ushered in the era of proletarian democracy ... That is why Leninism is the further development of Marxism.[47]

47 J. V. Stalin, "Foundations of Leninism", *Problems of Leninism*, Foreign Language Press Peking, 1976, p. 3.

Likewise, emphasizing the relevance of the definition of Leninism by Stalin, the declaration passed by the Second International Founding Conference (1984) of the RIM states:

> Stalin said, "Leninism is Marxism of the era of imperialism and the proletarian revolution." This is entirely correct. Since Lenin's death the world situation has undergone great changes. But the era has not changed. The fundamental principles of Leninism are not outdated, they remain the theoretical basis guiding our thinking today.[48]

Three things become clear from Stalin and RIM. The first is that Leninism is Marxism of the era of the imperialism and the proletarian revolution. The second, era of the imperialism and the proletarian revolution has not changed. Still, we are living under the era of imperialism and the proletarian revolution. And the third is that there is the same relevance of main principles of the Leninism as in the period of Lenin and Stalin. The facts conclude that to be a Marxist at present is to be Marxist-Leninist, not "principally Maoist". The claim that to be Marxist, at present is to be "principally Maoist", a claim of the propounder of Maoism, directly violates Stalin and Mao's recognition that "Leninism is the Marxism of the era of imperialism and the proletarian revolution" and the RIM's definition "the fundamental principles of Leninism are not outdated, they remain the theoretical bases for guiding our thinking today." Taking the thought of Mao to be a "third stage" in the development of scientific socialism is another example of taking Leninism as the past era. In the second era, seen in the development of capitalism, i.e. imperialism, some of the strategies and tactics of Marx and Engels of the competitive stage of capitalism became irrelevant and Lenin's developed thinking worked as a guideline. To say that Mao's thinking as a "new, third and superior stage" appeared in the existence of the development of scientific socialism is to regard most of the analysis of Lenin irrelevant to serve as a guide in deciding the strategy and tactics of revolution. Such thinking is totally wrong.

The recognizing views of Mao about "imperialism, world war, the worldwide proletarian class movement, the national liberation movement, the struggle between Marxism and revisionism" and the continuation of revolution under the proletarian dictatorship as the bases of Maoism brings forward the reference of relevance of Leninism to an end. The above bases presented by the supporters of Maoism are bases of Leninism.

By suggesting that Maoism is born amidst a situation of an upheaval in the present world, the supporters of Maoism do not accept this situation of upheaval as a by-product of the era of imperialism and proletarian revolution. This means the situation of upheaval is the product

48 *Declaration of the Revolutionary Internationalist Movement,* 1987, pp. 14-15.

of an era different from the era of Lenin. If this situation is the by-product of the era of Lenin, then the thinking of Lenin is still relevant, and it can be taken as a guiding principle. But they cannot be taken to be the bases for the birth of Maoism. If this situation provides the bases for the birth of Maoism, as supporters of Maoism believe, this situation should not be taken as the by-product of the epoch of imperialism and the proletarian revolution, or Leninism should not be regarded as the product of the era of imperialism and proletarian revolution. Whichever of the two is taken to justify Maoism, it is bound to push Leninism back.

Actually, Lenin's views about the characteristic of our era and revolutionary strategy and tactics are relevant even today and they can guide our activities even after the development of modern capitalism and the following of the laws established by Lenin even years after his death. In this perspective, to represent Mao's contributions as a "new, third and superior stage" in the development of scientific socialism is absolutely wrong. They take Maoism born out of imperialism, world war, worldwide proletarian revolution, national liberation movement and struggle between Marxism and revisionism. What comes out of it is that it is not Leninism that is Marxism of the era of imperialism and proletarian revolution, but it is Leninism-Maoism. According to this, it will be wrong to take the era of imperialism and proletarian revolution only as a Leninist era. The thinking that it should be called Leninist-Maoist era. It is Leninism that is Marxism of the era of imperialism and proletariat revolution, as stated by Stalin and Mao, and Leninism is sufficient basically to represent this. Theoretically itself, it becomes wrong to add Maoism with Leninism as Marxism of the era, or to create the synonym of the Leninist-Maoist era for the era of imperialism and the proletarian revolution.

Mao raised the context of "Two swords" with reference to the struggle against the modern revisionism. Mao's meaning of "two swords" refers to Lenin and Stalin. According to him, Russians not only abandoned the sword of Stalin, they also abandoned the sword of Lenin too "to a certain extent". He writes:

> As for the sword of Lenin, hasn't it too been discarded to a certain extent by some Soviet leaders? In my view, it has been discarded to a considerable extent. Is the October Revolution still valid? Can it still serve as the example for all countries? Khrushchev's report at the Twentieth Congress of the CPSU says it is possible to seize state power by the parliamentary road, that is to say, it is no longer necessary for all countries to learn from the October Revolution. Once this gate is opened, by and large Leninism is thrown away.[49]

---

49 Mao Tse-tung, "Speech at Second Session of Eighth Central Committee", *Selected Works*, Foreign Language Press, Peking, 1977, Vol. 5, p. 341.

The facts of a "new, third and superior stage", "mainly Maoism", argument of one revolution, or two revolutions, rejection of the"principle of era" and the invention of the principle of a stage," the "roots of Maoism", and thinking related to the development of Leninism-Maoism as presented by the supporters of Maoism are more dangerous than the thinking of the Soviet revisionists that power can be captured through the parliamentary path. The supporters of Maoism are apt to discard "the sword of Lenin". Revolutionary Marxist-Leninists of the world came forward to defend that "sword" under the leadership of Mao. In the same way, it is necessary for true followers of Marxism-Leninism-Mao Tse-tung Thought of the present world to come forward to defend that "sword" being abandoned once more. To defend the "sword" of Mao, it is necessary to defend the "sword" of Lenin too. The "sword" of Mao cannot be defended without defending the "sword" of Lenin.

Bharatpur, Chitawon, Nepal
July, 1993

Part V

Agreement and Disagreement

In Relation to the Evaluation of Stalin by Mao Tse-tung and the Communist Party of China

A controversy has cropped up in the international communist movement over the question of the role of Stalin after the Communist Party of Nepal(Mashal) (CPN (Mashal)) disagreed with some points on Mao Tse-tung's evaluation of Stalin, with an emphasis on the need of re-evaluation. The Committee of the Revolutionary Internationalist Movement (CoRIM) and other fraternal parties declared Mao to be correct, and the objections made by the CPN (Mashal) to be incorrect. Considering the seriousness of the issue and also the theoretical aspect of it, CPN (Mashal) has decided to put up a proposal for discussion in the upcoming Sixth Party Congress. It wants not to limit it within the party, and intends to make it a public debate with a view to making evaluation of Stalin more and more objective in the party congress. So, it needs to be discussed in an analytical way, not in a general sense. Accordingly, the subject matter has been presented here.

1
Mao and the Communist Party of China on Stalin

Mao and the CPC have had a high evaluation, from the very beginning, of Stalin. *On Practice* and *On Contradiction* are two of Mao's most famous philosophical works. Internationally, Marxist-Leninists hold that Mao developed dialectics in these works. In this situation, it is clear that the thoughts expressed by Mao in these books is specifically relevant to this question. In these books, he has a very high evaluation of Stalin theoretically. Mao said that Lenin and Stalin understood the particular laws of the era of the imperialism. As Mao said, "it was scientifically formulated by Marx, Engels, Lenin and Stalin"[1]. Mao used an example of the particularity and universality of contradiction and their interconnection analysed by Stalin as a "model". He states:

> Stalin analysed the universality of contradiction in imperialism, showing why Leninism is the Marxism of the era of imperialism and proletarian revolution, and at the same time analysed the particularity of Tsarist Russian imperialism within this general contradiction, showing why Russia became the birthplace of the theory and tactics of proletarian revolution and how the universality of contradiction is contained in this particularity. Stalin's analysis provides us with a model for understanding the particularity and the universality of contradiction and their interconnection.

Discussing Stalin's view on the study of contradiction, he further writes:

> On the question of using dialectics in the study of objective phenomena, Marx and Engels, and likewise Lenin and Stalin, always enjoin people not to be in any way subjective and arbitrary but, from the concrete conditions in the actual objective movement of these phenomena, to discover their concrete contradictions, the concrete position of each aspect of every contradiction and the concrete interrelations of the contradictions.[2]

Mao stated that Lenin along with Stalin have "developed" the great theory of dialectical and historical materialism. In the course of this, he explained that Stalin is one of "the great creators and continuers of Marxism". As he writes:

> The materialist-dialectical world outlook was discovered and materialist dialectics applied with outstanding success to analysing many aspects of

1 Mao Tse-tung, "On Practice", *Selected Works*, Eng. ed., Foreign Language Press, Peking, Third Printing, 1975, Vol. 1, p. 305.

2 Mao Tse-tung, "On Contradiction", *Selected Works*, Eng. ed., Foreign Language Press, Peking, Third Printing, 1975, Vol. 1, p. 330.

human history and natural history and to changing many aspects of society and nature (as in the Soviet Union) by the great creators and continuers of Marxism–Marx, Engels, Lenin and Stalin."[3]

Mao said that in studying any complicated process, in which two or more contradictions are present: "Marx taught us in his study of capitalist society. Likewise Lenin and Stalin taught us this method when they studied imperialism and the general crisis of capitalism and when they studied the Soviet economy."[4]

Mao always looked at the question of Stalin, linking it with victory of socialism in the Soviet Union and to the question of the liberation of oppressed nations and people of the world. It becomes clear from his expression at the sixtieth anniversary of Stalin:

> Congratulating Stalin is not a formality. Congratulating Stalin means supporting him and his cause, supporting the victory of socialism, and the way forward for mankind which he points out, it means supporting a dear friend. For the great majority of mankind today are suffering, and mankind can free itself from suffering only by the road pointed out by Stalin and with his help.[5]

Mao has claimed that the CPC's understanding about the Chinese revolution, i.e. not as part of the "old type of world revolution", but of a new type of world revolution, is also "based on Stalin's theory". Referring to an article by Stalin about the revolution in colonial and semi-colonial countries, Mao states that Stalin developed the theory more and more in his later days. As he states:

> "Stalin has again and again expounded the theory that revolutions in the colonies and semi-colonies have broken away from the old category and become part of the proletarian-socialist revolution. The clearest and most precise explanation is given in an article published on 30 June 1925, in which Stalin carried on a controversy with the Yugoslav nationalists of the time."[6]

In order to criticize weaknesses in the movement and to understand Marxism-Leninism within the CPC, Mao suggested:

> In studying Marxism-Leninism, we should use the *History of the CPSU (Bolsheviks), short course* as the principal material. It is the best synthesis and summing-up of the world communist movement of the past hundred years, a model of the integration of theory and practice, and so far the only

3 Ibid., pp. 315-16.

4 Ibid., p. 332.

5 Mao Tse-tung, "Stalin, Friend of the Chinese People", *Selected Works*, Eng. ed., Foreign Language Press, Peking, First ed., December 1965, Vol. 2, p. 335.

6 Mao Tse-tung, "On New Democracy", *Selected Works*, Eng. ed., Foreign Language Press, Peking, First ed., December 1965, Vol. 2, p. 345.

comprehensive model in the whole world. When we see how Lenin and Stalin integrated the universal truth of Marxism with the concrete practice of the Soviet revolution and thereby developed Marxism, we shall know how we should work in China.[7]

Highlighting the all-round role of Stalin, Mao says:

The victory of the Chinese people's revolution is absolutely inseparable from Comrade Stalin's unceasing care, leadership, and support of over thirty years. Since the victory of the Chinese people's revolution, Comrade Stalin and the people and government of the Soviet Union, under his leadership have rendered generous and selfless assistance to the Chinese people's cause of construction. Such a great and profound friendship as that which Comrade Stalin had for the Chinese people will be forever remembered with gratitude by the Chinese people. The immortal beacon of Comrade Stalin will forever illuminate the path on which the Chinese people march forward.[8]

Comrade Stalin's contribution to our era through his theoretical activities and practice is incalculable. Comrade Stalin represented our entire new age. ... After the death of Lenin, Comrade Stalin led the Soviet people in building into a magnificent socialist society the first socialist state in the world, which he, together with the great Lenin, created at the time of the October Revolution. The victory of socialist construction in the Soviet Union was not only a victory for the people of the Soviet Union, but also a common victory for the people of the whole world. First, this victory proved in the most real-life terms the infinite correctness of Marxism-Leninism and concretely educated working people throughout the world on how they should advance towards a good life. Second, this victory ensured that during the Second World War humanity would have the strength to defeat the fascist beast. The achievement of victory in the anti-fascist war, and the glory for these victories should be attributed to our great Comrade Stalin.

Comrade Stalin developed Marxist-Leninist theory in a comprehensive and epoch-making way and propelled the development of Marxism to a new stage. Comrade Stalin creatively developed Lenin's theory concerning the law of the uneven development of capitalism and the theory that it is possible for socialism to first achieve victory in one country; Comrade Stalin creatively contributed the theory of the general crisis of the capitalist system; he contributed the theory concerning the building of communism in the Soviet Union; he contributed the theory of the fundamental economic laws of present-day capitalism and of socialism; he contributed the theory of revolution in the colonies and semi-colonies. Comrade Stalin also creatively developed Lenin's theory of party-building. All these creative theories of

---

7 Mao Tse-tung, "Reform Our Study", *Selected Works*, Eng. ed., Foreign Language Press, Peking, Second Printing, 1967, Vol. 3, p. 24.

8 Mao Tse-tung, "Telegram to the USSR on Stalin's Death, March 6, 1953", *Selected Works*, Kranti Publications, Secundarabad, India, First ed., 1991, Vol. 7, p. 217.

> Comrade Stalin's further united the workers throughout the world, further united the oppressed classes and oppressed people throughout the world, thereby enabling the struggle of the world's working class and all oppressed people for liberation and well-being and the victories in this struggle to reach unprecedented proportions.
>
> All of Comrade Stalin's writing are immortal documents of Marxism. His works, *The Foundations of Leninism*, *The History of the CPSU [Bolsheviks]*, and his last great work, *Economic Problems of Socialism in the USSR*, constitute an encyclopedia of Marxism-Leninism, a synthesis of the experience of the world communist movement of the past hundred years. His speech at the Nineteenth Congress of the CPSU is a precious last testament bequeathed to the communists of all the countries of the world. We Chinese communists, like the communists of all countries, search for our own road to victory in the great works of Comrade Stalin.
>
> Since the death of Lenin, Comrade Stalin has always been the central figure in the world communist movement. We rallied around him, constantly asked his advice, and constantly drew ideological strength from his works. Comrade Stalin was full of warmth for the oppressed peoples of the East. "Do not forget the East"–this was Comrade Stalin's great call after the October Revolution. Everyone knows that Comrade Stalin warmly loved the Chinese people and regarded the might of the Chinese revolution as incalculable. On the question of the Chinese revolution, he contributed his exalted wisdom. It was by following the teachings of Lenin and Stalin, along with having the support of the great Soviet state and all the revolutionary forces of other countries, that the CPC and the Chinese people achieved their historic victory a few years ago."[9]

The question of Stalin came to be serious, complicated and even more important in the international communist movement after the Twentieth Congress of the CPSU. Mao and the CPC and the true Marxist-Leninists of the whole world expressed their opinion about Stalin in general before that. This was necessary, not only because Khrushchev blamed Stalin for several things in the Twentieth Party Congress, also because of the degeneration of socialism and restoration of capitalism in the Soviet Union took shape from that Congress. In that context it was not adequate to look at Stalin from the earlier perspective

The degeneration of socialism and the restoration of capitalism in the Soviet Union was an unprecedented event in human history. How did this event happen? Investigation was needed. An appropriate evaluation of Stalin and his policy was clearly necessary for the Soviet Union and the international communist movement. Stalin was the chief leader of the party and the state. How far were the objective aspects responsible for the degeneration of

9 Mao Tse-tung, "The Greatest Friendship, March 9, 1953", *Selected Works*, Kranti Publications, Secundarabad, India, First ed., 1991, Vol. 7, pp. 220-21.

socialism and how far were the subjective aspects responsible, i.e. the lines of Stalin? It is an investigation posed to revolutionaries by history. In this context, it was natural that the question of Stalin's role became more serious, complicated and important.

Facing the new situation, the CPC under the leadership of Mao defended the Marxist-Leninist style by launching an uncompromising struggle against the blame, abuse and attempt to blacken the picture of the history of the Soviet Union under Stalin by the modern revisionists. The party also exposed the mistakes of Stalin in the course of his leadership. We shall discuss both sides.

The CPC, under the leadership of Mao, defended Stalin strongly, declaring him a great Marxist-Leninist after the modern revisionists accelerated the attack on Stalin internationally. In response to blames and abuses attributed to Stalin by modern revisionists, CPC states as published in the *People's Daily* on April 1956:

> After Lenin's death Stalin, as the chief leader of the party and the state, creatively applied and developed Marxism-Leninism. In the struggle to defend the legacy of Leninism and against its enemies–the Trotskyites, Zinovievites and other bourgeois agents–Stalin expressed the will and wishes of the people and proved himself to be an outstanding Marxist-Leninist fighter. The reason why Stalin won the support of the Soviet people and played an important role in history was primarily because he, together with the other leaders of the CPSU, defended Lenin's line on the industrialization of the Soviet land and the collectivization of agriculture. By pursuing this line, the CPSU brought about the triumph of socialism in the Soviet Union and created the conditions for the victory of the Soviet Union in the war against Hitler; these victories of the Soviet people conformed to the interests of the working class of the world and all progressive mankind. It was therefore quite natural for the name of Stalin to be greatly honoured throughout the world.[10]

Discussing the two "swords" and two amounts of "capital", Mao compared Stalin with Lenin in the course of that struggle. He says:

> I would like to say a few words about the Twentieth Congress of the CPSU. I think there are two "swords": one is Lenin and the other Stalin. The sword of Stalin has now been discarded by the Russians. Gomulka and some people in Hungary have picked it up to stab at the Soviet Union and oppose so-called Stalinism. The Communist Parties of many European countries are criticizing the Soviet Union, and their leader is Togliatti. The imperialists use this sword to slay people with.

Further he says:

10 "On the Historical Experience of the Dictatorship of the Proletariat", *The Documents of the Great Debate* (February 1956-June-1963, First ed., December 2005, Antararashtriya Prakashan, India, Vol. 1, p. 276.

> How much capital do you have? Just Lenin and Stalin. Now you have. abandoned Stalin and practically all of Lenin as well, with Lenin's feet gone, or perhaps with only his head left, or with one of his hands cut off.[11]

The CPC, under the leadership of Mao, declared the question of Stalin as "worldwide importance" and an "important question of principle involving the whole international communist movement." It is not only a question of the evaluation of a person, but also a question of the evaluation of the international communist movement after the death of Lenin. It states:

> The CPC has consistently maintained that the question of how to evaluate Stalin and what attitude to take towards him is not just one of appraising Stalin himself; more important, it is a question of how to sum up the historical experience of the dictatorship of the proletariat and of the international communist movement since Lenin's death.

The CPC makes explicitly clear that there were "some hidden reasons" behind the opposition to Stalin by Krushschev, and that "opposition to the cult of personality" was only an excuse by Krushschev. The "struggle against the cult of personality" disobeys all "Lenin's teaching on the interrelationship of the leaders, party, class and masses and contravenes the principle of democratic-centralism in the party." Highlighting the real intention of the "combat against the personality cult" of the leaders of the CPSU, the CPC states:

> It has become increasingly clear that in advocating the "combat against the personality cult" the leaders of the CPSU do not intend, as they themselves claim, to promote democracy, practise collective leadership and oppose exaggeration of the role of the individual but have ulterior motives. What exactly is the gist of their "combat against the personality cult? To put it bluntly, it is nothing but the following:
>
> (1) on the pretext of "combating the personality cult", to counterpose Stalin, the leader of the party, to the party organization, the proletariat and the masses of the people; (2) on the pretext of "combating the personality cult", to besmirch the proletarian party, the dictatorship of the proletariat, and the socialist system; (3) on the pretext of "combating the personality cult", to build themselves up and attack revolutionaries loyal to Marxism-Leninism so as to pave the way for revisionist schemers to usurp the party and state leadership; (4) on the pretext of "combating the personality cult", to interfere in the internal affairs of fraternal parties and countries and strive to subvert their leadership to suit themselves; and (5) on the pretext of "combating the personality cult", to attack fraternal parties which adhere to Marxism-Leninism and to split the international communist movement.

---

11 Mao Tse-tung, "Speech at the Second Session of the Eight Central Committee", *Selected Works*, Eng. ed., Foreign Language Press, Peking, First ed., 1977, Vol. 5, pp. 341-42.

The CPC stated that the slogan raised by the revisionist leadership of the Soviet Union, the "struggle against the personality cult", has passed through Bakunin, Kautsky, Trotsky and Tito, and all of them had been using it to attack the proletarian leaders and undermine the proletarian revolutionary movement. At that time, the CPC was confident that as "opportunists were unable to negate Marx, Engels or Lenin in the history of the international communist movement," in the same way "Khrushchev will be unable to negate Stalin." Clarifying all revolutionary activities in the course of an uncompromising struggle based on the principle launched against the modern revisionists over the question of Stalin, the CPC states:

> Stalin fought tsarism and propagated Marxism during Lenin's lifetime; after he became a member of the Central Committee of the Bolshevik Party headed by Lenin he took part in the struggle to pave the way for the 1917 Revolution; after the October Revolution he fought to defend the fruits of the proletarian revolution.
>
> Stalin led the CPSU and the Soviet people, after Lenin's death, in resolutely fighting both internal and external foes, and in safeguarding and consolidating the first socialist state in the world.
>
> Stalin led the CPSU and the Soviet people in upholding the line of socialist industrialization and agricultural collectivization and achieving great success in socialist transformation and socialist construction.
>
> Stalin led the CPSU, the Soviet people and the Soviet army in an arduous and bitter struggle to great victory of the anti-fascist war.
>
> Stalin defended and developed Marxism-Leninism in the fight against various kinds of opportunism, against the enemies of Leninism, the Trotskyites, Zinovievites, Bukharinites and other bourgeois agents.
>
> Stalin made an indelible contribution to the international communist movement in a number of theoretical writings which are immortal Marxist-Leninist works.
>
> Stalin led the Soviet party and government in pursuing a foreign policy which on the whole was in keeping with proletarian internationalism and in greatly assisting the revolutionary struggles of all peoples, including the Chinese people.
>
> Stalin stood in the forefront of the tide of history guiding the struggle, and was the irreconcilable enemy of the imperialists and all reactionaries.
>
> Stalin's activities were intimately bound up with the struggles of the great CPSU and the great Soviet people and inseparable from the revolutionary struggles of the people of the whole world.
>
> Stalin's life was that of a great Marxist-Leninist, a great proletarian revolutionary.

The statements from the CPC about Stalin are clear in themselves and need no further explanation. They present a living picture of Stalin's revolutionary life and the activities far more accurately than so many heavy volumes written about Stalin.

In the course of struggle against modern revisionists, the CPC also discussed the mistakes made by Stalin. The mistakes made by Stalin in the course of carrying on his responsibilities should not have been kept secret. Identification of his mistakes were completely integrated with the job of defending him. It would not have been possible to find objective and subjective causes of the degeneration of socialism and the restoration of capitalism, and to learn how to stop the repetition or lessen the possibility of that type of counter-revolution in future. By utilizing a dialectical analysis of Mao, the CPC under the leadership could develop a correct understanding and ideological-political line to find the causes of the restoration of capitalism. When pointing to the mistakes of Stalin, the CPC under the leadership of Mao listed three aspects. The first was that some mistakes of Stalin "could have been avoided and some were scarcely avoidable at a time when the dictatorship of the proletariat had no precedent to go by."

The second aspect was the merits and faults of Stalin:

> A comparison of the two shows that his merits outweighted his faults. He was primarily correct, and his faults were secondary. In summing up Stalin's thinking and his work in their totality, surely every honest communist with a respect for history will first observe what was primary in Stalin. Therefore, when Stalin's errors are being correctly appraised, criticized and overcome it is necessary to safeguard what was primary in Stalin's life, to safeguard Marxism-Leninism which he defended and developed.

The third aspect was Stalin's self-criticism. For example, citing the example of self-criticism by Stalin about some wrong guidelines given to the Chinese revolution after the success of the Chinese revolution and some mistakes taken at purification of the Communist Party of the Soviet Union, the party states:

> When Stalin did something wrong, he was capable of criticizing himself. For instance, he had given some bad counsel with regard to the Chinese revolution. After the victory of the Chinese revolution, he admitted his mistake. Stalin also admitted some of his mistakes in the work of purifying the party ranks in his report to the Eighteenth Congress of the CPSU(B) in 1939.[12]

---

12 "On the Question of Stalin", *The Great Debate,* The Polemic on the General Line of the International Communist Movement, Mass Line Publications, Kerala, November 1994, pp. 89, 101, 90-91, 98.

2
Disagreement Over Stalin's Evaluation by Mao and the Communist Party of China

Some aspects of Stalin's evaluation by Mao and the CPC do not agree with the objective reality. In the course of the evaluation of Stalin, the CPC and Mao have criticized some philosophical, ideological, political and organizational questions. The CPC states:

> In his way of thinking, Stalin departed from dialectical materialism and fell into metaphysics and subjectivism on certain questions and consequently he was sometimes divorced from reality and from the masses. In struggles inside as well as outside the party, on certain occasions and on certain questions he confused two types of contradictions which are different in nature, contradiction between ourselves and the enemy and contradictions among the people, and also confused the different methods needed in handling them ... In the matter of Party and government organization, he did not fully apply proletarian democratic-centralism and, to some extent, violated it. In handling relations with fraternal Parties and countries he made some mistakes. He also gave some bad counsel in the international communist movement. These mistakes caused some losses to the Soviet Union and the international communist movement.[13]

Mao's criticism is less authentic and more unauthentic, which poses a great problem before us. Considering the uniformity in the authentic and unauthentic thoughts, the above quote can be attributed to Mao. Whether or not this was actually a comment by Mao is not the issue, the major question is whether the above comments are true. Our disagreement with that criticism is related to the thought. So, it makes no difference whether the statements that appeared in Mao's name are his own or not. Our criticism on those thoughts is an ideological one, irrespective of Mao or not. So, they do not change our position. The other problem we have is that the comments of this type on Stalin are not analytical presentations. Those comments are made simply with reference to talks among party comrades usual in the party committees or programmes of the CPC or informal type of works.

I shall first discuss that type of comment made by Mao and the CPC, after clarifying several points. The meaning of some of the disagreements of the "mistakes" of Stalin as indicated by Mao and the CPC is not to disagree with their evaluation on Stalin on the whole, but to emphasize the need for re-evaluation of some aspects. Comparing the right and wrong sides of the evaluation of Stalin made by Mao and the CPC, the right aspect

13 Ibid., p. 91.

is seen as more important than the wrong aspect. That evaluation is mainly true and its wrong side is secondary. Taking into account the evaluation of Stalin made by Mao and the CPC, every honest communist respecting the history will certainly respect the evaluation and will accept it. Therefore, it is necessary to defend the main aspect of the above evaluation. On the issue of defending the evaluation of Stalin made by Mao and the CPC, we must defend the right side. From that evaluation we must defend the aspect of defending the glorious history of struggle of the first state of proletarian dictatorship, built by the October Revolution, and the aspect of defending the glorious history of the CPSU.

While defending the evaluation of Stalin made by Mao and the CPC, we must not defend the wrong aspect of that evaluation. Mistakes of that evaluation are needed to be taken as historical lessons. If historical facts are taken correctly without twisting the facts, both positive and negative aspects will be useful for the communist movement. In brief, this is the correct method of the total evaluation of any great person of history, i.e. the Marxist-Leninist method about the evaluation of merits and demerits. The emphasis given by the CPN (Mashal) on the need to re-evaluate some aspects of the evaluation of Stalin by Mao and the CPC is based on the right method.

The disagreement of the CPN (Mashal) on some points of evaluation of Stalin by Mao and the CPC is not a new thing. The CPN (Mashal) disagreed with the criticism of Stalin on dialectics by Mao in the document presented at the Second International Conference (1984) and passed by the Fifth Party Congress. That disagreement of CPN (Mashal) was related to the statement that Stalin "had a fair amount of metaphysics in him and he taught many people to follow metaphysic." It discusses the criticism of Mao towards Stalin.

> Based on that criticism some quarters in the international Marxist-Leninist movement today are accusing Stalin's views as not being dialectical to a significant extent and of him as not being able to see and comprehend correctly the struggle and unity between the opposites. In that context Stalin's conception of monolithic party and monolithic unity are also criticized as metaphysical thinking. We vehemently reject the above accusations against Stalin.

Further it states:

> Some mistakes were committed by him in the context of the analysis of the situation, policy formulation or their implementation. Thus it would not be correct to allege that his view itself was metaphysical on account of such mistakes.[14]

14 Communist Party of Nepal (Mashal), *Revolutionary Perspectives of the International Communist Movement After the Counter-Revolution in China*, pp. 24-25.

It is necessary to discuss the views of the CPN(Unity Centre) to some extent. The leadership of the CPN(Unity Centre) disagrees with the CPN (Mashal) over some points on the evaluation of Stalin by Mao, which the party takes to be "minimizing the contributions of Comrade Mao and following the Hoxaite tendency of Albania by concealing some mistakes of Comrade Stalin"[15] and "a terrible attack on Maoist dialectics by the leadership of 'Mashal' "[16]. The above quoted statements by the CPN (Mashal) regarding Mao's evaluation by Mao are not new; rather they are the earlier views of the party presented at the Extended Meeting of the RIM. It is to remember that the line of Fifth Congress on the above question is the line accepted by the leaders of the Unity Centre, Comrade Kiran and Prachanda too. Kiran was the General Secretary of the party while Prachanda was a central leader. For many years, they continued to support many points about the party's disagreement in regard to the evaluation of Stalin by Mao. It is clear that calling the thinking of CPN (Mashal) to be the "Hoxhaite tendency" and a "terrible attack on Maoist dialectics" today means, they also agreed with that "tendency" and they also made a "terrible attack on the Maoist dialectics for long." The thing is not limited just to that much. We agree that changes may occur in the thinking and vision of any person or political party and they can make changes in their previous thinking. Therefore, it is not to say Kiran and Pranchanda are not allowed to make changes from their previous thinking. If they found the analysis of the above question they accepted for long to be wrong, first of all they should have made self-criticism and should have brought their new thinking forward. However, they did not ever do so. So, it is clear that there is a lack of proletarian morality in the struggle against CPN (Mashal)'s so-called Hoxhaite tendency and "terrible attack" on the dialectics of Mao. Mao and the CPC emphasized: "An overall objective and scientific analysis ... by the method of historical materialism and the presentation of history as it actually occurred"[17]

With reference to the evaluation of Stalin by Mao and the CPC, they mainly used "an overall objective and scientific analysis" and "method of historical materialism". However, they deviated to a certain extent from what they themselves exhorted others to follow.

a. Dialectics and Stalin

Mao and the CPC reached the conclusion that Stalin made serious mistakes in the sphere of dialectics. Mao writes:

---

15 Prachanda, General Secretary, CPN (UC), *Naya Morcha Daily*, 25 March 1994.

16 Kiran, *Janadesh Weekly*, 19 April 1994.

17 "On the Question of Stalin", *The Great Debate*, The Polemic on the General Line of the International Communist Movement, Mass Line Publications, Kerala, November 1994, p. 90.

> Stalin had a fair amount of metaphysics in him and he taught many people to follow metaphysics. In the *History of the CPSU (Bolsheviks), Short Course*, Stalin says that Marxist dialectics has four principal features. As the first feature he talks of the interconnection of things, as if all things happened to be interconnected for no reason at all. What then are the things that are interconnected? It is the two contradictory aspects of a thing that are interconnected. Everything has two contradictory aspects. As the fourth feature he talks of the internal contradiction in all things, but then he deals only with the struggle of opposites, without mentioning their unity. According to the basic law of dialectics, the unity of opposites, there is at once struggle and unity between the opposites, which are both mutually exclusive and interconnected and which under given conditions transform themselves into each other. ... Stalin failed to see the connection between the struggle of opposites and the unity of opposites.[18]

Besides this, they said many mistakes occurred because of Stalin's metaphysical outlook, which will be discussed below separately. Here, the topic is closed only at the limit that Mao and the CPC thought that the source of mistakes of Stalin was "metaphysics." Certainly, there have been many weaknesses in principle and practice from Stalin as Mao and the CPC indicated. But "some of these could have been avoided," whereas some could not as there was no previous example or experience, "it was really difficult to avoid some mistakes at that time." Our difference of opinion with Mao and the CPC is mainly on the source of Stalin's mistakes. They claim the source of his mistakes and weaknesses was "a fair amount of metaphysics"–we reject this charge.

Metaphysics or dialectics is an issue of world outlook. It is not correct to confine this with reference to any particular mistake or event. This means had Stalin "a fair amount of metaphysics" or dialectics? Did Stalin teach many people to follow the metaphysics or to follow the dialectics? Was Stalin confused in the different processes needed for their mobilization, or unable to tackle it successfully? According to Lenin, the thing should be concluded on not only a particular question, but on the basis of an all-round analysis of the interrelationship and their development and not in fragments. Whether a sufficient quantity of metaphysics, or dialectics was present in Stalin should be examined and concluded not on the ground in fragments, but on total activities and contributions of his whole life. The conclusion that "there was a sufficient quantity of metaphysics" in Stalin and that "he taught many people to follow metaphysics" are against the dialectical point of view that Lenin emphasized to adopt in the course of study, i.e. on the basis of facts in fragments discarded by him. This conclusion of Mao and the CPC is against the facts available in the history and the method of historical materialism,

18 Mao Tse-tung, "Talk at Conference of Party Committee Secretaries", *Selected Works*, Eng. ed., Foreign Language Press, Peking, First ed., 1977, Vol. 5, pp. 367-69.

which they emphasized to adopt themselves over the question of Stalin in the struggle against the modern revisionism.

As Marx, Engels and Lenin, Stalin too was a great dialectical materialist. This is not only our view but also the view of Mao himself. We have referred to so many statements of Mao to show how he accepted Stalin as a great dialectical materialist along with Marx, Engels, and Lenin, not only in the field of theory, but also in the field of practice. The great dialectical thinking of Stalin is open to us like an open book. His dialectical skill can be clearly seen in his analysis of the world situation, after the death of Lenin and in the policies adopted by him in the international communist movement and in building socialism in the Soviet Union. The present epoch is the era of imperialism and proletarian revolution. This is a Leninist era and Marxism-Leninism is the basic principle of this era, but after the death of Lenin, it was not a simple task to realize Lenin's views in practice.

Although the theory of imperialism and proletarian revolution was Lenin's, it cannot be understood properly without the explanation and analysis of Stalin. Mao himself accepted the fact that Stalin developed this theory of Lenin. In his analysis of the then world situation, the danger of fascism and economic and political crisis of the capitalist world are especially remarkable. He analysed the economic and political crisis in the developed capitalist countries dialectically as revealed in the reports presented at the Seventeenth Congress of the CPSU on January 26, 1934, and at the Eighteenth Congress in 1939. Stalin's analysis can be taken as a model analysis. The views expressed by him in those reports proved to be correct by the situations that developed later. Stalin warned the world about the danger looming large on the world level immediately after the emergence of fascism in Germany. He emphasized the need for a counter-fascist power to come jointly ahead to stop the danger of fascism. But countries like America, England and France paid no attention. They adopted the strategy of using the fascist group against the Soviet Union. Consequently, after the war started, they were compelled to form a joint front against fascism as proposed by Stalin long before. During the Second World War and the period around it, if the contradictions had not been mobilized correctly on the world level and within the Soviet Union, the relationship between universal and particular contradictions could not have been understood correctly, and the primary and secondary aspects of contradictions could not have been identified correctly. It would not have been possible to form a joint front against fascism on the world level, to defeat fascism, to defend Soviet Union, and to form a world socialist camp. His thinking related to the solution of complicated contradictions present in some colonial and feudal countries under the imperialist epoch shows his deep understanding of the contradictions.

Mao's greatest contribution is the development of dialectics. The point of view of Mao on the change in the situation of struggle and unity between two opposite poles along with emphasis on the law of contradiction, on the question of inter-relationship between universality and particularity of contradiction, on the question of correct mobilization of contradictions, on the question of friendly and hostile aspects of contradiction and change in their position and on the question of primary and secondary forms of contradictions, and the change in their position are especially remarkable. In this regard, he has developed dialectics explaining it further. Stalin has not used many of these words. He did not use the terminology as used by Mao, but it does not mean that he did not understand the dialectics correctly in the field of revolutionary practice. After the study of Stalin's whole revolutionary life, we find this clear that all those views and contributions for which Mao is regarded as a great dialectical materialist, practically Stalin was too well-versed with the same points of view and characteristics. The statement of Mao and the CPC that there was "a fair amount of metaphysics in Stalin and taught many people to follow metaphysics", creates a need of re-evaluation of the relations of dialectics in the pre-Mao period. Mao indicates "a fair amount of metaphysics" in Stalin for mainly two reasons. According to him, the first thing is that Stalin could not understand struggle and the unity of opposites correctly.

The second thing is that he spoke of the four characteristics of the dialectics. Undoubtedly the reasons on which Mao derived the conclusion of "a fair amount of metaphysics" present in Stalin are related not only to evaluation of Stalin, but also apply to the evaluation of Marx, Engels and Lenin as well. The discussion about this should not begin with Stalin but from Marx and should end with Stalin. Here, the first main question is the issue of struggle and unity between two opposite poles and the second is that of laws of dialectics. If these two reasons are present in all three, it becomes obligatory to accept the fact of there being present in them "a fair amount of metaphysics". If these two are the criteria to evaluate, we conclude the fact of "a fair amount of metaphysics" not only in Stalin but also in Marx, Engels and Lenin as well. It is true about Mao too. But concentrating ourselves to discover the degree of metaphysics or dialectics in their particular cases is against the procedure of Marxist analysis.

Mao presented Stalin's criticism only on the ground that unity is not mentioned in the *History of the Communist Party of the Soviet Union (Bolsheviks).* He indicated that it was because of his non-dialectical thinking that Stalin made mistakes in politics and other fields. It should be remembered that in the period immediately before and after the death of Stalin and for a certain period, Mao supported that book and commented on it as "a synthesis of the experience of the world communist movement of the past hundred years" and "an encyclopedia of Marxism-Leninism." The great appreciation of that book by Mao cannot be said to be because of his immature stage in dialectics. We have two works of Mao written in 1938. They are *On Practice* and *On Contradiction.* These works are of a very high standard on Marxist dialectics. They developed Mao's views thoroughly with clear elucidation there. So, it cannot at all be said that he evaluated Stalin's works on the ground of insufficient knowledge at that time. While reaching the conclusion of "a fair amount of metaphysics", we find no self-criticism of Mao about his previous evaluation about the book. Somebody may say that both admiration of Stalin's book and the criticism made by Mao are correct. He/she can argue that previous admiration of Stalin by Mao that being the main aspect and the criticism being secondary, so Mao was correct on both (admiration and criticism). A person who cannot understand the issue of struggle and unity between opposite poles and who talks of being four characteristics instead of the only one basic law of dialectics, cannot make the best synthesis and conclusion of the communist movement of one hundred years, and cannot present a model of combining theory and practice.

We agree that Stalin made some mistakes in the course of practice. We should look at them not in an absolute and mechanical way, but from the perspective of historical materialism. Some of them were avoidable, whereas others were unavoidable in the absence of any experience of building socialism. Stalin failed to understand the struggle and unity between the class and the basis as well in a concrete way. It is not correct to describe such mistakes as the weaknesses as a result of metaphysical thinking. Whether Stalin had a dogmatic or metaphysical thinking in abundance can be ascertained on the basis of a comprehensive evaluation of his contribution and the activities of his whole life, not merely on the basis of fragmentation of his thoughts. If we evaluate in a fragmented way, metaphysics can be found not only in Stalin, but also in Marx, Engels and Lenin too. The difference is that of quantity, not the quality. It applies to Mao too. Without differentiating it, if we try finding out the percentage of metaphysics, it will be against synthesizing method of Marxism.

The other reason for the "a fair amount of metaphysics" by Mao is the mention of four characteristics of dialectics in the *History of the Communist Party of the Soviet Union (Bolsheviks).* Mao's view of looking at the basic law of dialectics is different from the traditional points of view. He maintains only one fundamental law, i.e. the law of struggle and unity between opposite aspects. According to him, the other two laws cannot be taken to be fundamental because they are not universal. The other two laws come under the law of contradiction itself and they do not have an independent existence. Here is an expression of Engels that explains the pre-Mao dialectical laws: "The law of the transformation of quantity into quality and vice versa; the law of the interpenetration of opposites; the law of the negation of the negation."[19]

Showing his disagreement to the above thinking of Engels, Mao says: "Engels talked about the three categories, but as for me I don't believe in two of those categories."

On the other two laws of dialectics as explained by Engels, Mao further says: "The transformation of quality and quantity into one another is the unity of the opposites quality and quantity, and the negation of the negation does not exist at all." He thought that Engels' 'three categories' is 'triplism' not monism". [20]

The topic of this article is not about Mao's views on the laws of dialectics. However, is the law of dialectics only one, as Mao says? Is it wrong to maintain three laws? We shall answer the questions somewhere else. Here the question is how to see a fair amount of metaphysics present in Stalin by maintaining more than one feature in dialectics? The leaders of the CPN (Unity Centre) have presented the ideas of Mao about the laws of dialectics quite wrongly. Regarding the CPN (Mashal) stance, denying the existence of two other basic laws Mao presented the law of unity and struggle between opposite aspects only the basic law of dialectics, Comrade Kiran says: "Mao's disagreement with Engels is not on the fact of dismissing the other two laws by saying the law of unity and struggle between opposite aspects but maintaining three main laws taking them all on the same level."[21]

To prove this, it quotes the following statement of Mao: "The juxtaposition, on the same level, of the transformation of quality and quantity into one another, the negation of the negation and the law of the unity of opposites is 'triplism', not monism."[22]

Taking this statement of Mao as the basis, the leaders of CPN (Unity Centre) have claimed that he has not rejected the two previously accepted laws, but has opposed them on the same level of the law of contradiction. It is necessary to pay attention to the words of Mao in the above statement, i.e. "triplism" and "not monism". With these two words, i.e. "triplism" and "not-monism", it becomes clear that he believes in only one law of dialectics. It is puzzling why the CPN (Unity Centre) leaders are trying hard to prove that

19 Frederick Engels, "Dialectics, Dialectics of Nature", Karl Marx and Frederick Engels, *Collected Works*, Eng. ed., Progress Publishers, Moscow, 1987, Vol. 25, p. 356.

20 Mao Tse-tung, "Talk on the Question of Philosophy", *Mao Tse-tung Unrehearsed, Talks and Letters: 1956-71*, edited by Stuart Schram, Penguin Books, 1974, p. 226.

21 Kiran, *Janadesh Weekly*, 19 April 1994.

22 Mao Tse-tung, "Talk on the Question of Philosophy", *Mao Tse-tung Unrehearsed, Talks, and Letters: 1956-71*, edited by Stuart Schram, Penguin Books, 1974, p. 226.

Mao is an opponent only of "arranging in that order, not of three laws." The declaring transformation of quality and quantity into one another to be the "unity of opposites" and declaring no existence of "negation of the negation" simply to be the opposition only of the means arranging of order, or keeping at the same level is not correct. Another statement of Mao too proves their bankruptcy. For example, Mao says: "In my view there is only one basic law and that is the law of contradiction. Quality and quantity, positive and negative, external appearance and essence, content and form, necessity and freedom, possibility and reality, etc., are all cases of the unity of opposites."[23]

Mao has expressed this view with reference to a talk where three or four laws of dialectics were maintained. Mao has mentioned that Stalin had stated "four laws".

Stalin has not mentioned that there are "four great laws" of dialectics. He has discussed four prominent features of dialectics under the chapter *Dialectical and Historical Materialism*, but not four fundamental laws. If we mention four points or features with reference to make a distinction between metaphysics and dialectics to be taken as four great laws, it should be accepted that Stalin maintained four great laws of metaphysics. Stalin has talked about dialectics and many features of materialism as well. He has indicated three features of materialism. Should it mean that Stalin maintained that there are three fundamental laws of Marxist materialism? If on the basis of his talk of four main features of Marxist dialectics we conclude that he maintained four fundamental laws, it must be synthesized with reference to materialism as well for the fact that Stalin maintained three fundamental laws of materialism too. If they conclude that there are four fundamental laws on the basis of pointing out four main features of dialectics by Stalin is incorrect, then what would they say of the sixteen elements of dialectics by Lenin? Mao does not say anything about that. In *Conspectus of Hegel's Science of Logic*, Lenin refers to three main elements of dialectics and that, in greater details, they can be defined in the form of sixteen elements.[24] About the first feature of dialectics of Stalin, Mao says to be nothing more than "two contradictory aspects of a thing that are interconnected" and suggests that there is no need to talk separately on that feature. What about Lenin's explanation of the first three main elements of dialectic as being the inter-relationship and development of things? They do not say anything about that.

It is wrong to see "a fair amount of metaphysics" in Stalin because of his analysis of four features or interconnectivity between things. In

23 Mao Tse-tung, "Speech at Hangchow", *Mao Tse-tung Unrehearsed, Talks, and Letters: 1956-71*, edited by Stuart Schram, Penguin Books, 1974, p. 240.

24 V. I. Lenin, "Conspectus of Hegel's Science of Logic", *Collected Works*, Eng. ed., Progress Publishers, Moscow, Fifth Printing, 1980, Vol. 38, pp. 220-22.

general, there was an assumption of three fundamental laws of dialectics before Mao. But, Marx, Engels, Lenin, and Stalin did not synthesize it in the same manner. In essence, they have expressed basically the same thing. Marx has reviewed the dialectical system in general. He has not specified the fundamental laws by number. But, we can get three basic laws in his analysis. Engels has analysed three general laws of dialectics. Lenin has also based himself on Engels' analysis in the course of the analysis of Marxist dialectics. In later days, he gave comparatively more emphasis to the law of contradiction. Stalin has analysed it very generally in this regard. He did not move Lenin's thinking on the law of contradiction forward. Various terminologies have been used to present the basic laws of dialectics. At various places, Engels has said "very general laws of dialectics" and "basic laws of dialectics".

Lenin, as well, has mentioned at various places the "characteristics of dialectics", main elements, various elements, etc. "In brief", he has said, "dialectics can be defined as the doctrine of the unity of opposites." Although once indicated that dialectics in brief, could be explained in the form of unity of opposites, and he (Lenin) had not rejected the other two laws accepted in practice by that time, or had not claimed the axiom to be only one. More than that he has talked of many characteristics or elements of dialectics. Stalin has analysed four principal features of dialectics. All these facts make it clear that it is wrong to say that Stalin could not understand dialectics or see "a fair amount of metaphysics" in him. If the analysis of Stalin by Mao and the CPC is taken to be correct, it is to be accepted that Lenin as well could not understand dialectics adequately, or that a fair amount of metaphysics was present in him as well. But, this type of thinking about Engels, Lenin and Stalin is not correct.

With reference to criticism of Stalin by Mao on the question of dialectics, it will be appropriate to refer to the criticism of Engels by Lenin on the same question. Lenin has explained that both Engels and Plekhanov have paid "inadequate attention" to the "identity of opposites"[25]. The same is true about Stalin. He paid inadequate attention to the identity of opposites. What should be taken to be the cause of weakness in Engels, if the cause of a fair amount of metaphysics being present in Stalin was the cause of those types of weaknesses? It is a fact available in the history that the cause Mao saw in Stalin for that weakness is the case of Engels, and Lenin simply made a general comment that Engels paid "inadequate attention" to that. Lenin did not see a fair amount of metaphysics for that weakness. The same phrase that Lenin used for Engels is sufficient about Stalin as well.

25 V. I. Lenin, "On the Question of Dialectics", *Collected Works*, Eng. ed., Progress Publishers, Moscow, Fifth Printing, 1980, Vol. 38, p. 357.

The conclusion should not mean that dialectics had developed to the fullest in the period of Marx and Engels themselves and that no further development of it was necessary. According to dialectics, nothing is extreme, absolute and pure forever. The thinking of Marx, Engels, Lenin, Stalin and Mao as well about dialectics cannot be final, and absolute according to the laws of dialectics itself. The following statements of Engels about it are worth considering:

> For it (dialectical philosophy) nothing is final, absolute, sacred. It reveals the transitory character of everything and in everything; nothing can endure before it except the uninterrupted process of becoming and of passing away, of endless ascendancy from the lower to the higher. And dialectical philosophy itself is nothing more than the mere reflection of this process in the thinking brain. ... dialectics reduced itself to the science of the general laws of motion, both of the external world and of human thought.[26]

Engels' statement, clarifies that dialectics exists not as final and absolute, but in a state of motion. It lies in the endless process of birth and ruin. Dialectics is always in a state of its development. This means that great experiences of the development of natural science, workers' movements, imperialism, proletarian revolutions, building of socialism, disintegration of socialism, national liberation movements and so on, always raises dialectics upwards. Understanding dialectics in this way is to look at it from the dialectical point of view.

Mao's thinking about dialectics represents a higher stage of the development of dialectics. He has not only applied the Marxist dialectics successfully in the field of practice, but he raised it theoretically to a higher level. We accept this type of Mao's higher contribution in the field of dialectics, on the other, greatly respect the criticism of Stalin by him on this question.

b. Personality Cult and Stalin

Mao and the CPC have charged Stalin for having encouraged the personality cult in later days. However, there is a distinction between the nature of the "struggle against the personality cult" of Khrushchev and the criticism of Stalin's activities of encouraging a personality cult in later days by Mao and the CPC. In spite of that, we emphasize the re-evaluation of the criticism with an attention to the seriousness of Stalin's criticism presented by Mao and the CPC. Mao says that "Stalin has highlighted his role wrongly and put his personal authority on an equal status of collective leadership." He further says:

---

26 Frederick Engels, "Feurbach and the End of Classical German Philosophy", *Karl Marx and Frederick Engels Selected Works,* Eng. ed., Progress Publishers, Moscow, Fourth Printing, 1977, Vol. 3, pp. 339, 362.

> During the latter part of his life, Stalin took more and more pleasure in this cult of the individual, and violated the party's system of democratic-centralism and the principle of combining collective leadership with individual responsibility. As a result, he made some serious mistakes such as the following: he broadened the scope of the suppression of counter-revolution; he lacked the necessary vigilance on the eve of the anti-fascist war; he failed to pay proper attention to the further development of agriculture and the material welfare of the peasantry; he gave certain wrong advice on the international communist movement, and, in particular, made a wrong decision on the question of Yugoslavia. On these issues, Stalin fell victim to subjectivism and one-sidedness, and divorced himself from objective reality from the masses.

In the beginning itself, Mao criticized Stalin for his alleged tendency of the personality cult and supported the "struggle against the personality cult" of Khrushchev. For example, he says:

> The struggle against the cult of the individual which was launched by the Twentieth Congress is a great and courageous fight by the communists and the people of the Soviet Union to clear away the ideological obstacles in the way of their advance. ... The CPC congratulates the CPSU on its great achievements in this historic struggle against the cult of the individual.[27]

The article titled as 'More On the Historical Experience of the Proletariat Dictatorship' in the *People's Daily* on December 29, 1956 is based on Mao's statement on this question. It says:

> A series of victories and the eulogies which Stalin received in the latter part of his life turned his head. He deviated partly, but grossly, from the dialectical materialist way of thinking and fell into subjectivism. He began to put blind faith in personal wisdom and authority; he would not investigate and study complicated conditions seriously or listen carefully to the opinions of his comrades and the voice of the masses. As a result, some of the policies and measures he adopted were often at variance with objective reality. He often stubbornly persisted in carrying out these mistaken measures over long periods and was unable to correct his mistakes in time.
>
> The CPSU has been taking measures to correct Stalin's mistakes and eliminate their consequences. These measures are beginning to bear fruit. The Twentieth Congress of the CPSU showed great determination and courage in doing away with the blind faith in Stalin, and exposing the gravity of Stalin's mistakes and in eliminating their effects. Marxist-Leninists throughout the world, and all those who sympathize with the communist cause, support the efforts of the CPSU to correct mistakes, and hope that the efforts of the Soviet comrades will meet with complete success.

---

27 "On the Historical Experience of the Dictatorship of the Proletariat", *The Documents of the Great Debate* (February 1956-June 1963), First ed., Antararashtriya Prakashan, India, December 2005, Vol. 1, pp. 277-79.

> It is obvious that since Stalin's mistakes were not of short duration, their thorough correction cannot be achieved overnight, but demands fairly protracted efforts and thoroughgoing ideological education. We believe that the great CPSU, which has already overcome countless difficulties, will triumph over these difficulties and achieve its purpose.[28]

We have already discussed how Mao and the CPC have opposed Khrushchev's struggle against the personality cult. However, in the early days they supported the policies on that stand, which reflects some influence of Khrushchev regarding Stalin's overall evaluation.

Although Mao and the CPC opposed Khrushchev's struggle against the "personality cult", later on, they did not give any self-criticism on their previous understanding regarding that question. So, it is necessary to talk about the understanding that continued later. Did that type of tendency develop in Stalin in his later days? Was that tendency growing in him as the source of his other mistakes? Our answers are negative. First of all, it is necessary to discuss Stalin's view on the question of the personality cult. Stalin was a great Marxist-Leninist and his point of view on this question was fully congruent with Marxism-Leninism. He was always thoroughly against any exaggerated expression from anybody about his role. He emphasized publicly the Marxist-Leninist point of view about it. The facts presented below explain Stalin's view.

Workers in 1926 welcomed him as a hero of the October Revolution, leader of the Communist Party of the Soviet Union, leader of Communist International, brave warrior and so on. Responding to their praise, he said, "a hero of the October Revolution, the leader of the CPSU, the leader of the Communist International, a legendary warrior-knight" and so on as "absurd" and "quite unnecessary exaggeration". He described himself as a "pupil of the advanced workers of the Tiflis railway workshops".[29]

Likewise, on the occasion of his 50th birthday, different organizations and comrades sent him good wishes. His point of view towards the good wishes must be discussed here. On December 21, 1929, he addressed the good wishes and said:

> Your congratulations and greetings I place to the credit of the great party of the working class which bore me and reared me in its own image and likeness. And just because I place them to the credit of our glorious Leninist party. ... You need have no doubt, comrades, that I am prepared in the

---

28 "More On the Historical Experience of the Dictatorship of the Proletariat", The *Documents of the Great Debate* (February 1956-June 1963), First ed., Antararashtriya Prakashan, India, December 2005, Vol. 1, pp. 341-42.

29 J. V. Stalin, "Reply to the Greetings of the Workers of the Chief Railway Workshops in Tiflis, June 8, 1926", *J. V. Stalin Works*, Foreign Languages Publishing House, Moscow, 1954, Vol. 8, p. 182.

> future, too, to devote to the cause of the working class, to the cause of the proletarian revolution and world communism, all my strength, all my ability and, if need be, all my blood, drop by drop.[30]

In March 1930, Stalin wrote an article titled *Dizzy With Success*, refuting many types of wrong thinking on the question of collectivization. Many people praised Stalin for this article. About this, he wrote:

> There are some who think that the article *Dizzy With Success* was the result of Stalin's personal initiative. That, of course, is nonsense. It is not in order that personal initiative is a matter like this to be taken by anyone, whoever he might be, that we have a central committee.[31]

In the same way, in a letter sent to Comrade Shatunovsky in 1930, he said:

> You speak of your "devotion" to me ... if the phrase was not accidental, I would advise you to discard the 'principle' of devotion to persons. It is not the Bolsheviks way. Be devoted to the working class, its party, its state. That is a fine and useful thing. We do not confuse it with devotion to persons, this vain and useless bauble of weak-minded intellectuals.[32]

During a talk with German writer Emil Ludwig in December 1931, Stalin spoke on the role of great persons in history so far:

> As for myself, I am just a pupil of Lenin's and the aim of my life is to be a worthy pupil of his ... Marxism does not at all deny the role played by outstanding individuals or that history is made by people. But ... great people are worth anything at all only to the extent that they are able correctly to understand these conditions, to understand how to change them. If they fail to understand these conditions and want to alter them according to the promptings of their imagination, they will land themselves in the situation of Don Quixote.
>
> Individual persons cannot decide. Decisions of individuals are always, or nearly always, one-sided decisions ... In every collegium, in every collective body, there are people whose opinion must be reckoned with ... From the experience of three revolutions we know that out of every 100 decisions taken by individual persons without being tested and corrected collectively, approximately 90 are one-sided.
>
> Never under any circumstances would our workers now tolerate power in the hands of one person. With us personages of the greatest authority are

30 J. V. Stalin, "To all Organizations and Comrades Who Sent Greetings on the Occasion of Comrade Stalin's Fiftieth Birthday", *J. V. Stalin Works*, Foreign Languages Publishing House, Moscow, 1954, Vol. 12, p. 146.

31 J. V. Stalin, "Replied to Collective-Farm Comrades", *J. V. Stalin Works*, Foreign Language Publishing House, Moscow, 1954, Vol. 12, p. 218.

32 J. V. Stalin, "Letter to Comrade Shatunovsky", *J. V. Stalin Works*, Foreign Languages Publishing House, Moscow, 1954, Vol. 13, p. 20.

> reduced to nonentities, become mere ciphers, as soon as the masses of the workers lose confidence in them. Plekhanov used to enjoy exceptionally great prestige.
>
> As soon as he began to stumble politically the workers forgot him. They forsook him and forgot him. Another instance: Trotsky. His prestige too was great, although, of course, it was nothing like Plekhanov's ... As soon as he drifted away from the workers they forgot him.[33]

Similarly, the point of view of Stalin on the above question becomes clearer in an extract of a talk with Colonel Robins in May, 1933:

> Robins: I consider it a great to have the opportunity of paying you a visit.
>
> Stalin: There is nothing particular in that. You are exaggerating.
>
> Robins: What is most interesting to me is that throughout Russia I have found the names Lenin-Stalin, Lenin-Stalin, Lenin-Stalin, linked together.
>
> Stalin: That, too, is an exaggeration. How can I be compared to Lenin?[34]

In 1938, many people emphasized the stories of the childhood of Stalin. But Stalin opposed that book. He said:

> I am absolutely against the publication of the *Stories of the Childhood of Stalin*. The book abounds with a mass of inexactitudes of fact, of alterations, of exaggerations and unmerited praise. ... The important thing resides in the fact that the book has a tendency to engrave on the minds of Soviet children (and people in general) the personality cult of leaders, of infallible heroes. This is dangerous and detrimental. The theory of 'heroes' and 'crowd' is not a Bolshevik, but a Social-Revolutionary theory. ... I suggest we burn this book.[35]

In the last part of his life, there was a proposal to add a chapter in a textbook named Lenin and Stalin as founders of the political economy of socialism. Rejecting that proposal and calling it completely unnecessary, he emphasized to "exclude it from the textbook".[36]

The study of the Nineteenth Congress of the CPSU report (on October 1952) that Mao termed as a "testament for all communists of the world" presented by Stalin, clarifies that the accusation of encouraging a personality cult is completely baseless. It is true that during the period of

---

33 J. V. Stalin, "Talk With the German Author Emil Ludwig, December 13, 1931", *J. V. Stalin Works*, Foreign Languages Publishing House, Moscow, 1954, Vol. 13, pp. 107-09, 113.

34 J. V. Stalin, "Talk With Colonel Robins, May 13, 1933", *J. V. Stalin Works*, Foreign Languages Publishing House, Moscow, 1954, Vol. 13, p. 267.

35 J. V. Stalin, "Letter On Publications for Children Directed to the Central Committee of the All Union Communist Youth, 16 February 1938", *J. V. Stalin Works*, Red Star Press Ltd., England, 1978, Vol. 14, p. 327.

36 J. V. Stalin, "Economic Problems of Socialism in the USSR", *The Essential Stalin, Major Theoretical Writing 1905-52*, edited and with an Introduction by Bruce Franklin, Re-printed by: Rahul Foundation, Lucknow, p. 459.

Stalin, especially around the Second World War and post-war period, the tendency of Stalin's personality cult emerged strongly. But, only on that ground, the thinking that Stalin encouraged his personality cult in his latter days is not correct. There was no role of Stalin behind the personality cult that grew around him in his latter days. Instead, the reality is that Stalin was against such a trend.

If Stalin is taken to be responsible for that "personality cult", what to say about Mao. The personality cult of Mao in China, especially during the period of the Great Proletarian Cultural Revolution, was prevalent too. At that time, slogans such as this is the "era of Mao Tse-tung Thought", "Mao is the sun to brighten the world on the whole", "Mao incompatible great personality in human history", "Mao knows all", "Mao's thoughts are top of Marxism", " Mao did all", "if anybody, at anytime, in any country wants a solution to any problem, one must read Mao's works, one must be inspired by Mao's thought", "one copy of valuable red quotes for all revolutionaries of the world", "Mao being here, we do not have to learn from the Soviet Union", "a great personality like Mao in the world in some countries and in China to be seen once in some thousands of years", "Mao's works to be studied by ninety-nine per cent in classical Marxist-Leninist literature" were common. If it is agreed that Stalin encouraged the personality cult, then it must be accepted that Mao also encouraged the personality cult on the basis of the tendency of the personality cult seen in the period of the Great Proletarian Culture Revolution in China. But this is wrong about both Stalin and Mao. As Stalin maintained the thinking of personality cult to be anti-Marxist-Leninist, Mao too maintained that thinking to be wrong. Just as Stalin, he also criticized the thinking of encouraging a personality cult.

If there was no role of Stalin and Mao behind the "personality cult" in the Soviet Union and China, whose role was there? It is clear that it was the role of different types of opportunists in the party. In the Soviet Union, Khrushcev and others led Stalin's personality cult in a well planned way, while Lin Piao and Company led that campaign in China. By leading the personality cult they wanted to finish them off. It will be wrong to think that Stalin and Mao did not understand the conspiracy or they themselves were part of those campaigns. The sources of the personality cult are a small production system, the existence of bourgeois rights, tradition, difference of thinking between communist principles and masses and so on. Although Stalin and Mao were very clear in themselves, they could not stop the personality cult.

c. The Chinese Revolution and Stalin

In the previous sub-headings, we have discussed the recognition of the great role of Stalin in the Chinese revolution led by Mao Tse-tung and the CPC. But, the expressions of Mao on the occasions completely negate the great role of Stalin in the Chinese revolution. With reference to such attempts of modern revisionists to win favour by exerting pressure on the determination of China, Mao denotes such attempts and trends of leaders of the CPSU not to be new but with its roots in the "past". By "past" he means from the time of Stalin itself. It is that the CPSU adopted the policy of putting pressure on the CPC as adopted by Khrushchev in the 1960s. He says:

> They did not permit China to make revolution: that was in 1945. Stalin wanted to prevent China from making revolution, saying that we should not have a civil war and should cooperate with Chiang Kai-shek, otherwise the Chinese nation would perish. But we did not do what he said. The revolution was victorious. After the victory of the revolution he next suspected China of being a Yugoslavia, and that I would become a second Tito. Later when I went to Moscow to sign the Sino-Soviet Treaty of Alliance and Mutual Assistance, we had to go through another struggle. He was not willing to sign a treaty. After two months of negotiations he at last signed.[37]

On another occasion, pointing to a long talk with Stalin on the China-Soviet Treaty of Alliance and Mutual Assistance in 1950, Mao says:

> In 1950 I argued with Stalin in Moscow for two months. On the questions of the Treaty of Mutual Assistance, the Chinese Eastern Railway, the joint-stock companies and border we adopted two attitudes: one was to argue when the other side made proposals we did not agree with, and the other was to accept their proposal if they absolutely, insisted. This was out of consideration for the interests of socialism. Then there were two 'colonies' that is the North-East and Sinkiang, where people of the third country were not allowed to reside. Now this has been rescinded. After the criticism of Stalin, the victims of blind faith had their eyes opened slightly. In order that our comrades recognize that the old ancestor also had his faults, we should apply analysis to him, and not have blind faith in him.[38]

Mao's analysis of Stalin on the Chinese revolution does not agree with his previous analysis about it. It has been already said that Mao held that the programme of the Chinese revolution was based on the principles of Stalin and the victory of the Chinese revolution was absolutely linked with Stalin's continuous leadership and support for thirty years. These two pieces of analysis about the role of Stalin on the Chinese revolution by Mao do not agree in themselves, but one negates the other outright. Had Stalin really stopped Chinese communists from launching the revolution, and had an unequal policy been signed between the two socialist countries in 1950, as Mao suggested, it would be totally wrong to say that the programme of the Chinese revolution was based on the principles of Stalin or the victory

37 Mao Tse-tung, "Speech At the Tenth Plenum", *Mao Tse-tung Unrehearsed, Talks and Letters: 1956-71*, edited by Stuart Schram, Penguin Books, 1974, p. 191.

38 Mao Tse-tung, "Talk At Chengtu: On the Problem of Stalin", *Mao Tse-tung Unrehearsed, Talks and Letters: 1956-71*, edited by Stuart Schram, Penguin Books, 1974, p. 101.

of the Chinese revolution was linked with the thirty years long continuous care, leadership and support of Stalin. How can the man who wants to stop revolution or opposes revolution be linked with the victory of revolution?

If the argument that the Chinese revolution was linked with the absolute thirty years long care, leadership and support is agreed, then accusing Stalin for stopping or opposing the Chinese revolution becomes baseless. It is true that some mistakes had been committed by Stalin regarding the Chinese revolution. Some suggestions sent by him for the revolution of China were wrong and Mao's thinking about that was right as is proved by the outcome. Facts available by now prove that there was no ideological and fundamental difference of opinion in relation to the revolution in China between Stalin and Mao. Minor differences between them on the Chinese revolution were on a tactical level. On the basis of wrong suggestions at a tactical level, it is not reasonable to say that he attempted to stop the Chinese revolution or to oppose the Chinese revolution. It will be right to take them if differences were of an ideological and fundamental level, but not at a tactical level. Therefore, Mao's accusation that Stalin was against the Chinese revolution is quite baseless. If only on the basis of Stalin having given suggestions in relation to the tactical level of issues of the Chinese revolution, he is regarded as opposed to the Chinese revolution, what should be said of Marx's stand in relation to the Paris Commune? Marx opposed the revolt of Paris in the beginning before it started. Only later, he supported it strongly. If that analysis of Mao about Stalin is taken as correct, we have to say it was the opposition of the Paris Commune of Marx and Engels' suggestion as well. But, that cannot be accepted. Afterwards, Stalin admitted that some suggestions he gave to the Chinese revolution were wrong, and that Mao and the CPC were correct about that. He has accepted self-criticism for that. The CPC itself has acknowledged the fact that the case of some mistakes committed by him were accepted and Stalin underwent a self-criticism. In that situation, it is wrong to present the subject matter as Stalin attempted to stop the Chinese revolution or oppose it.

d. Fundamental Principles of Marxism and Stalin

According to Mao, after the Second World War, Stalin did not work according to the fundamental principles of Marxism, i.e. class-struggle, proletarian revolution, party leadership, democratic-centralism and the ties between the party and masses. However, he has not mentioned Stalin by name. He said that the Soviet Union and some countries of Eastern Europe did not adopt these principles rightly. However, the statement "the Soviet Union after the Second World War and ...", leaves no puzzle that this criticism is aimed at Stalin too. The other thing is that the fundamental principles of Marxism that he has included in his saying on many occasions. He has criticized Stalin on those very issues. He writes:

> After World War II, the CPSU and certain East European Parties no longer concerned themselves with the basic principles of Marxism. They no longer concerned themselves with class struggle, the dictatorship of the proletariat, party leadership, democratic-centralism and the ties between the party and the masses, and there wasn't much of a political atmosphere.[39]

This criticism of Stalin by Mao is not correct. It is certain that on the issues mentioned by Mao above, there have appeared some weaknesses in Stalin in understanding and putting them into practice. But those weaknesses have been committed not because of deviation from the fundamental principles of Marxism or because of not having a relation with them. They occurred in the absence of historical facts while executing certain tasks. It is not correct to treat them as theoretical deviation that cropped up in the course of solving problems, especially to a great Marxist-Leninist personality like Stalin.

It is necessary to discuss Stalin's thinking on the issue of the class struggle raised by Mao above. In 1937 and 1939, Stalin reached the conclusion that antagonistic (hostile) classes did not exist[40] and need for a proletarian dictatorship ended internally, but it remained intact due to the imperialists' enclosure. Stalin was clear on the existence of the hostile class contradiction for long even after the proletarian revolution. When the old exploiting class was abolished as a class in the Soviet Union, he concluded that hostile class contradictions also got dissolved. What situation and form of classes existed after the end of the old exploiting class?

This question did not have a ready-made answer. Lenin did not have to solve that problem. At that time, there was a new situation in the international communist movement and it required an analysis of this new situation. Rightly, here appeared the weakness of Stalin. He could not make a concrete analysis of the new situation. He could not understand that a new exploiting class could come into existence after the end of old exploiting class because of the social grounds for this to rise were present in society after the completion of the socialist transformation of the instruments and the means of production. The credit of understanding this problem dialectically goes to Mao, first of all, in the history of the international communist movement. He raised the fact that a new exploiting class could come into existence after the end of the old exploiting class, and that the social bases for their rise were present in society itself. We, on the one

39 Mao Tse-tung, "Talk At Conference of Party Committee Secretaries", *Selected Works*, Eng. ed., Foreign Language Press, Peking, First ed., 1977, Vol. 5, pp. 377-78.

40 J. V. Stalin, "On the Draft Constitution, and Report to the Eighteenth Party Congress", *Problems of Leninism*, Foreign Language Press, Peking, 1976, pp. 800, 912.

hand, take Stalin's thinking to be wrong, whereas we accord a high rank of the evaluation to Mao's thinking about the issue. But, we reject that the source of this weakness was metaphysics or not relating to the fundamental principles of Marxism, i.e. class struggle. Mao's great contribution to this field was not any wonder of his mind, but the product of social practice. It was the experience of the restoration of capitalism in Yugoslavia and the Soviet Union and the direct experience of a transitional period running through the struggle between the capitalist road and the socialist road in China itself, of which Stalin had no experience at all and in the absence of which it would not have been possible for Mao to analyse the new situation correctly.

Actually, not only Stalin, for some years after the restoration of capitalism in Yugoslavia and the Soviet Union too, Mao did not agree that a new exploiting class could come into existence and classes have an antagonistic contradiction in socialism. He says:

> The transition to communism certainly is not a matter of one class overthrowing another. But that does not mean there will be no social revolution, because the superseding of one kind of production relations by another is a qualitative leap, i.e. a revolution.
>
> Although classes may be eliminated in a socialist society, in the course of its development there are bound to be certain problems with "vested interest groups" which have grown content with existing institutions and unwilling to change them.
>
> Under socialism there may be no war but there is still struggle, struggle among sections of the people; there may be no revolution of one class overthrowing another, but there is still revolution. The transition from socialism to communism is revolutionary. The transition from one stage of communism to another is also revolutionary. Then there is technological revolution and Cultural Revolution.

Mao observes the statement to be "correct" that "under socialism there is no class energetically plotting to preserve outmoded economic relations". He further writes: "In a socialist society there are still conservative strata and something like "vested interest groups". There still remain differences between mental and manual labour, city and countryside, worker and peasant. Although these are not antagonistic contradictions, they cannot be resolved without struggle".[41] We have quoted above only those views of Mao on classes and class-struggle in socialism that were expressed years after the restoration of capitalism in Yugoslavia and the Soviet Union. Mao's thinking on the above questions is not fundamentally different from that of Stalin on the related issue. By that time, Mao had not understood the objective need

41 Mao Tse-tung, "Reading Notes on the Soviet Text Political Economy (1961-1962)", *A Critique of Soviet Economics*, Progressive Publications, New Delhi, 1982, pp. 62-63, 71.

of continuing revolution in socialism by one class overthrowing another. He took the question of transition into socialism as the same as the transition of stages under communism. His views expressed at that time do not agree with those expressed later on. If we take a wrong impression of Stalin in the situation when no example was available to him to say that he had metaphysics or that he could not relate himself to principle of class struggle, what should we say to the thinking of Mao expressed after vast practical examples had been available?

If we take the criticism of Stalin by Mao on the above question to be correct, we become obliged to accept that Mao committed the same type of mistake for a long period of time, and that should mean he had metaphysics and he did not show an interest in the fundamental principle of Marxism, i.e. class struggle. But this type of criticism for both is wrong. Stalin's fundamental weakness about proletarian dictatorship lies with his saying that after 1936, its need continued not because of internal causes but because of external reasons, i.e. imperialist enclosure. At that time, proletarian dictatorship was necessary for both internal as well as external reasons, and not only external reasons.

It is important that after that type of expression, he launched an uncompromising struggle to strengthen the proletarian state power not only against external enemies, but also against the internal enemies. The purge movement that he launched in 1939 proves that on the question of class struggle and proletarian dictatorship, he was correct on practical grounds. In days later on as well, he was determined to strengthen proletarian dictatorship in the Soviet Union. The criticism that he neglected the party leadership is also unarguable. Probably, this criticism by Mao is not targeted at Stalin, but at the then leaders of East European communist parties of that time.

The thinking that Stalin did not apply the principle of democratic-centralism correctly in the practical field is also not correct. Certainly, in later days in the Soviet Union, there was somehow greater attention paid to centralism. But, we should see the situation linking it with the concrete situation mainly of the then world situation. The other thing giving emphasis to centralism is not to neglect the aspect of democracy. His thinking of emphasizing centralism stood on the ground of exclusive democracy. Centralism without democracy is dictatorship and to analyse Stalin's policy in this sense would be absolutely wrong. The wide participation of the Soviet people in the recovery of the post-world war period in the great campaign of economic reform to recover from the loss caused by the war and during the fight against fascism would not have been possible without broad democracy. So, Stalin's thinking on democratic-centralism fully agreed with the dialectics theoretically and on the practical ground too.

Out of the questions on which Mao presented a criticism of Stalin or the criticism that Stalin showed no interest to fundamental principles of Marxism in the Soviet Union after the Second World War, other than those related to philosophy, almost all are related not to the fundamental principles of Marxism, but to policies adopted in particular situations. Let's take the example of the criticism that "Stalin squeezed peasants." Firstly, this criticism is wrong. Secondly, this criticism is related to some particular events and not with the fundamental viewpoint to deal with the question of the peasants in socialism. Likewise, the accusation that Stalin could not understand the question of class struggle in the Soviet Union after 1936 also is not of fundamental character, but is a specific weakness. He expressed such a view in particular situations of a particular country, and not on an ideological level or worldwide. Other criticisms made by Mao and the CPC also belong to the same type of characteristics. Did Stalin show an interest in the fundamental principles of Marxism-Leninism or not? The question should be answered not on the basis of any particular policy he adopted, but on the totality of policies adopted in his entire political life.

Bharatpur, Chitawon, Nepal
May 6, 1994

Part VI

Remarks on the RIM Declaration

In the Context of Ten Years Since the Publication of the Declaration

The Revolutionary Internationalist Movement (RIM) was established by the Second International Conference comprised of different communist parties and organizations in 1984. It passed a declaration, which helps to understand the position of the international communist movement of that time, especially with some problems in the world communist movement after the death of Mao Tse-tung and restoration of capitalism in China. At that time, some communist parties of the world, mainly the Revolutionary Communist Party of the United States of America (RCP, USA) and the Revolutionary Communist Party of Chile, put forward some new conclusions in the name of the study, evaluation and re-evaluation of the dissolution of the world socialist system. On the other, many communist parties of the world, mainly the Communist Party of Nepal(Mashal) (CPM(Mashal)), put forward the argument that the path outlined by Marx, Engels, Lenin, Stalin and Mao Tse-tung was basically sufficient for tackling the problems in the international communist movement at present. In that situation, the formation of RIM and its declaration were to pass through a complicated, troublesome and long process.

In that context, the declaration of the Second International Conference (*Declaration* onward) was going to be a declaration of compromise between the thinking of the "new" and "old", as clarified by the cursory study of the *Declaration*, which includes the history of Stalin and the Comintern after 1939, especially during the period of the Second World War, and then declaring their policy completely wrong. On the other, it contains criticism of the thinking of negating the experience of the proletarian class in the Soviet Union and rejecting Stalin from the rank of leaders of the proletarian over the question of the defence of the Soviet Union. I will not discuss everything in the *Declaration* in detail. I shall limit myself to comment on some questions that must be discussed.

1. Quoting these words from the Joint Communiqué of the First International Conference (in Autumn 1980), the *Declaration* starts: Today the world is on the threshold of momentous events. The crisis of the imperialist system is rapidly bringing about the danger of the outbreak of a new, third, world war as well as the real perspective for revolution in countries throughout the world.

Fully supporting the above view on the world situation, the the *Declaration* states: "The scientific accuracy of these words from the Joint Communiqué of our First International Conference in Autumn 1980 have not only been fully borne out by the recent developments in the world, but the world situation has been further accentuated and aggravated since that time".

Further it writes:

> All the major contradictions of the world imperialist system are rapidly accentuating: the contradiction between various imperialist powers, the contradiction between imperialism and the oppressed peoples and nations, and the contradiction between the bourgeoisie and the proletariat in the imperialist countries. All these contradictions have a common origin in the capitalist mode of production and its fundamental contradiction. The rivalry between the two blocs of imperialist powers led by the US and the USSR respectively is bound to lead to war unless revolution prevents it and this rivalry is greatly affecting world events.

In this regard, quoting Mao Tse-tung's "Either revolution will prevent war, or war will give rise to revolution", the *Declaration* takes "On Urgent Importance".

Further it writes:

> The very logic of the imperialist system and the revolutionary struggles is preparing a new situation. The contradiction between the rival bands of

> imperialists, between the imperialists and the oppressed nations, between the proletariat and the bourgeoisie in the imperialist countries, are all likely in the coming period to express themselves by the force of arms on an unprecedented scale.

To justify its own conclusion, the *Declaration* quotes Stalin: "The significance of the imperialist war which broke out ten years ago lies, among other things, in the fact that it gathered all these contradictions into a single knot and threw them on to the scales, thereby accelerating and facilitating the revolutionary battles of the proletariat."

It is true that the fundamental contradictions of the world imperialist system are sharpening. However, the world situation mentioned here is of a subjective type and not an objective one. Here the *Declaration* has compared the situation around 1984 with that of the First World War. This analysis concludes that the principal contradiction lies between the then Soviet Union and the United States of America, i.e. inter-imperialist by nature. If not solved by revolution, war is inevitable between two imperialist power groups under the leadership of the USA and the Soviet Union. The *Declaration* mentions contradictions between imperialism and the oppressed people and nations just in general and talks on inter-imperialist contradictions with emphasis. This is basically wrong thinking about the present world situation. At present as well, the contradiction between imperialism and oppressed peoples and nations is the principal contradiction of the world as analysed by the CPC under the leadership of Mao Tse-tung. The principal contradiction of the world affects the contradiction between the imperialist powers and the contradiction between the bourgeoisie and the proletariat in imperialist countries. In the present world situation, not to recognize the contradiction between imperialism and oppressed peoples and nations to be the principal contradiction of the world is, the pro-imperialist thinking in reality.

The conclusion of the *Declaration* states that if problems are not solved by revolution, war is inevitable out of the competition between the two power groups of the imperialist powers under the leadership of the USA and the Soviet Union. This was proved completely wrong in later years. Although a long period has passed after the conclusion, inter-imperialist contradiction could not take the form of world war. Neither was there a situation of that type to appear immediately, nor is it so even after the Soviet social-imperialism collapse. But, all these are not natural outcomes of revolution. Although, the *Declaration* declared the contradiction among imperialists to be the principal contradiction, the world is going in the same way, i.e. to the direction of contradiction between imperialism and oppressed people and nations.

The analysis of the world situation is simply a vulgar copy of the analysis of the then world situation by the International Conference in the days before the First World War under the leadership of Lenin. The analysis of the then world situation under the leadership of Lenin was fully objective and the result proved its validity. But, the analysis under a different world situation made under Lenin's leadership is not true in reference to the present world situation, the results as well have proved this analysis wrong.

2. Since imperialism has integrated the world into a single global system (and is increasingly doing so) the world situation increasingly influences the developments in each country; thus revolutionary forces all over the world must base themselves on a correct evaluation of the overall world situation. This does not negate the crucial task they face of evaluating the specific conditions in each country, formulating specific strategy and tactics and developing revolutionary practice. Unless this dialectical relationship between the overall situation at the global level and the concrete conditions in each country is grasped correctly by Marxist-Leninists they will not be able to use the extremely favourable situation at the global level in favour of revolution in each country.

At a glance, this expression appears to comply with the Marxist-Leninist philosophy. But, when studied deeply, it is clear in this statement that the driving force (both internal and external) of the development process of a thing or event is amalgamated here. The view of dialectical materialism suggests that the basic causes of development of an event are internal and the external aspect is only a condition, not present here clearly. Putting two different points of view on an equal scale on one issue together is not dialectics but rather eclecticism. After the death of Mao, some deviations appeared in the international communist movement, in the driving forces of development of events. I would like to say something on the statement of the *Declaration*: "Tendencies in the international movement to view the revolution in one country apart from the overall struggle for communism must be struggled against". The *Declaration* has expressed this view not mentioning the name of any leader or any party here. But, there are some communist leaders and some communist parties who are the target of this criticism. Indeed, they are Lenin, Stalin and Mao Tse-tung and parties under their leadership and the Comintern. After the death of Mao Tse-tung, serious deviations appeared in the international communist movement. The RCP, USA is especially worth mentioning in this regard. The RCP, USA and its Chairman Bob Avakian have blamed Stalin, the Comintern, Mao Tse-tung, and to a certain extent Lenin too, viewing the revolution in one country as separate from the world revolution. The RIM is badly influenced by the view of the RCP, USA and its Chairman Bob Avakian. The facts below make it clear:

Regarding the role of internal and external factors in changing society, Mao says:

> According to materialist dialectics, changes in nature are due chiefly to the development of the internal contradictions in nature. Changes in society are due chiefly to the development of the internal contradictions in society, that is, the contradiction between the productive forces and the relations of production, the contradiction between classes and the contradiction between the old and the new; it is the development of these contradictions that pushes society forward and gives the impetus for the supersession of the old society by the new. Does materialist dialectics exclude external causes? Not at all. It holds that external causes are the condition of change and internal causes are the basis of change, and the external causes become operative through internal causes. In a suitable temperature an egg changes into a chicken, but no temperature can change a stone into a chicken, because each has a different basis. There is constant interaction between the peoples of different countries. In the era of capitalism, and especially in the era of imperialism and proletarian revolution, the interaction and mutual impact of different countries in the political, economic and cultural spheres are extremely great. The October Socialist Revolution ushered in a new epoch in world history as well as in Russian history. It exerted influence on internal changes in the other countries in the world and, similarly and in a particularly profound way, on internal changes in China. These changes, however, were effected through the inner laws of development of these countries, China included.[1]

Countering Mao's views, Chairman Bob Avakian writes:

> In "On contradiction" the way it's presented is that China is the internal and the rest of the world is the external. And what we've emphasized in opposition to this is viewing the process of the world historic advance from the bourgeois epoch to the communist epoch as something which in fact takes place in an overall sense on a world scale, is a world process and both arises out of and is ultimately determined by the fundamental contradiction of capitalism which, with the advent of imperialism, has become the fundamental contradiction of this process on a world scale. If we want to look to see what is the underlying and main driving force in terms of the development of revolutionary situations in particular countries at particular times, then too we have to look to the overall development of contradictions on a world scale, flowing out of and ultimately determined by this fundamental contradiction and not mainly to the development of the contradictions within a particular country, because that country and the process there is integrated in an overall way into this larger world process. It's not simply as it was in the feudal era or the beginning of the bourgeois era where you had separate countries more or less separately developing

1 Mao Tse-tung, "On Contradiction", *Selected Works*, Eng. ed., Third Printing, 1975, Foreign Language Press, Peking, Vol. 1, p. 313.

> with interpenetration between them; now they've been integrated into this larger process.[2]

This is Comrade Bob Avakian's anti-Marxist-Leninist view which has occupied a place in its *Declaration* by the founding conference of the RIM. This will be taken as a blunder in the history of the world communist movement. A genuine struggle should be waged against the tendency of the international communist movement for its act of separating the revolution in one country from the total struggle for communism.

Further the *Declaration* observes:

> Tendencies in the international movement to view the revolution in one country apart from the overall struggle for communism must be struggled against. To justify our own view on the subject matter, *Declaration* quotes Lenin: "There is one, and only one, kind of real internationalism, and that is–working wholeheartedly for the development of the revolutionary movement and the revolutionary struggle in *one's own* country, and supporting (by propaganda, sympathy and material aid) *this struggle*, this, *and only this*, line in every country without exception." Lenin stressed that proletarian revolutionaries must approach the question of their revolutionary work not from the point of view of "my" country but "from the point of view of *my share* in the preparation, in the propaganda, and in the acceleration of the world Proletarian revolution.

In general, the statement is true. But if we understand this concretely, we know the secret behind this. This expression of the *Declaration* has been targeted especially against the policy of Stalin and the Comintern around the Second World War. The RCP, USA and its Chairman Bob Avakian have been saying regularly and publicly that Stalin and the Comintern adopted a policy of national chauvinism, and isolated the question of world revolution over the question of defence of the Soviet Union at the time of the Second World War. The emphasized tendency of the struggle in the *Declaration* is not anything other than the struggle against the policy that Stalin and the Comintern adopted, especially during the civil war in Spain and at the same time after German fascism attacked the Soviet Union. Regarding this, the fact is that policies adopted by Stalin and the Comintern were correct. Their policies regarding Spain's civil war and Soviet Union's defensive war were fully based on Lenin's above quoted statements. The RIM has given importance in its Declaration to the point of view of the RCP, USA that declares those correct and true Marxist-Leninist policies to be wrong. Those policies were adopted from the point of view of the share in the world proletarian revolution.

---

2 Bob Avakian, "Conquer the World? The International Proletariat Must and Will", *Revolution,* Special Issue, Number 50, pp. 34-35.

3. Stalin said: "Leninism is Marxism of the era of imperialism and the proletarian revolution." This is entirely correct. Since Lenin's death the world situation has undergone great changes. But the era has not changed. The fundamental principles of Leninism are not outdated, they remain the theoretical basis guiding our thinking today. We affirm that Mao Tse-tung Thought is a new stage in the development of Marxism-Leninism. Without upholding and building on Marxism-Leninism-Mao Tse-tung Thought it is not possible to defeat revisionism, imperialism and reaction in general.

This is totally correct. Though a widespread change has come into the world, the era is the same. Lenin's principles are still relevant today, and they can be our guide for a theoretical base, we can say with certainty that Mao's thought is further development of Marxism-Leninism. We cannot defeat imperialism, revisionism and reactionary forces without adopting Mao's Thought.

This thinking is the soul of the *Declaration.* Its significance is far-reaching and long lasting. This must be defended.

4. The *Declaration* writes on the history of the international communist movement:

> Today, the Revolutionary Internationalist Movement, together with other Maoist forces, are inheritors of Marx, Lenin, Stalin and Mao, and they must firmly base themselves on this heritage. ... Mao Tse-tung's great battle to oppose the modern revisionists and their negation of the experience of building socialism in the USSR under Lenin and Stalin while carrying out a thorough and scientific criticism of the roots of revisionism are evidence of this.
>
> Today a similar approach is necessary to the thorny questions and problems of the history of the international communist movement. A serious danger comes from those who, in the face of setbacks in the international communist movement since the death of Mao Tse-tung, declare that Marxism-Leninism has failed or is outmoded and the entire experience acquired by the proletariat must be put into question. This tendency would negate the experience of the dictatorship of the proletariat in the Soviet Union, eliminate Stalin from the ranks of proletarian leaders, and in fact, attack the basic Leninist thesis on the nature of the proletarian revolution, the need for a vanguard party and the dictatorship of the proletariat. As Mao powerfully expressed: "I think there are two 'swords': one is Lenin and the other Stalin" , once the sword of Stalin has been discarded "once this gate is opened, by and large Leninism is thrown away". This statement made by Mao Tse-tung in 1956 has been shown by the experience of the international communist movement till today to retain its validity.

> Lenin and his successor Stalin were faced with the necessity of safeguarding the gains of the revolution in the USSR and carrying through the establishment of a socialist economic system in the Soviet Union alone. ... In 1935 an extremely important Congress of the Communist International was held in the midst of a severe world economic crisis, the growing threat of a new world war and imperialist attacks on the Soviet Union, the coming to power of fascism in Germany and the smashing of the German Communist Party, and the establishment of fascism or menace of the same in a number of other countries. It was necessary and correct for the Communist International to try to develop a tactical line concerning all these questions.
>
> Then the Communist International mobilized millions of workers against class enemies and led heroic struggles against reaction such as the organizing of the International Brigades to fight against fascism in Spain in which many of the best sons and daughters of the working class shed their blood in an inspiring example of internationalism.
>
> The Communist International also gave, correctly, great emphasis to the defence of the Soviet Union, the land of socialism. ... In circumstances of imperialist encirclement of (a) socialist state(s) defending these revolutionary conquests is a very important task for the international proletariat. It will also be necessary for socialist states to carry out a diplomatic struggle and at times to enter into different types of agreements with one or another imperialist power.
>
> The Second World War cannot be considered a mere repetition of the First World War, for, even if the same murderous logic of the capitalist system was responsible for it, it was a complex combination of contradictions. At its beginning in 1939 it was, as Mao then pointed out "unjust, predatory and imperialist in character." But a major change with global implications took place when Hitler's Germany turned its troops on the Soviet Union. This just war on the part of the Soviet Union drew the support and sympathy of the working class and oppressed peoples the world over who were greatly inspired by the heroic resistance of the Red Army and the Soviet working class and people. This was no mere sympathy for a victim of aggression but the profound conviction that the defence of the Soviet Union was also the defence of the socialist base area of the world revolution.

The RCP, USA and its Chairman Bob Avakian were bringing forward their "new thinking" publicly on some historical issues about four years before the commencement of the Second International Conference. Regarding this, the negative view of an antagonistic level on the formation of a united front against fascism, the civil war of Spain, the role of the Comintern in the Second World War and the question of Stalin are especially remarkable. Bob Avakian declared the policy of Stalin and the Comintern on the front against fascism to be "absolutely wrong in principle", "the subordination of everything to the defence of the Soviet Union", "being acceptable to the imperialist bourgeoisie" and so on. Likewise, over the revolutionary civil war in Spain, he said that "the possibilities for big revolutionary advances in that country and worldwide were sacrificed to the defence–on a state-to-state level–of the Soviet Union", "At the root of it was the Comintern's entirely wrong–and disastrous–view of the kind of historic conjucture into which the world was heading at that time." Comrade Bob Avakian condemned the patriotic war conducted by the Soviet Union in this way: "The fact that there was indeed a contradiction, as I said, at times a very acute and potentially antagonistic contradiction between the maintaining of power in one socialist state and the advance of the world revolution overall, could in a certain sense be mitigated and buried under the fact that the Soviet national interests, or the national interests, if you will, of the proletariat in power in the Soviet Union went parallel with the world revolution at that time and the policies that were being adopted by the Soviet state did not come sharply into conflict with the overall revolutionary struggle in other parts of the world." To mention the above facts with emphasis of the *Declaration* in the context of that kind of thinking in the international communist movement can be taken as a great achievement.

5. On Stalin's errors on a so-called ideological basis, the *Declaration*, often quoting Mao, states:

> Mao explained the ideological basis for Stalin's errors: "Stalin had a fair amount of metaphysics in him and he taught many people to follow metaphysics", "Stalin failed to see the connection between the struggle of opposites and the unity of opposites. Some people in the Soviet Union are so metaphysical and rigid in their thinking that they think a thing has to be either one or the other, refusing to recognize the unity of opposites. Hence, political mistakes are made." Stalin's most fundamental error was to fail thoroughly to apply dialectics in all spheres and thus draw serious wrong conclusions concerning the nature of the class struggle under socialism and the means to prevent capitalist restoration.
>
> This incorrect understanding of the nature of socialist society also contributed to Stalin's failure to adequately distinguish the contradictions between the people and the enemy and the contradictions among the people themselves. This in turn contributed to a marked tendency to resort to bureaucratic methods of handling these contradictions and gave more openings to the enemy.
>
> First the distinction between fascism and bourgeois democracy in the imperialist countries, while certainly of real importance for the communist parties, was treated in a way that tended to make an absolute of the difference between these two forms of bourgeois dictatorship and also to make a strategic stage of the struggle against fascism. Secondly, a thesis was developed, which held that the growing immiseration of the proletariat would create in the advanced countries the material basis for healing the split in the working class and its consequent polarization that Lenin had

> so powerfully analysed in his works on imperialism and the collapse of the Second International. While it is certainly true that the depth of the crisis undermined the social base of the labour aristocracy in the advanced capitalist countries and led to real possibilities that the communist parties needed to make use of to unite with large sections of the workers previously under the hegemony of the Social Democrats, it was not correct to believe that in any kind of a strategic sense the split in the working class could be healed. Thirdly, when fascism was defined as the regime of the most reactionary section of the monopoly bourgeoisie in the imperialist countries, this left the door open to the dangerous, reformist and pacifist tendency to see a section of the monopoly bourgeoisie as progressive.
>
> In practical political terms, the diplomatic struggle and international agreements of the Soviet Union became increasingly confounded with the activities of the communist parties making up the Comintern. This problem also contributed to strong tendencies to portray the non-fascist powers as something other than what they truly were–imperialists who would have to be overthrown. In the European countries occupied by German fascist troops it was not incorrect for the communist parties to take tactical advantage of national sentiments for the standpoint of mobilizing the masses, but errors were made due to raising such tactical measures to the level of strategy. Liberation struggles in colonies under the domination of the allied imperialist powers were also held back owing to such erroneous views.

The above quoted parts are the wrong pictures of the history, or an inappropriate comprehension of the history. This is the success of the RCP, USA in incorporating such an anti-Marxist-Leninist analysis on Stalin in the historic *Declaration* passed by the second International Conference. Those hostile to Stalin may make Mao's wrong analysis as a pretext to hide themselves behind Mao easily. It is a serious problem in the international communist movement. Just as Mao, Stalin was a great dialectician and he always taught people to follow dialectics, not metaphysics. The issue should be presented in this very way and never otherwise.

Stalin and the Comintern's dividing fascist and anti-fascist imperialist powers, was not a strategic, but tactical one. The thinking that poverty in the proletariat in the developed countries would bridge the gap between the working class, and as a result, it would prepare the objective ground for polarization, was not taken as a strategic awareness, or as a thinking that could avoid a split within the working class. Leninism has clarified in this regard. The analysis that while forwarding such a thought, it would be just like abandoning Leninism, proves the helplessness of such analysts.

In the course of the Second World War, with the background of Stalin and the Comintern adopting the united front, the communist parties of some countries and democratic forces being included in the Soviet front did not adopt a policy of struggling against their oppressor imperialists. This was a great mistake from them. However, it is not correct to say that the policy of the united front of Stalin and the Comintern to be wrong. In the course of the united front, they emphasized always for struggling independently in their own way against the bourgeoisie of their own country. If the result is wrong, that is a matter related to the communist party, democratic forces in the concerned countries. Some people and some Communist Parties bring forward the example of China and try to prove that Stalin and the Comintern were wrong and Mao was right. This attempt is futile. Evidently, Mao was in favour of forming the anti-fascist united front and concluded it to be true.

Under the leadership of Mao Tse-tung, the New Democratic Revolution was successful in China. Some national and international factors were instrumental for this. In being so, of course, credit goes to Mao's correct political and military line. However, China not being a colonial but a semi-colonial country, and the defeat of Japanese imperialism in the Second World War were other important factors. In the course of an anti-fascist united front as well, Mao continued the policy of leading a struggle against the British imperialism and American imperialism independently, although communist parties of some countries gave up the struggle against the British imperialism and American imperialism with the excuse of forming a united front formed on the international scale. In this reference, the decision of the Communist Party of India in 1942 not to struggle against the British imperialism is especially remarkable. This was a serious mistake. Therefore, the analysis of the *Declaration* that because of the policy of anti-fascism of Stalin and the Comintern, the "Liberation struggles in colonies under the domination of the allied imperialist powers were also held back due to such erroneous views" is wrong.

6. Criticizing *A Proposal Concerning the General Line of the International Communist Movement,* the *Declaration* states:

> Yet, on a number of questions, the criticism of revisionism was not thorough enough and some erroneous views were incorporated even while criticizing others. Exactly because of the important role these polemics and Mao and the CPC played in giving birth to a new Marxist-Leninist movement, it is correct and necessary to consider the secondary, negative aspect in the polemics and in the struggle waged by the CPC in the international communist movement.
>
> In relation to the imperialist countries, the *Proposal* expressed the view that "In the capitalist countries which US imperialism controls or is trying to control, the working class and the people should direct their attacks mainly against US imperialism, but also against their own monopoly capitalists and other reactionary forces who are betraying the national interests."

> This view, which seriously affected the development of the Marxist-Leninist movement in these types of countries, obscures the fact that in imperialist countries the " national interests" are imperialist interests and are not betrayed, but on the contrary defended, by the ruling monopoly capitalist class despite whatever alliances it may make with other imperialist powers and despite the inevitably unequal nature of such an alliance. The proletariat of these countries is thus encouraged to strive to outbid the imperialist bourgeoisie as the best defenders of its own interests. This view had a long history in the international communist movement and should be broken with.

At another place, it states:

> As was pointed out, the polemics of the CPC contained serious errors in this regard, errors which were incorporated by the Marxist-Leninist movement. The correct internationalist desire to fight against US imperialism (correctly singled out as the main bastion of world reaction at that time) increasingly mingled with a promotion of the national interests of the imperialist states insofar as they came into contradiction with the US and (especially from the early 1970s on) with the Soviet Union. Increasingly wrong positions were taken by a great many Marxist-Leninist parties concerning world affairs, positions which went against internationalism and objectively aligned the positions of these parties on these issues with imperialist war preparations and counter-revolutionary suppression. As pointed out earlier, some Marxist-Leninist parties in the imperialist countries had already adopted a thoroughly social-chauvinist line even before the coup d'état in China in 1976.

Actually, the *Declaration* on this point of the *Proposal* is not new in the international communist movement. Bob Avakian, Chairman of the RCP, USA, had presented earlier this type of view on that point of *Proposal.* As he has said:

> There is the specific criticism to be made of Mao ... in the case of the General Line polemic, US imperialism was seen as the main enemy at that stage and in the other imperialist countries the advice was to struggle against the monopoly capitalists and reactionary forces who betrayed the national interest, in other words who were allying with US imperialism; overall this was not correct.[3]

After the quote of Comrade Bob Avakian's statement on that point of *Proposal*, it is very clear that the base of that view on this subject of *Declaration* is the RCP, USA and its Chairman Bob Avakian's view. Actually, it is a success of the RCP, USA to get its absolute view on "national interests" penetrated in the historic *Declaration* passed by the Second International Conference. The Proposal indicates clearly that workers and people of the

3 Bob Avakin, "Conquer the World? The International Proletariat Must and Will", *Revolution,* Special Issue, Number 50, p. 35.

countries controlled or in the process of control by American imperialism must direct their attacks against American imperialism along with the monopolist capitalists of their own country and other reactionary powers, who betrayed the national interest. The *Declaration* indicates this statement of Mao and the CPC to be the defender of the imperialist bourgeoisie.

The *Declaration* says that in imperialist countries "national interests are imperialist interests". In general, the statement is true. The greatest mistake of the *Declaration* with this reference is that it takes this general meaning as the absolute one. Therefore, it has drawn a totally wrong conclusion on the above thinking about the *Proposal*. This analysis by the CPC is necessary to be observed as it is based on a concrete analysis of the concrete situations, and not as an absolute point of view. In *Proposal*, the emphasis given in regard to the struggle waged by the working class and the people against the reactionaries, who betray the cause of national interest, in the capitalist countries either controlled or under an attempt of American imperialism, is related to adopting policies by taking into consideration the situation of contradiction among the imperialist powers. The *Proposal* mentioned above is related to a special meaning, not in a general sense in regard to the capitalist countries. That is said not in regard to the capitalist countries in a general sense, but in the context of the countries either controlled or about to be controlled by American imperialism.

Then what is the general line for revolution in regard to the capitalist countries? Some lines from the *Proposal* will answer this question properly.

> In the imperialist and the capitalist countries, the proletarian revolution and the dictatorship of the proletariat are essential for the thorough resolution of the contradictions of capitalist society. In striving to accomplish this task the proletarian party must under the present circumstances actively lead the working class and the working people in struggles to oppose monopoly capital, to defend democratic rights, to oppose the menace of fascism, to improve living conditions, to oppose imperialist arms expansion and war preparations, to defend world peace and actively to support the revolutionary struggles of the oppressed nations.
>
> The proletarian parties in imperialist or capitalist countries must maintain their own ideological, political and organizational independence in leading revolutionary struggles. At the same time, they must unite all the forces that can be united and build a broad united front against monopoly capital and against the imperialist policies of aggression and war.

American imperialism successfully accumulated power in the Second World War, and adopted the strategy of control over the fascist countries defeated in the war and with friendly countries of the war period in the decades after the war, and it took some capitalist countries under control and took steps to put some other countries under its control. The reactionary forces of those countries took the role of assisting American imperialism with the above strategy. In that situation, the *Proposal* has done the correct thing by emphasizing the fact of targeting the struggle of workers and people of those countries against American imperialism, along with the monopolist capitalists and other reactionary forces who betrayed the national interest of their own countries.

The situation among the capitalist countries that the *Proposal* has talked about here is not a general, but a special situation as explained above. That is related to the special situation of the existence among the great powers and American imperialism on the other. Some capitalist countries are controlled by the US, or are under an attempt of being controlled. Even with reference to capitalist countries, raising the question of "national interests" in a special situation of this type as witnessed at different turning points of history complies with Marxism-Leninism. In that situation too, understanding the question in general principles is not dialectics, but metaphysics. The issue of national interests that the *Proposal* has raised for countries controlled by American imperialism or countries where there is a plan to be controlled is not related to the defence of imperialist interests, but the defence of sovereignty of these countries. It is the right way to build a broad united front against the main enemy. It is tactics to isolate the main enemy. To see the defence of sovereignty and the defence of imperialist interests as the same thing is wrong. There are important differences between the two, although, with reference to imperialist countries, the difference between the two is the product of a special situation. This evaluation by the *Declaration* is quite objectionable. It declares this *dialectical* analysis of the *Proposal* to be the same as the line of revisionists, by representing the interests of imperialists over a long period in the international communist movement and emphasizes a break off with it. It is self-evident that to break relations with such a thinking of the *Proposal* on the above question means breaking from Marxism-Leninism and adopting a "left" sectarianism view. It is a shame to compare the *Proposal's* line with the revisionist line.

7. While the CPC paid great attention to the development of Marxist-Leninist parties in opposition to the revisionists they did not find the necessary forms and ways to develop the international unity of the communists. Despite contributions to the ideological and political unity this was not reflected by efforts to build organizational unity on a world scale. The CPC had an exaggerated understanding of the negative aspects of the Comintern, mainly those caused by over-centralization, which led to crushing the initiative and independence of constituent communist parties. While the CPC correctly criticized the concept of the paternal party, pointed out its harmful influence within the international communist movement, and stressed the

principles of fraternal relations between parties, the lack of an organized forum for debating views and achieving a common viewpoint did not help resolve this problem but in fact exacerbated it.

The analysis of the *Declaration* that the CPC did not discover the required ways and system to develop the unity of communists are subjective and absolute. It has accepted the fact that the "CPC paid great attention to the development of Marxist-Leninist parties in opposition to the revisionists" and made important "contributions to the ideological and political unity." Along with attempts for ideological and political unity of the communists of the world, attempts for their organizational unity on a world scale and the discovery of required ways and systems are necessary and important. But to understand the question of building organizational unity of communists on a world scale on the view of this general principle absolutely in all situations is non-Marxist-Leninist thinking. The main thing is to emphasize ideological and political unity itself. According to the *Declaration* itself, the CPC under the leadership of Mao Tse-tung made a great contribution in this respect.

In the history of the world communist movement, the First International was dissolved. Thereafter, almost for two decades, the world communist movement was deprived of the international organization's leadership. Second International organization of communists was founded under the leadership of Engels towards the end of his lifetime. At the beginning of the 20th century sharp contradictions appeared over the political and ideological issues among the communists and it ultimately led to the dissolution of the Second International synchronizing with the beginning of the First World War. Again, the world communist movement could not get leadership of any international organization. After the October Revolution in Russia the Third International was founded under the leadership of Lenin. It was dissolved again during the Second World War period. After the end of the war, Stalin was found making an attempt to establish the Cominform with a view to building an international level organization. However, Stalin's plan could not be realized in the light of differences of opinions in the then international communist movement. After Stalin's death the Cominform was dissolved.

In that situation it becomes a matter of primary importance to struggle against revisionism and to work for ideological and political unity in the international communist movement. The CPC was correct to concentrate itself on that work. This work went on through the whole life span of Mao on a world scale. Glancing at the situation of this period in the world communist movement, the forming of a world organization could not have been fruitful.

The contention of the *Declaration* that it would have been easier "for debating views and achieving a common viewpoint", had there been an organization of communists of world level formed is one-sided too. It was equally possible that in such a national and international situation of the communist movement, there might have developed a stronghold of revisionists. The position of Mao and the CPC on the issue of ideological and political unity might have been comparatively weaker. Paying no attention to this whole situation, the *Declaration* that the CPC's "Contribution to the ideological and political unity" instead of solving the problem, further exacerbated it.

It will be appropriate to quote the following statement written in the *Declaration* with reference to the criticism of the CPC on the above mentioned context. It says:

> Despite the tremendous victories of the Cultural Revolution the revisionists in the Chinese party and state continued to maintain important positions and promoted lines and policies which did considerable harm to the still fragile efforts to rebuild a genuine international communist movement. The revisionists in China, who controlled to a large degree its diplomacy and the relations between the Communists Party of China and other Marxist-Leninist parties, turned their backs on the revolutionary struggles of the proletariat and the oppressed peoples or tried to subordinate these struggles to the state interests of China.

In that situation, if an international organization had been formed, it would have developed as a spot to debate revolutionary thinking and would work less to form a common thinking and would change into a revisionist thinking. If an international organization of communists had come into existence in that situation, it would possibly have spoiled the attempts for renovation of a true international communist movement. They would have used them as well in the same way in their favour.

8. The revisionists in the Chinese Party and State continued to maintain important positions ... Reactionary despots were falsely labelled as "anti-imperialists" and increasingly under the banner of a worldwide struggle against "hegemonism" certain imperialist powers of the Western bloc were portrayed as intermediate or even positive forces in the world. Even during this period many of the pro-Chinese Marxist-Leninist parties supported by the revisionists in the CPC began to shamelessly tail the bourgeoisie and even support or acquiesce in imperialist adventures and war preparations aimed at the Soviet Union which was increasingly seen as the "main enemy" in the whole world. All these tendencies blossomed fully with the coup d'état in China and the revisionists' subsequent elaboration of the "Three Worlds Theory" which they attempted to shove down the throats of the international communist movement. The Marxist-Leninists have correctly refuted the revisionist slander that the "Three Worlds Theory" was put forward by Mao Tse-tung. However, this is not enough. The criticism of the "Three Worlds Theory" must be deepened by criticizing the concepts underlying it, and the origins must be investigated.

The *Declaration* statement about China's revisionists is correct. Its analysis of the principles of the so-called "Three Worlds Theory" is equally correct. But in the course of support and welcome of the right aspect of this, not to comment on the non-Marxist-Leninist deviation implied in it is wrong. The *Declaration* has not been able to adopt the correct view in relation to the contradictions among the enemy powers, especially between the imperialist and some reactionary powers. It presents differentiating the contradictions and using them as far as possible just as China's activities of revisionists, Mao was against utilizing them. Calling reactionaries and dictators anti-imperialist, and recognizing certain imperialist powers of the Western bloc to be "middle" or positive is not revisionist thinking in itself. Analysing the world situation of that time, Mao himself had put forward an analysis of that type. For example, he said in the course of a talk with a foreign leader in 1974: "In my opinion, the United States of America and the Soviet Union fall in the first world. Japan, Europe and Canada come in the mid part of the second world. Leaving Japan, the whole of Asia is in the third world. The whole of Africa and Latin America fall in the third world."

In the same way, the CPC and the government adopted the policy to support some reactionary rulers as part of the struggle against imperialism. Long before Mao, Stalin himself adopted such a policy. He indicated the struggle mobilized for the freedom by the Amir in Afghanistan to be revolutionary. Policies that Mao and Stalin both adopted basing themselves on concrete historical situation and using even small contradictions among the enemy comply with a Marxist-Leninist principle. With reference to this, revisionists should be criticized because they bring forward the policy of support for a certain ruler of some country in some special situation or utilizing contradictions among them as the general line for all communist parties and for the international communist movement of the Socialist Countries.

Chinese revisionists put forward as a principle Mao's policy of using of contradictions among enemies. However, to state the same to be a strategy of the world proletarian class is something different. There are fundamental differences. The greatest mistake of the *Declaration* is related to this, as it has made no differentiation between them and has criticized both taking them at the same level. The *Declaration* has not criticized these two fundamentally different policies but has taken them as one, and it has emphasized to investigate the origin of the "Three Worlds Theory". There is no need to wonder if the writers of the *Declaration* discover in Lenin after their deeper "investigation" the origin of the "Three Worlds Theory" or in Stalin or Mao in the background of criticizing these two different policies.

> **9.** The Cultural Revolution represents the most advanced experience of the proletarian dictatorship and the revolutionizing of society. For the first time the workers and other revolutionary elements were armed with a clear understanding of the nature of the class struggle under socialism; of the necessity to rise and overthrow the capitalist roaders who would inevitably emerge from within the socialist society and which are especially concentrated in the leadership of the party itself and to struggle to further advance the socialist transformation and thus dig away at the soil which engenders these capitalist elements. Great victories were won in the course of the Cultural Revolution which prevented the revisionist restoration in China for a decade and led to great socialist transformations in education, literature and art, scientific research and other elements of the superstructure. Millions of workers and other revolutionaries greatly deepened their class consciousness and mastery of Marxism-Leninism in the course of fierce ideological and political struggle and their capacity to wield political power was further increased. The Cultural Revolution was waged as part of the international struggle of the proletariat and was a training ground in proletarian internationalism, manifested not only by the support given to revolutionary struggles throughout the world but also by the real sacrifices made by the Chinese people to render this support.

This is a correct analysis of the Great Proletarian Cultural Revolution of China and should be established strongly in the communist movement.

> **10.** Lenin said, "Only he is a Marxist who *extends* the recognition of class struggle to the recognition of the *dictatorship of the proletariat*". In the light of the invaluable lessons and advances achieved through the great proletarian Cultural Revolution led by Mao Tse-tung, this criterion put forward by Lenin has been further sharpened. Now it can be stated that only he is a Marxist who extends the recognition of class struggle to the recognition of the dictatorship of the proletariat and the recognition of the objective existence of classes, antagonistic class contradictions and of the continuation of the class struggle under the dictatorship of the proletariat throughout the whole period of socialism until communism. As Mao so powerfully stated: Lack of clarity on this question will lead to revisionism.

This is the most important lesson from the history of the proletarian dictatorship since the Paris Commune to now. The *Declaration* has done a commendable job establishing the historic importance of this lesson in the international communist movement as a yardstick measurement to differentiate true Marxist-Leninists from the phony Marxist-Leninists in the present.

> **11.** In the oppressed countries of Asia, Africa and Latin America a continuous revolutionary situation generally exists. But it is important to understand this correctly: the revolutionary situation does not follow a straight line; it has its ebbs and flows. The communist parties should keep this dynamic in mind. They should not fall into one-sidedness in the form of asserting that the commencement and the final victory of people's war depends totally on the subjective factor (the communists), a view often associated with "Lin Piaoism".

Further it says:

> It is necessary to combat any erroneous view which would postpone the commencement of armed struggle or the utilization of any form of armed struggle until conditions become favourable for revolutionary warfare throughout the country. This view negates the uneven development of revolution and revolutionary situations in these countries, in opposition to Mao's statement, "a single spark can start a prairie fire". It is also important to note that the overall international situation has an influence on the revolution in a particular country; not taking this into account leaves the Marxist-Leninists unprepared to seize the opportunity when the revolutionary process is hastened by developments on the world scale.

The *Declaration* has criticized Lin Piaoist thinking properly about the beginning of the people's war and final victory. But on the basis of the statement below, there remains, the *Declaration* has not been able to adopt a correct Marxist-Leninist point of view on the issue of armed struggle. The way, the *Declaration* presents itself in words: "Although at all times some form of armed struggle is generally both desirable and necessary to carry out the tasks of the class struggle in these countries, during certain periods armed struggle may be the principal form of struggle and at other times it may not be." This is a situation of ambiguity. Neither has it been able to say clearly that in oppressed countries, the main form of struggle is not always armed struggle, nor has it said that the form of struggle must be decided on concrete analysis of a concrete situation. Notably like other legal forms of struggle, we cannot adopt or leave within hours/days illegal forms, like people's war or armed insurrection, of struggle. Armed insurrection or people's war is the highest form of struggle. Once we raise arms its consequences can be more serious and more prolonged than any other legal form, such as demonstrations, general political strikes, etc. After entering into armed struggle, taking a shift in the name of tactics as we do in the case of legal forms of struggle, can lead to defeat. So, we must be very careful while we handle this issue.

In the present world situation, the violent path of struggle is the universal path beyond controversy. But it does not mean that violence is the main form of struggle all the time. Such a view about the struggle to be waged in the oppressed countries, instead of leading clearly and strongly in accordance with the Marxist-Leninist direction, is fraught with the serious danger of directing to deviation.

Kathmandu, Nepal
May 10, 1994

Part VII

Mao's Comment on Stalin's 'Economic Problems of Socialism in the Soviet Union'

Stalin's *Economic Problems of Socialism in the USSR* written in 1952, is an analysis of the political economy of socialist society. The book was prepared not with the aim of making an analysis of the political economy of socialism, rather it is a collection of comments, written in the form of replies to certain questions raised over a draft textbook of the political economy in the Soviet Union at that time. Stalin answered the questions raised at the talks as he thought necessary to reply. Perhaps all the replies were not published in this book. The book does not give a whole explanation of socialist political economy, and this limitation should be taken into consideration while studying the book.

Stalin has spoken about the questions like character of economic law, commodity production, law of value, elimination of the difference between physical and mental labour as well as between town and countryside, and the relationship between the productive forces and the relations of production in the socialism. This book has faced criticism since its publication. Modern revisionists "defended" their principles with a sharp attack on Stalin against the ideas expressed in the book. This book has invited sharp criticism not only from outside the proletarian movement, but also from inside. To begin with, Mao appraised this book as a "great work" and "an encyclopedia of Marxism-Leninism" and a "synthesis of experience of the past one hundred years of the world communist movement".

However, after the Twentieth Congress of the Communist Party of the Soviet Union (CPSU), Mao criticized this book in sharp words with an exception to some questions only. Certainly there were some weaknesses in Stalin's book. However, it has not presented a comprehensive analysis of the political economy of socialism. It is one thing to point out this or that issue not included in this book, but to argue that it is totally wrong is a different issue. Mao's saying that there are wrong arguments in the book is not correct for two reasons.

The first point is that instead of being a book with reference to political economy, it is simply a collection of comments. To answer all questions satisfactorily was not possible in it. In that condition, it is not correct to take it to be wrong just because of not finding a satisfactory or holistic answer to the problems discussed in it. If Stalin's book is said to be wrong on that ground, what about the book *A Critique of Soviet Economics* by Mao himself? Mao has raised many important questions in this collection, but he has not answered all the problems in detail. They may sound wrong or unsatisfactory because of the absence of detailed analysis.

Likewise, let us take Mao on dialectics. Mao has talked about only one fundamental law, i.e. the law of contradiction. But the study of his entire works clarifies that he has not presented a clear explanation and analysis in that book. Does this mean that his thinking in criticism of Soviet Economics and the fundamental law of dialectics is wrong or unsatisfactory? This type of thinking about the works of both Mao and Stalin is not correct. It is the responsibility of a true Marxist-Leninist to analyse satisfactorily their own understanding, be it in brief or in the form of notes. The other point is that most of the economic problems of socialism were not discussed in any major Marxist-Leninist works. Stalin has discussed some very important issues in this book, which are new problems of political economics, seen in the course of building socialism. This does not mean that Stalin was successful in understanding all the new problems practically in the building of socialism. He could not correctly understand the relations of production and antagonistic contradictions between two classes under socialism, and between the superstructure and economic foundation. In spite of this, his understanding of those problems of the political economy of socialism in the field of Marxist political economy is incomparable. Therefore, as Mao said previously, Stalin's book is a "great work", the "encyclopedia of Marxism-Leninism" and the "synthesis of experience of one hundred years of the world communist movement".

In spite of some weaknesses in this book, it is the fundamental basis of Mao's thinking on the character of economic laws, commodity production, the law of value, the distinction between the town and the countryside, mental and physical labour, relations between forces of production, and the distribution under socialism. It is the fundamental basis of the *Shanghai Text-book of Political Economy* on the political economics of socialism. Although, Mao and the team of editors of that book have not mentioned Stalin's book as the main theoretical basis of their thinking.

Mao's contribution in the field of political economics is a different topic. It is necessary to talk about the contribution of Mao in that field so that confusion may not arise in the course of the analysis made by Mao on the *Economic Problems of Socialism in the USSR* by Stalin. Mao has further developed the thinking that Stalin has expressed in the *Economic Problems of Socialism in the USSR*, especially under socialism to the characteristics of economic laws, commodity production, law of value, differences between town and countryside, mental and physical labour, and the relation between productive forces and the relations of production. Not only this, having understood antagonistic classes under socialism, i.e. the proletarian class and the capitalist class and antagonistic contradictions between them and the relation between superstructure and economic base, which Stalin did not understand. Mao analysed them scientifically, basing himself on Leninism, and he explained the contradictions between industry and agriculture under socialism, contradictions among different branches of industry, contradictions between small-scale production system and the socialist form of production, contradictions among different forms of exchange and so on under socialism. Basing himself on the thought of Lenin and Stalin and taking lessons from the experience of the building of socialism and the counter-revolution in the USSR, and Yugoslavia Mao Tse-tung developed the Marxist thinking on the political economy of socialism. So, it is not possible to get full knowledge of the political economics of socialism without Mao Tse-tung Thought.

1. Economic Laws Under Socialism

Stalin wrote about the nature of economic laws under socialism in the first chapter of *Economic Problems of Socialism in the USSR*. In the then Soviet Union, some people had wrong ideas about the nature of economic laws of socialism. Especially, they denied the objective character of laws of political economics. They did not believe that those laws were objective and thought that Soviet power and its leaders could make new laws by ordinance or declaration and with the annulment of the existing laws of political economics, if they wished. In that book, criticizing the wrong thinking of this type, Stalin presents the Marxist-Leninist point of view clearly. Stalin says:

> Marxism regards laws of science–whether they be laws of natural science or laws of political economy–as the reflection of objective processes which take place independently of the will of man. Man may discover these laws, get to know them, study them, reckon with them in his activities and utilize them in the interests of society, but he cannot change or abolish them. Still less can he form or create new laws of science. – J. V. Stalin, *Economic Problems of Socialism in the USSR,* Foreign Language Press, Peking, 1972, p. 2
>
> The same must be said of the laws of economic development, the laws of political economy–whether in the period of capitalism or in the period of socialism. Here, too, the laws of economic development, as in the case of natural science, are objective laws, reflecting the process of economic development which takes place independently of the will of man. Man may discover these laws, get to know them and, relying on them, use them in the interests of society, impart a different direction to the destructive action of some of the laws, restrict their sphere of action, and allow fuller scope to other laws that are forcing their way to the forefront; but he cannot destroy them or create new economic laws.
>
> One of the distinguishing features of political economy is that its laws, unlike those of natural science, are impermanent, that they, or at least the majority of them, operate for a definite historical period, after which they give place to new laws. However, these laws are not abolished, but lose their validity owing to the new economic conditions and depart from the scene in order to give place to new laws, laws which are not created by the will of man, but which arise from the new economic conditions." –Ibid., pp. 3-4.

Presenting his comments on Stalin's view on the nature of economic laws, Mao Tse-tung said: "Grasping the laws, but without proposing a method." –Mao Tse-tung, "Critique of Stalin's Economic Problems of Socialism in the USSR", *A Critique of Soviet Economics*, Progressive Publications, New Delhi, 1982, p. 136.

Further, he writes:

> In Chapter 1 he says only a few things about objective laws and how to go about planning the economy, without unfolding his ideas; or it may be that to his mind Soviet planning of the economy already reflected objective governing principles. ... In Chapter 1: he suggested the objective governing principles, but he failed to provide satisfactory answers. –Mao Tse-tung, "Concerning Economic Problems of Socialism in the USSR, November 1958", *A Critique of Soviet Economics*, pp. 129-130.

However, it is marked after deep study that the things Mao has indicated to be lacking are not completely absent. They are present there only in brief or in clues. The doubt Mao has raised above by saying that Stalin's thinking might be that "Soviet planning of the economy already reflected objective governing principles," is not correct. Stalin's statement below is a good answer to Mao's review. As he says:

> It is said that the necessity for balanced (proportionate) development of the national economy in our country enables the Soviet government to abolish existing economic laws and to create new ones. That is absolutely untrue. Our yearly and five-yearly plans must not be confused with the objective economic law of balanced, proportionate development of the national economy. The law of balanced development of the national economy arose in opposition to the law of competition and anarchy of production under capitalism. It arose from the socialization of the means of production, after the law of competition and anarchy of production had lost its validity. It became operative because a socialist economy can be conducted only on the basis of the economic law of balanced development of the national economy. That means that law of balanced development of the national economy makes it *possible* for our planning bodies to plan social production correctly. But *possibility* must not be confused with *actuality*. They are two different things. In order to turn the possibility into actuality, it is necessary to study this economic law, to master it, to learn to apply it with full understanding, and to compile such plans as fully reflect the requirements of this law. It cannot be said that the requirements of this economic law are fully reflected by our yearly and five-yearly plans. –J. V. Stalin, *Economic Problems of Socialism in the USSR*, Foreign Language Press, Peking, 1972, p. 7.

Mao himself said in one place: Even Stalin said that the plans of the Soviet Union could not be regarded as already fully reflecting what the laws demanded. –Mao Tse-tung, "Reading Notes on the Soviet Text Political Economy, 1961-1962", *A Critique of Soviet Economics*, p. 76.

It is puzzling how Mao wrote two different and contradictory things on the same topic on two separate occasions.

In the course of commenting on the economic laws under socialism, Mao has said that Stalin "did not lay enough emphasis on the light industry and agriculture, they did not point out the main aspect of the contradictions in the relationships among departments of heavy industry. They exaggerated the importance of heavy industry, claiming that steel was the foundation, machinery the heart and soul" –Ibid., pp. 129-30.

This comment of Mao will be discussed in detail in another sub-topic somewhere else. Basically supporting Stalin's view on economic law, Mao criticizes two points:

> First, the conscious activity of the party and the masses is not sufficiently brought out; second, it is not comprehensive enough in that it fails to explain that what makes government decrees correct is not only that they emerge from the will of the working class but also the fact that they faithfully reflect the imperatives of objective economic laws.–Mao Tse-tung, "Critique of Stalin's Economic Problems of Socialism in the USSR", *A Critique of Soviet Economics*, p. 136.

Mao's quoted statement makes it clear that Stalin has talked on conscious activities of the party and people. His disagreement with Stalin is on not discussing these topics sufficiently. So far as the fact of not throwing light sufficiently is concerned, that cannot be at all a cause of criticism. At that time the thinking that economic laws can be "transformed" or "abolished" in the Soviet Union was strong. At that stage, it was needed to emphasize especially the objective character of the economic laws and Stalin did just that. We have the world famous philosophical works by Mao *On Practice*. Some claim that Mao neglected theory. It will be wrong to say that Mao neglected theory on the basis of the topic and content of that work that emphasizes practice. The reality is that this writing is a great work throwing light on the dialectical relation between theory and practice. At that time, dogmatism was rooted within the CPC. Dogmatists emphasized isolating the Marxist-Leninist principles from the revolutionary practice. In that situation, it was needed to emphasize practice. Because of this, Mao chose the topic. Likewise, so many articles are written according to the need at a particular time with an emphasis on a particular content. Such type of articles may not touch all aspects or may not throw sufficient light on many aspects. Therefore, criticizing Stalin by raising the question of sufficient light not thrown on the role of a conscious aspect is not correct.

The other point noted by Mao in his comment on Stalin is related to economic laws; Mao says orders of government are correct not simply because they are the outcome of the working class will, but also by the dint of reflecting reliably the needs of the objective economic laws.

The two elements of government orders that Mao talked on are correct. Orders issued by the government in a proletarian state are correct only if they represent working class will and the needs of the objective economic laws. In Stalin's quoted statement about government, these two elements are not present. But to reach a conclusion on that basis, as done by Mao, is wrong. From the above quoted statement, it is clear that Stalin, just as Mao, also believed that government of the laws are correct not reliably simply because they come out of the will of the working class, but by the dint of representing the needs of the objective economic laws. The government orders that Stalin has talked above are not the ones that reliably reflect the needs of the objective economic laws. At that time, some people in the Soviet Union rejected the objective aspect of economic laws. Stalin's statement came in the light of Soviet power and leaders reversing the objective economic laws of socialism and making laws subjectively to fulfil the demands of some people. The laws mentioned by Mao cannot be included in the laws made by the government in that particular context and manner. Another statement made by Stalin clarifies this confusion:

> Some comrades deny the objective character of laws of science, and of laws of political economy particularly, under socialism. They deny that the laws of political economy reflect law-governed processes which operate independently of the will of man. They believe that in view of the specific role assigned to the Soviet state by history, the Soviet state and its leaders can abolish existing laws of political economy and can "form", "create", new laws.

On one occasion, Stalin said that: "Leaving aside astronomical, geological and other similar processes, which man really is powerless to influence, even if he has come to know the laws of their development, in many other cases man is very far from powerless, in the sense of being able to influence the process of nature." –J. V. Stalin, *Economic Problems of Socialism in the USSR*, Foreign Language Press, Peking, 1972, p. 2.

Declaring Stalin's saying to be wrong, Mao writes: "This argument is wrong. Human knowledge and the capability to transform nature have no limit. Stalin did not consider these matters developmentally. What cannot now be done, may be done in the future" –Mao Tse-tung, *A Critique of Soviet Economics*, p. 137.

Here Stalin has raised the issue of control over astronomy, geology, etc., not related to the future, but only to the present . His statement certainly does not mean that there can be no control of nature by man in the future too. From the whole thinking expressed by him under the above sub-topic related to the laws of nature and the activities of natural forces and the knowledge of man, can it be said that Stalin never had the thought of not having control over those fields and processes? This becomes quite clear from the study of the book that, just as Mao, Stalin also understood the issue of knowledge and the transformation of nature related to the process of development in incessant form itself. But, there is some confusion as he presented this view only in relation to the present. Mao's criticism of Stalin with reference to those fields and processes presented as his thinking on the whole, i.e. even in the future is not correct. Further lines clarify Stalin's position on this subject:

> In many other cases man is very far from powerless, in the sense of being able to influence the process of nature. In all such cases, having come to know the laws of nature, reckoning with them and relying on them, and

> intelligently applying and utilizing them, men can restrict their sphere of action, and can impart a different direction to the destructive forces of nature and convert them to the use of society.
>
> To take one of numerous examples. In olden times the overflow of big rivers, floods, and the resulting destruction of homes and crops, was considered an unavoidable calamity, against which man was powerless. ... The action of the destructive forces of water and of utilizing them in the interests of society takes place without any violation, alteration or abolition of scientific laws or the creation of new scientific laws. On the contrary, this procedure is effected in precise conformity with the laws of nature and the laws of science, since any violation, even the slightest, of the laws of nature would only upset matters and render the procedure futile.

2. Commodity Production Under Socialism

At that time, some people in the Soviet Union believed that the party had made a mistake by not ending the production of commodity even after the party had assumed power and the instruments and the means of production were nationalized. According to them, after the revolution the production of commodities should have immediately ended. This type of thinking was not correct. Immediately after the proletarian revolution, Lenin declared that the production of commodities should be allowed in socialism too. He said that production of commodities should be kept in existence as a need at that time in Russia existing small and middle scale production system to develop them in a collective farming system gradually and to make modern technical base of production available to collective farming for large-scale production and to establish an economic relation between the town and countryside and between industry and agriculture. In the course of discussion, Stalin not only defended and re-established the thinking of Lenin, he developed it to a new height. In the discussion held about 35 years after the revolution on whether the production of commodities should be continued under socialism or not, Stalin emphasized that the production of commodities should be allowed. Presenting the objective reasons for the production of commodities under socialism he said:

> Today there are basic forms of socialist production in our country: state, or public-owned production, and collective farm production, which cannot be said to be publicly owned. In the state enterprises, the means of production and the product of production are national property. In the collective farm, although the means of production (land, machines) do belong to the state, the product of production is the property of the different collective farms, since the labour, as well as the seed, is their own, while the land, which has been turned over to the collective farms in perpetual tenure, is used by them virtually as their own property, in spite of the fact that they cannot sell, buy, lease or mortgage it.

> The effect of this is that the state disposes only of the products of the state enterprises, while the products of the collective farms, being their property, is disposed of only by them. But the collective farms are unwilling to alienate their products except in the form of commodities, in exchange for which they desire to receive the commodities they need. At present, the collective farms will not recognize any other economic relations with the town except the commodity relation–exchange through purchase and sale. Because of this, commodity production and trade are as much a necessity with us today as they were, say, thirty years ago, when Lenin spoke of the necessity of developing trade to the utmost. –J. V. Stalin, *Economic Problems of Socialism in the USSR*, Foreign Language Press, Peking, 1972, p. 15.

Basically agreeing with Stalin about commodity production, Mao expresses some of his differences like this:

> Commodity Production Under Socialism, Stalin has not comprehensively set forth the conditions for the existence of commodities. The existence of two kinds of ownership is the main premise for commodity production. But ultimately commodity production is also related to the productive forces. For this reason, even under completely socialized public ownership, commodity exchange will still have to be operative in some areas.–Mao Tse-tung, *A Critique of Soviet Economics*, p. 140.

So, Mao's disagreement with Stalin about the main premise for commodity production is not correct. The above explanation by Stalin on the main premise for commodity production fully complies with Leninism. Expressing Lenin's thought in his own language, Stalin writes:

> In order to ensure an economic bond between town and country, between industry and agriculture, commodity production (exchange through purchase and sale) should be preserved for a certain period, it being the form of economic ties with the town which is *alone acceptable* to the peasants, and Soviet trade–state, cooperative, and collective farm–should be developed to the full and the capitalists of all types and descriptions ousted from trading activity. –J. V. Stalin, *Economic Problems of Socialism in the USSR*, Foreign Language Press, Peking, 1972, p. 13.

Mao himself has said, "On commodity production we still have to take from Stalin, who in turn, got it from Lenin". In his works, Mao supports Lenin's thinking in relation to commodity production given by Stalin. What these things make clear is that Mao takes the thinking of Stalin related to commodity production as based on Lenin's thinking. But, it is an irony that he has criticized only Stalin and not Lenin, saying that he did not present the necessary situation for the existence of commodity production in detail. Stalin writes on a statement of Engels about this subject matter:

> Engels has in mind countries where capitalism and the concentration of production have advanced far enough both in industry and in agriculture to permit the expropriation of *all* the means of production in the country and

> their conversion into public property. Engels, consequently, considers that in *such* countries, parallel with the socialization of *all* the means of production, commodity production should be put an end to. And that, of course, is correct. –Ibid., p. 10.

It must be remembered that Mao has said, "Stalin's analysis of Engels' formulae is correct."–Mao Tse-tung, *A Critique of Soviet Economics*, p. 140. No third cause is presented to be necessary for the continuation of commodity production in the above formulae of Engels that is analysed by Stalin. Mao's saying that commodity production is linked with the productive forces, is true. Just because it is not discussed in that very way, it is wrong to think that Stalin did not understand the importance of the productive forces. Mao has raised a new idea that exchange remains active in some fields even under the socialized public ownership. It is a good thing to discuss. He has not explained this himself. But, this is mentioned in the works of Stalin, Engels and Lenin. The main argument of people who pleaded that commodity production has been abolished in the Soviet Union at that time was that if commodity production was kept in existence, it would restore capitalism in the country. Stalin rejects it:

> It is said that commodity production must lead, is bound to lead, to capitalism all the same, under all conditions. That is not true. Not always and not under all conditions! Commodity production must not be identified with capitalist production. They are two different things. Capitalist production is the highest form of commodity production. Commodity production leads to capitalism only *if* there is private ownership of the means of production, *if* labour power appears in the market as a commodity which can be bought by the capitalist and exploited in the process of production, and *if*, consequently, the system of exploitation of wage workers by capitalists exists in the country. Capitalist production begins when the means of production are concentrated in private hands, and when the workers are bereft of the means of production and are compelled to sell their labour power as a commodity. Without this there is no such thing as capitalist production.
>
> Well, and what is to be done if the conditions for the conversion of commodity production into capitalist production do not exist, if the means of production are no longer private but socialist property, if the system of wage labour no longer exists and labour power is no longer a commodity, and if the system of exploitation has long been abolished–it can be considered then that commodity production will lead to capitalism all the same? No, it cannot. Yet ours is precisely such a society, a society where private ownership of the means of production, the system of wage labour, and the system of exploitation have long ceased to exist.
>
> Commodity production must not be regarded as something sufficient unto itself, something independent of the surrounding economic conditions.

> Commodity production is older than capitalist production. It existed in slave-owning society, and served it, but did not lead to capitalism. It existed in feudal society and served it, yet, although it prepared some of the conditions for capitalist production, it did not lead to capitalism. Why then, one asks, cannot commodity production similarly serve our socialist society for a certain period without leading to capitalism, bearing in mind that in our country commodity production is not so boundless and all embracing as it is under capitalist conditions, being confined within strict bounds thanks to such decisive economic conditions as social ownership of the means of production, the abolition of the system of wage labour, and the elimination of the system of exploitation? –J. V. Stalin, *Economic Problems of Socialism in the USSR*, Foreign Language Press, Peking, 1972, pp. 13-14.

Mao has fully supported the above analysis by Stalin, though he has termed Stalin's analysis of commodity production as "a little exaggerated." However, Mao's interpretation of "a little exaggerated" in regard to Stalin's analysis is not correct. Actually Mao also has not gone out of that framework:

> In a capitalist context it is capitalist commodity production. In a socialist context it is socialist commodity production. Commodity production has existed since ancient times. ... The thing that determines commodity production is the surrounding economic conditions. The question is, can commodity production be regarded as a useful instrument for furthering socialist production? I think commodity production will serve socialism quite tamely.–Mao Tse-tung, *A Critique of Soviet Economics*, p. 144.

This saying can be taken as the summary of what Stalin has said above. It was necessary to talk in some detail on the issue in the light of the voices forcefully raised against the existence of commodity production in the Soviet Union. The thinking could not be adequately refuted, putting it as briefly as Mao did. Therefore, the criticism of "a little exaggeration" against Stalin's analysis on commodity production under socialism is not correct. Stalin has not only written on the compulsion of commodity production under socialism, he has explained it further. On the one hand, he has criticized the thinking of those who tried to banish commodity production under socialism subjectively, on the other, he has also pointed out the existence of commodity production under socialism as an obstruction to go ahead to communism. Referring to production relations appearing as obstruction to the further development of productive forces, he writes:

> The task of the directing bodies is therefore promptly to discern incipient contradictions, and to take timely measures to resolve them by adapting the relations of production to the growth of the productive forces. This, above all, concerns such economic factors as group, or collective farm, property and commodity circulation. At present, of course, these factors are being successfully utilized by us for the promotion of the socialist economy,

> and they are of undeniable benefit to our society. It is undeniable, too, that they will be of benefit also in the near future. But it would be unpardonable blindness not to see at the same time that these factors are already beginning to hamper the powerful development of our productive forces, since they create obstacles to the full extension of government planning to the whole of the national economy, especially agriculture. There is no doubt that these factors will hamper the continued growth of the productive forces of our country more and more as time goes on. The task, therefore, is to eliminate these contradictions by gradually converting collective farm property into public property, and by introducing–also gradually–products-exchange in place of commodity circulation. –J. V. Stalin, *Economic Problems of Socialism in the USSR*, Foreign Language Press, Peking, 1972, pp. 69-70.

The concept of the contradiction between the existence of commodity production under socialism and the essential solution of that to lead to communism is a new extension added to the field of Marxist-Leninist political economy by Stalin.

3. Law of Value Under Socialism

Stalin says:

> Wherever commodities and commodity production exist, there the law of value must also exist. ... The law of value extends, first of all, to commodity circulation, to the exchange of commodities through purchase and sale, the exchange, chiefly, of articles of personal consumption. Here, in this sphere, the law of value preserves, within certain limits, of course, the function of a regulator.
>
> But the operation of the law of value is not confined to the sphere of commodity circulation. It also extends to production. True, the law of value has no regulating function in our socialist production, but it nevertheless influences production, and this fact cannot be ignored when directing production. As a matter of fact, consumer goods, which are needed to compensate the labour power expended in the process of production, are produced and realized in our country as commodities coming under the operation of the law of value. It is precisely here that the law of value exercises its influence on production. In this connection, such things as cost accounting and profitableness, production costs, prices, etc., are of actual importance in our enterprises. Consequently, our enterprises cannot, and must not, function without taking the law of value into account. –Ibid., pp. 18-19.

The issue of understanding the law of value has a great importance under socialism. Even a slight negligence of the law of value will shake the whole economy. Even under socialism, it is necessary to regulate production on logical grounds, to maintain discipline in production, to link outcome of the production rightly and understand the actual production rightly, to find out things implied indirectly in production and consume them, to improve the production system to cut investment cost, to estimate investment, and regulate one's industry in profit. We cannot escape from this historical need. To escape from these problems is to orient socialism (under formation period) towards defeat. For this, the law of value should be thanked as it improves the efficiency of administrators of socialist countries and makes them capable leaders for socialist production. Stalin too says that the law of value is a "competent practical school", but all these things cannot be accomplished simply by accepting the law of value. After the existence of value is accepted, the main objective is to understand its value rightly, and to study it with a proper attention in one's organization. If it is not understood adequately, it cannot manage properly with mobilizing production rightly, setting the right quantity of production, improving the process of production, cutting investment costs, running industry on profit and fixing right value. Its meaning should not be taken as the working procedure of the law of value. Stalin says further:

> The law of value can be a regulator of production only under capitalism, with private ownership of the means of production, and competition, anarchy of production, and crises of overproduction ... in our country the sphere of operation of the law of value is limited by the social ownership of the means of production, and by the law of balanced development of the national economy, and is consequently also limited by our yearly and five-yearly plans, which are an approximate reflection of the requirements of this law. –Ibid., p. 23.

On another occasion, he says:

> Actually, the sphere of operation of the law of value under our economic system is strictly limited and placed within definite bounds. It has already been said that the sphere of commodity production is restricted and placed within definite bounds by our system. The same must be said of the sphere of operation of the law of value. Undoubtedly, the fact that private ownership of the means of production does not exist, and that the means of production both in town and country are socialized, cannot but restrict the sphere of operation of the law of value and the extent of its influence on production. –Ibid., p. 21.

In his comment, Mao does not have a different view on the law of value from that of Stalin. On one occasion, linking politics with a plan in production, he mentioned it as a regulating element. This is not an issue of difference of opinion. There can be no proletarian plan in the absence of proletarian politics. Not to mention a regulating factor does not mean that Stalin neglected the importance of proletarian politics.

Mao has also mentioned only the plan in the form of the determinant element under socialism, for example, he writes: "In our society the law of value has no regulative function, that is, has no determinative function. Planning determines production, e.g. for hogs or steel we do not use the law of value; we rely on planning. –Mao Tse-tung, *A Critique of Soviet Economics*, p. 147.

Actually, Stalin has not mentioned only the plan in the form of the determinant element under socialism. He mentions two other factors that are really important in relation to the law of value. The first is the division of labour in different sections of production under socialism. It is not done under socialism on a "proportional" law of value. The control of value in this issue means to engage workers in industries that give profit and not to engage workers that give no profit or show loss. The division of labour in different sections of production is controlled by the state, and not by the law of value. In a proletarian state, such things are not allowed at all. In different sections of production under socialism, the division of labour is to be regulated by the state, not by the law of value.

Stalin has repudiated the thinking that the law of value can be applicable as a permanent law at all stages of historical development:

> It is said that the law of value is a permanent law, binding upon all periods of historical development, and that if it does lose its function as a regulator of exchange relations in the second phase of communist society, it retains at this phase of development its function as a regulator of the relations between the various branches of production, as a regulator of the distribution of labour among them.
>
> That is quite untrue. Value, like the law of value, is a historical category connected with the existence of commodity production. With the disappearance of commodity production, value and its forms and the law of value also disappear.

4. Antithesis Between Town and Country and Mental and Physical Labour

The proletarian revolution in the Soviet Union brought an end to the economic bases of hostile contradictions between town and country and between industry and agriculture in capitalism, i.e. exploitation of countryside by the town through business, loans, and the destruction of peasants in the countryside, and the population as a whole. In the course of destroying the bases of exploitation of peasants and the countryside, under socialism, peasants were given assistance to root out landlords, and they were provided with tractors for collective farming. It is how the gap between the town and the countryside was abolishing and, as a result, the contradiction between industry and agriculture was abolished under socialism.

It is equally true also about the contradiction between mental and physical labour. After the proletarian revolution in the Soviet Union, the economic bases of discrimination between mental and physical labour under capitalism, i.e. exploitation of physical workers by mental workers was abolished. Here, Stalin's main concern is not the differences between town and countryside and mental and physical labour, but the problem of differences between the town and countryside, and mental and physical labour existing in socialist society. For the world proletarian class, and especially for the proletarian class of the Soviet Union, this was a quite serious problem and immediate corrective steps were necessary. This was a problem of a type that socialist construction of the Soviet Union raised practically. As Stalin has said that: "This problem was not discussed in the Marxist classics. It is a new problem, one that has been raised practically by our socialist construction." –J. V. Stalin, *Economic Problems of Socialism in the USSR*, Foreign Language Press, Peking, 1972, p. 27.

In that condition, the question of a solution to the above problem, especially for the proletarian class of the Soviet Union, was a serious challenge. Having given theoretical and practical contributions for the solution to this new problem, Stalin developed Marxism-Leninism. After the proletarian revolution and establishment of the socialist society, the economic bases of difference between town and countryside and between mental and physical labour will exist here and there or differences of a new type will appear in the course of practice. Stalin has indicated two types of causes which bring forward differences under socialism between town and countryside and industry and agriculture. Firstly, the difference of labour between industry. He has said that differences caused by this situation cannot be wiped out in a short period. Secondly, in industry production relation and ownership of production acquire public form, whereas in agriculture the ownership is not public, but the form of collective farming. Stalin considers the second to be the main and major cause of difference. Stalin noticed the difference between mental and physical labour present under socialism and concluded that the development was not achieved to the expected extent in industry. He has suggested two causes also for differences of two types. The first is the difference caused by the management authorities and the working situation of workers. According to him, the difference caused by this situation cannot be wiped out in a short period. The second is the difference seen because of the distinction in cultural and technical standards. Stalin has said that this difference can be removed by raising the cultural and technical standard of workers to the standard of technical authorities. Here the situation that Stalin has discussed is about working situations and differences caused by them, which are very important. Under socialism as well, working situations of industries are not the same. Working situations in different sections of industry are not the same. Differences remain in the working situation of different branches of agriculture as well. Differences exist in the working situation of mental and physical labour. Likewise, differences exist in the working situations of different sections of mental labour. Differences continue in working situations in different sections of physical labour. Even after the cultural and technical standard of workers is raised to technical expertise, i.e. even in the second stage of socialism, there exist certain differences (however secondary they might be) caused because of the differences in working situations.

5. Relation Between Productive Forces and Relations of Production Under Socialism

At that time, non-Marxist-Leninist thinking arose on the question of relations between the productive forces and the relations of production under socialism in the Soviet Union. Regarding that, the thinking of L. D. Yaroshenko on the above question is remarkable. He believed that under socialism relations of production would become part of the organization of productive forces. For example, he says:

> The chief problem of the *Political Economy of Socialism*, therefore, is *not* to investigate the relations of production of the members of socialist society; *it is* to elaborate and develop a scientific theory of the organization of the productive forces in social production, a theory of the planning of economic development.
>
> Disputes as to the role of any particular category of socialist political economy–value, commodity, money, credit, etc.,–which very often with us are of a scholastic character, *are replaced* by a healthy discussion of the rational organization of the productive forces in social production, by a scientific demonstration of the validity of such organization.
>
> Under socialism, the basic struggle for the building of a communist society reduces itself to a struggle for the proper organization of the productive forces and their rational utilization in social production. ... Communism is the highest scientific organization of the productive forces in social production.–Taken From Stalin's book above, pp. 61-62.

In relation to Yaroshenko's chief error in the above statement, Stalin says:

> Comrade Yaroshenko's chief error is that he forsakes the Marxist position on the question of the role of the productive forces and of the relations of production in the development of society, that he inordinately overrates the role of the productive forces, and just as inordinately underrates the role of

> the relations of production, and ends up by declaring that under socialism the relations of production are a component part of the productive forces. –J. V. Stalin, *Economic Problems of Socialism in the USSR*, Foreign Language Press, Peking, 1972, p. 60.

The thinking of Yaroshenko on the productive forces and relations of production under socialism represent a quite dangerous revisionist theory of productive forces in the history of the international communist movement. Stalin has refuted this wrong thinking from a high theoretical ground and he has guided Marxist-Leninists of the whole world to refute the revisionist theory of productive forces. Yaroshenko's thinking is wrong on four issues. The first issue is the economic base of political economy. What becomes clear from the above statement is that he does not observe relations of production in political economy at all. According to him, it is the study of productive forces that is the main content of the study of the political economy of socialism. Quoting Marx, Stalin says:

> In the social production of their life (that is, in the production of the material values necessary to the life of men–J. Stalin), men enter into definite relations that are indispensable and independent of their will, relations of production which correspond to a definite stage of development of their material productive forces. The sum total of these relations of production constitutes the economic structure of society, the real foundation, on which rises a legal and political superstructure and to which correspond definite forms of social consciousness. –Karl Marx, Preface to *A Contribution to the Critique of Political Economy.*
>
> This means that every social formation, socialist society not excluded, has its economic foundation, consisting of the sum total of men's relations of production." –J. V. Stalin, *Economic Problems of Socialism in the USSR*, Foreign Language Press, Peking, 1972, pp. 65-66.

Yaroshenko's above line under socialism about the relations of production as the organ of productive forces presents socialism as a system without an economic base, which is incorrect.

The second is the main subject matter of political economy in socialism. Yaroshenko's observation means he treats the productive forces as the main problem of political economy of socialism. Stalin describes Yaroshenko's thinking as the "political economy without economic problems."

A well known fact is that the main content of the study of political economy is not of things, but to study relations among men and finally relations among classes. Stalin defended this Marxist-Leninist principle firmly. What Stalin made clear analytically is that the above tenet of Marxism-Leninism is true regarding other systems as well as about socialism. He explained that two aspects of social production are also present in socialism as well. One is the relations of man with nature (productive forces) and the other is inter-personal relations of man with other men in the process of production. In that situation also the main problems of political economics of socialism are the relations of the production itself. The meaning of separating relations of production from the content of political economics of socialism is to separate ownership from the instruments and the means of production, the position of people in production and the distribution of production from the study of political economics. This was what Yaroshenko tried his best to do and what the CPSU under the leadership of Stalin foiled at that time.

The third issue is of contradiction between productive forces and relations of production under socialism. The above quotes clarify that Yaroshenko believes that there is no situation of contradiction between the productive forces and relations of production under socialism. He limits contradiction between these two aspects only unto capitalism. Criticizing Yaroshenko's thinking, Stalin writes:

> Comrade Yaroshenko is mistaken when he asserts that there is no contradiction between the relations of production and the productive forces of society under socialism. Of course, our present relations of production are in a period when they fully conform to the growth of the productive forces and help to advance them at seven-league strides. But it would be wrong to rest easy at that and to think that there are no contradictions between our productive forces and the relations of production. There certainly are, and will be, contradictions, seeing that the development of the relations of production lags, and will lag, behind the development of the productive forces. Given a correct policy on the part of the directing bodies, these contradictions cannot grow into antagonisms, and there is no chance of matters coming to a conflict between the relations of production and the productive forces of society. It would be a different matter if we were to conduct a wrong policy, such as that which Comrade Yaroshenko recommends. In that case conflict would be inevitable, and our relations of production might become a serious brake on the further development of the productive forces. –Ibid., p. 69.

The fourth issue is the transition from socialism to communism. Yaroshenko maintains struggle for the formation of a socialist society is the rational organization of forces of production under socialism and their wise utilization in the social production. Stalin thinks his concept as a great confusion and proof of his lack of understanding of the law of economic development of socialism, suggesting the path to communism from socialism to be as easy as indicated by Yaroshenko. He clearly writes "at least three main preliminary conditions" have to be fulfilled to pave the way for transition to communism:

> It is necessary, in the first place, to ensure, not a mythical "rational organization" of the productive forces, but a continuous expansion of all social production, with a relatively higher rate of expansion of the production of the means of production. The relatively higher rate of expansion of production of the means of production is necessary not only because it has to provide the equipment both for its own plants and for all the other branches of the national economy, but also because reproduction on an extended scale becomes altogether impossible without it.
>
> It is necessary, in the second place, by means of gradual transitions carried out to the advantage of the collective farms, and, hence, of all society, to raise collective farm property to the level of public property, and, also by means of gradual transitions, to replace commodity circulation by a system of product-exchange, under which the central government, or some other social-economic centre, might control the whole product of social production in the interests of society.
>
> It is necessary, in the third place, to ensure such a cultural advancement of society as will secure for all members of society the all-round development of their physical and mental abilities, so that the members of society may be in a position to receive an education sufficient to enable them to be active agents of social development, and in a position freely to choose their occupations and not be tied all their lives, owing to the existing division of labour, to some one occupation. – Ibid., pp. 68-70.

Stalin has also suggested some processes to fulfil the above three conditions for the transition into communism. The three conditions as discussed above by Stalin for transition into communism are the touchstones.

Kathmandu, Nepal
April 1995

Part VIII

Serious Accusation and Serious Situation

The Committee of the Revolutionary Internationalist Movement (CoRIM) has said that serious accusations have been levelled within the Revolutionary Internationalist Movement (RIM), creating a serious situation in the current international communist movement. It is correct that grave accusations have been levelled within the RIM. The questions arise–who is responsible for those serious accusations? And who is responsible to create this situation? There is a fundamental difference between the analysis made by the CoRIM and the Communist Party of Nepal (Mashal) (CPN (Mashal)). According to the CoRIM, the CPN (Mashal) has made serious accusations against the CoRIM and Mao, creating a serious situation within the RIM. In the analysis of the CPN (Mashal), the Revolutionary Communist Party, USA(RCP, USA) made serious accusations against Marx, Engels, Lenin, Stalin and Mao and condemned certain turns in the glorious history of the communist movement, creating a drive in the international communist movement that could lead towards a non-Marxist-Leninist direction.

The CoRIM finds fault with the CPN (Mashal) mainly on these issues:

1. Evaluation of the Contribution of Mao Tse-tung

The CPN (Mashal) accepts the analysis and evaluations of Mao by the Communist Party of China (CPC) during the leadership of Mao himself. It accepts the contributions of Mao in the form of Mao Tse-tung

Thought. However, a new analysis has been put forward in the international communist movement a few years after the demise of Mao Tse-tung. The Communist Party of Peru (PCP) under the leadership of Comrade Gonzalo claimed the contributions of Mao to be the same as the contributions of Lenin in terms of representing a new qualitative stage in the development of Marxism, and called it a new stage, that is, 'Maoism'. So, a controversy began in the RIM based on the established recognition in relation to contributions of Mao (Mao Tse-tung Thought). Having led the issue of Maoism, the RCP, USA along with some other parties and organizations within the RIM went ahead lately towards recognizing this new analysis in relation to the contributions of Mao. In spite of the recognition of Mao Tse-tung Thought by the Second International Conference (1984); the CoRIM was successful in establishing Maoism as a theoretical foundation.

The decision of the CoRIM and the PCP, along with some other parties and organizations to bring forward Mao's contributions in the form of Maoism and to replace Marxism-Leninism-Mao Tse-tung Thought established in the form of guiding principles in the international communist movement is wrong. Mao is a great Marxist-Leninist. His contributions to international communist movement in theoretical and practical fields are things in the Leninist era, i.e. the era of imperialism and proletarian revolution. Certainly, Mao has developed Lenin's theory, strategy and tactics, which were just in embryo. He has enriched Marxism-Leninism in the course of the struggle against imperialism, feudalism, comprador and bureaucratic capitalism, modern revisionism, and wrong thinking and trend seen within the party. However, having made this objective reality as the base, to put the contributions of Mao on an equal footing with the contributions of Lenin is completely non-objective. Because the thought of Lenin represents a specifically different world situation–imperialist–from the competitive capitalist world situation of Marx and Engels, while Mao's thinking does not represent any new world situation specifically different from that of Lenin.

The thinking and contributions of Mao come under the world situation of Lenin's era. This means that contributions of Mao are contributions under the Leninist theory, strategy and tactics, and they are related to the development of science to the solution of particular problems of revolution. Certainly, the struggle against imperialism, reactionaries and revisionism, the formation of a socialist system and leading the revolution ahead and making it successful in oppressed countries would not be possible without the guidance of Mao Tse-tung Thought. But the situation equally verifies that the contributions of Mao do not represent the third stage of Maoism in the development of Marxism-Leninism.

Such an extremist view in relation to the contribution of Mao is not new in the international communist movement. In the life of Mao himself, the conspirator Lin Piao and his clique in the CPC had presented Mao Tse-tung's Thought as: "Marxism-Leninism at its highest in the present era."–"Hail the Mass Publication of Chairman Mao's Works", *Chinese Literature*, No. 3, 1968, p. 11. The thinking of the PCP presents Maoism as "a new, third and superior stage", and adopting "Marxism-Leninism-Maoism, principally Maoism" to solve the problems of revolution at the present time and this type of thinking of other parties and organizations participating in the RIM comply with the above mentioned stale arguments of Lin Piao and his clique. It does not mean that the new analysis brought forward by the RIM and other parties and organizations is to kill the thought of Mao, as Lin Piao and his clique had plotted. They have brought it forward with good intentions, but as Lenin has explained, the validity of such a thinking is not proved only because of good intentions. The main thing is whether it is objective or not. If we forward our analysis with good intentions and it gives the wrong results, then we must be responsible for that. As the analysis stands on a non-objective ground and it is the product of subjective thinking, with whatever good intentions the presentation might have been brought forward, it is a fatal outcome appearing in the international communist movement.

The CPN (Mashal) has made it clear that the way Maoism is being explained and analysed pulls down Leninism from the position of being the Marxism of the era of imperialism and proletarian revolution. Any thinking to establish Maoism as the Marxism of the present era is completely wrong. The present world is under the era of imperialism and proletarian revolution and Leninism is the Marxism of this era as defined by Stalin, Mao and the declaration of RIM. Leninism is the guiding principle of the world proletariat and all oppressed classes and nations even today.

The CPN (Mashal) has been rejecting this proposal of Maoism by the CoRIM from the very beginning. For example, the proposal passed at the Extended Meeting of its Central Organizing Committee (COC) (September 17-19, 1992) says:

> Although Mao Tse-tung, a great Marxist-Leninist of Lenin's era, has contributed greatly in the fields of philosophy, political economy, scientific socialism, military science, party organization, united front and two-line struggle under the rubric of socialism and the revolution in colonial and semi (neo)-colonial countries are of great historical importance. However, we should clearly understand that the present era, as defined by Stalin is still an era of imperialism, socialist revolution, and Leninism. Although in Mao Tse-tung's Thought, the science of Marxism-Leninism has reached its

highest stage of development, it should not be taken as something outside the Lenin era but within it.

The Communist Party of Nepal (CPN (Mashal)) holds the view that the stand of the declaration is correct even today. The question of Maoism does not substantiate the characteristics of an era of Leninism as defined by Stalin. Instead, it distorts Mao Tse-tung Thought, devaluates Leninism, and deviates the world communist movement from the right track of Marxism-Leninism. Therefore, the extended meeting of the COC of the CPN (Mashal) unanimously decides to reject the proposal on Maoism by the Committee." –"On Maoism", A Resolution Adopted by the CPN (Mashal) held from September 17-19, 1992.

On the contributions of Mao and the thinking of Maoism of the CoRIM and other fraternal parties and organizations, the CoRIM has said that the position of the CPN (Mashal) on Maoism has "negated" or "denigrated" the contributions of Mao. Expressing its view forcefully, the CoRIM said that "negating or denigrating Mao's path-breaking contributions to our revolutionary science will prevent us from solving the difficult problems we face and worse, will guarantee revisionist rather that revolutionary solutions." Mao says that ideological and political line decides everything. So, we should grasp the gravity of Mao's contributions and then wage a struggle to justify why his contribution does not represent revolutionary science's third and the highest peak. CoRIM writes to CPN (Mashal):

On December 26, 1993 on the occasion of the Mao Tse-tung Centenary the Revolutionary Internationalist Movement took the historic step of adopting Marxism-Leninism-Maoism as its ideology. The decision was taken after a long and vigorous debate within RIM which had gone on over a number of years. In the course of these discussions your party has repeatedly and vociferously argued against this position of our Movement.

The dispute between RIM and the CPN (Mashal) is by no means limited to a question of terminology. The debate has revealed that the dispute over Marxism-Leninism-Maoism concentrates a whole series of political and ideological questions. These questions involve but are not limited to the applicability of Mao Tse-tung's teachings on the path of the protracted people's war in the oppressed countries, Mao's summation of the experience of building socialism in the Soviet Union, the lessons of the Great Proletarian Cultural Revolution and other vital questions.

Our Movement adopted the document long live Marxism-Leninism-Maoism! To serve, together with the Declaration of RIM as its ideological and political foundation. The opposition of CPN (Mashal) to this document and to this very ideology, has resulted in the untenable situation in which one of the participating parties of our movement has publicly rejected the very foundation of our movement."–Letter of the CoRIM to CPN (Mashal) August 21, 1996.

2. Evaluation of Stalin

The CPN (Mashal) takes the evaluation of Stalin made by the CPC under the leadership of Mao basically correct. But on one aspect of this evaluation, which is very important, the CPN (Mashal) has had a difference of opinion with Mao and the CPC and that perspective is the source of the mistakes of Stalin. Mao and the CPC think "metaphysics" to be the source of some mistakes, whereas the CPN (Mashal) has basically a different opinion regarding this. It looks at the type of mistakes and weaknesses of Stalin to be the natural outcome of the historical situations in the building of socialism in the Soviet Union under the then world situation, and not the outcome of "a fair amount of metaphysics". For example, the proposal passed by an Extended Meeting of the CPN (Mashal) says:

> The CPN (Mashal) fundamentally differs from a criticism made against Stalin by Chairman Mao. We hold the view that the main cause behind Stalin's mistake, i.e. Stalin's inability to grasp the nature of class struggle within socialism, was not due to a fair amount of metaphysics in him or his failure to apply dialectics in all spheres of life and his failure to analyse socialist society as pointed out by Mao, but it was due to a particular historical situation of the Soviet Union. –"On Maoism", A Resolution Adopted by the Communist Party of Nepal (Mashal) held from September 17-19, 1992.

The CoRIM is not prepared to accept this. For example, in the above *Message*, CoRIM has presented this view explicitly in this way:

> While upholding Stalin's contributions in the historical experience of the dictatorship of the proletariat and against the revisionist slanders launched at Stalin by Khrushchev, Mao made serious criticism of Stalin's metaphysics. Mao demonstrated that Stalin failed to understand the unity and struggle of opposites and therefore was unable to understand the nature of the class struggle under socialism and the means to prevent capitalist restoration. Stalin did not understand that under socialist society contradictions still exist between the productive forces and the relations of production, and the importance of carrying out revolution in the superstructure as well as in the relations of production. Stalin failed to distinguish the contradictions between the people and the enemy and the contradictions among the people themselves.

The CoRIM suggests that not to agree with the evaluation of the CPC under the leadership of Mao on the source of Stalin's mistakes will be a blunder. It challenges the stance of the CPN (Mashal) which disagrees with the evaluation of Mao and the CPC regarding the source of Stalin's mistakes. As it says: "Today, anyone who refuses to recognize Stalin's mistakes and attempts to take refuge in them, will resolve this contradiction by putting themselves in opposition to Marxism as it has actually developed and will end up not mistaken, but revisionist." According to the CoRIM, the CPN (Mashal) has not identified the mistakes of Stalin, which is a mistaken presentation of the problem. Accepting the fact that Stalin could not understand the issue of class struggle in socialism and the issue of the restoration of capitalism in the socialist period, the CPN (Mashal) has clarified that Mao, on that point, was right. With that exception, Stalin certainly made many mistakes about the revolutionary struggle in China and in Eastern Europe. If a lesson is not learnt from these mistakes of Stalin, the result will be indeed revisionism, as indicated by the CoRIM. How can the CoRIM, neglecting the basically different evaluation of Stalin, relate the evaluation of Stalin made by Enver Hoxha to the CPN (Mashal)? Whether such a 'doubt' and 'prophecy' made by the RIM will return to itself in the form of rightist revisionism as exemplified by Khruschev after his criticism of Stalin. We do not have an answer to this possibility, and we have to wait for the future for this. However, we do not want such an end for RIM.

There is fundamental difference between the nature of the evaluation done by Mao and the CPC and the evaluation of Stalin made by the CoRIM and the RCP, USA. Although Mao and the CPC reached fundamentally the same wrong conclusion about the source of the mistakes of Stalin, they did not adopt an antagonistic attitude to Stalin. However, some parties and organizations have adopted an antagonistic attitude to Stalin, which must be made public and explain that a Trotskyite evaluation is being revived in the present international communist movement over the question of the world communist movement and formation of socialist system under Stalin's leadership.

3. Mao's Military Line

There is a serious division of opinion on the application of Mao's military line in the oppressed countries as advocated by Mao. The CPN (Mashal) assumes that the preparation of the objective and subjective conditions are the starting point in this regard. However, the CoRIM and the majority of the parties and organizations within the RIM consider the view of the CPN (Mashal) to be wrong. According to them, the preparation of the objective and subjective situations in the capitalist or the imperialist countries is needed for socialist revolution, not for New Democratic Revolution in oppressed countries. This kind of point of view is against the Marxism-Leninism-Mao Tse-tung Thought. Sadly, the CoRIM and majority of parties and organizations of the RIM are presenting this view in the form of view of Maoism. In reality, such a view corresponds not with the Marxism-Leninism-Mao Tse-tung Thought, but with the anarchism.

In the proposal passed at the Extended Meeting of the CPN (Mashal) on September 17-19, 1992, it states:

> Lenin has thrown sufficient light on the question of armed struggle and laws governing it. According to Lenin, armed struggle is both art and science having its own laws and violation of such laws will lead the movement either right or left deviation. Therefore, our attitude towards armed struggle should not be guided by our own subjective thinking or arbitrary way of thinking, but it should be based on the concrete analysis to the subjective as well as objective condition. For various parties and organizations who support Maoism, such a line of Leninism is outdated and even a right deviation in the present world context. So far as the military line developed by Mao Tse-tung is concerned, it basically conforms with the military line of Lenin. Such a correct thinking of Mao Tse-tung based on Leninism is often distorted to accommodate their arbitrary way of thinking.

The CoRIM has commented on the *Message* on many occasions about the above point of view of the CPN (Mashal), especially on the beginning of the people's war in the oppressed countries in this way:

> The central task for a revolutionary party in an oppressed country should not be focused on leading a militant mass movement in the cities but on solving the ideological, political and organizational problems to start people's war in the countryside. Before starting the people's war all practical work must serve that effort. After the war is initiated, all efforts must be made to develop it. This is the yardstick one must use to measure whether the work and activities carried out by a party is in line with its reason for existing. Mao says that people's war itself is the best organizing tool to arouse and unleash the broad masses of peasants. The people's war will not be an outgrowth of mass struggles in the city and countryside, nor mobilizing around local or national elections. These activities might create a quantitative buildup of the party and it's followers, but they will not somehow go over to people's war. In studying the particularities of a country the goal is not to find reasons why one should not take armed struggle and not go over to people's war. But rather on the positive side, we study in order to understand how best to prepare for starting people's war as soon as possible given the contradictions and difficulties that inevitably exist.

In another section of the above letter, it states: "In the countries, where the revolutionary road to revolution exists is protracted, mainly rural warfare from the beginning."

In the letter sent to the CPN (Mashal) on August 21, 1996, the CoRIM writes that the "denunciation of the launching of the people's war" is "the most serious political consequence" of the "opposition to Marxism-Leninism-Maoism". –Letter of CoRIM to CPN (Mashal), August 21, 1996.

CoRIM's presentation of Mao's thought on the people's war distorts the whole point of view of Mao, and it is just one part of its anarchistic view from Mao's comprehensive perspective regarding the people's war. The CoRIM has presented only those aspects that modern revisionists have been quoting out of his whole point of view to prove Mao an anarchist. Comrades of the CoRIM see only one tree and not the whole forest. If not understood the above quoted Mao's saying in regard to the people's war, specifically "the people's war is the best weapon to raise the wider community of peasants", within the limitation of the analysis of concrete conditions, it will push the movement into an anarchic marsh. Can a political strike in the situation, when it is expanding nationwide, not be said to be the best weapon of workers and peasants themselves to raise and lead them? As this saying does not take the form of political strike to be an absolute form of struggle, the thought of Mao on people's war does not take people's war to be the only major and absolute form of struggle from the beginning to the end. This is extreme distortion of Mao's Marxist-Leninist military line regarding the revolution in the oppressed countries.

4. Mao's Struggle Against Opportunism

Some mistakes were committed by Mao in the course of struggle against different types of opportunist trends within the CPC. The weak position of the revolutionaries and the restoration of capitalism in China after the death of Mao, to some extent, is the outcome of Mao's mistakes. Certain mistakes by Mao in relation to the struggle against "centrists" opportunism seen in the party and government are noteworthy. Clarifying this issue, the proposal passed at the Extended Meeting of CPN (Mashal) writes:

> The result of the past, particularly the collapse of the world socialist system, has proved that the mission of Mao or struggle against revisionism was correct. However, we should not overlook the mistake Mao has made in the course of struggle against opportunism. He was keen enough to take a correct stand against the right opportunism, but was unable to understand properly the importance of the struggle against centrist opportunism upon what Lenin has sufficiently thrown light in his theoretical as well as practical works. The mistake made by Chairman Mao or the question of centrism has definitely caused no less damage to the socialist system in China." –"On Maoism", A Resolution Adopted by the CPN (Mashal) September 17-19, 1992.

The CoRIM takes this analysis of the CPN (Mashal) as a "serious accusation" on Mao. The CoRIM has been arguing loudly against this position of CPN (Mashal) repeatedly. Why is the CoRIM so excited about pointing out the mistakes of Mao? Is the CoRIM really honest to revolutionary thinking and theory? Even a cursory glance at the history of the international communist movement after the death of Mao, clarifies CoRIM's the lowest level of honesty to this issue. After the death of Mao, there was an attack on Mao Tse-tung Thought not only from the angle of Hoxha's dogmato-sectarianism but by some parties and organizations inside the international communist movement itself too. Those parties and organizations attacked not only Stalin but Marx, Engels, Lenin and Mao too. The CoRIM is making a big fuss against the statements of CPN (Mashal) for pointing out that Mao did not struggle sufficiently against the centrist opportunists. However, it is silent on the accusations made by parties such as the RCP, USA on Marx, Engels, Lenin and Stalin. The CoRIM has never shown determination in the two-line struggle in a non-compromising way against those types of attack within the RIM. That does not mean that, the CoRIM, which is not mobilizing a struggle against the RCP, USA's, attack on Marx to Mao, has no right to say that the position of the CPN (Mashal) is wrong. If it thinks CPN (Mashal)'s position is wrong regarding this, it has the right to criticize. But the CoRIM has to understand the dangerous and fatal thinking of the RCP, USA and most forward struggle against it. Below, I have quoted that type of problematic thinking without any explanation and analysis, from the Chairman of RCP, USA, Bob Avakian and other leaders:

> Within the international communist movement (before as well as after Stalin's influence became dominant in the Comintern) there were already developing economist, reformist and bourgeois-democratic deviations. ... Especially after the crushing defeat of the communists in Germany with the rise of the fascist form of bourgeois dictatorship (1933), heavy defensive and defeatist tendencies grew in the leadership of the Soviet Union and the Comintern. Together with the growing danger of world war, especially of attack on the Soviet Union, openly rightist deviations, of a fundamental nature, became predominant–the promotion of nationalism, reformism and bourgeois democracy, the subordination of everything to the defence of the Soviet Union, etc., in a qualitatively greater way than before ... All this was concentrated in the Dimitroff Report to the Seventh World Congress of the Comintern (1935) and the implementation and further development of this line –which, as we know, involved, among other things, as one of its key ingredients, the basic repudiation of the Leninist position on "defence of the fatherland." This whole line was in its essence erroneous.

> More essentially, it must be summed up that the anlaysis which our party has upheld, that with the invasion of the Soviet Union the nature (the principle aspect) of the war changed–from an inter-imperialist war to one whose main aspect was that between socialism and imperialism–is *not correct* ... I believe, that its nature remained *mainly* an inter-imperialist war.

And generally, in the contradiction between defending the Soviet Union on the one hand and supporting and advancing revolutionary struggle elsewhere and on the international level as a whole on the other hand, not only was the first aspect (incorrectly) treated as the principal one but the other aspect (which should have been treated as principal) was liquidated insofor as it conflicted with the (narrowly, one-sidedly conceived) defence of the Soviet Union (The dissolution of the Comintern itself during the war, and especially the explanation given for this, is a sharp expression of this). The fundamental deviations during this war were concentrated in Stalin's speeches. 'On the Great Patriotic War of the Soviet Union', where the erroneous, anti-Leninist positions consistently put forward are so thoroughly (and extremely) incorrect that they cannot be explained merely by the necessity Stalin faced but must be taken as the expression of fundamental departures from Marxism-Leninism.

When a new historic conjuncture was shaping up, when that major spiral was reaching its concentration point and resolution–raising qualitatively greater possibilities for revolutionary advance on a world scale, which the Soviet and Comintern leadership's line largely worked against.

I am struck by the superficiality of the arguments. To cite a flagrant example, in the original Party *Programme*, in the section "The Present Situation," it merely says that since the end of WWI the Soviet Union had been established as a socialist state ... "So with the German invasion of the USSR in 1941, WWII changed ...It became a battle for the defence of the future, as it was already being realized by the Soviet working people in building socialism" (p. 11, emphasis added). Similarly, in the article "On the Character of World War 2" (*The Communist*, Vol.1, No.1) at one point it is simply stated that "Everything described above changed with drastic swiftness on June 22, 1941 ... This changed the nature of the war and required a totally new orientation. (p. 90)

That the character of the war did change, has represented in fact a rationalization for–and an attempt to give the best interpretation to–the overall erroneous line of the leadership of the USSR (and the Comintern... as long as it existed) on WW2. This was actually a line of *incorrectly* subordinating everything to the defence of the Soviet Union and *along with that* downplaying or even denying the need to advance revolutionary struggles elsewhere that conflicted with this narrowly (and overall erroneously) conceived defence of the USSR, and it seriously deviated from the correct, Leninist analysis of imperialism and imperialist war and from the Marxist-Leninist stand on the nature of the state (as opposed to bourgeois-democratic camouflage of this nature) and other cardinal questions. In short, while we have criticized a number of the particular deviations associated with this overall line, we have not (up until now) made a deep-going analysis of this–nor *fully* broken with the overall erroneous orientation of Stalin, et al. on this question, which represents a concentration of much of what constitutes the roots of revisionism in the international communist movement.

In sum: the Second World War, from beginning to end, was the second world *inter-imperialist* war–this was its principal aspect and overall character even after the Soviet Union was invaded and became involved in the war." –Bob Avakian, "Outline of Views on the Historical Experience of the International Communist Movement and the Lessons for Today", *Revolution,* June 1981, pp. 5-6, 8-9.

Stalin went so far as to imply that in the whole period before the outbreak of the war, the US-British bloc of imperialists had been real peace lovers. "It is a fact that the aggressor nations in the present war had an *army of invasion* ready even before the war broke out, whereas the peaceful nations did not even have a fully satisfactory *covering army* for mobilization. Unpleasant facts such as the Pearl Harbour "incident", the loss of the Philippines and other islands in the Pacific, the loss of Hong Kong and Singapore, when Japan, as an aggressor nation, proved to be better prepared for war than Great Britain and the United States who pursued a peace policy, cannot be regarded as accidents." (Stalin's italics) What is really a fact here is that this is a fundamental departure from Marxism-Leninism on the nature of the state and imperialism and represents in fact the subordination of Marxism to nationalism in the form of the defence of the Soviet Union."–"Some Notes on Military and Diplomatic History of the Second World War" by a comrade of RCP, USA, *Revolution,* June, 1981, pp. 14-15.

Imperialist countries were classified into "aggressor" (i.e. fascist) and "non-aggressor" (bourgeois-democratic imperialist) states. In the first category, the fascist bourgeoisie was accused of being "destroyers of the nation" and upholders of "barbarism" (something different from capitalism). In the second "non-aggressor" camp, the bourgeoisie was (at least for a while in the 1930s) also accused of betraying the nation, but here the charge was that it was doing so by giving in, appeasing, surrendering to the fascist aggressors. In common between both these analyses was the idea that the proletariat should "oppose" the bourgeoisie in the imperialist countries on the basis of being the "true defenders of the nation." Increasing, and especially after the Soviet Union was attacked, the mask of "opposing" was thrown aside and the open line taken up of uniting with the bourgeoisie... increasingly under the bourgeois and chauvinist banner of defending the (imperialist) nation.

In *Imperialism* Lenin saw and analysed all the essential decadent and reactionary tendencies of the imperialist countries, and showed why they were due to the features common to all capitalism in its highest stage–and to nothing else. He analysed why imperialism tends towards repression and violations of bourgeois democracy, and why it aggressively seeks world domination and redivision of the world through war. He even noted that, leading up to World War 1, Germany was the openly lusting, up-and-coming imperialist which had been largely cut out from the imperialist feast, so it was the more openly aggressive. But all this did not lead him to talk about "aggressor" and "non-aggressor" states to take sides." –"On the Question of So-called 'National Nihilism', You Cannot Beat the Enemy While Raising His Flag", *Revolution,* June 1981, p. 25.

In Spain, to be blunt, the possibilities for big revolutionary advances in that country and worldwide were sacrificed to the defence–on a state-to-state level–of the Soviet Union."

There is Stalin's line that the defence of the USSR and the world revolution were identical, and that the world revolution, in order to progress should everywhere be subordinate to the defence of the USSR. ... Stalin and the Comintern opposed revolution in Spain." –"The line of the Comintern on the Civil War in Spain", *Revolution,* June 1981, pp. 34, 53.

We can see some confusion in Marx and Engels, again especially viewed with the perspective we have from history and the lessons summed up from history, on this question of the nation and on whether or not it is correct to view the working class as being the inheritors and those best carrying forward the tradition, the "best" tradition, of the nation. This question is not completely clear, even in Marx, although it hardly needs saying, but should be said, just in case what I'm arguing might lead to any confusion, that Marx and Engels, both in their summation of the Commune as well as in their practice around the Commune itself, were obviously outstanding supporters and promoters of proletarian internationalism: that's clear all the way through the summation of the Commune. Theirs is not a summation done from the narrow point of view of the French nation, but there is that confusion.

Now just in passing, one thing that should be said is that in Lenin himself, and not simply later in the Soviet Party and the international movement, there is a wrong view, a view contrary to a certain degree to Leninism, in fact, on the question of the Versailles Treaty and how to deal with it in Germany, which is not totally unconnected with these things I've been discussing. Earlier Lenin took and fought for a basically correct position, for example in *Left-Wing Communism*, on the question of the Versailles Treaty where he said that on the basis of internationalism, German communists should not put themselves in a position of allowing the bourgeoisie to corner them into coming out and saying they're against the Versailles Treaty and should determine their attitude towards the Versailles Treaty on the basis of the interests of the international proletariat and the world revolution. But then there begins to creep in the view, even somewhat appearing in Lenin and certainly carried forward after him, of pushing the communists in Germany sightly–and this is not accidental and ties in somewhat with his sort of early and partial analysis of the three parts of the world, if you will–to raise the national banner in Germany against the Versailles Treaty and against the victors' feast at the expense of Germany.

Stalin's position is a muddle, whereas Khrushchev resolved the muddle; and in that contradiction Stalin's muddle is infinitely preferable to Khrushchev's resolution, but it's still a muddle and not very good.

Stalin did what he could do (and in some cases it wasn't insignificant) to kill the revolutionary struggle of the masses in order not to bring down the wrath of US imperialism.

Returning to the question of Mao: also linked to the general erroneous tendencies in Mao–too much of a country-by-country perspective, the tendency to see things too much in terms of nations and national struggle–something else that should be reviewed here briefly is confusion and some of Mao's errors on the question of internal and external, and in particular the internal basis of change and the external conditions of change and how this applies in the relationship between revolutions in particular countries, on the one hand, and the overall world struggle and the world situation, on the other ... Even in Mao, despite and in contradiction to his contributions to and development of materialist dialectics, there were some metaphysical tendencies which interpenetrated with nationalist tendencies on this question.

For example in "On Contradiction" the way it is presented is that China is the internal and the rest of the world is the external. And what we've emphasized in opposition to this is viewing the process of the world historic advance from the bourgeois epoch to the communist epoch as something which in fact takes place in an overall sense on a world scale, is a world process and both arises out of and is ultimately determined by the fundamental contradiction of capitalism which, with the advent of imperialism, has become the fundamental contradiction of this process on a world scale. ... This was something that Lenin began to stress with his analysis of imperialism but was not fully developed by Lenin, at least in an all around way and specifically in a philosophical sense; and was got away from very sharply by the international communist movement after Lenin. And here again it was a case where there was not a radical rupture in a throughgoing way on the part of Mao.

All this, in turn, is linked with a wrong view of, or a wrong method of dealing with, the question of the development of conjunctures. It's not that Mao totally failed to grasp the question and the importance of conjunctures shaping up; certainly he grasped this in a certain way in relationship to World War 2, for example, and how that interpenetrated with the Chinese revolution. But we have to understand how Mao's approach to such historic situations reflected certain errors that go along with what I said earlier about this orientation as set forth in "On Policy", of attempting to line up all the progressive forces, or all the forces that can be lined up, against one main enemy, especially in the face of a developing conjuncture like that and in particular of a world war.

We also have to guard against a view that can develop spontaneously in the movement of presenting the course of the Chinese revolution as a "model" in the incorrect, metaphysical sense. In the main–although there are, very secondarily, some tendencies towards this in Mao–he overwhelmingly

> struggled against just such an error. But still it crops up and it goes along with the kind of error... In particular, there is a tendency towards a kind of absolute, mechanical, metaphysical view that there are two types of countries in the world and one of them has one-stage revolutions and the other has two-stage revolutions and the way you make revolution in a country that has a two-stage revolution is the way they did it in China, more or less, with *some* concrete application to conditions in your country; that is, you put forward new democracy as your programme, you go to the countryside, surround the cities from the countryside, wage protracted people's war and eventually capture power.
>
> There is the specific criticism to be made of Mao on the question of nations, national struggle and the world revolution: not only in the Anna Louise Strong interview and in "On Policy" but also in the General Line polemic, the tendency shows up to see things too much country-by-country separated from each other, too much in terms of nations and national struggle, and too much in terms of identifying one enemy and rallying everybody against it. In the case of the General Line polemic, US imperialism was seen as the main enemy at that stage and in the other imperialist countries the advice was to struggle against the monopoly capitalists and reactionary forces who betrayed the national interest, in other words who were allying with US imperialism; overall this was not correct.–Bob Avakian, "Conquer the World? The International Proletariat Must and Will", *Revolution,* Special Issue No. 50, pp. 3, 16-17, 28, 34-35.

How did Bob Avakian dare to make such a great accusation in relation to Marx, Engels, Lenin, Stalin, Mao and the communist movement and the building of socialism? True Marxist-Leninists will not accept these accusations from Avakian. This is an irony that the CoRIM is silent about it. Why is the CoRIM not serious on such a wrong thinking? Anything cannot be considered under the present structure of the CoRIM. Given the situation, it is not possible for the CoRIM to be serious about the issue in the RIM. In fact, the present CoRIM is not an elected body from the founding Conference of 1984. After the Communist Party of Turkey (ML) and CRC, CPI (ML) left the CoRIM, only the RCP, USA remained of the original elected body. The present CoRIM is constituted with the nomination by the minority RCP, USA. The RCP, USA constituted CoRIM in its interest. The activities of the CoRIM after this development are crystal clear. Since immediately after the formation of RIM, an attempt was made to establish the non-Marxist-Leninist line of the RCP, USA, as an official line of the RIM. It has not stopped its attempt, continuously in trying to establish the non-Marxist-Leninist line, as an official line of the RIM.

5. Election Under the Reactionary System

The CPN (Mashal) maintains that the question of the utilization or the boycott of election under a reactionary system to be a tactical one. At present, we are living in the era of imperialism and proletarian revolution. Leninism is our guiding principle even now, even according to Stalin, Mao Tse-tung and the *Declaration* of the RIM. As the *Declaration* of RIM has said that: "The tactics and style of work developed by the Bolsheviks Party and summed up by Lenin still remain the basic guideline."

Supporting Stalin's above view *Declaration* writes: "Since Lenin's death the world situation has undergone great changes. But the era has not changed. The fundamental principles of Leninism are not outdated, they remain the theoretical basis guiding our thinking today."–*Declaration of the Revolutionary Internationalist Movement*, pp. 42, 14-15.

In this context this question should be seen in the spirit of Leninism. With the background of Leninism, the issue of utilizing or boycotting of elections conducted under a reactionary system is tactics and seeing it as something else ultimately leads to anarchism or parliamentary cretinism. On the question of election in the RIM, different opinions have surfaced from the established thinking. Many of the parties and organizations in the RIM believe that Lenin's view on election can be true only about socialist revolution in capitalist countries. According to them, it is a "raw revisionism" to apply this policy in the oppressed countries. They have brought forward this view in the name of Mao's thought that the nature of election in oppressed countries is of a strategic type. This type of thinking is against Mao Tse-tung Thought. Mao also took the question of election to be tactical, just as Lenin did. Mao and the CPC expressed their view on the above question in the course of the great historical struggle against the modern revisionism is before us. On the question of election, the CPN (Mashal) states:

> To Lenin, the question of election was a matter of tactics to be used or boycotted according to the particular situation of the movement of the country. But the parties and organizations that support Maoism have a tendency to take it as a strategically boycott without providing any acceptable argument. Why have Lenin's lines been replaced by the policy of strategically boycott? Neither have we got any evidence of such a boycott policy in Mao Tse-tung Thought nor in any theory expounded by him. This again shows how Maoists are playing with the principles of Mao Tse-tung to accommodate their arbitrary thought in the name of Maoism. –"On Maoism", A Resolution Adopted by the Extended Meeting of the COC of the CPN (Mashal) held from September 17-19, 1992.

The CoRIM considers this point of view of the CPN (Mashal) in relation to elections to be wrong. It suggests that any body can wrap himself up in Lenin. Many revolutionary groups take situations in Russian history to prove their view to be correct and quote sayings of Lenin related to that and forsake the unmistakable point of view of Mao, which begins with a proposal of developing revolutionary war as the main form of class struggle in China. The CoRIM has concluded that, parliamentary elections are tricks to pull people into the reactionary state mechanism. In the name of using legal opportunities the organization sinks into the electoral system and this policy is not far fetched for immature revisionism. The stance on election by the CoRIM, and other parties as well as organizations, believing in Maoism, have not to hide themselves behind Lenin and their wrong interpretation of Mao Tse-tung Thought regarding the question of the parliamentary elections will lead them nowhere, except the anarchism, if they do not correct themselves in time. We can just expect them to follow the Marxist-Leninist line, rejecting their anarchist line.

The CoRIM has presented Mao's view regarding the elections quite wrongly. It is wrong to define Lenin's view as mistakable and of Mao unmistakable. To disguise their anarchic thinking of boycotting elections, the CoRIM has mentioned the basic and class character of parliament and election under it and so on. The question is not of what fundamental form of those things are and what class character they have, but whether under their reactionary class character, in some particular situations, they can be used in favour of the movement, although in a secondary manner.

6. On Working Style

The CPN (Mashal) has stated that the working style of the CoRIM is wrong and it has adopted a non-Marxist-Leninist working style on important issues in relation to making decisions. The CoRIM has been trying to establish it as a shadow of the RCP, USA and it has succeeded to a great extent. Furthermore, the CoRIM replaced Marxism-Leninism-Mao Tse-tung Thought established as the guiding principle at the founding Conference of the RIM, in 1984, quite arbitrarily. It has adopted a wrong practice to influence parties and organizations that firmly oppose its non-Marxist-Leninist thinking and working style within the RIM, to the extent of a split in a CIA style and this has been successful in some situations. It has been plotting a conspiracy to oust the parties and organizations that go against its non-Marxist thinking and working procedure. The CPN (Mashal) has been victim of the wrath of the CoRIM for some time. The CoRIM finds the determination of the CPN (Mashal) on the above questions as a "serious accusation, serious situation". To put it in another way, it can be put like this: if the CPN (Mashal) drops this position or the CPN (Mashal) is ousted, the RIM will be free from such a "serious accusation and serious situation" and can move ahead without interruption. For this, the CoRIM tried hard to pressurize the CPN (Mashal) to drop its stance. When this was not successful, the CoRIM started to take steps to oust the CPN (Mashal) from the RIM. The letter on August 21, 1996 makes it clear:

> In our view, it is necessary to conclude this period of clarification and debate between your party and our movement which has lasted over two years now.
>
> The participating parties and organizations of RIM as well as its Committee, treasure the ideological and political unity of RIM which has been achieved through ideological struggle and in the course of revolutionary practice. If your party continues to maintain its opposition to the ideological foundation of the Revolutionary Internationalist Movement the correct and principled response on your part would be your voluntary resignation from our movement. We hope that you will give urgent attention to this matter and respond within three months. –Letter of CoRIM to CPN (Mashal), 21 August 1996.

The CPN (Mashal) could not drop its stance and it did not do so. In response to the above suggestion, CPN (Mashal) has said:

> The Central Committee (CC) of CPN (Mashal) (hereafter CC or Mashal only) in its meeting held on 24 October 1996 has concluded that the letter of the Committee of the Revolutionary Internationalist Movement (thereafter CoRIM) to the former (Mashal) dated August 21, 1996, is unjustified, arbitrary, unprincipled, splitter, sectarian and even against the norms and tradition of RIM itself. The CC meeting especially called to discuss the letter of CoRIM decided unanimously, unlike requested by CoRIM, to continue its stand on Mao Tse-tung Thought and not respond with "voluntary" (forced?) resignation "within three months" from RIM and continue to maintain opposition to "Maoism". –Resolution on the Letter of CoRIM, Adopted by the Meeting of the CC of the CPN (Mashal) held on 24 October 1996.

After having discussed briefly the thinking of the RCP, USA and the CoRIM, as well as the comment of the CPN (Mashal) on it, we present some facts that clarify the struggle of the CoRIM against the position of the CPN (Mashal) on different issues (to the extent of ousting the CPN (Mashal) from the RIM) was not oriented to lead to the solution of the "serious accusations" made on Marx, Engels, Lenin, Stalin and Mao and the "serious situation" born in RIM, but only for the purpose of establishing the wrong line of the RCP, USA in the international communist movement. It is an open fact to the public that the CPN (Mashal) has been opposing the non-Marxist-Leninist line of the RCP, USA. The presence of the CPN (Mashal) in the RIM is the main obstacle to get their non-Marxist-Leninist line established. The struggle of the CoRIM against the determination of the CPN (Mashal) is being led ahead with a view to get rid of the obstacle and hindrances. If the line of the RCP, USA really becomes established as the 'authorized' line of RIM, what form and direction will RIM take?

The above mentioned facts reveal that the serious accusations have been made to the international communist movement and a serious situation has appeared. The responsible side for this is not the CPN (Mashal) as the CoRIM says, but the RCP, USA and the CoRIM and the servitude of many parties and organizations to the non-Marxist-Leninist line of the RCP, USA. In this situation, it is vital for true Marxist-Leninists of the world to expose their anti-revolutionary line vehemently and vigorously.

Bharatpur, Chitawon, Nepal
November, 1996

Part IX

On Bob Avakian's New Synthesis of Communism

1
New Synthesis of Communism

Basically rupturing with the past understanding and practices of the international communist movement, the Chairman of the RCP, USA, Bob Avakian, has brought forward a New Synthesis of Communism (NSC). Avakian has said that a "whole stage of the communist revolution has ended, and it ended with defeat", "and the beginning of–and the need to launch, in fact–a new stage of the communist revolution."[1] He has claimed that the new stage of the communist revolution has begun, and the communist revolution cannot embark under the guidance of Marxism-Leninism in this "new" stage. Then, naturally the question arises–how to embark on a new stage of revolution? Responding to this query, a leader of RCP, USA writes:

> In this situation, Bob Avakian has led in defending, upholding and building on the monumental achievements of those revolutions and the illuminating insights of its greatest thinkers and leaders. But he has also deeply analysed the mistakes, and the shortcomings in conception and method that led to those mistakes. And on that basis, he has forged a coherent, comprehensive and overarching theoretical framework–that is, a *synthesis*. While this definitely comes out of and builds on what has gone before, this advance

---

1 What Humanity Needs Revolution, and the New Synthesis of Communism, *An Interview with Bob Avakian,* By A. Brook, pp. 37, 106.

> has also involved real ruptures with the past understanding and experience as a crucial element, which is why we call it the *new* synthesis.[2]

What Bob Avakian himself says about his 'New Synthesis'? Let us see:

> In a sense, it could be said that the new synthesis is a synthesis of the previous experience of socialist society and of the international communist movement more broadly, on the one hand, *and* of the criticisms, of various kinds and from various standpoints, of that experience, on the other hand. That doesn't mean that this new synthesis represents a mere "pasting together" of that experience on the one hand, and the criticisms on the other hand. It is not an eclectic combination of these things, but a sifting through, a recasting and recombining on the basis of a scientific, materialist and dialectical outlook and method, and of the need to continue advancing towards communism, a need and objective which this outlook and method continues to point to–and, the more thoroughly and deeply it is taken up and applied, the more firmly it points to this need and objective.

Further, he writes:

> In concluding on this point, I want to stress that it is very important not to underestimate the significance and potential positive force of this new synthesis: criticizing and rupturing with significant errors and shortcomings while bringing forward and *recasting* what has been positive from the historical experience of the international communist movements and the socialist countries that have so far existed; in a real sense *reviving*–on a new, more advanced basis–the *viability* and, yes, the *desirability* of a whole new and radically different world, and placing this on an even firmer foundation of materialism and dialectics.[3]

The NSC is not a particular work of Bob Avakian. It is a synthesis of his works for three and a half decades. Bob Avakian himself has said that "since the time that socialism faced reverses in China, shortly after Mao died in 1976, for three and a half decades, for 35 years", he worked, and he waged a struggle "in the realm of theory–summing up historical experience, positive and negative, drawing from many different spheres of human activity, and bringing forward a new synthesis of communism"[4]

Bob Avakian has said that he, "didn't set out to bring forward a new synthesis of communism", he "just set out to meet the needs" and it has resulted in bringing forward a new synthesis of communism." On the whole, development process of NSC, Bob Avakian writes:

2 Re-envisioning Revolution and Communism: What is Bob Avakian's New Synthesis?, p. 2.

3 Bob Avakian, "Making Revolution and Emancipating Humanity, Part 1: Beyond the Narrow Horizon of Bourgeois Right", *Revolution and Communism: A Foundation and Strategic Orientation*, pp. 35-37.

4 What Humanity Needs Revolution, and the New Synthesis of Communism, *An Interview with Bob Avakian,* by A. Brook, p. 40.

> There is a need to sum up this experience: What happened in China, and why? How does this relate to what happened in the Soviet Union? What are the underlying causes of this? How do we understand this in terms of what's going on in the world now? And what are the implications of this in terms of how we go about pursuing the struggle for communism in the world and applying the communist outlook and method? So, there was a need there. And I felt the responsibility to rise to the need–to dig into this deeply; and then to pursue, after that, looking more deeply into the history of socialist society in the Soviet Union and then China, including the experience of the Cultural Revolution in China, but also the experience of the communist movement more broadly and historically, beginning all the way back with Marx.

Responding to these questions what did Bob Avakian do? Let us see in his language:

> So I did a lot of reading and studying. I found myself in a position where I both was able to be and had to be–was able to study, but also was forced to be separated from a lot of the ongoing struggle at the time. So this, on the other hand, did provide the opportunity for me to do a lot of digging into the historical experience, a lot of studying, whilc I continued to pay attention to and provide the leadership that I could to the ongoing revolutionary movement. And, once again, it was a matter of: there's a need and, if you see the need and it's not being fulfilled, you have to rise to that the best you can and fulfil that need, to take that responsibility. That's what it means to act as leadership of a revolutionary process, a leader of a revolutionary party, to take the responsibility–which is what it is–to do that. And over the decades since that time, this was what was necessary–I did my best to rise to what was necessary in order to draw the lessons that needed to be drawn, to more deeply ground myself in the communist outlook and method that would enable the lessons to be drawn correctly, and to struggle to make those lessons accessible to growing numbers of people.

He further adds:

> That is what's been the driving force in what I've been doing–feeling for some time, going way back for decades now, that there were needs and that they needed to be met, and that once you became convinced of the need and the possibility of this communist revolution and you saw the world was continuing on as it was, and it was causing tremendous suffering, you had to rise to those responsibilities. So that's what I've sought to do, and it's resulted in bringing forward a new synthesis of communism. But I didn't set out to bring forward a new synthesis of communism. I just set out to meet the needs that I could recognize were there, if the movement for communism was not going to be set back even more than it was with the loss in China, with the reversal there–and the need to forge, if we could, the basis and the foundation to go forward again.[5]

5 Ibid., p. 121.

So, it is very clear that to synthesize Bob Avakian's NSC, we should start from the very beginning, that is, Bob Avakian's views on the historical experience of the international communist movement and the socialist transformation of society in the past. This is the crux of the matter. "Marxism-Leninism is a science, and science fears no debate. Anything which fears debate is no science."[6] Based on this truth, I welcome Bob Avakian's emphasis to sum up the historical experience of the international communist movement and the practices of the socialist transformation of society in the past in the context of the degeneration of the socialist system. In this regard, I want to emphasize that our method of summation and apprehension should be dialectical, not idealistic, while its conception of history, its theory should be materialistic, not metaphysical–that is, historical materialistic. Being historical materialists, we must oppose historical idealism. Under the leadership of Mao Tse-tung, the Communist Party of China (CPC) and all Marxist-Leninists all over the world had applied this method and conception in the study of the international communist movement and socialist movements in the context of the degeneration of socialism in the USSR. In the present context too, I mean after the degeneration of socialism in China, we should follow the same way which was chartered by Mao Tse-tung in the historical struggle against modern revisionism.

2
Communist Philosophy

The RCP, USA has claimed that "to critically interrogate, or analyse, the philosophical foundations of communism–and to put those foundations on a more fully scientific basis" is "the very heart of new synthesis". Leaders of the RCP, USA have seen limitations in Marx and Engels, and serious methodological shortcomings on the part of Stalin and Mao's straining against an inherited framework, and not being free from its influences in the realm of philosophy. As they have written:

> There were, not surprisingly, limitations in the way that Marx and Engels went at this, and these problems got compounded by serious methodological shortcomings on the part of Stalin, who led the Soviet Union and the international communist movement for nearly 30 years following Lenin's death. What's worse, these errors came at the very time an advance in understanding was urgently called for. Mao–the leader of the Chinese Revolution–fought against some of these problems, but Mao

6 "The Leaders of the CPSU are the Greatest Splitters of our Times", Seventh Comment on the Open Letter of the Central Committee of the CPSU (February 4, 1964), *The Great Debate*, Mass Line Publications, Kerala, India, 1994, p. 266.

himself was straining against an inherited framework and was not free from its influences.

According to the RCP, USA, Bob Avakian has identified and deeply criticized the weaknesses of communist philosophy. Regarding the questions on which Bob Avakian has "corrected" the philosophical foundations of communism, a leader of RCP, USA writes:

> Bob Avakian has identified and deeply criticized weaknesses along four different dimensions of communist philosophy. These concern: one, a fuller break with idealist, even quasi-religious, forms of thought that had found their way into the foundation of Marxism and had not been ruptured with; two, a further and qualitatively deeper grasp of the ways in which matter and consciousness mutually interpenetrate with and transform each other; three, a critique of a host of problems associated with pragmatism and related philosophical tendencies; and four, a radically different epistemology, or way of getting at the truth. In doing all this, he has put Marxism on a more fully scientific basis.

2.1–On the First Dimension of Communist Philosophy, they write:

> To begin with, Avakian has excavated, criticized, and broken with certain secondary but still significant religious-type tendencies that have previously existed within the communist movement and communist theory–tendencies to see the achievement of communism as an "historical inevitability" and the related view of communism as almost like a heaven, some kind of "kingdom of great harmony", without contradictions and struggles among people.[7]

The RCP, USA and its other leaders have carried on Bob Avakian's view blindly. Bob Avakian has synthesized that there was an idealistic, even quasi-religious way of thinking in Marxism to some degree. He has not only criticized Stalin, but also Marx, Engels, Lenin and Mao. He thinks that past practices of the process of the socialist transformations of society and the advance to communism were based, in a significant degree, on idealism and the religious way of thinking. As he says:

> Previously, there were some aspects of how communism was conceived that actually, and ironically, incorporated some metaphysical thinking. For example, Engels, and Marx as well, talked about moving from the realm of necessity to the realm of freedom, with the achievement of communism, as though–I'm exaggerating, or overstating, but there was a certain tendency towards thinking that–when you get to communism you will be in a realm of freedom in relation to necessity in a whole different way. And this, Mao came to see, is not really correct–does not correctly grasp the essence of things.

7 Re-envisioning Revolution and Communism; What is Bob Avakian's New Synthesis? pp. 2, 4.

> Even in Mao's early writings you see references (invoking some traditional Chinese terms) that talk about communism as the "kingdom of Great Harmony." Well, the more Mao went on and dealt with reality, and the revolutionary struggle, the more he came to see: that's not exactly the way it is. But that notion of the "Kingdom of Great Harmony" corresponds, in significant measure, to at least much of the understanding in the international communist movement prior to Mao. You can see it in Stalin: In his discussions of socialism, you see things tending towards a notion of the end of contradiction. Not that he literally said all contradiction has come to an end in socialist society, but he did say in the mid-1930s, that class antagonisms had come to an end in the Soviet Union. There is a need to leap beyond and rupture ... with all expressions of religious tendencies, within the communist movement.[8]

The view of Bob Avakian and the RCP, USA concerning the question of Marxism-Leninism-Mao Tse-tung Thought (MLM) and its practices of the socialist transformation of society and the advance to communism in the past is absolutely wrong. It is a subjective presentation of problem. They have invented the theory like "religious-belief", the "historical inevitability" in Marxist philosophy. Actually, their view totally slanders and vilifies Marxist philosophy and, accordingly, practices in the past. There is no space for religious-type tendency, "inevitabilism" in communist philosophy. Karl Marx and Frederick Engels made a historical breakthrough from the mechanical way of thinking, idealism and religiosity in materialism. Stripping its mechanical way of thinking, idealism and religiosity in materialism to the full, they enriched materialism with the great Hegel's dialectics stripping with its idealism base. Two major contributions they made in the sphere of philosophy–firstly, they developed dialectical materialism; secondly, they extended the recognition of nature as the recognition of human society. Doing this, they developed historical materialism to human society. On its achievement, Lenin writes:

> *Historical materialism* was a great achievement in scientific thinking. The chaos and arbitrariness that had previously reigned in views on history and politics were replaced by a strikingly integral and harmonious scientific theory, which shows how, in consequence of the growth of productive forces, out of one system of social life another and higher system develops.[9]

The basic assumption of historical materialism on history and politics is that the development of history and politics does not move arbitrarily, but it moves forward due to the struggle between forces, i.e. productive

8 Bob Avakian, "Making Revolution and Emancipating Humanity, Beyond the Narrow Horizon of Bourgeois Right", *Revolution and Communism: A Foundation and Strategic Orientation*, pp. 10, 16.

9 V. I. Lenin, "The Three Sources and Three Component Parts of Marxism", *Collected Works*, Eng. ed., Progress Publishers, Moscow, Fifth Printing, 1980, Vol. 19, p. 25.

forces and relations of production which coexist and struggle within every phenomenon and process. As a consequence of the growth of productive forces, one system of social life develops into another higher system of social life. Within a particular system, there arise varied stages of social life because of the continuous growth of the productive forces. It is equally true to the socialist transformation of society and the advance towards communism. The MLM long ago made it clear that the socialist transformation of society and the advance to communism is full of contradictions. It is ridiculous that Bob Avakian and other leaders of the RCP, USA have blamed Marx, Engels, Lenin, Stalin and Mao saying that they could not understand the contradictory character of socialist society and the advancement of communism. It is due to their idealistic, metaphysical and mechanical materialistic philosophical ground that they could not see (or were unable to see) the basic understanding of MLM on the question of the character of socialist society and the advance to communism. Just a couple of points are enough to expose the bankruptcy of their "correction" of Marxist philosophy on this issue. From Marx to Mao they were philosophically very clear about the character of socialist society and communism. Marx and Engels analysed socialism "the *declaration of permanence of the revolution*"[10] and they said that the transition from capitalist society to advance communism is impossible without "a political transition period." They have said that in this period "*the revolutionary dictatorship of the proletariat*" is a must.[11]

The presentation of the question–the transition from capitalism to communism–by Marx and Engels is most important. There are two major objectives to achieve one's own emancipation–first of all, the proletariat must overthrow the bourgeoisie; and secondly, establish its revolutionary dictatorship–they have preceded analysing the different levels or stages of communist society to make a concrete analysis of the socialist society and the advance to communism. According to them, there are two phases of communist society. The first phase, which is usually called socialism, and the higher phase which in real terms can be called communism. The first phase of communist society is that type of society which has not "*developed* on its own foundations. On the contrary, as it *emerges* from capitalist society; which is in every respect, economically, morally and intellectually, still stamped with the birth marks of the old society from whose womb it emerges." It means the situation of inequality of right, in its content, still exists. As Marx has said, "these defects are inevitable in the first phase of communist society." The higher phase of communist society develops on its own foundations. It develops from the first phase of communist society; which is in every respect,

10 Karl Marx, "The Class Struggle in France", *Karl Marx and Frederick Engels Selected Works*, Eng. ed., Progress Publishers, Moscow, Fourth Printing, 1977, Vol. 1, p. 282.

11 Karl Marx, "Critique of the Gotha Programme", *Karl Marx and Frederick Engels Selected Works*, Eng. ed., Progress Publishers, Moscow, Fourth Printing, 1977, Vol. 3, p. 26.

economically, morally and intellectually different and free from birth marks of the old capitalist society. It means in the higher phase of communist society "the narrow horizon of the bourgeois right can be crossed in its entirety and society inscribe on its banners: From each according to his ability, to each according to his needs!"[12]

Their masterly analysis of the universality and particularity of contradiction in all phenomena and process of nature–including mind and society–clears their view. Frederick Engels has said, "Motion itself is a contradiction.":

> If simple mechanical change of place contains a contradiction, this is even more true of the higher forms of motion of matter, and especially of organic life and its development ... life consists precisely and primarily in this–that a being is at each moment itself and yet something else. Life is therefore also a contradiction which is present in things and processes themselves, and which constantly originates and resolves itself; and as soon as the contradiction ceases, life, too, comes to an end, and death steps in... also in the sphere of thought we could not escape contradictions, and that for example the contradiction between man's inherently unlimited capacity for knowledge and its actual presence only in men who are externally limited and possess limited cognition finds its solution in what is–at least practically, for us–an endless succession of generations, in infinite progress.[13]

Whenever we apply Engels to the above philosophy to the socialist transformation of society and the advance to communism, it becomes clear: For Marx and Engels, socialist society is in motion. It is a totality of contradictory aspects. A motionless socialist society has never been in existence and will not exist in future either. Whenever socialist society becomes motionless, it disappears from existence. It means, one who accepts "motion itself is a contradiction" must also accept that socialist society is contradictory. Contradiction between contradictory aspects in socialist society determines its existence. As soon as the contradiction ceases, socialist society, too, comes to an end. Mao Tse-tung has rightly said that: "The interdependence of the contradictory aspects present in all things and the struggle between these aspects determine the life of all things and push their development forward. There is nothing that does not contain contradictions; without contradictions nothing would exist."

In the course of socialist construction and the advance to communism under the dictatorship of the proletariat and revolutionary communist party's leadership, some old contradictions gradually resolve and some new

12 Karl Marx, "Critique of the Gotha Programme", *Karl Marx and Frederick Engels Selected Works*, Eng. ed., Progress Publishers, Moscow, Fourth Printing, 1977, Vol. 3, pp. 17, 19.

13 Frederick Engels, "Dialectics, Quantity and Quality", *Anti-Duhring,* Eng. ed., Progress Publishers, Moscow, Sixth Printing, 1975, p. 140.

contradictions emerge. In socialist society, communists do not think of the presence or absence of contradiction, but they think and discuss which contradiction has been resolved, and which has not still been resolved and what new contradiction has emerged. Because, for them, contradiction is universal and absolute. Mao Tse-tung writes:

> In the course of socialist construction we are gradually resolving this contradiction in the course of the advance from socialism to communism. The question is one of different kinds of contradiction, not of the presence or absence of contradiction. Contradiction is universal and absolute, it is present in the process of development of all things and permeates every process from beginning to end.
>
> What is meant by the emergence of a new process? The old unity with its constituent opposites yields to a new unity with its constituent opposites, whereupon a new process emerges to replace the old. The old process ends and the new one begins. The new process contains new contradictions and begins its own history of the development of contradictions.[14]

What Mao has said in the above paragraphs is very important. It is a brilliant philosophical history of the advancement of socialism to communism. In the course of socialist construction in the Soviet Union, it is clear how Lenin and Stalin handled contradictions well. With a masterful skill, this is Mao's philosophical interpretation. But because of their metaphysical outlook, Bob Avakian and leaders of the RCP, USA fail to see this truth. Mao upheld and developed Marxist philosophy in the course of socialist construction in China, basing himself on the experience of the new process (degeneration of socialism and restoration of capitalism in the USSR). He developed Marxist philosophical thinking on the character of socialist society.

A person who lost his or her senses or who is not a genuine Marxist-Leninist, but is just pretending to be, can think "within the communist movement and communist theory", there were "secondary but still significant religious-type" or "inevitabilism" or "view of communism as almost like a heaven", some kind of "kingdom of great harmony", without contradictions and struggle among people's tendencies. In the course of the advance from socialism to communism, the view from Marx to Mao on the dictatorship of the proletariat, uninterrupted revolution, correct handling of contradictions, superstructure and relations of production, world revolution, and imperialism does not leave any loophole for the above allegations.

Certainly, in the course of the advance from socialism to communism, any genuine communist must not take the victory of communism as an

14 Mao Tse-tung, "On Contradiction", *Selected Works*, Foreign Language Press, Peking, Third printing, 1975, Vol. 1, pp. 316, 318.

"inevitable" and "driven forward by history." This type of view is anti-historical materialistic. It represents the revisionist (old and modern revisionists) outlook. Based on this outlook, modern revisionists abandoned the dictatorship of the proletariat, uninterrupted revolution, correct handling of contradictions among people, development of superstructure and relations of production in the course of the advance from socialism to communism, and they advocate the theory of peaceful transition from capitalism to communism, they replaced the dictatorship of the proletariat by the "state of the whole people", they replaced the party of the proletariat by the "party of the entire people", they replaced the practice of uninterrupted revolution by, "all-round cooperation", they replaced the practice of class struggle by class collaboration, in the course of the advance from socialism to communism. I wonder how and on what basis Bob Avakian and leaders of the RCP, USA have seen "significant religious-type tendencies" in Marx, Engels, Lenin, Stalin and Mao Tse-tung?

The central point of the whole criticism by Bob Avakian and the RCP, USA is Stalin. They have claimed that there was some kind of utopian thinking in Stalin about communism. They have said that Stalin saw the advance from socialism to communism as a society without contradictions and struggle as a society of great harmony. As quoted above, Bob Avakian has said that "In his discussion of socialism, you see things tending towards a notion of the end of contradiction. Not that he literally said all contradictions have come to an end in socialist society, but he did say, in the mid-1930s, that class antagonism had come to an end in the Soviet Union." Certainly this type of thinking of Stalin in regard to the advance from socialism to communism is basically wrong. It does not interpret the objective reality of socialist society. But it is not correct to interpret that Stalin saw the advance from socialism to communism as a society without contradiction and struggle as a society of great harmony. There are some points to be noted: Historical limitations and objective conditions.

The Soviet Union was first and the only country at that time, which was building socialism. There was no precedent on the solution of problems of socialism. So, Stalin made a mistake on correctly understanding the nature of class struggle in the course of the advance from socialism to communism. After the declaration of Stalin "no longer contains antagonistic, hostile classes"[15] in the Soviet Union, Stain did not stop class struggle in practice. After that too, Stalin went on and dealt with the objective reality of society. Under the leadership of Mao Tse-tung, the CPC has said that Stalin's view "was wrong both in theory and practice. Nevertheless, Stalin remained a great Marxist-Leninist. As long as he led the

15 J. V. Stalin, "Report to the Eighteenth Congress of the CPSU (B) On the Work of the Central Committee, March 10, 1939", *Problems of Leninism*, Eng. ed., Foreign Language Press, Peking, 1976, p. 912.

Soviet Party and state, he held fast to the dictatorship of the proletariat and the socialist course, pursued a Marxist-Leninist line and ensured the Soviet Union's victorious advance along the road of socialism."[16] When Stalin was advocating the above mentioned wrong view on class struggle in the course of the advance from socialism to communism (not in general terms, but at a certain stage of socialism) in the USSR, for a moment too, he did not leave the dictatorship of the proletariat in theory and practice. Till his death, he was a great supporter, analyser and applier of the dictatorship of the proletariat. He forwarded the socialist course in the Soviet Union. For the Soviet Union's victorious advance along the road to socialism, Stalin always pursued a Marxist-Leninist line. Actually, anyone who accepts inevitability of the dictatorship of the proletariat, in the course of the advance from socialism to communism, his or her view cannot be basically wrong on the character of socialist society. Because, the base of the dictatorship of the proletariat is class struggle, i.e. class struggle finally leads to the dictatorship of the proletariat. Not just that, whenever the dictatorship comes to exist it becomes an instrument for the abolition of classes. It is its historical responsibility, when classes are abolished the dictatorship of the proletariat loses its own necessity in society. As Marx has said: "Class struggle necessarily leads to the *dictatorship of the proletariat*, ...this dictatorship itself only constitutes the transition to the *abolition of all classes* and to a *classless society*."[17] Lenin has said on the relation between the existence of classes and struggle between them, and dictatorship of the proletariat: "The dictatorship of the proletariat is *also* a period of class struggle, which is inevitable as long as classes have not been abolished".[18]

Are the above statements of Marx and Lenin not clear? Undoubtedly, anyone who accepts the inevitability of the dictatorship of the proletariat and the socialist state, naturally he, or she accepts the existence of classes and struggle between them in theory and practice. It is not possible to accept the inevitability of the dictatorship of the proletariat, and socialist state not to accept the existence of classes and struggle between them in socialist society. By taking his wrong understanding about the existence of antagonistic classes and class conflicts, after the socialist ownership of the instrument and means of production, in the course of the socialist transformation of society, it is not correct to present Stalin's "view of communism as almost like a heaven", some kind of "kingdom of great harmony". His deeds do not permit us to conclude in this way.

16 "On Khrushchev's Phony Communism and its Historical Lessons for the World", Ninth Comment on Open Letter of the Central Committee of the CPSU (July 14, 1964), *The Great Debate*, Mass Line Publications, 1994, Kerala, p. 322.

17 "Marx to Joseph Weydemeyer in New York, London, March 5, 1852", *Marx-Engels Selected Correspondence*, Progress Publishers, Moscow, Third, revised ed., 1975, p. 64.

18 V.I. Lenin, "A Great Beginning", *Collected Works*, Eng. ed., Third Printing, 1977, Progress Publishers, Moscow, Vol. 29, p. 420.

2.2–On the Second Dimension of Communist Philosophy, leaders of the RCP, USA have said that "previously, the importance of the economic base (that is, the production relations) was not just recognized–but over emphasized." They have said that this tendency and practices undermined the potential role and power of consciousness. They say further:

> While both Lenin and especially Mao made very important contributions towards a more correct and dialectical understanding of how this relation between the base and superstructure "works", neither quite grasped the scope and fluidity of this relative independence deeply enough, or in a layered enough way." They have claimed that "Avakian has developed a far deeper understanding of the potential role and power of consciousness.[19]

It is better to enter into the subject matter and discussion to quote Bob Avakian's original view here:

> In the historical experience of socialist states so far, ... there have also been secondary but nonetheless important ways in which things have gone off track, and in some instances seriously so, with undeniably negative consequences. There has been a definite tendency towards positivism and reductionism–towards, if you will, flattening out contradictions and applying a mechanical approach, including in the manner of treating the superstructure as too closely linked to the goal of economic transformation at any given time, linking things in the superstructure too closely to the immediate tasks at hand, particularly with regard to the economic base. And then, in turn, economic transformation, especially in the experience of the Soviet Union, even when it was socialist, was too much reduced to mere economic expansion on the basis of state ownership, without sufficient attention to the transformation of the relations among people in production, in various aspects, as well as other social relations, and the expression of all this in the superstructure.[20]

The accusations of Bob Avakian and other leaders of the RCP, USA, are baseless. In fact, the above criticism shows their bankruptcy of thought about the revolutionary dialectics. If they had grasped revolutionary dialectics on this issue, they could have seen correct handling of the relation between the economic base and superstructure in the course of the socialist transformation of society and moving towards communism in the past. Lenin, Stalin and Mao Tse-tung upheld and practised that, basing themselves on the materialistic dialectical approach of Marx and Engels on the question of economic base and superstructure. According to the theory of knowledge, they looked at the economic base as primary and superstructure as secondary. According to dialectics, in the course of development, they did not take base as the only determining factor. It emphasized interaction between economic

19 Re-envisioning Revolution and Communism: What is Bob Avakian's New Synthesis?, p. 5.

20 Bob Avakian, "Making Revolution and Emancipating Humanity", *Revolution and Communism: A Foundation and Strategic Orientation*, p. 34.

base and superstructure. But it always held that basically the economic base was primary and was the determining factor on this interaction.

The question of the relation between economic base and superstructure is a philosophical question, i.e. question of the relation between thinking and being. Scientific materialism already has set that problem. For this, "matter as primary and regards consciousness, thought, sensation as secondary, because in its well-defined form sensation is associated only with the higher forms of matter (organic matter)". Elaborating it further, Lenin said:

> Matter acting upon our sense-organs produces sensation. Sensation depends on the brain, nerves, retina, etc, i.e. on matter organized in a definite way. The existence of matter does not depend on sensation. Matter is primary. Sensation, thought, consciousness are the supreme products of matter organized in a particular way.[21]

Idealist philosophy, to the contrary, assumes consciousness, thought, and sensation as primary. The existence of sensation does not depend on matter or it divorces thought, sensation from objective reality, from the external world; it divorces motion from matter. Marx puts his materialistic theory of knowledge of society in this way:

> In the social production of their life, men enter into definite relations that are indispensable and independent of their will, relations of production which correspond to a definite stage of development of their material productive forces. The sum total of these relations of production constitutes the economic structure of society, the real foundation, on which rises a legal and political superstructure and to which correspond definite forms of social consciousness. The mode of production of material life conditions the social, political and intellectual life process in general. It is not the consciousness of men that determines their being, but, on the contrary, their social being that determines their consciousness.[22]

Marx and Engels were not just materialist; they were dialectical too. Marxist philosophy is a brilliant combination of materialism and dialectics too. It means dialectical materialism is the world outlook of communists. As Stalin says: "Its approach to the phenomena of nature, its method of studying and apprehending them, is *dialectical*, while its interpretation of the phenomena of nature, its conception of these phenomena, its theory, is *materialistic*."[23]

---

21 V. I. Lenin, "Materialism and Empirio-Criticism", *Collected Works*, Eng. ed., Fourth Printing, Progress Publishers, Moscow, 1977, Vol. 14, pp. 46, 55.

22 Karl Marx, "Preface to A Contribution to the Critique of Political Economy", *Karl Marx and Frederick Engels Selected Works*, Eng. ed., Fourth Printing, Progress Publishers, Moscow, 1977, Vol. 1, p. 503.

23 J. V. Stalin, "Dialectical and Historical Materialism", September 1938, *Problems of Leninism*, First edition, Foreign Language Press, Peking, 1976, p. 835.

Extending Stalin's statement in social life, historical materialism's approach to social life can be expressed in this way: Its method of studying and apprehending them is dialectical, while its interpretation of the events of social life, its conception of these events, and its theory is materialistic. It means the economic situation is the basis and determining factor, and superstructure as secondary. But, we should not take it that the superstructure is always a passive effect of the economic base. In the course of the development process, between base and superstructure, there is a constant interaction. In many cases the superstructure also exercises an influential role. Likewise, we must not forget for a moment too the truth that in the ultimate sense the determining factor in history is economic life, not the superstructure. Many people criticize Marx and Engels for not writing on the superstructure in detail or more on both factors–base and superstructure–and their interaction in the development process. Regarding this, Engels writes:

> Marx and I are ourselves partly to blame for the fact that the younger people sometimes lay more stress on the economic side than is due to it. We had to emphasize the main principle vis-à-vis our adversaries, who denied it, and we had not always the time, the place or the opportunity to give their due to the other factors involved in the interaction. But when it came to presenting a section of history, that is, to applying the theory in practice, it was a different matter and there no error was permissible.

Stating their complete position on the subject, Engels writes:

> According to the materialist conception of history, the *ultimately* determining factor in history is the production and reproduction of real life. Neither Marx nor I have ever asserted more than this. Hence if somebody twists this into saying that the economic factor is the *only* determining one, he transforms that proposition into a meaningless, abstract, absurd phrase. The economic situation is the basis, but the various elements of the superstructure–political forms of the class struggle and its results, such as constitutions established by the victorious class after a successful battle, etc., juridical forms, and especially the reflections of all these real struggles in the brains of the participants, political, legal, philosophical theories, religious views and their further development into systems of dogmas–also exercise their influence upon the course of the historical struggles and in many cases determine their *form* in particular. There is an interaction of all these elements in which, amid all the endless host of accidents (that is, of things and events whose inner interconnection is so remote or so impossible of proof that we can regard it as non-existent and neglect it), the economic movement is finally bound to assert itself.[24]

24 Engels to Joseph Bloch in Konigsberg, September 21-22, 1890, *Marx and Engels Selected Correspondence*, Third revised ed., Progress Publishers, Moscow, 1975, pp. 396, 394-95.

Bob Avakian and other Leaders of the RCP, USA have not said anything about Lenin, Stalin and Mao, who went off the track? Who treated the superstructure too closely to the immediate task at hand, particularly with regard to the economic base? The accusation of "a definite tendency towards positivism and reductionism", on the question of base and superstructure, is serious. Undoubtedly, their sayings, "in the historical experience of socialist states", "in the experience of the Soviet Union, even when it was socialist", cover Lenin, Stalin and Mao, all three in general. But as in other questions their criticism's focal point is Stalin. But, none of them went off the track from dialectical materialism. Successfully and brilliantly, all three travelled on that track; the materialistic dialectical track. None of them treated superstructure as an instrument to achieve economic development. As far as the question of Stalin, it is true that, as Lenin and Mao, particularly Mao, he has not used the terminology 'superstructure' except here and there. But, if we study in depth, basically there is not any difference. In this regard, I want to pose a question here. What is superstructure? As Bob Avakian says: "The political institutions, legal structures, habits, customs, artistic conventions, philosophies, ways of thinking and looking at the world, etc., of a given society and epoch all belong to the superstructure."[25]

Again, a question arises: If superstructure is the combination of the above things, we should accept that Stalin was not only good, but he was the best as he did his best to develop proletarian political, cultural, legal and military institutions.

2.3+4. On the Third and Fourth Dimension of Communist Philosophy, the leaders of the RCP, USA have said that there were tendencies towards pragmatism and empiricism in the course of the process of the socialist transformation of society and the advance to communism. Further, they have said that Mao criticized and opposed these types of tendencies, but "had not been fully identified as such and systematically ruptured with prior to Avakian."[26] On the contribution of the NSC on the communist philosophy, Bob Avakian writes: "This new synthesis is bound up with and interpenetrates closely with key ruptures in the realm of epistemology–ruptures with instrumentalism and *apriorism*, dogmatism and religiosity, positivism, empiricism and pragmatism, as well as nationalism in the realm of how we view the whole process of advancing to communism."

In some detail, he further writes:

25 Bob Avakian, "Culture and the Superstructure", *Mao Tse-tung's Immortal Contributions*, Rahul Foundation, Lucknow, India, 2008, p. 211.

26 Re-envisioning Revolution and Communism: What is Bob Avakian's New Synthesis?, p. 6.

> There is a need to leap beyond and rupture with a definite legacy of the communist movement in terms of tendencies (which still exist and exert a significant influence) towards pragmatism and empiricism, reification of the proletariat, and reification of socialism (or the process of the socialist transformation of society and the advance to communism), ... some teleological process that's all working out towards some predetermined end. ... These kinds of viewpoints and approaches, along with reductionism and positivism–and the tendency to mechanical materialism and determinism in general–lead to reducing everything to the more immediate and narrow dimensions and to acting as if things that happened were *bound* to happen, and/or were determined by a linear progression of causes (or seeming causes), without leaps and qualitative changes from one state of matter to another, and without the interaction of different levels of matter in motion.

On the other forms of this tendency, Bob Avakian writes: "In the outlook and method of people–including communists–reducing things to the most narrow terms, looking for the causes of things just in the most immediate thing that suggests itself, not looking at the deeper dynamics and the larger picture–along with a lot of *apriorism* and instrumentalism."[27]

Here Bob Avakian and other leaders of the RCP, USA have accused the international communist movement in the past for its serious philosophical weaknesses and shortcomings. In this context, they have used some philosophical terminologies–mechanical materialism, pragmatism, positivism, instrumentalism, empiricism, reductionism, etc. These accusations are very serious and related to the communist world outlook. On so-called socialist states and revisionist leaders, these accusations are correct. We must expose their philosophical bankruptcy. But to follow the same type of method in the summation of Marx to Mao Tse-tung and their working method is absolutely wrong.

Bob Avakian and other leaders have accused revolutionary leaders of pragmatism, positivism and instrumentalism. **Pragmatism** is a philosophy of action. This word is from the Greek word "*pragma*"–it means action. It is a subjective, idealist philosophical trend of bourgeois, mainly of American origin. The pragmatists consider that cognition is purely psychological, subjective process of achieving religious belief. They thought that true knowledge comes from individual knowledge, not from human social practice. For them, subjective phenomena of consciousness is the criterion of the truth of knowledge. The main point of pragmatism is that a thing or event, if it is to a man's advantage, it is acceptable and vice versa. Expositions of pragmatism were brought forward by Charles Pierce, which

27 Bob Avakian, "Making Revolution and Emancipating Humanity", *Revolution and Communism: A Foundation and Strategic Orientation*, pp. 37, 16.

were further developed by William James and Ferdinand Schiller. Beyond that, pragmatism takes an evolutionary approach on the present system. In sociology, it is the personality cult, and in bourgeois democracy partisanship, racism and fascism are its essence. **Positivism** is nothing but a trend in bourgeois philosophy in the 20th century.

Instrumentalism is a further developed form of pragmatism. It regards all scientific theories, moral principles and social institutions as mere instruments to achieve the personal aims of an individual. Instrumentalists think that cognition need not reflect objectivity. Its attitude towards truth is subjective. Progress is not achievement of a targeted goal set by society, but it consists of the dynamic of motion itself. This trend in philosophy is the further development of pragmatism by John Dewey. **Reductionism** is a trend in philosophy which believes that complicated things and events can be analysed in a simple way. It assumes that it is possible to reduce complex phenomena into simple. It is possible to go from higher to lower to solve complicated phenomenon. This is the essence of reductionism. **Empiricism** is a philosophy of experience. It believes that all knowledge derives from experience and denies the objective content of experience. It does not recognize that there is an objective source of our knowledge, independent of us. If I am not mistaken, Bob Avakian and other leaders of the RCP, USA have taken **determinism** in a mechanical and absolute sense. In this sense, determinism does not accept the objectivity of casualty and made it analogous with necessity.

Whenever communist philosophy is being criticized in this way and on that level, I think, there is nothing to be appreciated and followed. We can make this accusation when the two-line struggle in regard to philosophy reaches its peak and turns into an antagonistic one. What does it mean if we say "there is a need to leap beyond and rupture with a definite legacy of the communist movement in terms of tendencies (which still exist and exert a significant influence) towards pragmatism, empiricism, ... reductionism, positivism, instrumentalism, determinism." It means: there were pragmatist, empiricist, instrumentalist, positivist, reductionist, and determinist, philosophical deviations in the international communist movement, "which still exist and exert a significant influence."

In reality, whenever communist philosophy is contaminated by these types of bourgeois philosophical tendencies, as Bob Avakian has said, "there is a need to leap beyond and rupture." But to accuse the general communist philosophy is absolutely wrong. It has come from the antagonistic angle. We must flatly reject it.

3
Bob Avakian on the International Communist Movement and the Socialist Transformation of Society

3.1. Nation, National Struggle and the World Revolution

Bob Avakian has said that in Marx and Engels' understanding there was "some confusion" on the question of nation and the relationship of the struggle in a particular country to the international struggle. As he says:

> The question of the nation and the relationship of the struggle in a particular country to the international struggle was not clearly handled, not only in the Commune itself–in the outlook and policies of the people who were leading the Commune at the time, for example, in their appeals to the soldiers of the reactionary army on a patriotic basis–but even to a certain degree in the writings of Marx and comments of Engels in summing up the Commune. The distinction between the nation and internationalism was not as clearly drawn as it has been learned that it must be drawn.

Bob Avakian has criticized not only Communards for not "all the radical ruptures on the question of the nation *vis-à-vis*–internationalism were not thoroughly made." But he has criticized Marx in this regard: "Marx's summation of the Commune ... shows the limitations of the approach of viewing things from the standpoint of which the bourgeoisie's victory would be most favourable for the international proletariat."

He writes further:

> We can see some confusion in Marx and Engels, ... on this question of the nation and on whether or not it is correct to view the working class as being the inheritors and those best carrying forward the tradition, the "best" tradition, of the nation. This question is not completely clear, even in Marx.

Bob Avakian observes that Marx and Engels did not sum up the Commune as well as their practice around the commune itself, and they were outstanding supporters and promoters of proletarian internationalism. But, he thought that "there is that confusion." Bob Avakian says that Marx did not fully grasp the meaning and implications of even what he himself had said earlier. Summing up the Commune more than two decades before Marx had told the workers to make themselves fit "for the exercise of political power", they had to "pass through long struggles, through a series of historic processes, transforming circumstances and men". But, according to Bob Avakian, Marx did not fully grasp the way to change the existing conditions and change the proletarians to be able to exercise political power. He writes: "Marx did not fully grasp the meaning and implications of even what he himself had commented on earlier, both at the time of the Commune and twenty years earlier when he talked about the 15, 20 or 50 years of civil war."[28]

Thanks to Bob Avakian and the RCP, USA for fully grasping the meaning and implications of Marx's earlier view.

Bob Avakian and the RCP, USA have criticized not only Marx and Engels on the question of the relation between proletarian state power and world revolution, they have criticized, to some degree, Lenin too. Bob Avakian has said that "In Lenin himself, and not simply later in the Soviet party and the international movement, there is a wrong view, a view contrary to a certain degree to Leninism." Further he says: "there is Lenin*ism* and there is Lenin ... every act of Lenin is not necessarily Leninism. But there is Leninism."[29]

Leninism strongly supports the national pride of the oppressed masses. It supports progressive cultural heritage and the revolutionary movements of the toiling masses. As Lenin has said: "Is a sense of national pride alien to us, great Russian class conscious proletarians? Certainly not! We love our language and our country, and we are doing our very utmost to raise *her* toiling masses ... to the level of a democratic and socialist consciousness. ... "We are full of national pride because the great Russian nation, *too*, has created a revolutionary class, because it, *too*, has proved capable of providing mankind with great models of the struggle for freedom and socialism. ... "We are full of a sense of national pride."[30]

But Bob Avakian does "not believe that in a fundamental sense there is for a communist such a thing as national pride."[31] Bob Avakian's absurd logic is that he has separated Lenin's above view from Leninism–"Lenin went against Leninism." These are not any of Lenin's personal views. His view represents a higher stage of Marxism. His view is the Marxism of the era of imperialism and proletarian revolution. That is why, Bob Avakan's attempt of separation of Leninism into two is totally futile. What type of national pride, what type of sentiments, interests and movements of working class did Lenin support, it is always a part of internationalism and world revolution. Seeing this as against internationalism and world revolution is metaphysics, not dialectics.

---

28 Bob Avakian, "Conquer the World? The International Proletariat Must and Will", *Revolution,* Special Issue, Number 50, pp. 2-4.

29 Ibid., pp. 16-17.

30 V. I. Lenin, "On the National Pride of the Great Russians", *Collected Works*, Progress Publishers, Moscow, Third Printing, Eng. ed., 1980, Vol. 21, pp. 103-04.

31 Taken From "On the Question of So-called 'National Nihilism': You Can't Beat the Enemy While Raising His Flag", *Revolution,* June 1981, p. 22.

Bob Avakian has said that after the civil war in Russia, there was no rapid spread of the proletarian revolution in many parts of the world. Lenin's view on the questions of the Soviet Union tended to change. He quotes Lenin's previous view on the world revolution:

> Lenin was perfectly willing (as opposed to the idea that you can't export revolution) to export revolution, but he wanted to make sure that there would be somebody to use it if he exported it. In the conditions of the 1920s, he summed up that, unfortunately, there would not be yet. This is something that has also been lost sight of to a large extent since Lenin's time.[32]

Bob Avakian has expressed it as a proof that since Lenin "lost sight of world revolution to a large degree." He has presented Lenin in a sense that in the later years he gave more priority to maintain proletarian power in the Soviet Union. He thought that by doing this, Lenin placed Soviet national interest parallel with world revolution as he presented them in terms of absolute identity between the maintaining of power in one socialist state and the advance of the world revolution overall. This is a wrong presentation of history. Lenin was a great dialectical materialistic. His view on the relation between maintaining of power in one socialist state and the advance of the world revolution was perfectly analogous with the dialectical materialism. Of course, we may see some different views and different ways to solve the problem in different times and different places. This is not because of the changing of views on concerning questions. This is because he was always guided by a dialectical materialistic outlook. It means, he always presented his view basing himself on the concrete analysis of concrete situations. Because of his idealistic and mechanical materialistic outlook, Bob Avakian could not see this reality. On the question of the relation between maintaining power in the Soviet Union and the advance of the world revolution, Bob Avakian has opposed Stalin in an antagonistic way. For this reason, he stands with Trotskyites. Actually, Bob Aavkian's views on the historical experience of the international communist movement is basically concerned with his views on Stalin. As he (Bob Avakian) has said, "The basic overview can be expressed by using Stalin as the focus." This is the heart of his analysis. During the great debate with modern revisionists, on the question of Stalin, the CPC had correctly said that:

> The question of Stalin is one of worldwide importance which has had repercussions among all classes in every country and which is still a subject of much discussion today, with different classes and their political parties and groups taking different views. It is likely that no final verdict can be reached on this question in the present century.[33]

32 Bob Avakian, "Conquer the World? The International Proletariat Must and Will", *Revolution,* Special Issue, Number 50, p. 14.

33 "On the Question of Stalin", *The Great Debate*, Mass Line Publications, Kerala, India, 1994, p. 88.

Exactly, even after fifty years this statement is equally valid. The question of Stalin is of worldwide importance. Still it is a question of much more discussion in the international communist movement. Stalin is a most hated enemy of the world imperialism. Probably, no final verdict can be reached on the question of Stalin in the era of imperialism and proletarian revolution. After the death of Mao Tse-tung and the counter-revolution in China, Bob Avakian and the RCP, USA brought forward their views by summing up the historical experience of the international communist movement on the question of Stalin. Summing up the "third period", Bob Avakian writes:

> Especially after the crushing defeat of the communists in Germany with the rise of the fascist form of bourgeois dictatorship (1933), heavy defensive and defeatist tendencies grew in the leadership of the Soviet Union and the Comintern. Together with the growing danger of world war, especially of attack on the Soviet Union, openly rightist deviations, of a fundamental nature, became predominant–the promotion of nationalism, reformism and bourgeois democracy, the subordination of everything to the defence of the Soviet Union, etc., in a qualitatively greater way than before ... the basic repudiation of the Leninist position on "defence of the fatherland." This whole line was in its essence erroneous...[34]

Bob Avakian sees an "antagonistic contradiction"[35] between defending the Soviet Union and supporting and advancing the revolutionary struggle worldwide. He says:

> In the contradiction between defending the Soviet Union on the one hand and supporting and advancing the revolutionary struggle elsewhere and on the international level as a whole on the other hand, not only was the first aspect (incorrectly) treated as the principal one but the other aspect (which should have been treated as principal) was liquidated insofar as it conflicted with the (narrowly, one-sidedly conceived) defence of the Soviet Union (the dissolution of the Comintern itself during the war, and especially the explanation given for this, is a sharp expression of this). The fundamental deviations during this war were concentrated in Stalin's speeches "On the Great Patriotic War of the Soviet Union", where the erroneous, anti-Leninist positions consistently put forward are so thoroughly (and extremely) incorrect that they cannot be explained merely by the necessity Stalin faced but must be taken as the expression of fundamental departures from Marxism-Leninism.

Further Bob Avakian has said that to achieve "*communism* in one country!" "the tendency to sacrifice everything–in particular revolution in

34 Bob Avakian, "Outline of Views on the Historical Experience of the International Communist Movement and Lessons for Today", *Revolution,* June 1981, p. 5.

35 Bob Avakian, "Conquer the World? The International Proletariat Must and Will", *Revolution,* Special Issue, Number 50, p. 19.

other countries–for the defence of the Soviet Union, and by an erroneous line overall for the international communist movement" brought forward by Stalin and Comintern.[36] Here the question has been presented in this way that Bob Avakian and the RCP, USA are true Leninists on the question of the world revolution, and Stalin's view was of "the basic repudiation of the Leninist position" on this question. A brief look at Lenin's views on the subject shows the real picture; who is a true Leninist, and who is a phony Leninist. Lenin said that the week (February 18-24, 1918) of imperialist Germany's military offensive against the Soviet Socialist Republic was bitter, distressing, painful, but necessary, useful and beneficial one. He drew three conclusions from that historic lesson. As he writes: "On our attitude to the defence of the fatherland, its defence potential and to the socialist revolutionary war; on the conditions under which we may come into collision with world imperialism; on the correct presentation of the question of our attitude to the world communist movement."

These conclusions are very important and the correct reflection of the new development in the present era. The new development is nothing than the success of the Socialist Revolution in Russia. Ever since that revolution, we could talk on defence of the socialist fatherland and defend its potentiality; on the handling of the socialist countries' relations with imperialist countries; and on maintaining the proletarian state power in one country and the world proletarian revolution. Lenin addressed these problems in accordance with historical materialism. After Lenin, Stalin upheld and applied this relation extraordinarily. Lenin viewed that since the October Socialist Revolution, communists had been defensive of the socialist fatherland. As he says:

> We are and have been defencists since October 25, 1917, we champion the defence of the fatherland ever since that day. That is because we have shown *by deeds* that we have broken away from imperialism. We have denounced and published the filthy, bloodstained treaties of the imperialist plotters. We have overthrown *our own* bourgeoisie. We have given freedom to the peoples *we* formerly oppressed. We have given land to the people and introduced workers' control. We are in favour of defending the Russian Soviet Socialist Republic.
>
> And because we are in favour of defending the fatherland we demand a *serious* attitude towards the country's defence potential and preparedness for war. We declare a ruthless war against revolutionary phrases about revolutionary war. There must be a lengthy, serious preparation for it, beginning with economic progress, the restoration of the railways (for without them modern warfare is an empty phrase) and with the establishment of the strictest revolutionary discipline and self-discipline everywhere.

---

36 Bob Avakian, "Outline of Views on the Historical Experience of the International Communist Movement and Lessons for Today", *Revolution,* June 1981, p. 6.

Further, he writes: "From the point of view of the defence of the fatherland it would be a crime to enter into an armed conflict with an infinitely superior and well-prepared enemy".[37]

A brief note on Lenin's ruthless war against the view of "Left Communists" on the defence of socialist fatherland is of great value. Without his historical struggle a complete Marxist-Leninist view on the question of the defence of the socialist fatherland would not have been with us today. The "Left Communists" were against the defence of fatherland after the existence of the socialist state power in an imperialist encirclement. Actually, they had an antagonistic view on this question. Refuting their anti-communist view, Lenin gave throughout the idea of why and when the defence of the fatherland was correct. He forcefully said that after the proletarian class became the ruling class, and began to transform society from a private property ownership society to a public property ownership society, it was our duty to defend the socialist fatherland. A communist cannot stay neutral while the socialist fatherland is under military intervention by imperialists. On the "Left Communists" high-sounding phrases, Lenin wrote:

> I shall enlighten you, my amiable friends, as to why such disaster overtook you. It is because you devote more effort to learning by heart and committing to memory revolutionary slogans than to thinking them out. This leads you to write "the defence of the socialist fatherland" in quotation marks, which are probably meant to signify your attempts at being ironical, but which really prove that you are muddleheads. You are accustomed to regard "defencism" as something base and despicable; you have learned this and committed it to memory. You have learned this by heart so thoroughly that some of you have begun talking nonsense to the effect that defence of the fatherland in an imperialist *epoch* is impermissible (as a matter of fact, it is impermissible only in an imperialist, reactionary war, waged by the bourgeoisie). But you have not thought out why and when "defencism" is abominable.

He adds:

> To recognize defence of the fatherland means recognizing the legitimacy and justice of war. Legitimacy and justice from what point of view? Only from the point of view of the socialist proletariat and its struggle for its emancipation. We do not recognize any other point of view. If war is waged by the exploiting class with the object of strengthening its rule as a class, such a war is a criminal war, and "defencism", in *such* a war is a base betrayal of socialism. If war is waged by the proletariat after it has conquered the bourgeoisie in its own country, and is waged with the object of strengthening and developing socialism, such a war is legitimate and "holy".

37 V. I. Lenin, "A Painful But Necessary Lesson", *Collected Works*, Eng. ed., Third Printing, Progress Publishers, Moscow, 1977, Vol. 27, pp. 63-64.

Warning those people who do not give importance to the defence of the country in which proletarian class has already achieved victory, and in which country proletarian class is developing and consolidating socialism, Lenin further writes:

> Those who treat frivolously the defence of the country in which the proletariat has already achieved victory are the ones who destroy the connection with international socialism. When we were the representatives of an oppressed class we did not adopt a frivolous attitude towards defence of the fatherland in an imperialist war. We opposed such defence on principle. Now that we have become representatives of the ruling class, which has begun to organize socialism, we demand that everybody adopt a *serious* attitude towards defence of the country.

Lenin has said correctly, "Left Communists"... "flaunting of high-sounding phrases is characteristic of the declassed petty-bourgeois intellectuals."[38] Of course, Lenin supported the Treaty of Brest-Litovsk, but relating it to patriotism, let us see what he says:

> Patriotism is one of the most deeply ingrained sentiments, inculcated by the existence of separate fatherlands for hundreds and thousands of years. One of the most pronounced, one might say exceptional, difficulties of our proletarian revolution is that it was obliged to pass through a phase of extreme departure from patriotism, the phase of the Brest-Litovsk Peace."[39]

Lenin's above statement is a weighty answer to the present-day "Left Communists", who think that defence is something base and despicable. Based on Lenin's above view, we can say that it was not Stalin who deviated from the Leninist position, but it is Bob Avakian who has deviated from the Leninist position on the question of the defence of the socialist fatherland.

Bob Avakian has not spared Mao, too. Criticizing Mao on nations, national struggle and the world revolution, he writes: "There is the specific criticism to be made of Mao on the question of nations, national struggle and the world revolution."

He writes further:

> Also linked to the general erroneous tendencies in Mao–too much of a country-by-country perspective, the tendency to see things too much in terms of nations and national struggle–something else that should be reviewed here briefly is confusion and some of Mao's errors on the question of internal and external, and in particular the internal basis of change and the external conditions of change and how this applies in the relationship

---

38 V. I. Lenin, " 'Left-Wing' Childishness and the Petty-Bourgeois Mentality", *Collected Works*, Eng. ed., Third Printing, Progress Publishers, Moscow, 1977, Vol. 27, pp. 331-32, 330.

39 V. I. Lenin, "Valuable Admission of Pitrim Sorokin", *Collected Works*, Third ed., Progress Publishers, Moscow, 1981, Vol. 28, p. 187.

> between revolutions in particular countries, on the one hand, and the overall world struggle and world situation, on the other ... even in Mao, despite and in contradiction of his contributions to and development of materialist dialectics, there were some metaphysical tendencies which interpenetrated with nationalist tendencies on this question.[40]

Here Bob Avakian firstly criticizes Mao for his view on the national struggle; and secondly, he finds the reason of that mistake as philosophical one. He observes that the mistake is related to Mao's thinking on the question of internal and external, and in particular the internal basis of change and the external conditions of change. According to him, Mao's application of this philosophy in the overall struggle for world revolution was erroneous. Yes, Mao has said internal is the basis for a change and external is the condition for that. Basing himself strictly on this philosophical ground, he has presented his views in the relationship between revolutions in particular countries and the overall struggle for world revolution. As Mao writes:

> As opposed to the metaphysical world outlook, the world outlook of materialist dialectics holds that in order to understand the development of a thing we should study it internally and in its relations with other things; in other words, the development of things should be seen as their internal and necessary self-movement, while each thing in its movement is interrelated with and interacts on the things around it. The fundamental cause of the development of a thing is not external but internal; it lies in the contradictoriness within the thing. There is internal contradiction in every single thing, hence its motion and development. Contradictoriness within a thing is the fundamental cause of its development, while its interrelations and interactions with other things are secondary causes. Thus materialist dialectics effectively combats the theory of external causes, or of an external motive force, advanced by metaphysical mechanical materialism and vulgar evolutionism. It is evident that purely external causes can only give rise to mechanical motion, that is, to changes in scale or quantity, but cannot explain why things differ qualitatively in thousands of ways and why one thing changes into another. As a matter of fact, even mechanical motion under external force occurs through the internal contradictoriness of things.[41]

Bob Avakian has bluntly rejected Mao's above view on the fundamental causes of the development of a thing. He thinks that the way Mao posed the question in relation to revolution means, China is the internal and the rest of the world external. He sees the advent of imperialism in every country and revolutionary process has been integrated into world process. So, it is wrong to say any individual country's situation is fundamental and the

---

40 Bob Avakian, "Conquer the World? The International Proletariat Must and Will", *Revolution,* Special Issue, Number 50, pp. 35, 34.

41 Mao Tse-tung, "On Contradiction", *Selected Works*, Eng. ed., Third Printing, Foreign Language Press, Peking, 1975, Vol. 1, p. 313.

external factor is conditional. He thinks, with the advent of imperialism, the era of the existence of the individual countries and their individual development with interpenetration between them is over, now they have been integrated into the world process. Whenever each and every individual country, smaller or larger, has been already integrated into a larger world process, the fundamental contradictions on the world scale determines the development of the contradictions within a particular country. Let us see what Bob Avakian says:

> In "On Contradiction" the way it's presented is that China is the internal and the rest of the world is the external. And what we've emphasized in opposition to this is viewing the process of the world historic advance from the bourgeois epoch to the communist epoch as something which in fact takes place in an overall sense on a world scale, is a world process and both arises out of and is ultimately determined by the fundamental contradiction of capitalism which, with the advent of imperialism, has become the fundamental contradiction of this process on a world scale. If we want to look to see what is the underlying and main driving force in terms of the development of revolutionary situations in particular countries at particular times, then too we have to look to the overall development of contradictions on a world scale, flowing out of and ultimately determined by this fundamental contradiction and not mainly to the development of the contradictions within a particular country, because that country and the process there is integrated in an overall way into this larger world process. It's not simply as it was in the feudal era or the beginning of the bourgeois era where you had separate countries more or less separately developing with interpenetration between them; now they've been integrated into this larger process.[42]

Here what Bob Avakian says is that the integration of individual countries into the larger world process is correct. This is a fundamental feature of imperialism. Not a single Marxist disagrees with this. But, what Bob Avakian is trying to prove that is wrong from the basic law of contradiction. He has tried to delete the existence of particularity of contradiction. He has talked only about general contradictions of the present world, and not of the particular contradiction of individual countries. There are three fundamental contradictions on world level in the present world. Firstly, the contradiction between labour and capital in capitalist countries; secondly, the contradiction between the oppressed nations and imperialism; and, thirdly the contradiction among the various financial groups and imperialist powers. The intensification and sharpness of these contradictions developed the special stage of capitalism. This special stage is nothing else than the era of imperialism and proletarian revolution. Leninism paid attention to this

---

42 Bob Avakian, "Conquer the World? The International Proletariat Must and Will", *Revolution,* Special Issue, Number 50, pp. 34-35.

new stage which existed in the process of development of capitalism. That is why, it could deal with its contradictions well.

The integration of individual countries into the world process is the generalization of existing contradictions on the world level. In the process of development, relationship between general contradiction and particular contradiction is dialectical, not metaphysical. Bob Avakian has taken this relationship metaphysically. He puts emphasis only on the general, not on the particular. He cannot understand the particular character of a particular country. All individual countries have been integrated into a larger world process. It is correct. But how can all the world's basic contradictions be treated in the same way? They cannot. As, Mao says: "These contradictions cannot be treated in the same way since each has its own particularity; moreover, the two aspects of each contradiction cannot be treated in the same way since each aspect has its own characteristics."

Each of the world's basic contradictions should be resolved in different ways. The contradiction between labour and capital in capitalist countries and the contradiction between oppressed nations and imperialism are qualitatively different contradictions. Applying different methods they can be resolved. Mao has said explicitly:

> Qualitatively different contradictions can only be resolved by qualitatively different methods. For instance, the contradiction between the proletariat and the bourgeoisie is resolved by the method of socialist revolution; the contradiction between the great masses of the people and the feudal system is resolved by the method of democratic revolution; the contradiction between the colonies and imperialism is resolved by the method of national revolutionary war. ... The principle of using different methods to resolve different contradictions is one which Marxist-Leninists must strictly observe. The dogmatists do not observe this principle; they do not understand that conditions differ in different kinds of revolution and so do not understand that different methods should be used to resolve different contradictions; on the contrary, they invariably adopt what they imagine to be an unalterable formula and arbitrarily apply it everywhere, which only causes setbacks to the revolution or makes a sorry mess of what was originally well done.[43]

Avoiding this materialist dialectical philosophical ground completely, Bob Avakian advocates a Trotskyite line on the question of nations, national struggle and world revolution. Wearing the mask of "ultra-leftism", he has attacked Marx, Lenin and Mao Tse-tung on a Rightist track. Actually, his "ultra-leftism" is nothing but opposition to revolution, repudiation of revolution. In essence, wearing the mask of world revolution, he is opposing revolution in single countries by over emphasizing the role of the external

43 Mao Tse-tung, "On Contradiction", *Selected Works*, Eng. ed., Third Printing, Foreign Language Press, Peking, 1975, Vol. 1, pp. 322-23, 321-22.

factor. He is trying to kill revolution in particular countries. Doing this, he is liquidating world revolution. We can see Bob Avakian's metaphysical view on revolution in particular countries in his view about "one-stage" and "two-stage" of revolution. Actually, he is against the new democratic revolution in colonial, semi (or neo)-colonial countries. According to the Thought of Mao, socialist revolution is fit for all the industrially advanced countries and new democratic revolution for all the colonial, semi (or neo)-colonial countries. As Mao has said:

> The historical characteristic of the Chinese revolution lies in its division into the two stages, democracy and socialism, the first being no longer democracy in general, but democracy of the Chinese type, a new and special type, namely, New Democracy. ... It follows from the colonial, semi-colonial and semi-feudal character of present-day Chinese society that the Chinese revolution must be divided into two stages. The first step is to change the colonial, semi-colonial and semi-feudal form of society into an independent, democratic society. The second is to carry the revolution forward and build a socialist society. At present the Chinese revolution is taking the first step.[44]

Bob Avakian disagrees with Mao. Taking Lenin's "help" (or using Lenin) he has tried to prove Mao wrong. As he expresses his view:

> In particular, there is a tendency towards a kind of absolute, mechanical, metaphysical view that there are two types of countries in the world and one of them has one-stage revolutions and the other has two-stage revolutions and the way you make revolution in a country that has a two-stage revolution is the way they did it in China, more or less, with *some* concrete application to conditions in your country; that is, you put forward new democracy as your programme, you go to the countryside, surround the cities from the countryside, wage protracted people's war and eventually capture power ... there is a lot of concrete living reality and importance to the fact that there are two different types of countries in the world. But as Lenin said, these boundary lines are conditional and relative, not absolute; and, despite the general distinction, whether the revolutions there proceed in one stage or two is also relative and conditional, not absolute, and overall it is more determined by what's happening in the world as a whole than it is by what's happening in one country.[45]

Mao held no absolute, mechanical and metaphysical view on the revolution of colonial, semi (neo)-colonial and semi-feudal countries. "Go to the countryside, surround the cities from the countryside, wage protracted people's war and eventually capture power"–these are not universal laws of revolution in the era of imperialism and proletarian revolution. For both

44 Mao Tse-tung, "On New Democracy", *Selected Works*, Eng. ed., First ed., Foreign Language Press, Peking, 1965, Vol. 2, 342.

45 Bob Avakian, "Conquer the World? The International Proletariat Must and Will", *Revolution,* Special Issue, Number 50, p. 35.

type of countries, violent revolution is a universal law of revolution in the era of imperialism and proletarian revolution. These were strategies and tactics developed by Mao in the course of completing the New Democratic Revolution in China. In China's particular situation, it was revolutionary Marxist-Leninist strategy and tactics. How long that type of situation exists in other colonial, semi (neo)-colonial and semi-feudal countries and where they can be applied as strategy and tactics. What we should not forget is that the character of democratic and national revolutionary war in colonial, semi (neo)-colonial and semi-feudal countries and socialist revolution in capitalist countries is different.

In the first type of countries, in the present context, the centres of exploitation are concentrated in the countryside. It means centres of class struggle are concentrated in the countryside. But in the second type of countries, the problem is totally different. Because of the high development of industries, the centres of exploitation are concentrated in large cities. It means the centres of class struggle are concentrated in cities. Communists should resolve one more problem in the colonial and semi (neo)-colonial countries. They have to solve the contradiction between their own country and imperialism. This contradiction can be resolved only by national revolutionary war. Overnight or in a short period, this type of war cannot be won. Undoubtedly, it should be a protracted one. In this era a colonial or semi (neo)-colonial country's revolutionary war against imperialism, i.e. against the international bourgeoisie or international capitalism, cannot be victorious in a short period. Some people think that protracted war means only the armed struggle. It means the comprehensive and political struggle. Actually, the armed struggle is the culmination of the political struggle.

This objective reality determines the strategy and tactics of revolution in the first type of countries. Whenever changes occur, in the objective condition, we should change our strategy and tactics. In this order, so many strategies and tactics cannot be applied in the revolutions of the first type of countries at present. But anti-imperialist character is its essence. This essence is not altered and will not be. To present the Thought of Mao on revolution in the first type of countries or anything else is wrong.

Mao's two-stage of revolution in colonial, semi (neo)-colonial and semi-feudal countries was absolutely correct. Particularity of these countries must be passed through a two-stage revolution in the present world situation. To reject two-stage revolutions in these countries in the name of world revolution is to abolish the task of combating imperialism and neo-colonialism. Proposing this, the RCP, USA and its Chairman Bob Avakian are trying to stop the revolution of the oppressed countries.

3.2. Making Use of Contradictions Among the Imperialists

Lenin's policy of making use of contradictions among the imperialists in defence of the socialist fatherland is of great importance and great contribution too to the international communist movement. He did not see this question in an absolute manner. For him, the concrete situation decides what policy–direct armed conflict with imperialist interventionists or giving concessions or using contradictions between imperialists making military agreements with one of the imperialist coalitions against the other–we should adopt this attitude. We can see his dialectical thinking and practice in his adoption of different policies in different times to defend the socialist fatherland. Lenin has forcefully said that we should adopt a serious attitude towards the defence of a socialist country, which should not be taken superficially. What does a serious attitude imply? Lenin's following statements correctly address this question:

> Adopting a serious attitude towards defence of the country means thoroughly preparing for it, and strictly calculating the balance of forces. If our forces are obviously small, the best means of defence is *retreat into the interior of the country* (anyone who regards this as an artificial formula, made up to suit the needs of the moment, should read old Clausewitz, ... The "Left Communists", however, do not give the slightest indication that they understand the significance of the question of the balance of forces.[46]

If the balance of power is not in our interest, we should be ready to adopt concessions as a rule. Under such situation, we should try to avoid battle and we must take advantage of the contradictions which exist between imperialists or two blocs of imperialism. Lenin expresses his view brilliantly:

> From the political point of view, the fundamental thing in the question of concessions–and here there are both political and economic considerations–is a rule we have not only assimilated in theory, but have also applied in practice, a rule which will remain fundamental with us for a long time until socialism finally triumphs all over the world: we must take advantage of the antagonisms and the contradictions that exist between the two imperialisms, the two groups of capitalist states, and play them off against each other. Until we have conquered the whole world, and as long as we are economically and militarily weaker than the capitalist world, we must stick to the rule that we must be able to take advantage of the antagonisms and contradictions existing among imperialists.[47]

46 V. I. Lenin, " 'Left-Wing' Childishness and the Petit-Bourgeois Mentality", *Collected Works*, Eng. ed., Third Printing, Progress Publishers, Moscow, 1977, Vol. 27, p. 332.

47 V. I. Lenin, "Speech Delivered at a Meeting of Activists of the Moscow Organization of the RCP (B), December", *Collected Works*, Eng. ed., Third Printing, Progress Publishers, Moscow, 1977, Vol. 31, pp. 438-39.

In a very general but abstract sense, Bob Avakian and the RCP, USA have supported the policy of making use of contradictions among the imperialists in the course of revolution, and maintaining power in socialist countries and the advance to communism. As Bob Avakian has said:

> In general during this period of the last few years of his life did put a lot of emphasis on the necessity, and correctly so, of making use of rifts among the imperialists, because he correctly recognized that this was a life-and-death struggle and gave concrete leadership. It wasn't a question of principle in the abstract, but upholding principle while at the same time having that principle be applied in practice. ... It's a question of the synthesis of the two, of winning the masses, a question of actually seizing power, making revolution and transforming society; that's the ultimate test and Lenin treated it as the *ultimate* test. He treated it as a test and he also treated it ultimately, and not narrowly in an empiricist or mechanical revisionist way.

Bob Avakian thinks that in later years, after *Left-Wing Communism*, there began to creep in Lenin's earlier position on the question of the making use of rifts among the imperialists and he pushed the communists in Germany to take national interests and oppose the Versailles Treaty. He has said that the foundation of this deviation from the earlier position was avoidance of the contradiction between the state interests and world revolution. Avakian states:

> One thing that should be said is that in Lenin himself, and not simply later in the Soviet Party and the international movement, there is a wrong view, a view contrary to a certain degree to Leninism, in fact, on the question of the Versailles Treaty and how to deal with it in Germany, which is not totally unconnected with these things I've been discussing. Earlier Lenin took and fought for a basically correct position, for example in *Left-Wing Communism*, on the question of the Versailles Treaty where he said that on the basis of internationalism, German communists should not put themselves in a position of allowing the bourgeoisie to corner them into coming out and saying they're against the Versailles Treaty and should determine their attitude towards the Versailles Treaty on the basis of the interests of the international proletariat and the world revolution. But then there begins to creep in the view, even somewhat appearing in Lenin and certainly carried forward after him, of pushing the communists in Germany a little bit–and this is not accidental and ties in somewhat with his sort of early and partial analysis of the three parts of the world, if you will–to raise the national banner in Germany against the Versailles Treaty and against the victors', feast at the expense of Germany.[48]

Bob Avakian, thus, has brought forward a serious accusation against Lenin. He has also tried to separate Lenin and Leninism. Pretending to be a

48 Bob Avakian, "Conquer the World? The International Proletariat Must and Will", *Revolution,* Special Issue, Number 50, pp. 15-17.

staunch supporter of Leninism, he refutes Lenin. On this serious criticism of Lenin, clarity is needed to some questions. Firstly, Bob Avakian has presented Lenin to a certain degree as a national chauvinist, who abandoned the earlier view of internationalism in the interests of the Soviet Union. Even a single Marxist-Leninist does not accept this accusation aimed at Lenin and Leninism. Lenin was a great champion of proletarian internationalism, and he successfully connected Soviet national interests with the interests of the world revolution. In his analysis of the world situation, Lenin had talked about three types of countries at the Second Congress of the Communist International. Actually, the world was not divided into three. It was just a broad outline of the picture of the world as it appeared after the imperialist war. Analyzing the world situation, Lenin writes:

> In the oppressed colonies–countries which are being dismembered, such as Persia, Turkey and China, and in countries that were defeated and have been relegated to the position of colonies–there are 1,250 million inhabitants. Not more than 250,000,000 inhabit countries that have retained their old positions, but have become economically dependent on America, and all of which, during the war, were militarily dependent, once the war involved the whole world and did not permit a single state to remain really neutral. And, finally, we have not more than 250,000,000 inhabitants in countries whose top stratum, the capitalists alone, benefited from the partition of the world.[49]

Responding to the Chinese revisionists claim of *Peking Review* No. 45 from 1977, their major theoretical statement on the "three worlds" theory, Bob Avakian writes:

> "At that time he divided the world into three, too. What should we learn from Lenin? We should learn to divide the world into three. But, there is an element of truth in that if you read the essay they are referring to, Lenin did say that among the victor imperialist states there are the ones that won big; there are the ones that didn't win so big; then, finally, there's Germany which got creamed, there's us that made revolution and all the colonial and dependent peoples. He did make an analysis like that–not, however, to figure out which bourgeoisie it was best to suck up to, but how to make use of contradictions among them and, even more strategically and fundamentally, where to expect and where to concentrate work to develop a revolutionary upsurge in the next period. But, again, it's not that the Chinese revisionists, in scrounging around and looking for a Leninist cover–to the degree they want any (and that's decreasingly so) for their reactionary and counter-revolutionary international line as formulated, at least heretofore, in the "three worlds" theory, it's not that they can't find any elements of that in Lenin. Of course, as Lenin himself once said, you can always find any quote out of context to justify anything, which is one of the things that makes life

49 V. I. Lenin, "The Second Congress of the Communist International", *Collected Works*, Progress Publishers, Moscow, Eng. ed., 1977, Vol. 31, p. 218.

> so frustrating. But these are some problems, we aren't simply dealing with distortion, there are some things, certain elements which begin showing up, that can be marshalled for wrong arguments.[50]

The first part of the above statement of Bob Avakian is not so objectionable. But in the last part, he has tried hard to prove Lenin wrong. He tries to find the root of Chinese revisionism in the so-called three worlds theory in Lenin. That's why; he got some "elements" of their so-called three worlds theory in Lenin. He found "some things, certain elements" which "marshalled" Chinese revisionists to put wrong arguments this way. While Lenin was analysing the world situation at that time, he said:

> By means of the Treaty of Versailles, the war imposed such terms upon these countries that advanced peoples have been reduced to a state of colonial dependence, poverty, starvation, ruin, and loss of rights: this Treaty binds them for many generations, placing them in conditions that no civilized nation has ever lived in.

Further, he says: "The Treaty of Versailles has placed Germany and the other defeated countries in a position that makes their economic existence physically impossible, deprives them of all rights, and humiliates them."[51]

Lenin's above statement neither goes against Leninism nor does it go against the objective reality. His sober and correct view on the Treaty of Versailles helped to expose its essence and to unite peace and just-loving people of the world. Clashes with the Treaty of Versailles worldwide demonstrated the correctness of Lenin's line. Bob Avakian sees some "elements" in the general analysis of the Chinese revisionists' "three worlds" in Mao. As he says: "There may have been in Mao's analysis of world forces certain elements contained in the "three worlds" theory." Further, he says:

> There was a certain tendency in Mao to make a principle out of it. And while Mao was certainly *not* responsible for the counter-revolutionary international line of the Chinese revisionists in power now, there is on the other hand some aspect of truth to their tracing of elements of the general analysis of "three worlds" in the analyses made by Mao during various periods going back, for example, to his 1946 interview with Anna Louise Strong where he lays out the whole thing about an intermediate zone between US imperialism and the Soviet Union. Here Mao talks about the countries (except the Soviet Union) immediately subjected to the aggression of US imperialism, lumping all of them, including the imperialist countries, together. Bob Avakian also has bluntly said that Mao's analysis involves a frankly classless concept

50 Bob Avakian, "Conquer the World? The International Proletariat Must and Will", *Revolution,* Special Issue, Number 50, pp. 15-16.

51 V. I. Lenin, "The Second Congress of the Communist International", *Collected Works*, Progress Publishers, Moscow, Eng. ed., 1977, Vol. 31, p. 217.

> of aggression and, ironically, an error in the direction of blotting out the distinction between imperialist and colonial countries.[52]

This is a serious accusation against Mao. His whole talk does not give the sense of "classless concept of aggression" and "blotting out the distinction between imperialist and colonial countries." Bob Avakian's presentation seems a forced one. Mao was not delivering a speech on the concept of aggression on class. He was answering Anna Louise Strong's question, ("what do you think of the possibility of the United States starting a war against the Soviet Union? "). Observing the world situation, Mao said:

> The United States and the Soviet Union are separated by a vast zone which includes many capitalist, colonial and semi-colonial countries in Europe, Asia and Africa. Before the US reactionaries have subjugated these countries, an attack on the Soviet Union is out of the question. In the Pacific the United States now controls areas larger than all the former British spheres of influence there put together; it controls Japan, that part of China under Kuomintang rule, half of Korea, and the South Pacific. It has long controlled Central and South America. It seeks also to control the whole of the British Empire and Western Europe. Using various pretexts, the United States is making large-scale military arrangements and setting up military bases in many countries. The US reactionaries say that the military bases they have set up and are preparing to set up all over the world are aimed against the Soviet Union. True, these military bases are directed against the Soviet Union. At present, however, it is not the Soviet Union but the countries in which these military bases are located that are the first to suffer US aggression.[53]

As to the world situation, it was wrong to give the slogan of class struggle or to suggest to the Soviet Union to take the path of armed conflict with the US imperialism, or to overthrow capitalism and establish socialism in various countries. It was not the time of the First World War. It would be suicidal to take the path of establishment of socialism and call to convert imperialist war (if occurred) into a civil war. According to the objective situation, it was hard work to arouse the masses of the people to fight for the preservation of world peace and to awaken them about the rising danger of the Third World War. That is why Mao's analysis of the world situation was absolutely right. Bob Avakian and the RCP, USA have criticized Stalin and the Comintern's policy of making use of rifts among the imperialists in relation to the Second World War; they did not accept that policy as a particular and tactical manoeuvres, of making use of rifts among the imperialists by the Soviet Union. As Bob Avakian says:

---

52 Bob Avakian, "Conquer the World? The International Proletariat Must and Will", *Revolution,* Special Issue, Number 50, pp. 34, 31.

53 Mao Tse-tung, "Talk with Anna Louise Strong", *Selected Works*, Eng. ed., First edition, Foreign Language Press, Peking, April 1961, Vol. 4, p. 99.

> The Line(s) of the Soviet and Comintern leadership in relation to WWII overall (that is, during the period leading up to the war, from the mid-1930s on, and during the different phases of the war itself) was *basically wrong.* The point is not that particular policies and tactical manoeuvres of the Soviet thinking nuclear power with different imperialists and making use of contradictions among them, were absolutely wrong in principle, taken by themselves; the point is that the overall line guiding this was incorrect.[54]

At another place Bob Avakian has said that the concentration in the united front against fascism was a "departure in significant aspects from Leninism in the international communist movement."[55] Here we can see the criticism of Bob Avakian on the policy of the Soviet Union and Comintern leadership in relation to making use of rifts among the imperialists from an antagonistic angle. This type of criticism of Stalin's period is absolutely wrong, and we flatly reject it. Under the leadership of Stalin, the policy the Soviet Union and the Comintern took in relation to making use of rifts among the imperialists to defend the socialist fatherland was totally Leninist. Lenin's views noted above do not leave any confusion. The rise of fascism in Germany, western imperialism (American imperialism included) and Japanese imperialism were great threats to the Soviet Union. Certainly, there were serious contradictions between them, but at one point they could be united (on the international level or at least on the regional level). The point was–the elimination of the existence of the socialist Soviet Union by military intervention.

The situation of the balance of power of that time was of prime importance. Compared to the world imperialism, socialism and the movement of the proletariat in advanced countries and national liberation movements in colonial countries were weak. On that condition, it would be suicidal for the Soviet Union to collide with the world imperialism. Lenin has correctly said, "from the point of view of the defence of the fatherland it would be a crime to enter into an armed conflict with an infinitely superior and well-prepared enemy."[56] From the point of defence of the Soviet Union, Stalin and the Comintern's policy of not entering into an armed conflict with an infinitely superior and well-prepared world imperialism was absolutely correct. So, Stalin was fully utilizing the chance to defend the Soviet Union.

When it was not possible to enter into armed conflict with the world imperialism, Stalin did not just wait, but tried to find other alternatives to

---

54 Bob Avakian, "Outline of Views on the Historical Experience of the International Communist Movement and Lessons for Today", *Revolution,* June 1981, p. 5.

55 Bob Avakian, "Conquer the World? The International Proletariat Must and Will", *Revolution,* Special Issue, Number 50, p. 25.

56 V. I. Lenin, "A Painful But Necessary Lesson", *Collected Works*, Eng. ed., Third Printing, 1977, Vol. 27, p. 64.

paralyze the imperialists' strategy to eliminate the socialist Soviet Union. In this regard, he went back to great Lenin. Except armed conflict, there were other measures which helped to defend any socialist country from the attack of imperialism. These were concessions, manoeuvring, and military agreements. Basing himself on the world situation, Stalin adopted all of them. After prolonged attempts, Stalin became successful to manoeuvre Britain, France and USA. Finally, he succeeded in forming a military agreement with a bloc of imperialists–Britain, France and USA–against that of the fascists of the world imperialism. The united front against fascism was a political and military agreement between four countries–Soviet Union, Britain, France and USA.

Bob Avakian has said that the Soviet Union and Comintern's policy of making use of rifts among the imperialists in relation to the Second World War was not "particular and tactical manoeuvres", they were "absolutely wrong in principle." So, they were "basically wrong." Bob Avakian's charge is baseless. His criticism on the united front against fascism is equally baseless. Making the front was not a "departure in significant aspects from Leninism." For this, I want to quote Lenin: "We do not in general reject military agreements with one of the imperialist coalitions against the other in those cases in which such an agreement could, without undermining the basis of Soviet power, strengthen its position and paralyze the attacks of any imperialist power."[57]

All these facts make it clear that it was not Stalin whose policies were "absolutely wrong in principle", "basically wrong" and "departure from insignificant aspects of Leninism", but, to the contrary, it is the summation of historical experience by the RCP, USA and its Chairman Bob Avakian, which is "absolutely wrong in principle", "basically wrong" and a "departure insignificant from Leninism."

In general, Mao also made use of contradictions between the imperialists in certain cases. Bob Avakian has criticized Mao for his view on making use of contradictions among the enemies, defeating the enemies one by one. In this regard, he writes:

> Not only in the Anna Louise Strong interview and in "On Policy" but also in the General Line polemic, the tendency shows up to see... too much in terms of identifying one enemy and rallying everybody against it. In the case of the General Line polemic, US imperialism was seen as the main enemy at that stage and in the other imperialist countries the advice was to struggle against the monopoly capitalists and reactionary forces who betrayed the national

57 V. I. Lenin, "Theses on the Present Political Situation", *Collected Works*. Eng. ed., Third Printing, Progress Publishers, Moscow, 1977, Vol. 27, 361.

interest, in other words who were allying with US imperialism; overall this was not correct.[58]

Bob Avakian's main charge against Mao is that he elevated this policy "to the level of a general principle." Of course, Mao was clear on this issue, and he has presented his view explicitly and forcefully in the above mentioned essays. But, in this regard, Bob Avakian has not mentioned one fundamental matter here. It is so because he cannot criticize Mao in this manner if he mentions that fundamental point within Mao's view on making use of contradictions among imperialists. For Mao, it was just "tactics", and not a general principle.

Bob Avakian has said that Mao's military strategy in China might have led him to the wrong military strategy in the context of the Second World War. Drawing out the political lessons from Mao's military strategy adopted in the course of the Chinese revolution, Bob Avakian writes:

> The political point that I want to draw in particular, besides correcting that point in *Mao Tse-tung's Immortal Contributions* ... is refocusing attention on the question of what is there in the military strategy Mao fought for that might, spontaneously at least, lead him away from understanding that in the context of a world war it might be correct to in fact strike out in different directions, viewing the world as a whole; that is, to oppose the imperialists in general and to attempt to overthrow them wherever possible in *both* camps, of course taking into the account the particular situation in different countries.

Bob Avakian concludes that "the experience and strategy forged in the military sphere in China might tend to lead against that" to Mao. And he adopted the policy of "making use of contradictions, dealing with a superior enemy and in that way defeating enemies one by one." He also adds, "especially since it is necessary to make these criticisms of Mao."[59]

In the period of the War of Resistance Against Japan, Mao upheld and developed a united front policy with all the people favouring resistance. The Anti-Japan National United Front consisted of all anti-Japanese workers, peasants, soldiers, students, intellectuals, and businessmen. On making use of contradictions among anti-communist diehards, Mao writes: "In the struggle against the anti-communist diehards, our policy is to make use of contradictions, win over the many, oppose the few and crush our enemies one by one, and to wage struggles on just grounds, to our advantage, and with restraint."

58 Bob Avakian, "Conquer the World? The International Proletariat Must and Will", *Revolution,* Special Issue, Number 50, p. 35.

59 Ibid., p. 34.

Mao had given adequate importance to independence within the unity. He said, "within the united front our policy must be one of independence and initiative, i.e. both unity and independence are necessary." Regarding imperialism he writes:

> We deal with imperialism in the same way. The Communist Party opposes all imperialism, but we make a distinction between Japanese imperialism which is now committing aggression against China and the imperialist powers which are not doing so now, between German and Italian imperialism which are allies of Japan and have recognized "Manchukuo" and British and US imperialism which are opposed to Japan, and between the Britain and the United States of yesterday which followed a Munich policy in the Far East and undermined China's resistance to Japan, and the Britain and the United States of today which have abandoned this policy and are now in favour of China's resistance. Our tactics are guided by one and the same principle: to make use of contradictions, win over the many, oppose the few and crush our enemies one by one.[60]

In an interview with Anna Louis Strong, Mao identified the main enemy and the main cause of the possible Third World War, saying: "American people and the peoples of all countries menaced by the US aggression should unite and struggle against the attacks of the US reactionaries and their running dogs in these countries."[61]

It is written in the General Line polemic:

> This general line proceeds from the actual world situation taken as a whole and from a class analysis of the fundamental contradiction in the contemporary world, and is directed against the counter-revolutionary global strategy of US imperialism. ... This general line is one of forming a broad united front, with the socialist camp and the international proletariat as its nucleus, to oppose the imperialists and reactionaries headed by the United States; it is a line of boldly arousing the masses, expanding the revolutionary forces, winning over the middle forces and isolating the reactionary forces.[62]

The General Line's proposal of the formation of a broad united front, aiming to arouse the masses, expand the revolutionary forces, win over the middle forces, isolate and oppose the imperialist and reactionary forces proved that it was a true Marxist-Leninist Line. Mao Tse-tung upheld and developed the line of Lenin and Stalin on making use of contradictions among imperialists.

---

60 Mao Tse-tung, "On Policy", *Selected Works*, Eng. ed., First ed., Foreign Language Press, Peking, December 1965, Vol. 2, pp. 442-44.

61 Mao Tse-tung, "Talk with Anna Louise Strong", *Selected Works*, Eng. ed., First edition, Foreign Language Press, Peking, 1961, Vol. 4, p. 100.

62 "A Proposal Concerning the General Line of the International Communist Movement", *The Great Debate*, Mass Line Publications, Kerala, 1994, pp. 3-4.

3.3. Industry and Agriculture in the Course of the Socialist Transformation of Society

After summing up the historical experience of the international communist movement on the above question, Bob Avakian has reached the conclusion that not only did Stalin make serious deviations, but Lenin, too, made the same mistake by holding a wrong view that without the dominance of industry over agriculture, we cannot move ahead from socialism to communism. As he has said:

> There was a little bit too much the tendency towards one-to-one identification of industrialization, the dominance of industry over agriculture, with socialism–in other words, the idea, looking at it from the other side, that without the dominance of industry socialism was not viable, and this view was in general currency in the socialist and communist movement.[63]

He has said that Lenin's view is referred to in his famous article–'Better Fewer, But Better', and 'A Great Beginning'. Bob Avakian has said that to a certain degree Lenin had the thinking of the theory of productive forces. He thought that Lenin was not completely free from the theory of the productive forces.

Lenin's debate with the Mensheviks, Kautskyites, etc., on this question is of great importance in Russia's socialist and communist movement. In his famous article 'Our Revolution', Lenin has refuted their theory of productive forces. Their argument was that it was not possible to build socialism under backward economic conditions. Refuting their mechanical view, Lenin said:

> If a definite level of culture is required for the building of socialism (although nobody can say just what that definite "level of culture" is, for it differs in every West European country), why can't we begin by first achieving the prerequisites for that definite level of culture in a revolutionary way, and *then*, with the aid of the workers' and peasants' government and the Soviet system, proceed to overtake the other nations?[64]

Here Bob Avakian does not like the last part of this paragraph–that is, "why can't we begin by first achieving ... to overtake the other nations?" He has interpreted Lenin's saying as accepting certain views of the Mensheviks and Kautskyites that it was impossible to build socialism in Russia in the light of the backward economic and technical level. He says further:

> Even here–in rereading it I was struck by this–it's clear that he's refuting them but also accepting some of their terms. He's saying, "Well, fine, so you do have to have a certain level of civilization", then he puts in parenthesis,

---

63 Bob Avakian, "Conquer the World? The International Proletariat Must and Will", *Revolution,* Special Issue, Number 50, p. 14.

64 V. I. Lenin, "Our Revolution", *Collected Works*, Progress Publishers, Moscow, Eng. ed., Fourth Printing, 1980, Vol. 33, 478-79.

> and this is important, "although nobody can say just what that level is" which is also a refutation on a more profound level, it's a dialectical statement as opposed to mechanical materialism; he's saying, "Well, yes, it's true but let's not get too mechanical and too absolute about it." But at the same time, he is, to a certain degree, saying, "All right, well and good, but why can't we first seize power and *then* outdo the capitalist countries and capitalism in general in creating a higher level of technique and (in that sense) civilization.[65]

Bob Avakian has failed to understand the problems objectively. He has talked a lot on dialectics. But he has shown his poverty of ideas on his understanding of dialectics only. The theory of productive forces, advocated by Mensheviks and Kautskyites then was to be refuted. Lenin did it in a splendid way. Lenin's "why can't we begin by first achieving the prerequisites for that definite level of culture in a revolutionary way, and *then*, with the aid of workers and peasants' government and the Soviet system, proceed to overtake the other nations" doesn't accept "certain bases of" Mensheviks and Kautskyites' "orientation" as "some of their terms." Here Lenin emphasizes the role of consciousness and the historical role of the proletarian leadership in revolution. It means if the real force capable of resolving the contradictions of socialist society in a revolutionary way, we should not stay away from moving ahead in the name of (comparatively) backward productive forces of the country. In the present era, revolution has an international character, so, we should not confine our work within the narrow national boundary of our own country, we should go ahead. We should begin, as Lenin has said "by first achieving the prerequisite for that definite level of culture in a revolutionary way, and *then*, with the aid of workers' and peasants' government and the Soviet system, proceed" to develop productive forces to overtake other developed capitalist countries.

3.4. Bob Avakian on Lenin's "Left-Wing" Communism: An Infantile Disorder

A summation of Lenin's *"Left-Wing" Communism: An Infantile Disorder* is a part of Bob Avakian's overall summation on the historical experience of the international communist movement. Bob Avakian has said that this is not a "thorough summation" of that book, "but rather to make a few points to be part of a deeper summation of *Left-Wing Communism* in the context of the larger questions being touched on here." "In the context of the larger question" he has summed just a few points, which are just a part of a future, "deeper summation" is enough to be familiar as with the view on this book. I cannot imagine what would be Bob Avakian's "a deeper summation" of this book. Summation of *"Left-Wing" Communism: An Infantile Disorder* isn't just

65 Bob Avakian, "Conquer the World? The International Proletariat Must and Will", *Revolution,* Special Issue, Number 50, p. 15.

a question of evaluating the book itself, it is a question of how to sum up Leninism to a certain degree. The evaluation of *"Left-Wing": Communism: An Infantile Disorder* is the evaluation of strategy and tactics of Leninism. So, the appraisal of Lenin's book *"Left-Wing" Communism: An Infantile Disorder* is an important question of Marxism-Leninism involving the whole international socialist and communist movement.

He has given many thanks to Soviet revisionists for the reprint of *"Left-Wing" Communism: An Infantile Disorder.* He is against taking this book as the great work of strategy and tactics. However, he has said that the essence and main aspect of this book is "correct" as given below:

> Now these errors might not be so important if everybody–and I mean the leaders of the international communist movement and down to all the modern-day revisionists of various kinds almost without exception–had not insisted on reprinting and disseminating *Left-Wing Communism* as "the great work of strategy and tactics" which must be applied to the latter, and if it had not been used, as it has been used by such types, as a recipe everywhere for revisionism ... *Left-Wing Communism* has been seized on to promote revisionism, and the kind of mistakes in it that I have pointed to are given concentrated attention and expression at the same time that the correct things about it, which are the essence and main aspect of it, are taken out of context and turned into a recipe for revisionism, for economism, parliamentary cretinism, tailism and being the tail on the bourgeoisie generally. Everyone that's ever been in the movement and around these various forces more than a few months has been smacked in the face with quotations from and references to *Left-Wing Communism* in this kind of way, and it's time to sum this up correctly and uphold what's correct and say we have a few criticisms, on the other hand, to make about this.

There is a serious problem of using the quotations and references from the works of Marx to Mao Tse-tung out of context and turn it into a recipe for Right not only with *Left-Wing Communism,* but also with other major classical Marxist works. We cannot escape from this problem in absolute terms. Soviet revisionists did not publish only *Left-Wing Communism*; they published Lenin's whole Collected Works–as well as they published works of Marx and Engels in so many volumes. "Left" and Right revisionists will interpret in their own way, and revolutionaries will interpret in their own way. Forgetting this basic truth, Bob Avakian has slandered Lenin's work *Left-Wing Communism* for having been seized by modern revisionists to promote revisionism.

Bob Avakian has criticized *Left-Wing Communism* mainly on the strategy and tactics of revolution. This is a great work of strategy and tactics of revolution. While moving towards socialist transformation in Russia and addressing the debate seen in the international communist movement, Lenin developed the strategy and tactics of the socialist revolution. Criticizing *Left-Wing Communism*, Avakian writes:

> Some points and approaches and even certain questions of method were wrong, even given the situation, reflecting on the one hand a certain lack of understanding of some of the concrete situations on the part of Lenin, but on the other hand going so far or trying so hard to take the lessons of the successful revolution in Russia and apply them to other circumstances in the crush and crunch of this still sharpening situation–to "squeeze as much as possible out of that conjuncture" (to use that very descriptive phrase)–that certain errors were actually made by Lenin, and in certain instances in any case, things begin to turn somewhat into their opposite in terms of tactics urged.[66]

What are those wrong and erroneous points, approaches and method–according to Bob Avakian–which were made by Lenin in his book *Left-Wing Communism*? Bob Avakian has said that Lenin's errors "begin to turn somewhat into their opposite in terms of tactics". In this regard, he has criticized Lenin on two points: first, on the formation of the British Communist Party ad participation in the British parliament. Lenin had suggested to the British Communists to unite four parties and groups into a single Communist Party on the basis of the principle of the Third International and obligatory participation in parliament. As Lenin had suggested:

> In my opinion, the British Communists should unite their four parties and groups ... into a single Communist Party on the basis of the principles of the Third International and of *obligatory* participation in parliament. The Communist Party should propose the following "compromise" election agreement to the Hendersons and Snowdens: let us jointly fight against the alliance between Lloyd George and the Conservatives; let us share parliamentary seats in proportion to the number of workers' votes polled for the Labour Party and for the Communist Party (not in elections, but in a special ballot), and let us retain *complete freedom* of agitation, propaganda and political activity. Of course, without this latter condition, we cannot agree to a bloc, for that would be treachery; the British Communists must demand and get complete freedom to expose the Hendersons and the Snowdens in the same way as (*for fifteen years*–1903–17) the Russian Bolsheviks demanded and got it in respect of the Russian Hendersons and Snowdens, i.e. the Mensheviks.[67]

Bob Avakian thinks that Lenin correctly employed the tactics of participation in parliament in the Russian Revolution, but he generalized that particular experience of the Russian Revolution in the case of Britain,

66 Ibid., pp. 11, 10.

67 V. I. Lenin, " 'Left-Wing' Communism: An Infantile Disorder", *Collected Works*, Progress Publishers, Moscow, Eng. ed., Third Printing, 1977, Vol. 31, p. 86.

he found fault in the suggestion to participate in parliament. I think that Bob has absolutely rejected the possibility of participating in parliament in a country like Britain even tactically. His statement, "regard to Merry Old England, with its long tradition of corruption and bourgeoisification of the working class which, along with its whole bourgeois parliamentary tradition", is nothing but only intended to prove Lenin wrong. Ridiculously he has seen "a point" in his favour in Stalin's saying–"In Russia, there is no parliament"*(Marxism and the National Question)*. This reference is nothing but like a rope support for a hanging man. Neither can it help him to prove correct, nor can he pull Stalin against Lenin. Stalin's view absolutely matches Lenin's view on this issue. Actually, he has done a frustrating job by quoting Stalin here in this regard. According to Bob Avakian's above quoted statement, where there is a long tradition of corruption and bourgeoisification of the working class, where there is a long bourgeois parliamentary tradition it is wrong to take part in parliament. It creates confusion and disorients among the advanced section of the proletariat. So, we should boycott parliamentary election. Marxism-Leninism always takes it as a tactical question. Of course, as Lenin has said, "The *era* of the bourgeois parliamentarianism is over, and the *era* of the proletarian dictatorship has *begun*. That is incontestable." But, alerting us, Lenin further says:

> Parliamentarianism has become "historically obsolete." That is true in the propaganda sense. However, everybody knows that this is still a far cry from overcoming it in *practice*. Capitalism could have been declared–and with full justice–to be "historically obsolete" many decades ago, but that does not at all remove the need for a very long and very persistent struggle *on the basis* of capitalism. Parliamentarianism is "historically obsolete" from the standpoint of *world history* ... But world history is counted in decades. Ten or twenty years earlier or later makes no difference when measured with the yardstick of world history; from the standpoint of world history it is a trifle that cannot be considered even approximately. But for that very reason, it is a glaring theoretical error to apply the yardstick of world history to practical politics.[68]

In a debate with modern revisionists, the CPC, continuing with Lenin's view on the above question, wrote:

> Lenin told us about the limitations of parliamentary struggle, but he also warned communists against narrow-minded, sectarian errors. In this well-known work *"Left-Wing" Communism: An Infantile Disorder* Lenin elucidated the experience of the Russian revolution, showing under what conditions a boycott of parliament is correct and under what other conditions it is incorrect. Lenin held that every proletarian party should make use of every possible opportunity to participate in necessary parliamentary struggles. It was fundamentally wrong and would only harm the cause of the

68 Ibid., Vol. 31, p. 56.

> revolutionary proletariat for a Communist Party member to engage only in empty talk about the revolution, while being unwilling to work perseveringly and painstakingly, and shunning necessary parliamentary struggles.[69]

Here we can see basically two different views on the question of Lenin's view on the participation in parliament, which is presented in *"Left-Wing" Communism: An Infantile Disorder.* Under Mao's leadership, the CPC analysed it as the developed thinking of Lenin based on the experience of the Russian Revolution. But, Avakian concluded it as a wrong generalization of a particular tactics. He sees there was a bourgeois logic to Lenin's argument. As he observes:

> Frankly, there is a certain bourgeois logic to Lenin's argument here. He even goes so far as to say at one point, that if you support Henderson and Snowden (who were the leaders of the phony socialist Labour Party) and if they gain the victory over Lloyd George and Churchill, then the majority of workers will, in a brief space of time, become disappointed in their leaders and come over to support the communists. Lenin says, and here's where I think bourgeois Logic begins to assert itself and even a certain amount of opportunism frankly, ... Well, they may or they may not, but that's not the question–that may be a tactical consideration, but it has to be based on something more fundamental. Lenin here is basing his argument on an erroneous assessment, and here is where he was trying so hard that he fell over backwards that's the only way I can put it, because he is not unaware of some of the points that I've been discussing, he reflects to a certain degree here an understanding of the role that parliamentarism has played in the British working class and British society. In fact, he even says to the effect that exactly because of the history of parliamentarism, it's all the more necessary to carry out the parliamentary form of struggle in Great Britain–and I think that is wrong, bourgeois logic and trying so hard that he fell over backwards.[70]

Lenin was fully aware and clear ideologically and politically on those points that Bob Avakian has been discussing here. What Lenin is taking about here is not in a historical sense or from the standpoint of world history, but he is talking about the practical politics of Great Britain. Bob Avakian here is basing his argument on an erroneous assessment. His assessment of Lenin's view on the above questions is metaphysical. So, it is not Lenin who fell over backwards, but it is Bob Avakian himself who has fallen over backwards.

Secondly, Bob Avakian has criticized Lenin's view on the question of trade unions and work in them. At that time the German "Lefts" were

---

69 "Long Live Leninism!" by The Editorial Department of "Red Flag." *The Documents of the Great Debate (February 1956-June 1963)*, Vol. 2, Antararashtriya Prakashan, Saharanpur, First ed., December, 2005, Vol. 2, pp. 87-88.

70 Bob Avakian, "Conquer the World? The International Proletariat Must and Will", *Revolution,* Special Issue, Number 50, p. 11.

against the working in "reactionary" and "counter-revolutionary" trade unions. Criticizing their view, Lenin said that it was fundamentally wrong, and "contains nothing but empty phrases." The article is vilified and has been described as "articles of faith of revisionism" by Bob Avakian. But for Lenin it "is aimed at applying to Western Europe whatever is universally practicable, significant and relevant in the history and the present-day tactics of Bolshevism."

Refuting the childish nonsense of the German "Lefts", Lenin writes:

> We cannot but regard as equally ridiculous and childish nonsense the pompous, very learned, and frightfully, revolutionary disquisitions of the German Lefts to the effect that communists cannot and should not work in reactionary trade unions, that it is permissible to turn down such work, that it is necessary to withdraw from the trade unions and create a brand new and immaculate "Workers' Union" invented by very pleasant (and, probably, for the most part very youthful) communists, etc., etc.

Further, he writes:

> The trade unions were a tremendous step forward for the working class in the early days of capitalist development, inasmuch as they marked a transition from the workers' disunity and helplessness to the *rudiments* of class organization. When the *revolutionary party of the proletariat*, the *highest* form of proletarian class organization, began to take shape (and the party will not merit the name until it learns to weld the leaders into one indivisible whole with the class and the masses) the trade unions inevitably began to reveal *certain* reactionary features, a certain craft narrow-mindedness, a certain tendency to be non-political, a certain inertness, etc. However, the development of the proletariat did not, and could not, proceed anywhere in the world otherwise than through the trade unions, through reciprocal action between them and the part of the working class.
>
> This ridiculous "theory" that communists should not work in reactionary trade unions reveals with the utmost clarity the frivolous attitude of the "Left" Communists towards the question of influencing the "masses", and their misuse of clamour about the "masses." If you want to help the "masses" and win the sympathy and support of the "masses", you should not fear difficulties, or pinpricks, chicanery, insults and persecution from the "leaders" (who, being opportunists and social-chauvinists, are in most cases directly or indirectly connected with the bourgeoisie and the police), but must absolutely *work wherever the masses are to be found.* You must be capable of any sacrifice, of overcoming the greatest obstacles, in order to carry on agitation and propaganda systematically, perseveringly, persistently and patiently in those institutions, societies and associations–even the most reactionary–in which proletarian or semi-proletarian masses are to be found.[71]

71 V. I. Lenin, " 'Left-Wing' Communism: An Infantile Disorder", *Collected Works*, Progress Publishers, Moscow, Eng. ed., 1977, Vol. 31, pp. 47, 49-50, 53.

This is the essence of Lenin's well-known book "*Left-Wing" Communism: An Infantile Disorder*, on the question of trade unions and work in them. Bob Avakian is not happy with Lenin. He has said that Lenin's view on trade unions and work in them disoriented the genuine proletarian movement in the West. Even with a cursory look, some errors can be found in "*Left-Wing" Communism*. Let us see what he says:

> In general we could say that some things that did apply then or mainly applied then and/or reflected errors to a certain degree, even if secondarily, have been carried along and built up as articles of faith and become in fact articles of faith of revisionism, for example, the emphasis on trade unions and work in them, which can also be found in *Left-Wing Communism*. It's not that Lenin does not recognize the limitations and shortcomings of trade unions, and certainly of trade unionism, and that he does not recognize the fact that in large part, especially in the West, the unions are controlled by outright reactionaries, not mere reformists. But there is a certain orientation that the trade unions, especially in the West, are, after all, the key mass organizations of the proletariat and that it is necessary to work in and win the trade unions to the cause of socialism. To the degree that this represented truth or much more of the truth at the time of *Left-Wing Communism*, at this stage of the proletarian struggle and of the situation of the working class in the advanced capitalist countries in particular, it certainly needs to be looked at critically and afresh now, as we and some others have begun doing.[72]

It is the vulgarization of Lenin's actual view on trade unions and works in them. Contrary to Bob Avakin's view, in reality, "Like all his other works, this book by Lenin can only serve as a weapon for Marxist-Leninists in the fights against various kinds of opportunism and can never serve as an instrument of revisionist apologetics."[73]

3.5. Bob Avakian has said that the rise of modern revisionism is a case of Khrushchev's resolving Stalin's "muddle." He thinks that during the Second World War and aftermath only in an overall sense the USSR was a socialist country. During that period "the socialist camp was in fact riddled with contradictions and more than that, the contradictions within it were coming to a head at the very time when it was at its height, that is, in the 1950s, more or less." In the post Second World War era, the Soviet Union, reviving socialism would have required. It means: The rise of modern revisionism in the Soviet Union "can largely be described as a case of Khrushchev's resolving Stalin's muddle."

72 Bob Avakian, "Conquer the World? The International Proletariat Must and Will", *Revolution,* Special Issue, Number 50, p. 11.

73 "The Proletarian Revolution and Khrushchev's Revisionism", Eighth Comment on the Open Letter of the Central Committee of the CPSU, *The Great Debate*, Mass Line Publications, Kerala, 1994, p. 299.

Let us see basing himself on Stalin's what "muddle" Khrushchev restored capitalism in the Soviet Union and gave final shape to the modern revisionism.

3.5 (a). Bob Avakian has called for attention to the question of the "state of the whole people" and the "party of the whole people." Taking Stalin's position on antagonistic classes under socialism (after 1936), he says:

> In a certain sense Stalin's policy or understanding on this represented a muddle, in that he said, on the one hand, there were no antagonistic classes and no one to suppress, other than foreign agents in the Soviet Union itself, but that the state and the dictatorship of the proletariat were still necessary because of foreign imperialist encirclement and the infiltration of its agents. We point out that really that's an argument that leads towards Khrushchev's point, because Khrushchev never said you do not need a state, he just said that because there are no longer antagonistic classes in the Soviet Union, you do not need a dictatorship of the proletariat; you just need a state to deal with the foreign enemies. Stalin did not go that far; Stalin said, well, we still need a state to deal with foreign enemies so we still need the dictatorship of the proletariat even though there are not antagonistic classes within the Soviet Union. We summed it up by saying that Stalin's position is a muddle; whereas Khrushchev resolved the muddle; and in that contradiction Stalin's muddle is infinitely preferable to Khrushchev's resolution, but it is still a muddle and not very good.[74]

This parallel is ridiculous. In his understanding of the law of the class struggle in socialist society, in the last part of his life, Stalin made theoretical mistakes. He subjectively declared, after the establishment of the socialist ownership of the instruments and the means of production, particularly after agriculture was basically collectivized in the Soviet Union, there were "no longer antagonistic classes." Under Mao's leadership, the CPC evaluated this mistake of Stalin, and it said two things–firstly, "The Soviet Union was the first, and at the time the only, country to build socialism and had no foreign experience to go by." On this ground, Stalin made that serious mistake. Secondly, except that mistake "Stalin remained a great Marxist-Leninist. As long as he led the Soviet Party and state, he held fast to the dictatorship of the proletariat and the socialist course, pursued a Marxist-Leninist line and ensured the Soviet Union's victorious advance along the road of socialism."[75]

Here, everyone can see two diametrically opposed lines on Stalin's wrong understanding of the law of the class struggle in socialist society–one

74 Bob Avakian, "Conquer the World? The International Proletariat Must and Will", *Revolution,* Special Issue, Number 50, p. 28.

75 "On Khrushchev's Phony, Communism, and its Historical Lessons for The World", Ninth Comment on the Open Letter of the Central Committee of the CPSU, *The Great Debate*, Mass Line Publications, Kerala, 1994, pp. 321-22.

is under Mao's leadership, a correct Marxist-Leninist line that all revolutionary communists stand for, and the other is that of the RCP, USA and its Chairman Bob Avakian's anti-Marxist-Leninist line, on which Trotskyites stand with. Avakian's parallel of Stalin's above mistake with Khrushchev's revisionist view on the state does not have any relation with the evaluation of the CPC on Stalin's above mistake. While Stalin was saying in the Soviet Union there were not hostile "class conflicts" and "antagonistic classes", he emphasized the inevitability of the socialist state and the dictatorship of the proletariat. Basing themselves on the ground of the elimination of the hostile "class conflicts" and "antagonistic classes" in the Soviet Union, the Soviet intelligentsia was asking to do away with the socialist state, to get rid of the state. Basing themselves on that ground, some people were expecting the end of the dictatorship of the proletariat as well. While Stalin was talking on the inevitability of the socialist state and the dictatorship of the proletariat after the "elimination" of the hostile "class conflicts" and "antagonistic classes" in the Soviet Union, he had associated these only with the military intervention by international imperialism. On this ground to present that Khrushchev's logic of "state of the whole people" was a further step as a consequence of Stalin's above mistake is absolutely wrong. There are so many facts which unduly prove the absurdity of Bob Avakian's comparison between Stalin's above mistake and Khrushchev's "state of the whole people".

In the context of the declaration of abolition of antagonistic classes and class conflicts too, Stalin had forcefully said that the Soviet Union was going forward to communism. What could be the meaning of going forward to communism? Finding a correct answer to this question is helpful to take a Marxist-Leninist attitude on Stalin's mistake. Not giving my own answer, I want to present some historical facts here, under the leadership of Mao Tse-tung regarding how the CPC replied to this question. According to the CPC, going forward to communism means:

> Moving towards the abolition of all classes and class differences. A communist society which preserves any classes at all, let alone exploiting classes, is inconceivable.
>
> Moving towards a unitary system of the ownership of the means of production by the whole people. A communist society in which several kinds of ownership of the means of production coexist is inconceivable.
>
> Moving towards a great abundance of social products and realization of the principle of "from each according to his ability, to each according to his needs." A communist society built on the enrichment of a handful of persons and the impoverishment of the masses is inconceivable.
>
> Moving towards enhancing the communist consciousness of the masses. A communist society with bourgeois ideas running rampant is inconceivable.

Moving towards the withering away of the state. A communist society with a state apparatus for oppressing the people is inconceivable.[76]

For Marxism-Leninism "development towards communism, proceeds through the dictatorship of the proletariat, and cannot do otherwise.[77]

The above quoted statements reveal that Stalin was not leading the Soviet Union from the highway of socialism to capitalism. In a real sense, he was committed to move towards communism. Even after the declaration of the end of antagonistic classes in the Soviet Union, all his efforts were concentrated to move the Soviet Union towards communism. A comparison of the above statements with his theoretical acceptance (i.e. dictatorship of the proletariat) and practices testify his position on the principles of scientific communism. Even after the declaration of the end of antagonistic classes in the Soviet Union, he did not abandon the dictatorship of the proletariat. Rather, to develop Soviet society towards communism, he upheld and practised the dictatorship of the proletariat in an all-round way. He strongly advocated the need of the socialist state. In the context of the "abolition" of antagonistic classes in the Soviet Union, some comrades thought, "there is no more need for the state; it must die away." Refuting such thinking, Stalin said: "The defects of our propagandist and ideological work is the absence of full clarity among our comrades on certain theoretical questions of vital practical importance, the existence of a certain amount of confusion on these questions."[78]

Although he was emphasizing the necessity of the socialist state to go forward to communism, he saw the enemy only as foreign attacks, not arising internally. However, he did not foster a new bourgeoisie, restore and extend the system of exploitation and accelerate class polarization in the Soviet Union. Till his death, the capitalist roaders could not occupy the ruling position in the CPSU and the government and the superstructure. Rather, he dedicated himself to eliminate all birth marks of capitalism, and preserved the proletarian character of the CPSU and the socialist character of the USSR. He did not create a situation to allow the degeneration of socialist ownership system into the capitalist one. He did not let people-owned enterprises as capitalist enterprises and farms, which were under the system of collective ownership, to fall into the Kulak economy. Rather he

---

76 "On Khrushchev's Phony Communism and its Historical Lessons for the World", Ninth Comment on the Open Letter of the Central Committee of the CPSU, *The Great Debate*, Mass Line Publications, Kerala, India 1994, pp. 346-47.

77 V. I. Lenin, "The State and Revolution", *Collected Works*, Progress Publishers, Moscow, Eng. ed., Fourth Printing, 1980, Vol. 25, p. 466.

78 J. V. Stalin, "Report to the Eighteenth Congress of the CPSU (B) On the Work of the Central Committee, March 10, 1939", *Problems of Leninism*, First ed., Foreign Language Press, Peking, 1976, p. 927.

was "moving towards a unitary system of the ownership of the means of production by the whole people." He did not degenerate the Soviet state owned economy into the market economy, he did not distort and violate the socialist principle of distribution of "from each according to his ability, to each according to his work." Rather, he was committed to move "towards a great abundance of social products and realization of the principle of "from each according to his ability, to each according to his needs." He did not revive bourgeois ideology in the Soviet Union. Rather, he enhanced the communist consciousness of the Soviet people. As a last attempt, we can see his views in his well-known works, *Economic Problems of Socialism in the USSR* and *Report of the CPSU to the Ninetieth Party Congress in October 1952.*

These facts make it clear that except for his mistake regarding classes and struggle between them in the Soviet Union, Stalin was a great Marxist-Leninist, who devoted his whole life to make a success of the October Socialist Revolution in Russia and keep going forward to communism. So, Bob Avakian's portrayal of the Khrushchevite revisionist theory of the "state of the whole people" and "party of the whole people" as a successor of Stalin's is not a genuine Marxist-Leninist criticism. To make an analysis of the changing class structure in the course of socialist transformation and the advance to communism is a difficult and complex problem. The Soviet Union was the first, and only country at that time which was building socialism in human history. In that context to make a scientific analysis of the changing class structure, was difficult and complex. According to Marxist-Leninist tenets, classes are:

> Classes are large groups of people differing from each other by the place they occupy in a historically determined system of social production, by their relation(in most cases fixed and formulated in law) to the means of production, by their role in the social organization of labour, and, consequently, by the dimensions of the share of social wealth of which they dispose and the mode of acquiring it. Classes are groups of people one of which can appropriate the labour of another owing to the different places they occupy in a definite system of social economy.[79]

Lenin has correctly said that "in the era of the dictatorship of the proletariat *every* class has undergone a change, and the relations between the classes have also changed."[80]

But what type of changes in every class, what type of changes in the relations between the classes that develop in the course of socialist transformation of society and advance towards communism? When in

79 V. I. Lenin, "A Great Beginning", *Collected Works*, Progress Publishers, Moscow, Eng. ed., Third Printing, 1977, Vol. 29, p. 421.

80 V. I. Lenin, "Economics and Politics in the Era of the Dictatorship of the Proletariat", *Collected Works*, Progress Publishers, Moscow, Eng. ed., Third Printing, 1977, Vol. 30, 115.

the course of socialist transformation of society and moving towards communism, and at a certain point the socialist ownership of the instruments and the means of production is completed? And what would be the economic foundation of the existence of antagonistic classes in society? When the exploiting classes are eliminated, when a small-producer economy has been replaced by a collective economy and a socialist society has been founded, and what would be the particular form of antagonistic classes? When Stalin had to respond to these questions, there wasn't a ready made answer in the Marxist treasury.

Still there are so many questions to be addressed. Basing himself on the experience of the restoration of capitalism in the Soviet Union, Mao has addressed some of them, but not all. In the course of the socialist transformation of society and advance towards communism, at a certain stage, some of (major, from the point of political economy) economic foundations disappear from society, but classes do not disappear. They still exist. But it is very difficult to show antagonistic classes or to say these are antagonistic classes, what we can say in capitalist society. Not only Stalin (in 1936), up to 1960, years after the restoration of capitalism in the Soviet Union, Mao Tse-tung also held the same view on the question. He had supported the view of the Soviet book, *Political Economy: A Textbook*, "Under socialism there is no class energetically plotting to preserve outmoded economic relations." In some detail he writes:

> Under socialism there may be no war but there is still struggle, struggle among sections of the people; there may be no revolution of one class overthrowing another, but there is still revolution. The transition from socialism to communism is revolutionary. The transition from one stage of communism to another is also. Then there is technological revolution and cultural revolution.

Further, he says:

> In a socialist society there are still conservative strata and something like "vested interest groups." There still remain differences between mental and manual labour, city and countryside, worker and peasant. Although these are not antagonistic contradictions they cannot be resolved without struggle.[81]

In the context of a decade later of Stalin's death, and the two-line struggle within the CPC in the course of going towards new democratic to socialist transformation of Chinese society, and a couple of years later of the restoration of capitalism in the Soviet Union, the above view of Mao Tse-tung is not different from that of Stalin. Mao and the CPC synthesized the

---

81 Mao Tse-tung, *A Critique of Soviet Economics*, Translated by Moss Roberts, Annotated by Richard Levy with an Introduction by James Peck, First Indian ed., Progressive Publications, New Delhi, 1982, p. 71.

experience that after the elimination of the exploiting classes, replacement of a small-producer economy by a collective economy and the building of socialist society, and how the capitalist roaders represent inside the party and government's bodies. They emerge as a privileged stratum. And in a planned way, they derive benefits from the rotten, poisonous ideological survivals of the old society, they influence people. Mao and the CPC have said that this privileged stratum represents an antagonistic class in socialist society. As, in the context of then (immediate of the capitalist restoration) Soviet society, they said: "The contradiction between the Soviet people and this privileged stratum is now the principal contradiction inside the Soviet Union, and it is an irreconcilable and antagonistic class contradiction."[82]

Still this analysis needs to be elaborated. It does not give a full size picture of socialist society.

3.5 (b). Bob Avakian has said that Stalin was the propounder of the theory of "Three Peacefuls." Particularly after the Second World War, Stalin promoted "three peacefuls", i.e. peaceful competition, peaceful coexistence and peaceful cooperation, in various forms. As he writes:

> In examining it more deeply, it is also largely the case that on Khrushchev's famous "three peacefuls", that is, peaceful competition, peaceful coexistence and peaceful transition to socialism, this again can largely be described as a case of Khrushchev's resolving Stalin's muddle. Khrushchev's resolution is infinitely and qualitatively worse than Stalin's muddle, but Stalin's policies were a muddle of the same sort; if you read Stalin's policy statements after the Second World War, even allowing for a certain amount of diplomatic doubletalk and so on (which may or may not be necessary but cannot be ruled out in principle in any case), it still becomes clear that he himself at times, particularly after the war, is promoting these "three peacefuls" in various forms, not only peaceful competition and peaceful coexistence but peaceful cooperation.[83]

I request Bob Avakian to respect historical facts. I urge him to present history objectively without aiming to fulfil any vested interest. It is unjust to history to compare Stalin's peaceful coexistence, peaceful cooperation with Khrushchev's revisionist "three peacefuls" theory. Khrushchev's "three peacefuls" wasn't quantitative development of Stalin's Leninist policy of peaceful coexistence. It was totally different, i.e. qualitatively different. That is why, it wasn't resolving Stalin's muddle by revisionist Khrushchev, but it was nakedly capitulations with imperialism and abandonment of proletarian internationalism and class struggle.

---

82 "On Khrushchev's Phony Communism and its Historical Lessons for the World", Ninth Comment on the Open Letter of the Central Committee of the CPSU, *The Great Debate*, Mass Line Publications, Kerala, 1995, p. 333.

83 Bob Avakian, "Conquer the World? The International Proletariat Must and Will", *Revolution,* Special Issue, Number 50, p. 28.

What Bob Avakian has mentioned above as Stalin's "three peacefuls" is actually one peaceful, i.e. peaceful coexistence. The other two are derived from the first one. When a socialist system was formed after the October Revolution in Russia, Lenin brought forward the policy of peaceful coexistence. It was not possible to advance the idea of peaceful coexistence before the existence of two basically different–socialist and capitalist systems. It took several years to be realized. Basing himself on real grounds, Lenin advanced that the socialist state should pursue a policy of peaceful coexistence with countries of different social systems. But the world imperialists did not accept the existence of basically different social systems–socialist system–side-by-side with the imperialist system. They did not think that there should be a policy which assumes that the coexistence of two opposite system is possible. On the contrary, imperialist powers attempted to strangle the Soviet State, launching all-round armed intervention. After a couple of years of defensive war, the Soviet people defeated them. Finally, their defeat and the victory of the Soviet people pressurized them to recognize the existence of basically different social systems side-by-side with capitalism. Gradually Lenin's idea of peaceful coexistence materialized.

The main part, the content, the strength of Lenin's policy of peaceful coexistence, is struggle. It was not searching peace with imperialists. Recognition of this policy by imperialist countries is the first proof of this truth. Without the life and death struggle of the Soviet people and without the defeat of the imperialist armed intervention, it was not possible to choose coexistence with a Soviet state by the imperialists. In the course of the great debate with modern revisionists, the CPC defended Lenin and Stalin's policy of peaceful coexistence. Differentiating between Lenin and Stalin's policy of peaceful coexistence and the modern revisionists' view on the question under the leadership of Mao, the CPC said: "Lenin's policy of peaceful coexistence is one followed by a socialist country in its relations with countries having different social systems, whereas Khrushchev describes peaceful coexistence as the supreme principle governing the life of modern society."

> Lenin's policy of peaceful coexistence constitutes one aspect of the international policy of the proletariat in power, whereas Khrushchev stretches peaceful coexistence into the general line of foreign policy for the socialist countries and even further into the general line for all communist parties.
>
> Lenin's policy of peaceful coexistence is based on the stand point of the international class struggle, whereas Khrushchev's peaceful coexistence strives to replace international class struggle with international class collaboration.

> Lenin's policy of peaceful coexistence proceeds from the historical mission of the international proletariat and therefore requires the socialist countries to give firm support to the revolutionary struggles of all the oppressed peoples and nations while pursuing this policy, whereas Khrushchev's peaceful coexistence seeks to replace the proletarian world revolution with pacifism and thus renounces proletarian internationalism.

Further, the CPC had said, "This is a brazen betrayal of Marxism-Leninism."[84]

It is absurd to say Khrushchev's "there peacefuls" were "resolving Stalin's muddle." According to Bob Avakian's logic, we should accept that Stalin was promoting the policy of peaceful coexistence (a) as the only principle governing the life of modern society; (b) into the general line of foreign policy for the socialist countries and even further into the general line of all communist parties; (c) to replace the international class struggle with class collaboration and (d) to replace the proletarian world revolution with pacifism and renunciation of proletarian internationalism. If anyone sees Stalin's practice of the policy of peaceful coexistence in this way that would be a brazen betrayal of history. There wasn't any confusion in Stalin on the question of the policy of peaceful coexistence. This policy was propounded by Lenin, but we should accept this truth that Stalin upheld and successfully applied this policy. The CPC has said correctly:

> Stalin upheld Lenin's policy of peaceful coexistence. In the thirty years during which he was the leader of the Soviet Union, he consistently pursued this policy. ... Lenin and Stalin's policy of peaceful coexistence, which all Marxist-Leninists, including the Chinese communists, stand for.[85]

On the one hand, the CPC has put Stalin's name with Lenin here and said all Marxist-Leninists, including the Chinese communists, stand with them, and, on the other, Bob Avakian says Khrushchev's "three peacefuls" was "resolving Stalin's muddle." Whenever a different social system accepts the existence of another basically different social system, undoubtedly, there should be a place for peaceful competition in general. Respecting another country's sovereignty and social system, we should try to make a healthy competition peacefully. For true Marxist-Leninists, peaceful competition between basically different systems must be guided by the basic principal of international class struggle, national liberation movement, proletarian world revolution or proletarian internationalism. Neither should it be the general line of foreign policy of socialist countries nor the general line of communist parties. Imperialists do not want to compete with socialist countries peacefully.

---

84 "Peaceful Coexistence: Two Diametrically Opposed Policies", Sixth Comment on the Open Letter of the Central Committce of the CPSU (December 12, 1963), *The Great Debate*, Mass Line Publications, Kerala, 1994, pp. 207-08.

85 Ibid., pp. 200, 195.

It is very difficult to go ahead for long. We should not forget for a moment too, only through struggle can socialist countries be able to live in the surroundings of imperialist countries. Supporting the international class struggle and national liberation movement can compel imperialist countries to accept peaceful competition with socialist countries. Khrushchev brought forward the policy of "peaceful competition" between socialist and imperialist countries. His "peaceful competition" between countries of different social systems was a general line of foreign policy of socialist countries and of communist parties. It replaced the international class struggle and national liberation movement by class capitulation and apology of neo-colonialism. It replaced proletarian internationalism by class collaborationism.

It is the same with peaceful cooperation between countries of basically different social systems, i.e. socialism and capitalism. But, as on the above questions–peaceful coexistence and peaceful competition between countries of basically different social systems (socialism and capitalism)–socialist countries can achieve peaceful cooperation through struggle. Through struggle they can stand on their ground; they can compel capitalist countries to accept a policy of cooperation with socialist countries. It means socialist countries can create a favourable atmosphere for cooperation between basically different social systems only through struggle.

3.5 (c). Bob Avakian has another serious accusation against Stalin. He has said that to kill the revolutionary struggle in various parts of the world and in order not to bring down the wrath of US imperialism, Stalin did what he could do. He also said what Khrushchev did later was a resolution of "Stalin's muddle". As he writes clearly:

> In fact, a question which I am grappling with and is worth pondering is: if Stalin had succeeded, for example, in forcing on Mao the policy that he attempted to enforce, that is, of killing the Chinese revolution after the Second World War and getting Mao to enter, in a subordinate position, into a coalition government with Chiang Kai-shek, would the US have then turned on the Soviet Union to the same degree that it did? Because in other places where he was able to, Stalin did what he could do (and in some cases it was not insignificant) to kill the revolutionary struggle of the masses in order not to bring down the wrath of US imperialism. I think we have to face up to this in the case of Greece and a number of other places. ... I think that at best it's a question of Stalin's muddle and Khrushchev's resolution.[86]

On Stalin's counsel with regard to the Chinese revolution, the CPC wrote: "When Stalin did something wrong, he was capable of criticizing himself. For instance, he had given some bad counsel with regard to the

86 Bob Avakian, "Conquer the World? The International Proletariat Must and Will", *Revolution,* Special Issue, Number 50, p. 28.

Chinese revolution. After the victory of the Chinese revolution, he admitted his mistake."[87]

When we compare the evaluation of the CPC and Bob Avakian on Stalin's counsel with regard to the Chinese revolution, we get two different results. The CPC said that it was "some bad counsel", but "after the victory of the Chinese revolution, Stalin admitted his mistake." Bob Avakian's criticism is basically different. It is antagonistic. "Some bad counsel" and admittance of that mistake after the victory of the Chinese revolution and "to enforce... of killing the Chinese revolution", these two views are basically different. In this regard, the more serious matter is that Bob Avakian has said: "Stalin did what he could do to kill the revolutionary struggle of the masses in order not to bring down the wrath of US imperialism." All Marxist-Leninists of the world should bluntly reject this type of slander on Stalin. Bob Avakian's statement quoted above tries to portray Stalin as a service holder of imperialists and portrays him as the one who served imperialism by killing the revolutionary struggles of the masses in the case of Greece and a number of other places. What does he want to prove by slandering Stalin? Undoubtedly, he wants to make the imperialist masters and Trotskyites happy.

3.5 (d). Bob Avakian has said that Stalin was not clear to connect inter-imperialists contradictions with revolution. He thinks that in his last part of life again Stalin raised the banner of democratic liberties and the banner of the nation. So, he could not take the correct policy to address challenges. According to him that was a situation of "muddle." Let us see in his words:

> The reason I say *muddle*, though, is that particularly after the US adopted a more hostile policy towards the Soviet Union, more specifically in the Korean War and so on, at the time of Stalin's last major work, *Economic Problems of Socialism in the USSR*, he is again talking about the inevitability of war among the imperialists and saying that it is necessary to eliminate imperialism before war can be eliminated. But exactly what that's all part of and how it links up with his views on revolution is not at all clear, because at the same time, that is at the 19th Congress of the Soviet Party in 1952, he's pushing the same line about the working class in the capitalist countries becoming the inheritors of the banner of democratic liberties and the banner of the nation and a lot of the same stuff that we're familiar with and which was very clear in the US party. I was just reading William Z. Foster's *History of the Three Internationals*, and the whole end of it is all the same peaceful transition, two-stage (non-)revolution, democracy going over someday into socialism and may be we'll have to curb the monopolies if they get uppity after we've basically implemented socialism and so on and so

87 "On the Question of Stalin", Second Comment on the Open Letter of the Central Committee of the CPSU (September 13, 1963), *The Great Debate*, Mass Line Publications, Kerala, 1994, p. 98.

> forth. All that stuff's in there and he was not that distant from the line that was being promoted by Stalin, even shortly before his death. So this needs to be looked at; ... Stalin's *Economic Problems* ... needs to be looked at again in this light and I think all this needs to be much more critically and much more deeply summed up, not just by ourselves but through struggle in the whole international communist movement.[88]

After the end of the Second World War, Western imperialism, headed by American imperialism, emerged strategically to stop revolution and to expand its influence around the world. The disintegration of a strong presence of Germany and Japan on an international level–politically, economically and militarily–was as a result of the Second World War. Their industry, agriculture, international trade, foreign policy and whole economic, political and military life came under the control of US imperialism. The situation of Britain and France was not much different to that of Germany and Japan. Because of direct war with the fascist axis, Britain and France lost their strong economic and military presence at an international level. Taking advantage of this situation, American imperialism took the leadership of world capitalism successfully. American imperialism came aggressively to control the capitalist world. Under the guise of the so-called Marshall Plan aid, American imperialism established its control on the British and French economy. With the existence of the Soviet Union and emerging socialist camp, it was impossible for American imperialism to realize their ambition of world domination. To achieve its goal, American imperialism seized the former British sphere of influence in the Pacific; it controlled members of the fascist axis. South Korea and South Pacific came under the control of the USA. Central and South America were already under its control. Using the pretext of democracy and the danger of communism, American imperialism made large-scale military arrangements under its leadership in various countries. In this context, in the Soviet Union and at the international level, so many people thought that the war between capitalist countries would not last longer. They thought that Lenin's thesis that imperialism inevitably generates war, had become obsolete. They thought that the socialist camp and other peace loving forces were capable of preventing another world war. We should see Stalin's view on the inevitability of war among the imperialists, which is expressed in his last major work, *Economic Problems of Socialism in the USSR* in that context. But Bob Avakian has twisted the truth. This part of his above statement is to be analysed in this regard. As it is written: "He is again talking about the inevitability of war among the imperialists, and saying that it is necessary to eliminate imperialism before war can be eliminated." The manner in which Bob Avakian has presented Stalin's view on the inevitability of war among the imperialists and elimination of the

88 "Bob Avakian, Conquer the World? The International Proletariat Must and Will", *Revolution,* Special Issue, Number 50, p. 28.

war between them is not correct. Basing himself on historical facts, Stalin was refuting the wrong view on war and peace after the Second World War which was rising as a powerful tide. As Stalin described the situation:

> Some comrades hold that, owing to the development of new international conditions since the Second World War, wars between capitalist countries have ceased to be inevitable. They consider that the contradictions between the socialist camp and the capitalist camp are more acute than the contradictions among the capitalist countries; that the USA has brought the other capitalist countries sufficiently under its sway to be able to prevent them going to war among themselves and weakening one another; that the foremost capitalist minds have been sufficiently taught by the two world wars and the severe damage they caused to the whole capitalist world not to venture to involve the capitalist countries in war with one another again–and that, because of all this, wars between capitalist countries are no longer inevitable.

Further, he writes: "It is said that Lenin's thesis that imperialism inevitably generates war must now be regarded as obsolete, since powerful popular forces have come forward today in defence of peace and against another world war."

To expose the futility and baselessness of their logic, presenting historical facts, Stalin's said:

> After the First World War it was similarly believed that Germany had been definitely put out of action, just as certain comrades now believe that Japan and Germany have been definitely put out of action. Then, too, it was said and clamoured in the press that the United States had put Europe on rations; that Germany would never rise to her feet again, and that there would be no more wars between capitalist countries. In spite of this, Germany rose to her feet again as a great power within the space of some fifteen or twenty years after her defeat, having broken out of bondage and taken the path of independent development. And it is significant that it was none other than Britain and the United States that helped Germany to recover economically and to enhance her economic war potential. Of course, when the United States and Britain assisted Germany's economic recovery, they did so with a view to setting a recovered Germany against the Soviet Union, to using her against the land of socialism. But Germany directed her forces in the first place against the Anglo-French-American bloc. And when Hitler Germany declared war on the Soviet Union, the Anglo-French-American bloc, far from joining with Hitler's Germany, was compelled to enter into a coalition with the USSR against Hitler's Germany.

What should be the duty of all Marxist-Leninists, particularly the leadership of the international communist movement in that context?

Undoubtedly, to defend the principle of Leninism on war and peace in the epoch of imperialism, Stalin defended Leninism on this question.

We should see his "the inevitability of wars between capitalist countries remains in force" statement in that context. What does Bob Avakian's mean when he says "he is again talking about the inevitability of war among the imperialists"? It means Stalin should not have talked of "the inevitability of wars between capitalist countries remains in force"? As far as Bob Avakian's accusation that, Stalin could not find the right way to link up revolution with the elimination of imperialism, is too baseless. He claims that Stalin pushed the working class in the capitalist countries to raise the banner of democratic liberty and the banner of nation. True, evaluating the then world situation, Stalin had emphasized the democratic aim of preserving peace. Undoubtedly, it wasn't call for the conversion of the possible imperialist war into civil war to achieve socialist aims. As he said:

> The object of the present-day peace movement is to rouse the masses of the people to fight for the preservation of peace and for the prevention of another world war. Consequently, the aim of this movement is not to overthrow capitalism and establish socialism–it confines itself to the democratic aim of preserving peace. In this respect, the present-day peace movement differs from the movement of the time of the First World War for the conversion of the imperialist war into civil war, since the latter movement went farther and pursued socialist aims.

Bob Avakian has presented Stalin in this way that he limited himself to the democratic aim of preserving peace. This is absolutely wrong. He was very clear on the possibility to develop a peace movement towards a socialist aim. But, for him it was possible only in a definite conjuncture of circumstances. Up to that day, such a conjuncture was not in existence. So, he did not call for the overthrow of capitalism, he limited himself to the democratic aim of preserving peace. As he said: "It is possible that in a definite conjuncture of circumstances the fight for peace will develop here or there into a fight for socialism. But then it will no longer be the present-day peace movement; it will be a movement for the overthrow of capitalism."

For Stalin, the success of the peace movement was not the permanent preservation of a permanent peace; it was temporary preservation of a particular peace. He was sure; it would not be able to eliminate the inevitability of wars between capitalist countries generally. In terms of the permanent solution to war and peace, he has said that "to eliminate the inevitability of war, it is necessary to abolish imperialism." He puts his view very explicitly:

> What is most likely is that the present-day peace movement, as a movement for the preservation of peace, will, if it succeeds, result in preventing a *particular* war, in its temporary postponement, in the temporary preservation of a *particular* peace, in the resignation of a bellicose government and its supersession by another that is prepared temporarily to keep the peace. That, of course, will be good. Even very good. But, all the same, it will not

be enough to eliminate the inevitability of wars between capitalist countries generally. It will not be enough, because, for all the successes of the peace movement, imperialism will remain, continue in force–and, consequently, the inevitability of wars will also continue in force. To eliminate the inevitability of war, it is necessary to abolish imperialism.[89]

4
Conclusion

Based on the above mentioned facts, the historical experience of the international communist movement and the scientific theory of communism, it is possible for everyone to draw some conclusions on Bob Avakian's NSC.

4.1. The RCP, USA and its leaders claim that "Bob Avakian has... developed a communist body of work and method and approach that responds to" the "great needs and challenges." It is not any "further development of the theoretical framework for carrying forward" the communist revolution. Their comparison of Bob Avakian's NSC with "what was done by Marx at the beginning of the communist movement" is baseless. Neither is it any "further development of the theoretical framework for carrying forward" the communist revolution, nor did it draw the positive and negative lessons correctly from the experience of the international communist movement, and raised "this to a new, higher level of synthesis."

Actually, it is the same wine, only in a different bottle. The way the RCP, USA and its Chairman Bob Avakian have brought forward the NSC, they are not defending and developing Marxism-Leninism, but negating it. Their conclusion of the "whole stage of the communist revolution has ended, and it ended with defeat", "and the beginning of–and the need to launch, in fact–a new stage of the communist revolution" means: their NSC is not a development of Marxism-Leninism under the new conditions of capitalist-imperialism and of class struggle of the proletariat. Actually, it has emerged negating the experiences and the lessons of the international communist movement and practices of the socialist transformation and advance to communism in the past.

Under the new conditions of imperialism and proletarian revolution, Marxism can be developed on the basis of the Marxist outlook. To accept Bob Avakian's synthesis as a further development of MLM means: To accept the distinctive and new (which represents a higher stage in the course of the development of scientific communism) thing in his synthesis. However, there is not this type of new thing in NSC, there is not even the possibility to

89 J. V. Stalin, *Economic Problems of Socialism in the USSR*, Foreign Language Press, Peking, 1972, pp. 32-33, 35-37.

accept it as a "new" synthesis of communism and take as a guiding thought of the communist revolution in a "new stage." Actually Bob Avakian's NSC is nothing more than a manifestation of the petty-bourgeois trend which strove to subordinate the working-class movement to the liberals, a petty-bourgeois, intellectualist opportunism. So, we should flatly reject Bob Avakian's revisionism which has appeared in the name of the NSC.

4.2. Bob Avakian's "Left doctrinarism" and "Left" opportunist practice has weakened the international communist movement, after the death of Mao Tse-tung and the counter-revolution in China. It was that prime time when the international communist movement was passing thorough an unprecedented crisis in its history. In the name of the summation of the historical experience of the international communist movement and the lessons for today, the RCP, USA and its Chairman Bob Avakian brought forward a Trotskyite line and tried to capture the leadership of the international communist movement. It was the main cause behind not organizing other true Marxist-Leninist parties and organizations in the Revolutionary Internationalist Movement (the RIM). After the formation of RIM, the RCP, USA and its Chairman Bob Avakian tried to dictate to other member parties and organizations to adopt their "left" doctrinarism, which was right liquidations in its essence. Their "Outline of Views on the Historical Experience of the International Communist Movement and the Lesson for Today" is actually rewriting the history of the international communist movement based on a faulty Trotskyites' view. The negation of the history of the international communist movement from 1928 to 1953 was a strong sign of their further direction of development. The NSC was the higher peak to be reached passing through that direction. Doing this, they pushed the RIM to the verge of dissolution. Now the RIM is a defunct body. The result has refuted the claim of the RCP, USA and its leaders that Avakian "played a crucial role in establishing the ideological and political basis for the regrouping of the remaining communists after the loss of China and the devastating effects of this on the revolutionary and communist movement throughout the world."[90]

Actually, Bob Avakian's "Outlines of Views on the Historical Experience of the International Communist Movement and the Lessons for Today, Conquer the World? The International Proletariat Must and Will", etc., played a crucial role in establishing the ideological and political basis to further split the communist movement throughout the world. So, the RCP, USA and its Chairman are not the pioneers of the "regrouping of the remaining communists after the loss of China and the devastating effects of it on the revolutionary and communist movement throughout the world". They are the greatest splitter of our times.

---

90 *Communism : The Beginning of A New Stage, A Manifesto from the Revolutionary Communist Party, USA*, RCP Publications, 2009, pp. 24, 23.

4.3. The RCP, USA and its Chairman Bob Avakian have talked about world revolution a lot. Their opposition to national and state distinctions among peoples and countries, to the two-stage revolution, to making use of contradictions among imperialists to forward revolution or to retain socialist power in a particular country, and to the patriotic war of the Soviet Union, make it clear that their talk on world revolution is futile. Actually, their opposition on these issues only protects the interests of the imperialism, and it is not for world revolution. Opposing national and state distinctions among peoples and emphasizing a stereotyped strategy and tactics for world revolution aborts revolution in individual countries and on the world level. The proletarian world revolution can be victorious step by step breaking the link of imperialism in individual countries where it is possible. Bob Avakian's opposition of making use of contradictions among imperialists and building of the united front with a bloc of imperialism against another bloc of imperialism is directed to abolish the task of combating imperialism. Actually, this opposition is nothing more than a prescription for abolishing the revolution in individual countries as well as world revolution. We should expose the anti-revolutionary essence of his revolutionary phrase of world revolution.

4.4. The rejection of the necessity of the maximum flexibility in tactics of the NSC is not Marxist-Leninist; it is a "Left" doctrinarism. Because of this, the RCP, USA and its Chairman Bob Avakian could not apply it in practice in the United States of America in the course of moving towards the socialist revolution. In the present international communist movement, "it is not only the Right doctrinarism that is erroneous; Left doctrinarism is erroneous too," though Right doctrinarism is much more of a danger than left doctrinarism. Right doctrinarism can be recognized easily. But, left doctrinarism can hide itself through revolutionary phrases for a long time in the communist movement. It is not rigid only on theory but on tactics too. The word flexibility, maximum flexibility is alien for "Left" doctrinarism. The essence of "Left" doctrinarism always stops to move ahead more confidently and firmly to victory in the communist movement. Lenin has rightly said:

> Only one thing is lacking to enable us to march forward more confidently and firmly to victory, namely, the universal and thorough awareness of all communists in all countries of the necessity to display the utmost *flexibility* in their tactics. The communist movement, which is developing magnificently, now lacks, especially in the advanced countries, this awareness and the ability to apply it in practice.[91]

91 V. I. Lenin, " 'Left-Wing' Communism: An Infantile Disorder", *Collected Works*, Eng. ed., Third Printing, Progress Publishers, Moscow, 1977, Vol. 31, pp. 103, 102.

So, it is an urgent job to defeat Bob Avakian's "Left" doctrinarism to move ahead more confidently and firmly to the victory of our revolution.

4.5. Bob Avakian's approach to the history of the international communist movement uses the method of studying and apprehending them is metaphysical, not dialectical, while his interpretation of the history of the international communist movement, his conception of this history and world events, is idealistic, not materialistic. Bob Avakian's NSC is a living-proof of his failure of the application of the principle of dialectical materialism to the history of society in general, and to the history of the international communist movement particularly.

Communists should always adopt a dialectical materialistic world outlook on the summation of the history in general, and on the summation of the history of the international communist movement particularly. Under the leadership of Mao Tse-tung, the CPC applied this world outlook very successfully on the summation of the history of the international communist movement. Two basically different world outlooks drew two basically different lessons from the summation of the history of the international communist movement. Negating the whole history of the international communist movement from 1928 to 1976, the RCP, USA said that the "whole stage of the communist revolution has ended, and it ended with defeat" and "a new stage of the communist revolution" begun, and this "new stage of the communist revolution" could be guided only by Bob Avakian's NSC.

On the contrary, Mao Tse-tung and the CPC summed up the history of the international communist movement and concluded that the degeneration of the socialist system in the USSR was basically under the general law of class struggle. Giving the continuity of the international communist movement, they moved to march forward more confidently and firmly to achieve a greater victory. They greatly appreciated the history of the international communist movement; they fully supported Stalin's policies concerning the Second World War's united front against fascism, and the patriotic war of the Soviet Union, the dissolution of the Comintern, etc. Rejecting this summation, Bob Avakian went towards a different direction. Actually, he put Mao and CPC, for their summation of the international communist movement, on trial.

To march forward more confidently and firmly to the communist victory, for continuity of the communist revolution, we should reject uncompromisingly Bob Avakian's metaphysical, mechanical materialistic and idealistic interpretation of the history of the international communist movement and lessons based on that.

4.6. Once Mao Tse-tung said:

> I think there are two "swords": one is Lenin and the other Stalin. The sword of Stalin has now been discarded by the Russians. Gomulka and some people in Hungary have picked it up to stab at the Soviet Union and oppose so-called Stalinism. The Communist Parties of many European countries are also criticizing the Soviet Union, and their leader is Togliatti. The imperialists also use this sword to slay people with.

Further, he asked: "As for the sword of Lenin, hasn't it too been discarded to a certain extent by some Soviet leaders?"

He answered: "In my view, it has been discarded to a considerable extent."

Further he says: "How much capital do you have? Just Lenin and Stalin. Now you have abandoned Stalin and practically all of Lenin as well, with Lenin's feet gone, or perhaps with only his head left, or with one of his hands cut off."[92]

I think that summing up the history of the international communist movement in this way, Bob Avakian has abandoned not only the sword of Stalin but also abandoned the swords of Marx, Engels, Lenin and Mao too negating the history of the international communist movement since its inception to now. All these he did not from Right doctrinarism, but from "Left" doctrinarism. Bob Avakian and the RCP, USA have presented their NSC as a new thought of communism which can lead the communist revolution around the world. This type of claim is baseless. Actually, their so-called new synthesis is nothing else, but liquidation away from communism and the communist revolution.

4.7. The NSC is an ideological and political form of the personality cult of Bob Avakian. For a long time, the RCP, USA and Bob Avakian himself has been promoting Bob Avakian's personality cult in a planned way. Decades ago, RCP, USA had presented "Three Ours", that is, "our ideology is Marxism-Leninism-Maoism; our Vanguard is the Revolutionary Communist Party; our leader is Chairman Avakian." Leaders can come and go. A revolutionary leader of a particular period can be changed into revisionist or can be inactive at another particular situation or period. But, how long a communist party exists, its world outlook and ideology (MLM) does not change, just develops; how long proletarian class exists, its vanguard cannot be anything except the communist party. To present paralleling, Bob Avakian's leadership with these universal truths is a blunder. The RCP, USA cannot put its leader on parallel with the science of revolution and its vanguard role. Further, they

---

92 Mao Tse-tung, "Speech at Second Session of Eighth Central Committee", *Selected Works*, First ed., Foreign Language Press, Peking, 1977, Vol. 5, pp. 341-42.

have moved more nakedly on the cult of Bob Avakian. On the occasion of the party's twentieth anniversary (1995), the RCP, USA passing a resolution on leadership said: "Bob Avakian is this leader of the leaders of our Party." The NSC is the climax of that campaign. Their emphasis on the promotion and popularization of the NSC makes clear their real intention. Emphasizing the appreciation, promotion and popularization of the NSC and his leadership, Bob Avakian says:

> The aim of this whole campaign that we're carrying out with its three objectives: making this revolution broadly and have a major impact in society; "making BA a household name", for short; and bringing forward new waves of initiators of the new stage of the communist revolution. And all this is concentrated now in the massive and multi-faceted fund-raising campaign to project this new synthesis (and my overall body of work and leadership) out into society, and make it a point of reference and a point of, yes, debate and struggle broadly in society. ... The "BA Everywhere" campaign, and the fund-raising to make it possible, is now a concentrated focus of working for those three objectives.

Further, he writes:

> The promotion and popularization of my leadership, my body of work and method and approach–this is now taking a concentrated expression in the "BA Everywhere" campaign. ... It is important to emphasize that this is about making the communist revolution a major question in society–it is a matter of spreading the new synthesis of communism into all corners of society. ... In other words, this "BA Everywhere" campaign is a concentrated means for pushing forward all three objectives–"making BA a household name" is a concentrated means for pursuing the three objectives of this overall campaign–the other two objectives being: to make this revolution, communist revolution, with the news synthesis of communism."[93]

Readers can judge for themselves. Amidst a big celebration, in April 2011 in Harlem, Bob Avakian unfolded his book B*Asics*, a collection of the quotations from the works of Bob Avakian. According to the leaders of the RCP, USA, this book is a concentrated form of more than 30 years of his works. They have also said that it is a concentration of the 'New Synthesis of Communism.' On its role and importance, Bob Avakian writes:

> It is intended to serve a purpose analogous to what the Red Book, the *Quotation from Chairman Mao Tse-tung*, served in relation to the movement and the upsurge of the 1960s: B*Asics* starts off with some exposure of the actual history of the US and of slavery as crucial in the development of the US; and then it speaks to the alternative, the socialist revolution and the goal of communism; it talks about the revolution that is needed and the strategic approach to that; it goes into questions of epistemology, that is the theory

93 What Humanity Needs Revolution, and the New Synthesis of Communism, *An Interview with Bob Avakian,* By A. Brook, pp. 41, 72.

of knowledge, how you know about the world, the method for knowing the world; and it speaks to morals in relation to revolution; and then gets into the revolutionary potential of the masses and the responsibility of leadership and the vanguard party.

On the planning of the book, Bob Avakian further writes:

In conceiving of and in planning of the book, I will say that we did deliberately organize it so it could be a counterpoint to and in opposition to the Bible. So that's why, like you have Leviticus 20:13 in the Bible, horrific things in there; and then you have B*Asics*. Or John 3:16: for God so loved the world, blah, blah, blah; and then you have B*Asics* 3:16, calling on the masses of people ... to rise up."[94]

Bob Avakian has said to Harlem celebration, "A Celebration of Revolution and the Vision of a New World."[95]

Here we can see how the RCP, USA and its Chairman Bob Avakian himself have erroneously exaggerated the NSC and Bob Avakian's role. They are trying to establish a superstitious belief in Bob Avakian's authority. Public manifestation on such a level with regard to NSC and Bob Avakian makes it clear how they are overtaken by the cult of an individual. By doing this, the RCP, USA and other leaders have tried to counterpoise Bob Avakian's individual authority to all communist parties and organizations. Marx, Engels, Lenin, Stalin and Mao Tse-tung all denounced this type of the exaggeration of the cult of the individual. During their lifetime, they strongly opposed such exaggerations, which were concerned personally with them. In this regard, once Marx said:

Neither of us cares a straw for popularity. A proof of this is, for example, that, because of aversion to any personality cult, I have never permitted the numerous expressions of appreciation from various countries, with which I was pestered during the existence of the International, to reach the realm of publicity, and have never answered them, except occasionally by a rebuke. When Engels and I first joined the secret Communist Society we made it a condition that everything tending to encourage superstitious belief in authority was to be removed from the Rules.

Marx was dissatisfied with Lassalle, because later on he "exerted his influence in the opposite direction."[96]

Under the leadership of Mao Tse-tung, the CPC had correctly said that: "The cult of the individual is a foul carry-over from the long history of mankind. The cult of the individual is rooted not only in the exploiting

94 Ibid., pp. 49-50, 52.

95 Ibid., p. 70.

96 Marx to Wilhem Blos in Hamburg, London, November 10, 1877, *Marx-Engels Selected Correspondence*, Third revised ed., Progress Publishers, Moscow, 1975, p. 291.

classes but also in the small-producers. As is well known, patriarchism is a product of small-producer economy."[97]

The USA is not a small-producer economy; it is the largest-producer and most developed economy. It means that the social root of the cult of the individual basically does not exist there. But the cult of the individual is not only in the small-scale production system. It is rooted in the exploiting classes too. In the USA, more developed more monopoly capitalist classes exist. The cult of Bob Avakian is rooted in that advanced monopoly capitalist classes of the USA. Even though the USA is not a country of a small producer economy, still small production system has spread worldwide and there still exist rotten, poisonous ideological survivals of the small production system. On this social basis, the RCP, USA decide to worship their leader.

4.8. Bob Avakian has talked extensively on imperialism. He has called for the abolition of imperialism. But, his opposition and hatred for imperialism is not genuine, particularly in the case of American imperialism. Various facts make it clear. In this regard, Bob Avakian's opposition to Lenin's policy of using contradictions among the imperialists in defence of the socialist fatherland, outline of the then world into three and his later view on Germany; Stalin, Comintern and Mao Tse-tung's view and policy of making use of contradictions among imperialists, formation of the United front, and call and support for the patriotic war and in defence of the socialist fatherland, etc., do not leave any confusion that he does not want to make imperialism weak and eliminate it. After the First World War, British imperialism was losing her empire and influences one after another. But, American imperialism started to rise. Ultimately, after the Second World War, American imperialism reached the top of the capitalist world. Politically and militarily, all former power countries became dwarves compared to the USA. Since that time, the counter revolutionary global strategy of US imperialism has become the number one threat for peace and justice-loving people and countries. Stalin, the Comintern and Mao Tse-tung always attempted to arouse the masses, to expand revolutionary forces, to win over the middle forces and isolate the reactionary forces, and to make the use of contradictions of other imperialists with US imperialism.

It has already been discussed that Bob Avakian has put his serious differences with the line of struggle against the imperialist and reactionaries headed by US imperialism. For this, he has said, Lenin went against Leninism,

97 On the Historical Experience of the Dictatorship of the Proletariat, *The Documents of the Great Debate*, First ed., Antararashtriya Prakashan, Saharanpur, India, December 2005, Vol. 1, p. 278.

Stalin and the Comintern deviated from Leninism. It means: They should not have taken that policy; they should not have targeted US imperialism as a number one enemy. He opposes imperialism, but he does not want to direct the struggle against the counter revolutionary global strategy of US imperialism. Actually, Bob Avakian's all out attack against imperialists, not differentiating them, safeguards the interests of US imperialism in the present world situation.

4.9. The RCP, USA and its Chairman Bob Avakian have abandoned the principles of scientific communism–MLM. Without MLM, there cannot be any revolution. For a couple of years, the RCP, USA and its Chairman Bob Avakian have left the usage of Marxism-Leninism-Maoism, as formerly they did. But, now they say just communism. The replacement of the Marxism-Leninism-Maoism by communism is theoretically wrong. Socialism and communism are social systems. And, MLM is a scientific guiding principle which guides us to prepare for the democratic and socialist revolution and make it successful to exercise the dictatorship of the proletariat, for a socialist transformation of society and the advance to communism. In this context, how can anyone replace MLM by 'communism'? Actually, this type of move is nothing else but liquidationism.

4.10. Presenting the NSC, the RCP, USA and its Chairman Bob Avakian have turned 180^0 from their earlier Marxist-Leninist view and stand on some ideological and political issues. In this regard, it is enough to present their historical struggle with the anti-Marxist-Leninist view of then Central Re-organization Committee, Communist Party of India (Marxist-Leninist) (CRC, CPI (ML)) and its secretary K. Venu. Then CRC, CPI (ML), an active Party of the RIM, published a document *On Proletarian Democracy* in 1990. Presenting that document, CRC, CPI (ML) and its secretary K. Venu repudiated the entire historical experience of the dictatorship of the proletariat; it abandoned the whole legacy of the proletarian revolution, socialist transformation of society and the advance of communism from the October Socialist Revolution to the Chinese Revolution and the Great Proletarian Cultural Revolution. Their summation on the historical experience of the international communist movement was wrong, the RCP, USA and its Chairman Bob Avakian took basically a Marxist-Leninist view and stand on the CRC document. They uncompromisingly fought and rejected K. Venu's Rightist liquidationist view. But for the last couple of years, the RCP, USA and its Chairman Bob Avakian have left their earlier correct position. To present their earlier view and stand in this regard, I would like to present their position on K. Venu's anti-Marxist-Leninist line. In its depth, Bob Avakian has raised so many ideological and political questions. Here I am not discussing all of them. I want to touch just a few of them.

4.10 (a) The Historical Experience of the Dictatorship of the Proletariat

The CRC document has openly repudiated the entire historical experience of the dictatorship of the proletariat beginning with the October Socialist Revolution in Russia to the Great Proletariat Cultural Revolution in China. On the CRC document, Bob Avakian writes:

> This document upholds only the Paris Commune of 1871 as a legitimate exercise of the dictatorship of the proletariat : it sets the very brief and limited experience of the Commune against the entire historical experience of the dictatorship of the proletariat in socialist society beginning with the October 1917 Soviet Revolution.

In this regard, he further writes:

> This document constitutes a complete degeneration into rather classical social-democratic opposition to communism and the proletarian revolution. That may sound extreme, but it is no more extreme than the open assertion in this document that the entire experience of the dictatorship of the proletariat, beginning with the Soviet Union, and the basic orientation guiding this experience–not only in the Soviet Union under the leadership of Lenin as well as Stalin but also of China under the leadership of Mao Tse-tung–that all this is fundamentally flawed and must be rejected and used as teaching material by *negative* example.

Further, he writes:

> This document openly repudiates the entire historical experience of the dictatorship of the proletariat beginning with the Soviet Revolution, and in opposition to this comes out with a call for what is barely disguised bourgeois democracy ... it is already becoming evident that this document regards the basic answers that have been given by Marxism-Leninism-Maoism to be insufficient or incorrect and that what it intends is a fundamental re-evaluation–and rejection

Bob Avakian has said that this view of the CRC document is nothing else "much in common with long-standing attacks on Leninism and with present day assault on communism in general."[98] What Bob Avakian has said above on the CRC document is absolutely correct. But later the RCP, USA and its Chairman Bob Avakian deviated from that position. Finally, more nakedly than CRC's document, they repudiated the entire historical experience of the dictatorship of the proletariat beginning with the Paris Commune to the October Socialist Revolution and Chinese Revolution and Great Proletarian Cultural Revolution. Their conclusion "With the revisionist coup and the restoration of capitalism in China, following after the rise to power of revisionists in the Soviet Union 20 years earlier, the

98 All Bob Avakian's quotations regarding his comments on the CRC document are taken from his long article "Democracy: Can't We Do Better Than That?", *A World to Win*, 1992/17.

first wave of communist revolution came to an end".[99] "It ended with defeat, and the beginning of–and the need to launch, in fact–a new stage of the communist revolution", and their strong presentation of NSC as a guiding thought to guide the communist revolution in this "new stage" and their rejection NSC as a "pasting together", that is, further development of Marxism is nothing more than complete repudiation of the entire historical experience of the dictatorship of the proletariat from the Paris Commune to counter-revolution in China in 1976. For the time being, forgetting his earlier summation of the international communist movement, Bob Avakian took the correct stand in the course of the struggle with the CRC document. But, later he went back to his earlier (1980) position. Actually, he has no consistency in his position. This situation can lead him towards the East-Europeanization path.

4.10 (b) Socialist Countries, a Situation of Encircled by Imperialism

Totally avoiding the difficult situation that has confronted the socialist countries as a consequence of the imperialists' encirclement, the CRC document evaluated the question of democracy and dictatorship in those countries. Bob Avakian criticized their method and apprehension of the problem. He correctly says:

> There is no serious attention paid–and apparently no real importance attached–to the very difficult problems that have confronted the socialist states as a consequence of their being in a position of being "encircled" by imperialism ... To attempt to discuss the questions of democracy and dictatorship apart from a serious examination of this problem betrays a lack of seriousness–and more specifically it betrays the classical bias and "blind spot" of social-democratic types who, with a typical bourgeois idealist outlook, purport to treat the question of democracy in some "pure" and "classless" way, in abstraction from its actual content and from the actual historical and social context.

On the one hand, the above comment is correct on the view of the CRC document; and on the other, the RCP, USA and its Chairman Bob Avakian themselves have suffered this bourgeois idealist outlook. Their summation of Stalin and the Comintern's period of the international communist movement is absolutely a departure from its actual content and from the historical and social context. They paid "no serious attention to the very difficult problems that have confronted" the Soviet Union "as a consequence of" her "being in a position of being "encircled" by imperialism". The RCP, USA and its Chairman Bob Avakian discussed the questions of the anti-fascist united front, civil war in Spain, dissolution of the Comintern and patriotic war of the Soviet Union. The difference

99 Bob Avakian, *Communism : The Beginning of A New Stage, A Manifesto from the Revolutionary Communist Party, USA*, RCP Publications, February 2009, p. 17.

between the CRC document and Bob Avakian, is that the former presented its view from the Right and the latter presented its view from the "Left". Basically both are the same–both are enemies of Marxism.

4.10 (c) Restoration of Capitalism

The document has said that "the traditional Marxist-Leninist interpretation of capitalist restoration", i.e. "basically correct in relation to the economic aspect of capitalist restoration. But it is not sufficient to answer the principal political issue." This conclusion of the CRC document is wrong. Flatly rejecting this, Bob Avakian has said, "this is a metaphysical separation of politics and economics–there cannot be an explanation that is correct in regard to the economic aspect but incorrect, or "insufficient" in fundamental terms, in regard to the political aspect." But, what have the RCP, USA and its Chairman Bob Avakian done? Just a cursory study of their summation of the international communist movement and the practice of the dictatorship of the proletariat from the October Socialist Revolution of Russia to the Great Proletarian Cultural Revolution of China, makes it very clear, not leaving any confusion, that their whole analysis is full of metaphysical separation of each and every event, policy from the actual historical and social context, not only separation between economics and politics.

4.10 (d) Socialist State Structures

The CRC document does not see any radical difference between a socialist state structure and the state structure after capitalist restoration. It says that "there is no difference between the essential structures of the social fascist political system and those which existed earlier when they were socialist", "Even in China, where the Cultural Revolution gave rise to a new political situation, the state structure under Teng is not essentially different from one which existed previously." Opposing the CRC's above view, he further said that "there was a radical difference between the Soviet Union when it was socialist and then when the revisionists seized power and restored capitalism."

Further, he says: "It is sheer idealism and metaphysics to argue that this radical difference was not reflected throughout the institutions of society."

Here Bob Avakian is correct. In actuality, the RCP, USA and its Chairman Bob Avakian are not free from the above mentioned blunder committed by the CRC document. Whenever we see Bob Avakian's summation of the international communist movement and the dictatorship of the proletariat from 1928 up to Stalin's death, particularly the prelude and aftermath of the Second World War period, they too have concluded not much more differently. In his summation of that period, Bob Avakian has portrayed the Soviet society and state institutions as a boiling point. His analysis of Soviet society was, "in a certain sense, ripe like a plum or ripe fruit to fall into the hands of the revisionists; and in fact they did resolve all the muddles and did thoroughly conclude the process–concluded it with a qualitative leap, however–of taking the Soviet Union onto the capitalist road", and his invention of the theory of "Khrushchev's resolving Stalin's muddle"[100] makes his position clear. What an astounding statements "ripe like a plum or ripe fruit to fall" and "Khrushchev's resolving Stalin's muddle"?! These statements are nothing but sheer idealism and metaphysics.

4.10 (e) Class Reductionism: Bob Avakian has severely criticized the CRC document for its "refusal to recognize the crucial role of Marxist analysis–such analysis is rejected in the name of opposing "class reductionism"! In his words, to insist on class analysis "is not 'class reductionism'–it is Marxist materialism." Further, he exposes opposition to "class reductionism" of the CRC document:

> The CRC document's opposition to "class-reductionism" is in actuality a petit-bourgeois demand for "freedom" from the Marxist method of class analysis and the whole proletarian world outlook and methodology–a demand which parallels the desire to be "free" of the proletariat and its dictatorship in the real world, to repudiate the entire historical experience of the dictatorship of the proletariat ("from Lenin onwards").

But later, Bob Avakian deviated from his earlier view and stand. His NSC has departed from the Marxist method of class analysis. His saying, "insistence on "class truth" and related reification of the proletariat, and generally an approach to communist theory and principles as some kind of dogma, akin to religious catechism–in essence."[101] is nothing more than repudiation of the importance of Marxist class analysis. To be clear about his actual position on the Marxist method of class analysis, let us take his view on intellectual, art, culture, and morality. It is his thought that in the history of the international communist movement and socialist transformation of society and the advance of communism, as a secondary phenomenon, the freedom of intellectuals, artists, and so on was curtailed. They could not develop their initiatives. That is why their creativity and innovations became constricted. I want to quote Bob Avakian in some detail to make clear his position. Slandering Marx, Lenin and Mao Tse-tung in this regard, he says:

> I do want to briefly make clear that prior communists, and in particular theoreticians and leaders of the communist movement such as Marx, Lenin and Mao, had a significant appreciation for the role of art and culture in relation to revolution; but ... there was a tendency–maybe this is a little oversimplified, but it does get at something–a tendency to see art and culture

---

100 Bob Avakian, "Conquer the World? The International Proletariat Must and Will", *Revolution,* Special Issue, Number 50, p. 30.

101 Bob Avakian, *Communism : The Beginning of A New Stage, A Manifesto from the Revolutionary Communist Party, USA*, RCP Publications, 2009, p. 31.

too much one-to-one with the political revolutionary movement. To see it as a part of the machinery of the revolution, in a more linear or direct sense. Not that they did not appreciate this at all, but perhaps there was a tendency working against fully appreciating the way in which the realm of art and culture has its own dynamics and has to explore many different questions or phenomena from a lot of different angles, including new and unusual angles.

Bob Avakian sees serious contradictions arising in the course of–"Giving the correct priority to the fundamental needs and interests of the masses of people, including their basic and immediate needs for essential material things, as well as their social and political needs, while, at the same time, not being too constricting, or even somewhat suffocating, in the realm of art, culture, and intellectual endeavour and working with ideas."

Further, he says:

There was a tendency for artistic work and intellectual efforts to be tied too much and too closely to whatever were identified as the needs of the time, in terms of the political objectives and the economic and social objectives of the government at that time. That was uneven, and it wasn't crudely the way it's generally presented. ... Nobody ever argued–or at least official policy did not articulate it–exactly in that way. But I do believe that a scientific analysis would reveal that there was some tendency in that direction, as a secondary phenomenon.

The RCP, USA and its Chairman Bob Avakian claim that the NSC has given the right vision to handle this difficult contradiction. In this way, it is an integrated part of the NSC. In this regard, Bob Avakian says:

I do think there was some narrowing in the past experience. Part of the new synthesis is analysing the ways in which there was some narrowing of that–of the second aspect–the dissent, the creativity, the ferment, the innovation in the realm of intellectual endeavour and artistic creation. There was not enough of allowing people to go off on their own initiative, and then working to embrace all this, in a large sense–not in a narrow, constricting sense, but in a large sense–giving large expression to it, but also embracing it and leading it to all contribute to going forward towards communism, together with the struggle throughout the world.[102]

Bob Avakian has boiled down his view in one sentence–**solid core with a lot of elasticity.**

Here I am not discussing Bob Avakian's view on the above question in detail. I am making just a brief note. Actually, RCP, USA and Bob Avakian have repudiated the crucial role of Marxist class analysis by their new invention, **solid core with a lot of elasticity**. Their criticism of earlier

102 What Humanity Needs Revolution, and the New Synthesis of Communism, *An Interview with Bob Avakian,* By A. Brook, pp. 54, 48, 46, 47.

practice in this regard is nothing than fundamental disagreement with Mao Tse-tung's view on this question: "In class society everyone lives as a member of a particular class, and every kind of thinking, without exception, is stamped with the brand of a class."[103]

The RCP, USA and its Chairman Bob Avakian's "political objective and the economic and social objectives of the government at that time" was achieved "at the cost of curtailing the freedom of the people, especially the intellectuals and artists and so on" statement is in actuality the petit-bourgeois demand for "freedom" from the Marxist method of class analysis. It insists on the "non-class aspect" of intellectuals, artists, culture and morality in socialist society and the advance of communism. To insist on the method of class analysis is not to curtail "the freedom of the people, especially the intellectuals and artists, and so on", but it is to insist on accepting the historical materialism, what Lenin, Stalin and Mao Tse-tung did in the course of the socialist transformation of society. In the final analysis, it is repudiation, from Lenin onwards, of the entire historical experience of the dictatorship of the proletariat.

Houston, Texas, USA
September 1-November 15, 2012

---

103 Mao Tse-tung, "On Practice", *Selected Works*, Third Printing, Foreign Language Press, Peking, 1975, Vol. 1, p. 296.